GST

A HANDBOOK FOR UG, PG AND PROFESSIONAL COURSES

Updated as per the Finance Act, 2023

SANT KUMAR

ATLANTIC
PUBLISHERS & DISTRIBUTORS (P) LTD

ATLANTIC
PUBLISHERS & DISTRIBUTORS (P) LTD
7/22, Ansari Road, Darya Ganj, New Delhi
Tel.: +91-11-4077 5252, 2327 3880
E-mail: orders@atlanticbooks.com
Web: www.atlanticbooks.com

Reprinted in 2025, 2026

Published by Atlantic Publishers & Distributors (P) Ltd.

Printed & bound in India by Atlantic Print Services

Acknowledgements

I express my gratitude to my teachers and guide, Dr. Narayan Prasad (Professor, IGNOU), Dr. Kaustuva Barik (Professor, IGNOU), Shri Saugato Sen (Associate Professor, IGNOU), Dr. Harsh Purohit (Professor, Banasthali Vidyapith, Rajasthan), Dr. Peeyush Bangur (Associate Professor Banasthali Vidyapith, Rajasthan), Dr. Nidhi Malhotra (Assistant Professor, Lal Bahadur Shastri Institute of Management, Delhi), Late C.S. Savita (Associate Professor, University of Delhi), Smt. Shanta Devi (Retired); to my friends CA Mukesh Prasad, CA Tarun Kumar, CA Harish Chaudhary, and CA Anuj Jain; to my colleagues; my family, and my students (Ms. Drishti Pahwa, Ms. Deepa Mishra, Ms. Dhriti, Ms. Isha Arora, Ms. Jasmeet, Ms. Khushi Didwani, Ms. Komal, Ms. Radhika Verma, Ms. Ruchi Khandelwal, Ms. Siddhi Verma, Ms. Tripti Bindal, Ms. Vishakha, Ms. Waniya Ashraf, Mr. Aakash, Mr. Aryan, Mr. Shivam Kumar) who helped me a lot in motivating, creating and improving the quality of the book.

I would further like to express my deepest gratitude to Atlantic Publishers & Distributors (P) Ltd. for making the publication of this book a reality. Your unwavering support, guidance and belief in my work have been instrumental in bringing my creative vision to life.

Sant Kumar

Preface

Goods and Services Tax (GST) is a significant tax reform introduced in India that aims to simplify the taxation system and reduce the cascading effect of taxes. Since its introduction in 2017, GST has brought a significant change in the way businesses operate, making it crucial for individuals and organizations to understand the concept and its implications. This book on GST is aimed at providing a comprehensive understanding of the GST system and its implications. The book is designed to cater to the needs of students, professionals, entrepreneurs and anyone interested in understanding the concepts of GST. The book starts with indirect taxes before GST. It then moves on to cover the different aspects of GST, including supply, exemptions, time of supply, place of supply, input tax credit, registration, exemptions, returns and so on. In addition to the theoretical aspects of GST, the book also includes numerous examples so that the complex provisions can be understood easily and wherever it has been felt necessary then, examples have been given in question-answer format so that students can learn how to write answers in their respective exams. Moreover, at relevant places, a general knowledge section has been inserted so that the readers can connect the provision with practical life easily.

I hope that the book will serve as a valuable resource for anyone interested in learning about GST and its implications. I welcome feedback and suggestions from readers, which will help us improve the book in future editions. Kindly connect with me at santk190398@gmail.com.

A special request: Although all the efforts have been made to keep this book error-free, yet if they may occur, I would be highly indebted to you for bringing them to the notice.

Sant Kumar

Contents

1

Indirect Taxes before GST

1.1 Introduction

Before GST, there were many indirect taxes at the Central, State and Local levels. One such state level tax was sales tax unless replaced by Value Added Tax (VAT) in 2005. Sales tax was a type of indirect tax levied by a state government on the sale of goods within its territory. Therefore, sales tax could be levied by a state in case of intra-state sale of goods. When goods moved from one state to another state or union territory, i.e., inter-state transaction, then the Central Sales Tax (CST) was applicable because of the Central Sales Tax Act, 1956. Although CST was levied by the Central Government, but collected and retained by the state from where the goods used to move. VAT and CST were both replaced by GST from 1.7.2017. The learning objectives of this chapter are as follows:

- Meaning of tax
- Difference between direct taxes and indirect taxes
- Major indirect taxes in India before GST
- Cascading effect in sales tax
- Value Added Tax—The solution to the problem of cascading effect at the state level
- Disadvantages of VAT
- Cascading effect in Excise Duty
- Problems of earlier tax system

1.2 Meaning of Tax

A tax is a mandatory payment made by a person to a government. Since any tax is backed by a law, therefore, a government cannot impose a tax without the authority of law. Taxes in India are of two types: (i) Direct taxes and (ii) Indirect taxes.

1. **Direct Taxes:** Suppose a government imposes a tax on Mr. A, then this tax is called a direct tax if its burden is borne by A only, i.e., the burden cannot be shifted to any other person. Thus, one cannot say that "the tax is imposed on me, but it is to be recovered from some other person by whatever way except a few cases". Income tax,

wealth tax, municipality tax, gift tax, inheritance tax, etc., are all examples of direct taxes because the burden of all these cannot be shifted to another person.

2. **Indirect Taxes:** Indirect taxes are those burdens that can be shifted to buyers. Value Added Tax (VAT), Central Sales Tax (CST), excise duty, customs duty, Goods and Services Tax (GST), etc., are all examples of indirect taxes. Whenever you buy a product, on its packaging, it is written: "price is inclusive of all the taxes". You know that those taxes are a liability of the producers/manufacturer/trader, but they are recovered from you by adding them to the price; therefore indirectly, you have borne the burden of those taxes. It is accepted that indirect taxes are levied on goods or services or both.

1.3 Difference Between Direct Taxes and Indirect Taxes

Based on the above discussion, we have the following points of difference:

Basis	Direct Taxes	Indirect Taxes
Meaning	Direct taxes are levied on a person's income and wealth.	These taxes are levied on goods or services supplied by a person, but the burden of taxation is borne by the buyers.
Shifting of Burden	Burden of tax cannot be shifted, i.e., the liability to pay a tax to the government falls on the same person on whom it has been imposed.	Burden of tax can be shifted, i.e., the liability to pay a tax to the government falls on a person, but it is recovered from some other person. However, in some cases, this is not done.
Examples	Income tax, wealth tax, municipality tax, inheritance tax, gift tax, etc.	Value Added Tax (VAT), Central Sales Tax (CST), customs duty, excise duty, etc.
Progressive or Regressive	Direct taxes are progressive in nature, i.e., the average rate of tax increases as the income increases. In simple words, the rich class pays more taxes, and the poor or middle class pays comparatively less or even zero taxes.	Indirect taxes are regressive in nature, i.e., they do not make a differentiation between the rich class and the poor class. Each class pays the taxes at the same rate.

1.4 Major Indirect Taxes in India Before GST

(1) **Central Excise Duty:** It means a duty imposed on a good manufactured in India. In India, excise duty was imposed by the Central Government on many goods under the Central Excise Act, 1944.

Note: Central Excise Duty is still applicable in case of:

(a) Petroleum crude

(b) High-speed diesel

(c) Motor spirit (or petrol)

(d) Natural gas

(e) Aviation turbine fuel
(f) Tobacco and tobacco products (subject to GST also)

(2) State Excise Duty: A state government, too, had the power to levy state excise duty on the following goods manufactured or produced in the state:

(a) Alcoholic liquor for human consumption
(b) Opium, Indian hemp and other narcotic drugs and narcotics

Note: The above goods are still subject to state excise duty as well as GST.

(3) Customs Duty: It means a duty imposed by the Central Government on the goods imported to and exported from India. Customs duty is levied and collected under the **Customs Act, 1962**. The following types of duties were levied before GST:

(a) Basic Customs Duty (BCD)
(b) Additional duty of customs or Countervailing Duty (CVD), i.e., compensation for loss of the central excise duty due to the import of goods
(c) Special additional duty of customs or special countervailing duty (Special CVD), i.e., compensation for loss of sales tax or VAT due to import of goods
(d) Protective duty, i.e., to protect domestic industries
(e) Safeguard duty, i.e., to protect domestic industries
(f) Anti-dumping duty, i.e., to discourage the practice of anti-dumping
(g) Natural Calamity Contingent Duty (NCCD) for specified goods

Note: After GST, the Customs Laws have also been amended, and therefore, CVD and Special CVD have been replaced by GST (i.e., IGST, to be specific).

(4) Service Tax: It was a type of tax levied and collected by the Central Government in 1994 on the services provided. There was no separate law for it; rather, it was governed by the Finance Act, 1994. Service tax was replaced by GST from 1.7.2017.

(5) Sales Tax: As the term implies, it is a tax on the sales of goods. Sales tax used to be a matter of the state government. Sales tax suffered from a serious problem known as the cascading effect; therefore, in 2005, almost all the state governments replaced their sales tax systems with Value Added Tax (VAT) to tackle the problem of cascading effect.

(6) Central Sales Tax (CST): When goods would move from one state to another, this was known as an inter-state transaction. In such cases, the central sales tax was levied by the Central Government under the **Central Sales Tax Act, 1956**, but collected by the state from where goods used to move. CST was, after all, a sales tax; therefore, it also suffered the problem of cascading effect.

(7) Value Added Tax (VAT): It was a tax levied and collected by a state government on the goods sold within its state. In fact, VAT was launched to replace sales tax by introducing the concept of input tax credit so that the problem of cascading effect can be dealt with. Each state had different VAT laws.

Common Note for (6) and (7): In case of the following goods, CST and VAT are still applicable:

(a) Petroleum crude

(b) High-speed diesel
(c) Motor spirit (or petrol)
(d) Natural gas
(e) Aviation turbine fuel

(8) **Octroi:** It means a tax or duty imposed by a state government while goods from other states enter their states.

1.5 Cascading Effect in Sales Tax

A serious problem with the sales tax system was the **cascading effect, i.e., tax on tax.** By introducing the concept of input tax credit in VAT, the state laws tried to reduce the cascading effect in their respective states. Let us first understand what the cascading effect is all about. Suppose that there are three business firms A, B and C. Further, suppose that A sells goods to B, and he quotes the price ₹10,000 plus 10% sales tax, then A prepares the following tax invoice/ retail invoice (in layman's language, it is a bill). So, A collects ₹11,000 (including the sales tax) from B and deposits the sales tax of ₹1,000 to the government. Now, B receives the goods and adds some value to them worth ₹5,000. He sells the goods to C for ₹16,000 plus 10% sales tax. Therefore, B collects ₹17,600 (including sales tax) from C and deposits the sales tax of ₹1,600 to the government.

Summary of the above Transactions

Invoice issued by A to B	Amount (in ₹)	Invoice issued by B to C	Amount (in ₹)
Cost of purchase	–	Cost of purchase	11,000
Add: Value addition	10,000	Add: Value addition	5,000
Sales price	10,000	Sales price	16,000
Add: Sales Tax @ 10% of Sales price	1,000	Add: Sales Tax @ 10% of Sales price	1,600
Invoice price	**11,000**	**Invoice price**	**17,600**

Total Sales Tax Collection by Government

Components	Amount (in ₹)
Sales tax deposited by A	1,000
Sales tax deposited by B	1,600
Total Sales Tax collection	2,600

Now, see the breakdown of the sales tax ₹1,600 (as shown below) collected by B from C.

₹1,600 = 10% × ₹16,000
= 10% × (₹11,000 + ₹5,000)
= 10% × (₹10,000 + ₹1,000 + ₹5,000)
= (10% × ₹10,000) + (10% × ₹1,000) + (10% × ₹5,000)

₹100 = Sales Tax rate × tax paid earlier
= Tax on tax

↓

Cascading effect

Therefore, out of the sales tax of ₹1,600, there is a sales tax of ₹100 on sales tax paid by B to A. This is known as the cascading effect. This cascading effect becomes bigger when the number of firms increases in the above supply chain. Now, a question arises here, i.e., **Is cascading effect philosophically and legally justified?** The answer is **No!** Why should one pay tax on tax? Another question is, **What is the impact of the cascading effect on inflation?** The answer is that it increases the price of the good under question. Think, if there were no cascading effects, then what would have been the invoice price? The answer is ₹16,500.

1.6 Value Added Tax—The Solution of the Problem of Cascading Effect at State Level

To remove the cascading effects, virtually all the states enacted their VAT laws in 2005, but some states did later. All the states and union territories in India adopted the VAT system except Puducherry, Andaman and Nicobar and Lakshadweep. VAT worked like sales tax only, but the difference was the concept of **input tax credit.** Input tax credit means adjusting the tax paid earlier from the tax liability of a seller. Let us understand the input tax credit in the last example. Suppose that B is asked not to add the tax paid earlier to his cost of purchase; then the following table shows the new calculations:

Summary of the above Transactions

Invoice issued by A to B	Amount (in ₹)	Invoice issued by B to C	Amount (in ₹)
Cost of purchase	–	Cost of purchase	10,000
Add: Value addition	10,000	Add: Value addition	5,000
Sales price	10,000	Sales price	15,000
Add: VAT @ 10%	1,000	Add: VAT @ 10%	1,500
Invoice price	**11,000**	**Invoice price**	**16,500**

From the above table, we see that the state government collects ₹1,000 from A. The liability of B appears to be ₹1,500. The government does not collect ₹1,500 from him, but it collects ₹500 only after adjusting the earlier tax of ₹1,000 paid by him to A.

Total VAT Collection by the State Government

Components	Amount (in ₹)	Net amount (in ₹)
VAT collected by A	1,000	
Less: Tax paid earlier by A	–	
VAT deposited by A		1,000
VAT collected by B	1,500	
Less: Tax paid earlier by B	1,000	
VAT deposited by B		500
Total VAT collected		1,500

VAT: As per its meaning

Value addition	Amount (in ₹)	VAT at 10%
Value addition by A	10,000	1,000
Value addition by B	5,000	500
Total value addition and VAT	**15,000**	**1,500**

1.7 Disadvantages of VAT System

Although the VAT system seems to be a perfect system, this is not so because of the following reasons:

(a) Input tax credit was not available in all the cases (e.g., purchases from an unregistered dealer, purchases without tax invoice, purchases from a different state, etc.). As a result, the cascading effect still remained in the system, making the goods expensive.

(b) Different states had different VAT laws. Therefore, one businessman needed to comply with different VAT laws to do business in different states. It used to cause financial and mental stress on him.

(c) Each state had exclusive power to control VAT rates, which would be increased or decreased as per economic and political needs. Consequently, some states had high VAT rates and some others low, causing their high or low inflation rate. It created a non-competitive environment in the country.

1.8 Cascading Effect in Excise Duty

Before GST, VAT was calculated on the value after adding the excise duty. As a result, there was VAT on excise duty, too, hence the cascading effect. For example, suppose that the value of the goods manufactured in India was ₹5,000, subject to 12% excise duty. Further, suppose that the VAT rate was 10%, then the invoice price was calculated like this:

Particulars	Amount in ₹
Value of the goods	5,000
Add: Excise duty at 12%	600
Value after excise duty	5,600
VAT at 10%	560
Invoice price	6,160

1.9 Problems of Earlier Tax System

Earlier tax systems suffered various serious problems which existed for a long time. These problems are as follows:

1. **Problem of double taxation:** There were different taxes for goods and services. Excise duty, sales tax/Value Added Tax, etc., were levied on goods, while there was service tax for services. The problem of double taxable would arise when a transaction was categorised as goods as well as services. Consequently, the transaction was subject to VAT as well as service tax. For example, the sale of software was subject to VAT and service tax.

2. **Problem of cascading effect:** The problem of the cascading effect means a tax on tax, and it unnecessarily increases the prices of goods and services. Sales tax suffered seriously from this problem. By introducing the concept of the input tax credit, VAT solved this problem, but this problem remained solved as long as the transaction was intra-state. As a transaction would turn into an inter-state, CST was levied, and the buyer could not avail of its credit. Consequently, cascading remained as it was before VAT. Apart, there was no credit of excise duty against the payment of VAT, causing a cascading effect again.

3. **Problem of various taxes:** There were various indirect taxes at central, state and local levels. These taxes increased the cost of production and services. Businessmen were required to comply with various laws of the centre, state and local authorities. As a result, the problem of multiple registrations under different laws and the numerous numbers of forms posed very serious issues and presented significant hurdles to the ease of doing business and attracting foreign companies to India. These problems would become more enticing when such compliances could not be performed online. As a result, a good amount of valuable time for a businessman was spent on offline compliances.

4. **Problem of litigation:** Earlier laws got very complex and difficult. As a result, numerous litigations were filed either by the tax department or the taxpayer for deciding various cases. On the same topic, many judgements by various High Courts and the Supreme Court of India, causing great confusion.

5. **Problem of corruption:** When a system becomes difficult, people indulge in the practice of corruption to get out of it. India was not exception to this. Complex procedures, multiple taxes, time consumption processes, etc., all were such factors that increased corruption.

6. **Problem of tax evasion:** Earlier laws had many loopholes in addition to being complex and challenging. Tax evasion was made possible by dishonest persons who took advantage of legal loopholes.

7. **Problem of long queues of goods carrier at various check posts:** Long queues of trucks, tempos, or other goods carriers were frequently seen at various check posts. These carriers used to have to wait for octroi payments and other formalities for many hours. Fuel wastage, time wastage, long travel time and corruption were all quite prevalent. Further, goods did not reach their destination at the scheduled time. As per a Business Standard Report published on 17.10.2017, after 4 months of GST, there was a reduction in travel time by 30%.

Theory Questions

1. What are the differences between direct and indirect taxes?
2. What do you mean by cascading effect? Explain it with a suitable example.
3. Do you think that cascading effected existed in the Sales Tax system only? Support your answer.
4. What were the main indirect taxes in India before GST in 2017?
5. Earlier indirect taxes in India were plagued with various issues or problems. Can you explain those issues or problems?
6. What is Value Added Tax? How is it different from sales tax?
7. How did Value Added Tax (VAT) tackle the problem of cascading effect? Was it able to completely remove the problem of the cascading effect?
8. Discuss the shortcomings of the previous tax structure in India prior to GST.

2

Constitutional Background of Indirect Taxes in India

2.1 Introduction

The Constitution of India is the supreme law, and from time to time, it has been amended as per the needs of the time. Till October 2021, there have been 105 amendments since 1950. One such amendment was the 101st amendment made in 2016, making Goods and Service Tax (GST) constitutionally valid. To understand the constitutional background of indirect taxes in India, it is important to see the status of the constitution before and after the 101st amendment. Let us see.

2.2 Constitutional Background Before and After GST

Article	Before 101st Amendment, i.e., before GST	After 101st Amendment, i.e., after GST
265	This article states that "no tax shall be levied or collected except by authority of law". Thus, a government cannot impose/levy or collect any tax unless it is authorised by law.	This article states that "no tax shall be levied or collected except by authority of law". Thus, a government cannot impose/levy or collect any tax unless it is authorised by law.
246	This article gives authority to the Central or State governments to levy or collect taxes. The article gives such authority or power under three lists known as List I, List II and List III. **Note:** In Appendix I, at the end of this chapter, the above said lists have been given.	This article gives authority to the Central or State governments to levy or collect taxes. The article gives such authority or power under three lists known as List I, List II and List III. **Note:** In Appendix I, at the end of this chapter, the above said lists have been given.

246A (New article)	Did not exist.	Whatever is written in Articles 246 and 254, the provisions of Article 246A shall prevail. According to this article: 1. Parliament and State legislature to make laws for GST. Simply put, the Centre and State Governments have power to levy and collect GST. 2. Parliament has power to make laws on GST on **inter-state supply** of goods or services or both.
248	Parliament has exclusive power to make any law with respect to any matter not enumerated in the Concurrent List or State List. Such power shall include the power of making any law imposing a tax not mentioned in either of those lists.	1. Subject to Article 246A, the Parliament has exclusive power to make any law with respect to any matter not enumerated in the Concurrent List or State List. 2. Such power shall include the power of making any law imposing a tax not mentioned in either of those lists.
249	1. Notwithstanding anything in the foregoing provisions of this Chapter, if the Council of States has declared by resolution supported by not less than two-thirds of the members present and voting that it is necessary or expedient in the national interest that Parliament should make laws with respect to any matter enumerated in the State List specified in the resolution, it shall be lawful for Parliament to make laws for the whole or any part of the territory of India with respect to that matter while the resolution remains in force. 2. A resolution passed under clause (1) shall remain in force for such period not exceeding one year as may be specified therein: Provided that, if and so often as a resolution approving the continuance in force of any such resolution is passed in the manner provided in clause (1), such resolution shall continue in force for a further period of one year from the date on which under this clause it would otherwise have ceased to be in force.	1. Notwithstanding anything in the foregoing provisions of this Chapter, if the Council of States has declared by resolution supported by not less than two-thirds of the members present and voting that it is necessary or expedient in the national interest that Parliament should make laws with respect to **[GST provided under article 246A or]** any matter enumerated in the State List specified in the resolution, it shall be lawful for Parliament to make laws for the whole or any part of the territory of India with respect to that matter while the resolution remains in force. 2. A resolution passed under clause (1) shall remain in force for such period not exceeding one year as may be specified therein: Provided that, if and so often as a resolution approving the continuance in force of any such resolution is passed in the manner provided in clause (1), such resolution shall continue in force for a further period of one year from the date on which under this clause it would otherwise have ceased to be in force.

	3. A law made by Parliament which Parliament would not but for the passing of a resolution under clause have been competent to make shall, to the extent of the incompetency, cease to have effect on the expiration of a period of six months after the resolution has ceased to be in force, except as respects things done or omitted to be done before the expiration of the said period.	3. A law made by Parliament which Parliament would not but for the passing of a resolution under clause (1) have been competent to make shall, to the extent of the incompetency, cease to have effect on the expiration of a period of six months after the resolution has ceased to be in force, except as respects things done or omitted to be done before the expiration of the said period.
250	1. Notwithstanding anything in this Chapter I of the Constitution, Parliament shall, while a Proclamation of Emergency is in operation, have power to make laws for the whole or any part of the territory of India with respect to any of the matters enumerated in the State List. 2. A law made by Parliament which Parliament would not but for the issue of a Proclamation of Emergency have been competent to make shall, to the extent of the incompetency, cease to have effect on the expiration of a period of six months after the Proclamation has ceased to operate, except as respects things done or omitted to be done before the expiration of the said period.	1. Notwithstanding anything in this Chapter of the Constitution, Parliament shall, while a Proclamation of Emergency is in operation, have power to make laws for the whole or any part of the territory of India with respect to [**GST under article 246A or**] any of the matters enumerated in the State List. 2. A law made by Parliament which Parliament would not but for the issue of a Proclamation of Emergency have been competent to make shall, to the extent of the incompetency, cease to have effect on the expiration of a period of six months after the Proclamation has ceased to operate, except as respects things done or omitted to be done before the expiration of the said period.
268	1. Such stamp duties and such duties of excise on medicinal and toilet preparations as are mentioned in the Union List shall be levied by the Government of India but shall be collected— (a) in the case where such duties are leviable within any Union territory, by the Government of India, and (b) in other cases, by the States within which such duties are respectively leviable. 2. The proceeds in any financial year of any such duty leviable within any State shall not form part of the Consolidated Fund of India, but shall be assigned to that State, i.e., the proceeds are not shareable with the Union.	1. Such stamp duties as are mentioned in the Union List shall be levied by the Government of India but shall be collected— (a) in the case where such duties are leviable within any Union territory, by the Government of India, and (b) in other cases, by the States within which such duties are respectively leviable. 2. The proceeds in any financial year of any such duty leviable within any State shall not form part of the Consolidated Fund of India, but shall be assigned to that State, i.e., the proceeds are not shareable with the Union.

268A	This article gave power to the Union to levy and collect service tax and appropriated by the Union and the States.	**Omitted**
269	1. Taxes on the sale or purchase of goods and taxes on the consignment of goods shall be levied and collected by the Government of India but shall be assigned and shall be deemed to have been assigned to the States on or after the 1st day of April, 1996 in the manner provided in clause (2). Explanation. —For the purposes of this clause, — (a) the expression "taxes on the sale or purchase of goods" shall mean taxes on sale or purchase of goods other than newspapers, where such sale or purchase takes place in the course of inter-State trade or commerce; (b) the expression "taxes on the consignment of goods" shall mean taxes on the consignment of goods (whether the consignment is to the person making it or to any other person), where such consignment takes place in the course of inter-State trade or commerce. 2. The net proceeds in any financial year of any such tax, except in so far as those proceeds represent proceeds attributable to Union territories, shall not form part of the Consolidated Fund of India, but shall be assigned to the States within which that tax is leviable in that year, and shall be distributed among those States in accordance with such principles of distribution as may be formulated by Parliament by law. 3. Parliament may by law formulate principles for determining when a [sale or purchase of, or consignment of, goods] takes place in the course of inter-State trade or commerce.	1. Taxes on the sale or purchase of goods and taxes on the consignment of goods [except as provided in article 269A] shall be levied and collected by the Government of India but shall be assigned and shall be deemed to have been assigned to the States on or after the 1st day of April, 1996 in the manner provided in clause (2). Explanation. —For the purposes of this clause, — (a) the expression "taxes on the sale or purchase of goods" shall mean taxes on sale or purchase of goods other than newspapers, where such sale or purchase takes place in the course of inter-State trade or commerce; (b) the expression "taxes on the consignment of goods" shall mean taxes on the consignment of goods (whether the consignment is to the person making it or to any other person), where such consignment takes place in the course of inter-State trade or commerce. 2. The net proceeds in any financial year of any such tax, except in so far as those proceeds represent proceeds attributable to Union territories, shall not form part of the Consolidated Fund of India, but shall be assigned to the States within which that tax is leviable in that year, and shall be distributed among those States in accordance with such principles of distribution as may be formulated by Parliament by law. 3. Parliament may by law formulate principles for determining when a [sale or purchase of, or consignment of, goods] takes place in the course of inter-State trade or commerce.

269A (New Article)		1. Goods and services tax on supplies in the course of inter-State trade or commerce shall be levied and collected by the Government of India and such tax shall be apportioned between the Union and the States in the manner as may be provided by Parliament by law on the recommendations of the Goods and Services Tax Council. GST on supplies in the course of inter-state trade or commerce shall be levied and collected by the Government of India and such tax shall be apportioned between the Union and the States in the manner prescribed by Parliament by a law on the recommendation of GST Council. 2. The amount apportioned to a State under clause (1) shall not form part of the Consolidated Fund of India. 3. Where an amount collected as tax levied under clause (1) has been used for payment of the tax levied by a State under article 246A, such amount shall not form part of the Consolidated Fund of India. 4. Where an amount collected as tax levied by a State under article 246A has been used for payment of the tax levied under clause (1), such amount shall not form part of the Consolidated Fund of the State. 5. Parliament may, by law, formulate the principles for determining the place of supply, and when a supply of goods, or of services, or both takes place in the course of inter-State trade or commerce.
270	1. All taxes and duties referred to in the Union List, except the duties and taxes referred to in articles [268 and 269], respectively, surcharge on taxes and duties referred to in article 271 and any cess levied for specific purposes under any law made by Parliament shall be levied and collected by the Government of India and shall be distributed between the Union and the States in the manner provided in clause (2).	1. All taxes and duties referred to in the Union List, except the duties and taxes referred to in [articles 268, 269 and 269A], respectively, surcharge on taxes and duties referred to in article 271 and any cess levied for specific purposes under any law made by Parliament shall be levied and collected by the Government of India and shall be distributed between the Union and the States in the manner provided in clause (2).

270	2. Such percentage, as may be prescribed, of the net proceeds of any such tax or duty in any financial year shall not form part of the Consolidated Fund of India, but shall be assigned to the States within which that tax or duty is leviable in that year, and shall be distributed among those States in such manner and from such time as may be prescribed in the manner provided in clause (3).	**[(1A) The tax collected by the Union under clause (1) of article 246A shall also be distributed between the Union and the States in the manner provided in clause (2).** **(1B) The tax levied and collected by the Union under clause (2) of article 246A and article 269A, which has been used for payment of the tax levied by the Union under clause (1) of article 246A, and the amount apportioned to the Union under clause (1) of article 269A, shall also be distributed between the Union and the States in the manner provided in clause (2).]** 2. Such percentage, as may be prescribed, of the net proceeds of any such tax or duty in any financial year shall not form part of the Consolidated Fund of India, but shall be assigned to the States within which that tax or duty is leviable in that year, and shall be distributed among those States in such manner and from such time as may be prescribed in the manner provided in clause (3).
271	Notwithstanding anything in articles 269 and 270, Parliament may at any time increase any of the duties or taxes referred to in those articles by a surcharge for purposes of the Union and the whole proceeds of any such surcharge shall form part of the Consolidated Fund of India. It simply means that, the Parliament has power to increase any of the duties or taxes mentioned in articles 269 and 270. This increase is called surcharge which is not shareable.	Notwithstanding anything in articles 269 and 270, Parliament may at any time increase any of the duties or taxes referred to in those articles **[except the goods and services tax under article 246A]** by a surcharge for purposes of the Union and the whole proceeds of any such surcharge shall form part of the Consolidated Fund of India. It simply means that, the Parliament has power to increase any of the duties or taxes mentioned in articles 269 and 270. This increase is called surcharge which is not shareable. However, GST is not covered here i.e., no surcharge can be imposed on GST.

Source: **https://cdnbbsr.s3waas.gov.in/s380537a945c7aaa788ccfcdf1b99b5d8f/uploads/2023/05/2023050195.pdf**

From the above, we can deduce the following significant points of the 101st Amendment.

1. **Insertion of new articles**
   - **Article 246A:** A new article 246A was inserted. According to the article, the Parliament and State Legislatures shall have the power to make laws on the Goods and Service Tax (GST). That is why we have a dual system of GST in India, i.e., Central Tax (CGST) and State Tax (SGST)/Union Territory Tax (UTGST) are levied in case of intra-state transactions. The power to levy and collect tax on inter-state transactions is vested in the hands of the Central Government. That is why IGST is levied on inter-state transactions.
   - **Article 269A:** Another new article 269A was inserted. According to the article, the tax levied and collected by the Central Government in the case of inter-state transaction/commerce shall be apportioned between the Centre and the States in a manner provided by the Parliament by law on the recommendations of the GST Council.
   - **Article 279A:** A new article 279A was inserted, which states that a joint forum of the Centre and States shall be constituted. Such forum shall be called as GST Council. The other aspects of the GST council have been explained in Chapter 3.
2. **Article 268A** has been omitted under which service tax was levied.
3. **Articles 249, 250, 268, 269, 270, 271** were amended.
4. **Deletion of Entries**
   - Entries 84, 92, 92C in the Union List were omitted.
   - Entries 52, 55 in the State List were omitted completely, while entries 54 and 62 of the same list were amended.

5. **Power to make the laws on the place of supply:** Laws relating to the place of supply and inter-state supply shall be made by the Parliament.

6. **No GST on alcoholic liquor:** GST shall be levied on all supply of goods and services except alcoholic liquor for human consumption.

7. **Goods not subject to GST:** GST shall not be levied on the following goods unless a date is notified on the recommendation of the GST Council.

(a) Petroleum crude
(b) High-Speed Diesel
(c) Motor Spirit (or petrol)
(d) Natural Gas
(e) Aviation Turbine Fuel (ATF)

8. **Goods subject to Central Excise Duty:** The Central Government has power to levy Central Excise duty on the following goods:

(a) Petroleum crude
(b) High-Speed Diesel
(c) Motor Spirit (or petrol)
(d) Natural Gas
(e) Aviation Turbine Fuel (ATF)
(f) Tobacco and tobacco products

Theory Questions

1. No government can levy and collect taxes in India without the authority of the law. In the light of the Constitution of India, explain the validity of the given statement.
2. What are Lists I and II under the Seventh Schedule of the Constitution of India?
3. What amendments to the Constitution of India have been made to bring GST in India?
4. Explain in brief the constitutional framework of Indirect Taxes before GST.
5. Write a short note on Article 246A.
6. Goods like petroleum crude, natural gas, diesel, aviation turbine fuel and petrol are not subject to GST as of now. What does the Constitution of India say about these goods?

Appendix I

List–I: Union List

Parliament has exclusive power to make laws, including the law for the levy of taxes in respect of the matter in the Union List. The matters of taxes range from entry 82 to 92C. These entries are explained below:

Entries	Before 101st Amendment, i.e., before GST	After 101st Amendment, i.e., after GST
Entry 82	Income tax other than agricultural income.	Income tax other than agricultural income.
Entry 83	Duties of customs including export duties.	Duties of customs including export duties.
Entry 84	Excise Duty on tobacco and other goods manufactured or produced in India except on (a) Alcoholic liquor for human consumption; (b) Opium, Indian hemp and other narcotic drugs and narcotics but including medicinal and toilet preparation containing alcohol or opium/Indian hemp/narcotic drugs/narcotics.	Duties of excise on the following goods manufactured or produced in India, namely: (a) Petroleum crude; (b) High-speed diesel; (c) Motor spirit (commonly known as petrol); (d) Natural gas; (e) Aviation turbine fuel; and (f) Tobacco and tobacco products
Entry 85	Corporation tax.	Corporation tax.
Entry 86	Taxes on the capital value of the assets, exclusive of agricultural land, of individuals and companies; taxes on the capital of companies.	Taxes on the capital value of the assets, exclusive of agricultural land, of individuals and companies; taxes on the capital of companies.
Entry 87	Estate duty in respect of property other than agricultural land.	Estate duty in respect of property other than agricultural land.

Entry 88	Duties in respect of succession to property other than agricultural land.	Duties in respect of succession to property other than agricultural land.
Entry 89	Terminal taxes on goods or passengers, carried by railway, sea or air; taxes on railway fares and freights.	Terminal taxes on goods or passengers, carried by railway, sea or air; taxes on railway fares and freights.
Entry 90	Taxes other than stamp duties on transactions in stock exchanges and futures markets.	Taxes other than stamp duties on transactions in stock exchanges and futures markets.
Entry 91	Rates of stamp duty in respect of bills of exchange, cheques, promissory notes, bills of lading, letters of credit, policies of insurance, transfer of shares, debentures, proxies and receipts.	Rates of stamp duty in respect of bills of exchange, cheques, promissory notes, bills of lading, letters of credit, policies of insurance, transfer of shares, debentures, proxies and receipts.
Entry 92	Taxes on the sale or purchase of newspapers and on advertisements published therein.	**Omitted**
Entry 92A	Taxes on the sale or purchase of goods other than newspapers, where such sale or purchase takes place in the course of inter-state trade or commerce.	Taxes on the sale or purchase of goods other than newspapers, where such sale or purchase takes place in the course of inter-state trade or commerce.
Entry 92B	Tax on consignment of goods in the course of inter-state transactions or commerce.	Tax on consignment of goods in the course of inter-state transactions or commerce.
Entry 92C	Service tax.	**Omitted**
Entry 97	Any other matter not enumerated in List II or List III including any tax not mentioned in those lists. This is a residuary entry.	Any other matter not enumerated in List II or List III including any tax not mentioned in those lists. This is a residuary entry.

List–II: State List

State legislature has exclusive power to make laws, including the law for levy of taxes in respect of the matter in the State list. The matters of taxes range from entry 46 to 63. These entries are explained below:

Entries	Before 101st Amendment, i.e., before GST	After 101st Amendment, i.e., after GST
Entry 46	Taxes on agricultural income.	Taxes on agricultural income.
Entry 49	Taxes on lands and buildings.	Taxes on lands and buildings.

Entry 51	Excise duty on goods manufactured or produced in the State and countervailing duties at the same or lower rates on similar goods manufactured or produced elsewhere in India: (a) Alcoholic liquor for human consumption; (b) Opium, Indian hemp and other narcotic drugs and narcotics But not including medicinal and toilet preparation containing alcohol or opium/Indian hemp/narcotic drugs/narcotics.	Excise duty on goods manufactured or produced in the State and countervailing duties at the same or lower rates on similar goods manufactured or produced elsewhere in India: (a) Alcoholic liquor for human consumption; (b) Opium, Indian hemp and other narcotic drugs and narcotics; But not including medicinal and toilet preparation containing alcohol or opium/Indian hemp/narcotic drugs/narcotics.
Entry 52	Octroi or Entry Tax.	**Omitted**
Entry 53	Taxes on the consumption or sale of electricity.	Taxes on the consumption or sale of electricity.
Entry 54	Taxes on the sale or purchase of goods other than newspapers.	**Taxes on the sale of petroleum crude, high speed diesel, motor spirit (commonly known as petrol), natural gas, aviation turbine fuel and alcoholic liquor for human consumption, but not including sale in the course of inter-state trade or commerce or sale in the course of international trade or commerce of such goods.**
Entry 55	Taxes on advertisements other than advertisements published in the newspapers [and advertisements broadcast by radio or television].	**Omitted**
Entry 56	Taxes on goods and passengers carried by road or on inland waterways.	Taxes on goods and passengers carried by road or on inland waterways.
Entry 57	Taxes on vehicles, whether mechanically propelled or not, suitable for use on roads, including tramcars subject to the provisions of entry 35 of List III.	Taxes on vehicles, whether mechanically propelled or not, suitable for use on roads, including tramcars subject to the provisions of entry 35 of List III.
Entry 58	Taxes on animals and boats.	Taxes on animals and boats.
Entry 59	Tolls.	Tolls.
Entry 60	Taxes on professions, trades, callings and employments.	Taxes on professions, trades, callings and employments.
Entry 61	Capitation taxes.	Capitation taxes.

Entry 62	Taxes on luxuries, including taxes on entertainments, amusements, betting and gambling.	**Taxes on entertainments and amusements to the extent levied and collected by a Panchayat or a Municipality or a Regional Council or a District Council.**
Entry 63	Stamp Duty in respect of documents other than those specified in List I.	Stamp Duty in respect of documents other than those specified in List I.

List–III: Concurrent List

Parliament and State legislature has power to make laws in respect of the matter in this list, e.g., legal, medical and other professions; prevention of the extension from one State to another of infectious or contagious diseases or pests affecting men, animals or plants.

3

Goods and Services Tax (GST): An Introduction

3.1 Introduction

As we learnt in the previous chapter, the earlier indirect tax system had a variety of shortcomings. If different taxes levied at the central, state, and local levels are replaced with one tax, many of these issues could be greatly alleviated. As a result, after a journey of around twenty years, we got a single tax known as Goods and Service Tax (GST) effective from 1.7.2017. The story of the birth of GST is quite interesting. Let us start our chapter with this story.

3.2 A Brief Story of the Birth of GST

The idea of GST took birth in the year 2000 when Bharat Ratna Atal Bihari Vajpayee was the Prime Minister of India. He had various meetings with renowned economists like C. Rangarajan, I.G. Patel, Bimal Jalan, and Asim Das Gupta in order for the idea of GST could come to fruition.

In 2004, the BJP-led alliance NDA was defeated by Congress-led alliance UPA 1. The then Prime Minister Dr. Manmohan Singh carried the wish of Atal Ji, and during the budget speech of 2006-07, the then Union Finance Minister P. Chidambaram announced to the implementation of GST in India from 1.4.2010. Congress-led alliance UPA 2 won the 2009 general election, and Dr. Manmohan Singh became the Prime Minister of India for the second time, and Bharat Ratna Pranab Mukherjee became the Union Finance Minister. However, due to various political and non-political reasons, GST could not be brought by 2010.

Further, BJP-led NDA won the 2014 general election with a clear majority in the Lok Sabha. During the same year, NDA presented the Constitution (122nd Amendment) Bill, 2014, which the Lok Sabha passed in May 2015 and the Rajya Sabha in August 2016. As a result, the Constitution (101st Amendment) Act, 2016 was notified on 8.09.2016. This Act cleared the way for bringing GST and making GST constitutionally valid. One of the amendments was Article 279A regarding the GST Council, and its first meeting was held in September 2016. The council, headed by the then Union Finance Minister Shri Arun Jaitley, recommended four bills to be presented in the Lok Sabha. These bills were:

(1) The Central Goods and Services Tax Bill, 2017
(2) The Integrated Goods and Services Tax Bill, 2017
(3) The Union Territory Goods and Services Tax Bill, 2017
(4) The Goods and Services Tax (Compensation to States) Bill, 2017

The Lok Sabha passed the above bills in March 2017 and the Rajya Sabha in April 2017. The assent of the then President of India, Bharat Ratna Pranab Mukherjee, was received on 12 April 2017. All the States (except Jammu and Kashmir) passed the State Goods and Services Tax Acts, 2017 by the end of 30 June 2017, while Jammu and Kashmir passed it on 8 July 2017.

Finally, the day came when a special midnight function was organised in the central hall of the Parliament to launch GST with effect from 1 July 2017. The GST was inaugurated by the Prime Minister of India, Shri Narender Modi, and the then President of India, Pranab Mukherjee. All the leading media channels telecasted the function. Since then, the following Acts are in force.

(1) The Central Goods and Services Tax Act, 2017 (CGST Act, 2017)
(2) The Integrated Goods and Services Tax Act, 2017 (IGST Act, 2017)
(3) The Union Territory Goods and Services Tax Act, 2017 (UTGST Act, 2017)
(4) The State Goods and Services Tax Act, 2017 (SGST Act, 2017)
(5) The Goods and Services Tax (Compensation to States) Act, 2017

3.3 Features or Characteristics of GST

The main features or characteristics of GST are as follows:

1. A Single Tax for Goods and Services: Before GST, there were separate taxes for goods and services. For example, excise duty and value-added tax were for goods, and service tax was for services, but in the GST regime, there is a single tax only whether it is case of goods or services.

2. Supply is Taxable Event: In earlier laws, various terms like sale, manufacture, service, etc., defined taxable events. But, at the same time, there were many litigations (decided and pending) regarding their interpretation in various cases. In the GST regime, the taxable event is supply. If there is no supply, then no GST can be levied.

3. Dual System: The constitution of India allows the Central and State Governments to levy tax simultaneously in the names of Central Goods and Services Tax (CGST) and State Goods and Services Tax (SGST), respectively. In the case of intra-state supply, CGST and SGST are charged, while in the case of inter-state supply, the centre levies Integrated Goods and Services Tax (IGST), which is a total of CGST and SGST.

4. Consumption-based Tax: GST is a consumption-based tax. It means the tax is levied in the state or union territory where the goods or services are consumed.

5. GST is Value-Added Tax only: GST can be considered value-added tax applied on goods and services. Value-added tax works on input tax credit system; similarly, GST too works on input tax credit system.

6. No Cascading Effect: Since GST is value-added tax only, therefore, it removes the cascading effect problem. However, in some cases, the GST law imposes some restrictions on availing input tax credit; therefore, a cascading effect may arise.

7. Technology-based system: You cannot imagine the functioning of GST the way it is working today. The credit goes to the technology. Faceless registration, filing of returns, payment of tax, refund, generation of various forms, including e-way bill, etc., are all being done online through the GST common portal, e-way bill system, and e-invoice system.

3.4 Benefits of GST

The main benefits of GST are as follows:

1. Ease of doing business and encourage to Make in India campaign.
2. Solution to the problem of cascading effect.
3. Special provisions for small taxpayers. Composition levy under section 10, exemption from registration upto a ₹20 lakhs or ₹10 lakhs (in case of Manipur, Meghalaya, Nagaland and Tripura) under section 22(1) are examples of special provision for small taxpayers.
4. Faceless or online registration and compliance through the GST Common portal.
5. Control on corruption.
6. Control on tax evasion.
7. Reduction in administrative costs.
8. Reduction in travel time of goods carriers or transporters.

3.5 GST Council

GST council is a national-level group/forum of central and state-level finance ministers constituted by the President of India under Article 279A (1). The council conducts its meetings from time to time to discuss and make decisions on various aspects of GST mentioned in Article 279A (4). Let us see the various aspects of the Goods and Services Tax Council.

1. Constitution of the Council—Article 279A (1): This article states that the President shall, by order, constitute a council to be called the GST Council. The council shall be created within 60 days from the date of commencement of the Constitution (One Hundred and First Amendment) Act, 2016. This is obvious that this article is a matter of history.

2. Members of the Council—Article 279A (2): This article states that the council has the following members:

(a) The Union Finance Minister as a Chairperson.
(b) The Union Minister of State, in-charge of Revenue of Finance as Member.
(c) The Minister in-charge of Finance or Taxation or any other Minister nominated by each State government as Members.

3. Who will be the Vice-Chairperson of the Council—Article 279A (3): This article states that each member shall elect one to serve as vice-chairperson of the council for such time as they may determine.

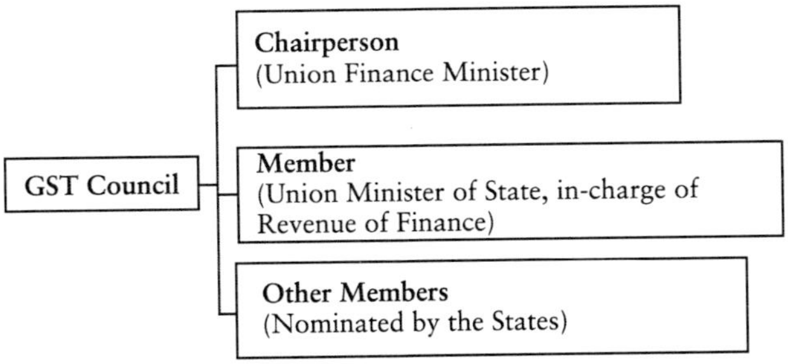

4. Matters which can be recommended by the GST Council–article 279A (4): This article states that the council shall make recommendations to the Union and the States on the following matters:

(a) The taxes, cesses and surcharges levied by the Union, the States and the local bodies may be merged with the GST.

(b) The goods and services may be subject to or exempt from the GST.

(c) Model GST laws, principles of levy, apportionment of GST levied on supplies in the course of inter-state trade or commerce and the principles that govern the place of supply.

(d) The turnover threshold below which GST exemption may apply.

(e) The applicable GST rates, including minimum rates with specific ranges.

(f) Provision for special rates during specific periods to generate additional resources in the event of natural calamities or disasters.

(g) Special provisions pertaining to

o	Arunachal Pradesh,
o	Assam,
o	Jammu and Kashmir,
o	Manipur,
o	Meghalaya,
o	Mizoram,
o	Nagaland,
o	Sikkim,
o	Tripura,
o	Himachal Pradesh, and
o	Uttarakhand.

(h) Any other matter related to GST, as the council may decide.

5. Some goods shall be taxable from a notified date—Article 279A (5): According to this article, the GST council shall recommend the date from which the GST be levied on

(a) Petroleum crude

(b) High speed diesel

(c) Motor spirit (or petrol)
(d) Natural gas
(e) Aviation Turbine Fuel (ATF)

6. Article 279A (6): While discharging the functions under Article 279A, the council shall be guided by the need for a harmonised structure of GST and for the development of a harmonised national market for goods and services.

7. Quorum of the meeting of the council–Article 279A (7): Quorum refers to the minimum number of members or participants required to be present at a meeting for the meeting to be legally valid and have the authority to make decisions or take action. According to the article, the quorum is 50% of the total council members for the council meeting.

8. Procedure of performance of the functions of the council–Article 279A (8): The council shall determine the procedure in the performance of its functions.

9. Weighted voting system—Article 279A (9): Every decision of the council is taken at its meeting by a majority of at least 3/4th of the weighted votes of the members present. Further,

(a) the Central Government has a weightage of 1/3rd of the total votes cast, and
(b) the State Government has a weightage of 2/3rd of the total votes cast.

Example 3.1: Suppose that the council consists of two members from the Central Government and thirty-one members from the State Governments. Further, suppose that the council is seeking voting for a proposal of change in the tax rate. Here are the details of the votes cast:

Members	Votes in favour	Votes against
Central Government	2	–
State Government	24	7
Total	26	7

Comment on the passing of the proposal as per article 279A (9).

Solution

Members	Votes in favour	Votes against	Total votes cast	Weighted votes in favour
Central Government	2	–	2	(2/2) × 1/3 = 0.33
State Government	24	7	31	(24/31) × 2/3 = 0.52
Total	26	7	33	0.85 = 85%

Special majority percentage = 75%

Since, weighted% of votes in favour = 85%

Therefore, the proposal can be said to have passed with a special majority.

10. Article 279A (10): No act or proceedings of the Council can be held invalid just because of

(a) any vacancy in, or any defect in, the Constitution of the Council or
(b) any defect in the appointment of a Member of the Council or
(c) any procedural irregularity of the Council not affecting the merits of the case.

11. Establishment of the mechanism to resolve the dispute—Article 279A (11): The Council shall create a system to resolve any dispute between the Central Government and one or more States regarding the suggestions made by the council.

3.6 Taxes Subsumed in GST

The following taxes subsumed in GST:

Central Taxes

(a) Central excise duty
(b) Additional excise duties
(c) Excise duty under Medicinal and Toilet Preparation Act
(d) Service tax
(e) Central sales tax
(f) CVD and Special CVD
(g) Central surcharges and Cesses related to supply of goods and services

State Taxes

(a) VAT/Sales tax
(b) Luxury tax
(c) Taxes on advertisements
(d) Entry tax and Purchase tax
(e) Entertainment tax (except those levied by local bodies)
(f) Tax on lottery, betting, and gambling
(g) State surcharges and cesses related to supply of goods and services

3.7 GST is not Leviable on the Supply of the following Goods unless the GST Council Notifies the date of Applicability of GST

(a) Petroleum crude
(b) High speed diesel
(c) Motor spirit (or petrol)
(d) Natural gas
(e) Aviation turbine fuel

Till then, VAT/CST is applicable on the above supplies.

3.8 What is included in GST law?

When we use the term GST law, then we mean the following laws:

1.	The Central Goods and Services Tax Act, 2017 (CGST Act, 2017)
2.	The Integrated Goods and Services Tax Act, 2017 (IGST Act, 2017)
3.	The Union Territory Goods and Services Tax Act, 2017 (UTGST Act, 2017)
4.	The State Goods and Services Tax Act, 2017 (SGST Act, 2017)
5.	The Goods and Services Tax (Compensation to States) Act, 2017
6.	The Central Goods and Services Tax Rules, 2017 (CGST Rules, 2017)
7.	Notifications issued by the Central Board of Indirect Taxes and Customs (CBIC)
8.	Circulars issued by the Central Board of Indirect Taxes and Customs (CBIC)
9.	The judgements by the State High Courts
10.	The judgements by the Supreme Court of India

3.9 Central Board of Indirect Taxes and Customs (CBIC)

Two boards of taxes are working under the Finance Ministry, Government of India. These boards are:

1. **Central Board of Direct Taxes (CBDT):** The Central Board of Direct Taxes is a statutory authority functioning under the Department of Revenue of the Finance Ministry. The board performs the functions relating to the levy and collection of direct taxes.
2. **Central Board of Indirect Taxes and Customs (CBIC):** The Central Board of Indirect Taxes and Customs Duty is also a statutory authority functioning under the Department of Revenue of the Finance Ministry. The board performs the functions related to the levy and collection of indirect taxes and customs duty, prevention of smuggling and evasion of duties and all administrative matters formations.

3.10 Basic definitions—Section 2 of the CGST Act

<table>
<tr><th>Terms</th><th>Meaning</th></tr>
<tr><td>Actionable claim
[Section 2(1)]</td><td>It means the actionable as defined under section 3 of the Transfer of Property Act, 1882. As per section 3 of the Transfer of Property Act, actionable claim means a claim to any debt, other than a debt secured by mortgage of immoveable property or by hypothecation or pledge of moveable property, or to any beneficial interest in moveable property not in the possession, either actual or constructive, of the claimant, which the Civil Courts recognise as affording grounds for relief, whether such debt or beneficial interest be existent, accruing, conditional or contingent.
Author's note
In simple words, an actionable claim refers to a claim to a debt or a beneficial interest in movable property. However, certain conditions need to be met for a claim to be considered actionable. An actionable claim can be any claim for a debt that is not secured by a mortgage of immovable property or by the use of movable property as collateral. It can also be a claim to a beneficial interest in movable property that is not currently in the possession of the person making the claim. In other words, the claimant doesn't have actual or legal control over the property.
To be recognized as an actionable claim, the claim should be something that a civil court would consider valid and provide legal relief for. The claim can be for an existing debt or beneficial interest, or it can be for a debt or interest that will arise in the future. It can also be a claim that is conditional or uncertain, meaning that it depends on certain conditions being fulfilled or events occurring.</td></tr>
<tr><td>Agent
[Section 2(5)]</td><td>An agent means a person who runs a business of supply or receipt of goods or services or both on behalf of some other person. The term agent also includes<ul><li>a factor,</li><li>a broker,</li><li>a commission agent,</li><li>an arhatia,</li><li>a del-credere agent,</li><li>an auctioneer,</li><li>any other mercantile agent, by whatever name called.</li></ul></td></tr>
<tr><td>Aggregate turnover
[Section 2(6)]</td><td><table><tr><th>Particulars</th><th>Amount</th></tr><tr><td>All taxable supplies (excluding inward supplies the tax on which is payable under reverse charge mechanism)</td><td>–</td></tr><tr><td>Exempt supplies</td><td>–</td></tr><tr><td>Export of goods or services or both</td><td>–</td></tr><tr><td>Inter-state supplies of persons having the same PAN</td><td>–</td></tr><tr><td>Aggregate turnover</td><td>–</td></tr></table>Notes:
1. All the components are exclusive of CGST, SGST/UTGST, IGST or Cesses.
2. All the above supplies are to be taken on all India basis.</td></tr>
</table>

Agriculturist [Section 2(7)]	An agriculturist means an individual or a Hindu Undivided Family (HUF) who cultivates a land (a) by own labour: This means that the individual or the HUF personally works on the land, putting in their own physical effort and labor to cultivate crops or manage agricultural activities. Or (b) by the labour of family: In this case, the cultivation is carried out with the help of family members. Family members contribute their labor and effort towards farming activities, such as planting, harvesting, and other tasks involved in agricultural production. Or (c) by **servants** on wages payable in cash or kind (e.g., food) or by **hired labour** under personal supervision or the personal supervision of any member of the family.
Business [Section 2(17)]	(a) any trade, commerce, manufacture, profession, vocation, adventure, wager or any other similar activity, whether or not it is for a pecuniary benefit, (b) any activity or transaction in connection with or incidental or ancillary to sub-clause (a), (c) any activity or transaction in the nature of sub-clause (a), whether or not there is volume, frequency, continuity or regularity of such transaction, (d) supply or acquisition of goods, including capital goods and services, in connection with commencement or closure of business, (e) provision by a club, association, society, or any such body (for a subscription or any other consideration) of the facilities or benefits to its members, (f) admission, for a consideration, of persons to any premises, (g) services supplied by a person as the holder of an office which has been accepted by him in the course or furtherance of his trade, profession or vocation, (h) activities of a race club, including by way of totalisator or a license to book maker or activities of a licensed book maker in such club, and (i) any activity or transaction undertaken by the Central Government, a State Government or any local authority in which they are engaged as public authorities.
Capital goods [Section 2(19)]	Capital goods means goods, the value of which is capitalized in the books of account of the person claiming input tax credit, and such goods are used or intended to be used in the course or furtherance of business.
Casual taxable person [Section 2(20)]	Casual taxable person means a person who occasionally makes supply of goods or services or both in the course or furtherance of business (whether as principal, agent or in any other capacity) in a State or a Union territory where he has no fixed place of business.
Commissioner [Section 2(24)]	Commissioner means the Commissioner of central tax and includes the Principal Commissioner of central tax appointed under section 3 and the Commissioner of integrated tax appointed under the IGST Act.

Consideration [Section 2(31)]	(a) any payment made or to be made, whether in money or otherwise, in respect of, in response to, or for the inducement of, the supply of goods or services or both, whether by the recipient or by any other person, but shall not include any subsidy given by the Central Government or a State Government, (b) the monetary value of any act or forbearance, in respect of, in response to, or for the inducement of, the supply of goods or services or both, whether by the recipient or by any other person, but shall not include any subsidy given by the Central Government or a State Government: **Note:** An amount deposited for the supply of goods or services or both is not considered as payment made for such supply unless the supplier applies such deposit as consideration for the said supply.
Document [Section 2(41)]	Document includes written or printed records of any type and electronic records as defined under the Information Technology Act, 2000.
Exempt supply [Section 2(47)]	Exempt supply means supply of any goods or services or both, which is • nil-rated supply or • *exempt from tax under section 11 of the CGST Act, or under section 6 of the IGST Act,* • *non-taxable supply.*
Goods [Section 2(52)]	Goods means every kind of movable property except money and securities. Goods also include the following: (a) Actionable claims but only *lottery, betting, gambling.* (b) Growing crops, grass and things attached to or forming part of the land which are agreed to be served before supply or under a contract of supply.
India [Section 2(56)]	India means the territory of India as referred to in article 1 of the Constitution, its territorial waters, seabed and sub-soil underlying such waters, continental shelf, exclusive economic zone or any other maritime zone as referred to in the Territorial Waters, Continental Shelf, Exclusive Economic Zone and other Maritime Zones Act, 1976, and the air space above its territory and territorial waters.
Input [Section 2(59)]	It means any goods other than capital goods used or intended to be used by a supplier in the course or furtherance of business.
Input service [Section 2(60)]	It means service used or intended to be used by a supplier in the course or furtherance of business.
Input Service Distributor [Section 2(61)]	Input Service Distributor (commonly known as ISD) means an office of the supplier of goods or services or both, which receives tax invoices for the receipt of input services and issues a prescribed document for distributing the credit of CGST, SGST, IGST or UTGST paid on the said services to a supplier of taxable goods or services or both having the same Permanent Account Number as that of the said office.

Input tax [Section 2(62)]	Input tax in relation to a registered person means the CGST, SGST, IGST or UTGST charged on any supply of goods or services or both made to him and includes (a) the IGST charged on import of goods, (b) the tax payable under section 9(3)/(4) of the CGST/SGST Act, i.e., reverse charge mechanism. (c) the tax payable under section 5(3)/(4) of section 5 of the IGST Act, i.e., reverse charge mechanism. (d) the tax payable under section 7(3)/(4) i.e., reverse charge mechanism. However, input tax does not include tax payable under composition levy under section 10 of the CGST Act.
Input tax credit [Section 2(63)]	It means credit of input tax.
Intra-state supply of goods [Section 2(64)]	Intra-state supply of goods has the same meaning as given to it in section 8 of the IGST Act. In fact, when the location of supplier and the place of supply falls in the same State/Union territory, then the supply is called intra-state supply. In this case, the Central Government levies Central Tax known as Central GST (CGST), and the State Government levies State tax known as State GST (SGST). However, in the case of a Union Territory UTGST is charged, not SGST.
Intra-state supply of services [Section 2(64)]	Intra-state supply of services has the same meaning as given to it in section 8 of the IGST Act.
Inward supply [Section 2(67)]	It means receipt of goods or services or both, whether by purchase/acquisition or any other means with or without consideration.
Local authority [Section 2(69)]	1. a "Panchayat" as defined in clause (d) of article 243 of the Constitution. 2. a "Municipality" as defined in clause (e) of article 243P of the Constitution. 3. a Municipal Committee, a Zilla Parishad, a District Board, and any other authority legally entitled to or entrusted by the Central Government or any State Government with the control or management of a municipal or local fund. 4. a Cantonment Board as defined in section 3 of the Cantonments Act, 2006. 5. a Regional Council or a District Council constituted under the Sixth Schedule to the Constitution. 6. a Development Board constituted under article 371 and article 371J of the Constitution. 7. a Regional Council constituted under article 371A of the Constitution.

Money [Section 2(75)]	Money means • the Indian legal tender or any foreign currency, • cheque, • promissory note, • bill of exchange, • letter of credit, • draft, • pay order, • traveller cheque, • money order, • postal, • electronic remittance or any other instrument recognised by the Reserve Bank of India where used as a consideration to settle an obligation or exchange with Indian legal tender of another denomination, but it does not mean any currency that is kept for its numismatic value. **Author's Note:** Numismatic value means the worth of a currency which exceeds its face value. It may be due to historical factors or some other reason.
Motor Vehicle [Section 2(76)]	Motor vehicle means the motor vehicle as by section 2 of the Motor Vehicles Act, 1988.
Non-resident taxable person [Section 2(77)]	Non-resident taxable person means any person who occasionally makes supply of goods or services or both (whether as principal or agent or in any other capacity) but who has no fixed place of business or residence in India. **Author's Note:** Thus, he is a foreigner who wants to make supply of goods or services or both on a temporary basis but has no fixed place of business or residence in India.
Output tax [Section 2(82)]	It means CGST, SGST/UTGST, IGST charged by a taxable person (or his agent) on taxable supply of goods or services or both, but it does not include tax payable under reverse charge mechanism.
Outward supply [Section 2(83)]	Outward supply means supply of goods or services or both, whether by sale, transfer, barter, exchange, licence, rental, lease or disposal or any other mode, made or agreed to be made by such person in the course or furtherance of business.
Person [Section 2(84)]	Person includes 1. an individual, 2. a Hindu Undivided Family (HUF), 3. a company, 4. a firm, 5. a Limited Liability Partnership (LLP), 6. an association of persons (AOP) or a body of individuals (BOI), whether incorporated or not, in India or outside India, 7. any corporation established by or under any Central Act, State Act or Provincial Act or a Government company as defined in clause (45) of section 2 of the Companies Act, 2013,

	8. any body corporate incorporated by or under the laws of a country outside India, 9. a co-operative society registered under any law relating to co-operative societies, 10. a local authority, 11. Central Government or a State Government, 12. society as defined under the Societies Registration Act, 1860, 13. trust, and 14. every artificial juridical person not covered above.
Place of business [Section 2(8)]	1. a place from where the business is ordinarily carried on, and it includes a warehouse, a godown or any other place where a taxable person stores his goods, supplies or receives goods or services or both; or 2. a place where a taxable person maintains his books of account; or 3. a place where a taxable person is engaged in business through an agent, by whatever name called.
Principal place of business [Section 2(89)]	Principal place of business means the place of business as mentioned in the registration certificate FORM GST REG-06.
Proper officer [Section 2(91)]	Proper officer in relation to any function to be performed under the CGST Act, means the Commissioner or the officer of the central tax who is assigned that function by the Commissioner in CBIC.
Quarter [Section 2(92)]	A quarter means a period comprising 3 consecutive calendar months, ending on the last day of March, June, September and December of a calendar year.
Recipient [Section 2(93)]	**Case I: Consideration is payable** The person who is liable to pay consideration is called recipient. **Case II: Consideration is not payable** (a) **Supply of Goods:** If no consideration is payable, the person to whom goods are delivered or made available or to whom possession or use of goods is given or made available is called recipient. (b) **Supply of Services:** The person who is rendered the services is called recipient. **Note:** An agent working on behalf of the above-said person is also included in the definition of recipient.
Registered person [Section 2(94)]	Registered person means a person who is registered under section 25 but does not include a person who has a Unique Identity Number (UIN).
Removal of goods [Section 2(96)]	(a) dispatch of the goods for delivery by the supplier or any other person acting on behalf of such supplier or (b) collection of the goods by the recipient or by any other person acting on behalf of such recipient.

<table>
<tr><td>Services
[Section 2(102)]</td><td>Services means anything other than goods, money and securities, but includes
(a) activities relating to the use of money or its conversion by cash or by any other mode, from one form, currency or denomination to another form, currency or denomination for which a separate consideration is charged (e.g., conversion of Indian rupee into US dollars by a bank),
(b) facilitating or arranging transactions in securities (e.g., brokers facilitating sale or purchase of shares or mutual funds).</td></tr>
<tr><td>State
[Section 2(103)]</td><td>State includes a Union territory with Legislature.
Author's Note:
In simple words, the Union Territories having their own chief ministers are treated as States. Thus, Delhi, Puducherry, and Jammu & Kashmir are also states under the CGST Act.</td></tr>
<tr><td>Supplier
[Section 2(105)]</td><td>The person (or his agent) who makes supply is called supplier.</td></tr>
<tr><td>Taxable person
[Section 2(107)]</td><td>Taxable person is a person who is registered or required to be registered under section 22 or section 24.</td></tr>
<tr><td>Taxable supply
[Section 2(108)]</td><td>Taxable supply means a supply of goods or services or both which is leviable to tax under this Act.</td></tr>
<tr><td>Taxable territory
[Section 2(109)]</td><td>It means the territory to which the provisions of the CGST Act apply. As per section 1, the CGST Act is applicable to the whole of India. Thus, taxable territory means India.</td></tr>
<tr><td>Turnover in state or turnover in Union Territory
[Section 2(112)]</td><td>Turnover in State or turnover in Union territory means
<table>
<tr><th></th><th>Particulars</th><th>Amount</th></tr>
<tr><td></td><td>All taxable supplies (excluding inward supplies on which tax is payable under reverse charge)</td><td>–</td></tr>
<tr><td>Add</td><td>Exempt supplies made within the State/UT</td><td>–</td></tr>
<tr><td>Add</td><td>Exports of goods or services or both made from the State/UT</td><td>–</td></tr>
<tr><td>Add</td><td>Inter-state supplies of goods or services or both made from the State/UT</td><td>–</td></tr>
</table>
Note: All the components are exclusive of CGST, SGST/UTGST, IGST or Cess.</td></tr>
<tr><td>Union Territory
[Section 2(114)]</td><td>Union territory includes
(a) the Andaman and Nicobar Islands,
(b) Lakshadweep,
(c) Dadra and Nagar Haveli and Daman and Diu,
(d) Ladakh,
(e) Chandigarh, and
(f) Other territory.
Author's Note:
Delhi, Puducherry and Jammu & Kashmir are also Union Territories as per our general knowledge, but under the CGST Act, they are treated as states because of section 2(103). We know that Delhi, Puducherry and J&K have their own legislature; therefore, as per section 2(103), they must be treated as states only.</td></tr>
</table>

Voucher [Section 2(118)]	A voucher is an instrument (or instrument or card) that can be used as payment or partial payment for goods or services or both. It specifies the goods or services that can be obtained or the potential suppliers who accept it. This information may be mentioned on the voucher itself or in accompanying documents, which also include the terms and conditions for its use.

3.11 Dual System of GST

India has adopted a dual GST system in the sense that in case of intra-state supply, two types of GST are levied, i.e., central tax (popularly known as Central Goods and Services Tax or CGST) and state tax (popularly known as state Goods and Services Tax or SGST). Further, in the case of inter-state supply, the Central Government levies an integrated tax (popularly known as Integrated Goods and Services Tax or IGST). Therefore, a supplier finds his invoice price in the following manner:

Nature of supply	Intra-state supply
Value of taxable supply	–
Add: CGST (levied by the Central Government)	–
Add: SGST (levied by the State Government)	–
Invoice price	–

Nature of supply	Inter-state supply
Value of taxable supply	–
Add: IGST (levied by the Central Government)	–
Invoice price	–

3.12 Format to Calculate GST Liability

Calculation of GST liability is very simple. We are required to have two amounts: (1) output tax, i.e., GST collected by the supplier (2) input tax, i.e., input tax paid on purchase of inputs/input services/capital goods. Once we have these two amounts, the input tax is subtracted from the output tax to determine GST liability.

The subtraction of the input tax from the output tax is called taking input tax credit, but this input tax credit cannot always be availed because various sections of the CGST Act and rules have to be followed to avail it. Such section rules have been discussed in the chapter on input tax credit. Thus, for numerical questions, we are going to use the following fundamental format:

Particulars	Amount (in ₹)
Output tax (CGST, SGST/UTGST, IGST collected)	–
Less: Eligible Input tax credit	–
GST liability which is to be paid using electronic cash ledger	–

3.13 GST Common Portal (www.gst.gov.in)

The GST Common Portal is a web-based platform designed to provide a single point of access for taxpayers, GST practitioners and other stakeholders to access the Goods and Services

Tax (GST) system in India. It serves as a one-stop shop for all GST-related activities, including registration, filing returns, payment of taxes and claiming refunds. The portal is managed by the Goods and Services Tax Network (GSTN), which is a non-profit organization responsible for developing and maintaining the IT infrastructure of the GST system. In fact, the GST portal is the biggest weapon of the GST system. It has merged the technology with the GST laws to serve the Governments and taxpayers.

3.14 GST Network (GSTN) (www.gstn.org.in)

GST Network (GSTN) is a government enterprise registered under section 25 of the Companies Act, 1956. It was established to provide the technological infrastructure for the implementation of the Goods and Services Tax (GST) in India. GSTN is responsible for creating a robust IT system that facilitates the registration, payment and return filing process for taxpayers under GST. Although it was registered as section 25 company, the Board of GSTN, in its 49th Board Meeting held on 30 June 2022, has decided to convert GSTN into a Government Company. The readers can scan the QR code to read about GSTN in more detail, but other notable points about GSTN are as follows:

1. **Unique PPP:** GSTN is a unique public-private partnership (PPP) between the government and private stakeholders. The Central Government and State Governments & EC separately own 24.5% of the stake in GSTN, while the rest is owned by private companies such as HDFC Bank, HDFC Ltd., ICICI Bank, NSE Strategic Investment Corporation, and LIC Housing Finance Ltd.

2. **Primary Objective:** The primary objective of GSTN is to provide a user-friendly interface that allows taxpayers to comply with the GST laws seamlessly.

3. **Development of GST portal:** GSTN is responsible for developing and maintaining the IT infrastructure for GST. This includes the GST portal, which serves as a one-stop shop for all GST-related activities. The portal provides various services, such as registration, return filing, payment, and refund processing. It also allows taxpayers to track the status of their applications and refunds.

4. **Role of Infosys:** GSTN has selected Infosys as the exclusive Managed Service Provider (MSP) responsible for designing, developing and implementing the GST system, which encompasses all application software, tools and infrastructure, as well as operating and maintaining the system for a five-year period following the Go-Live date.

Theory Questions

1. What are the characteristics of Goods and Services Tax?
2. What is the GST Council? What are the roles played by the GST council?
3. What are the taxes replaced by GST? Can you tell those which are still out of the ambit of GST?
4. VAT, Central Excise Duty and Central Sales do not exist at all in India after GST. Do you agree with this statement?
5. What is a GST Network? How is it related to the GST Common Portal?
6. What is the GST Common Portal?
7. Do you agree that India is using a Dual GST System? Explain.
8. Write short notes on the following:
   (a) Article 279A
   (b) Input tax
   (c) Output tax
   (d) Central tax
   (e) State tax
   (f) Union Territories under GST
   (g) Goods
   (h) Services
   (i) Intra-state supply
   (j) Inter-state supply
9. Why are Delhi, Jammu and Kashmir and Puducherry not union territories under GST despite they are union territories otherwise?
10. Explain briefly the history of the development of GST.

Appendix II

Current members of the GST Council as of 28th May 2023

S. No.	Government	Name of the Member	Portfolio
1.	Government of India	Smt. Nirmala Sitaraman	Union Finance Minister
2.	Government of India	Shri Pankaj Chaudhary	Union Minister of State (Finance)
3.	Andhra Pradesh	Shri Buggana Rajendranath	Finance Minister
4.	Arunachal Pradesh	Shri Chowna Mein	Deputy Chief Minister
5.	Assam	Smt. Ajanta Neog	Finance Minister
6.	Bihar	Shree Vijay Kumar Chaudhary	Finance Minister and Commercial Taxes Minister
7.	Chhattisgarh	Shri T.S. Singh Deo	Minister for Commercial Tax
8.	Delhi	Shri Kailash Gahlot	Transport & Environment Minister
9.	Goa	Shri Mauvin Godinho	Minister for Transport and Panchayat Raj, Housing, Protocol and Legislative Affairs

S. No.	Government	Name of the Member	Portfolio
10.	Gujarat	Shri Kanubhai Desai	Minister for Finance
11.	Haryana	Shri Dushyant Chautala	Deputy Chief Minister
12.	Himachal Pradesh	Shri Jai Ram Thakur	Hon'ble Chief Minister, Himachal Pradesh
13.	UT of J&K	Shri Rajeev Rai Bhatnagar	Advisor to Lieutenant Governor
14.	Jharkhand	Dr. Rameshwar Oraon	Minister for Planning cum Finance, Commercial Taxes and Food, Public Distribution and Consumer Affairs
15.	Karnataka	Shri Krishna Byre Gowda	Minister for Revenue Department
16.	Kerala	Shri K.N. Balagopal	Finance Minister
17.	Madhya Pradesh	Shri Jagdish Devda	Finance Minister
18.	Maharashtra	Shri Ajit Pawar	Deputy Chief Minister
19.	Manipur	Dr. Sapam Ranjan Singh	Minister For Medical, Health & Family Welfare Department and Publicity & Information Department
20.	Meghalaya	Shri Abu Taher Mondal	Community & Rural Development Minister
21.	Mizoram	Shri Lalchamliana	Hon'ble Minister, Home, Taxation, etc.
22.	Nagaland	Shri K.G. Kenye	Minister of Power and Parliament Affairs
23.	Odisha	Shri Bikram Keshari Arukha	Minister of Finance
24.	Puducherry	Shri K. Lakshminarayanan	Hon'ble Public Works Minister
25.	Punjab	Shri Harpal Singh Cheema	Finance Minister
26.	Rajasthan	Shri Shanti Kumar Dhariwal	Minister for Local Self Government, Urban Development & Housing, Law & Legal Affairs and Parliamentary Affairs
27.	Sikkim	Mr. Bedu Singh Pant	Hon'ble Minister for Tourism, Civil Aviation and Industries
28.	Tamil Nadu	Shri Thiru Thangam Thennarasu	Minister for Finance, Human Resource Management
29.	Telangana	Shri T. Harish Rao	Finance Minister
30.	Tripura	Shri Jishnu Dev Varma	Deputy Chief Minister
31.	Uttar Pradesh	Shri Suresh Kumar Khanna	Minister for Finance, Parliamentary Affairs, Medical Education
32.	Uttarakhand	Shri Premchand Aggarwal	Hon'ble Minister of Finance, Urban Development, Housing, Legislative and Parliamentary Affairs, Reorganization and Census
33.	West Bengal	Smt. Chandrima Bhattacharya	Minister of State for Finance

Source: https://gstcouncil.gov.in/gst-council-member

4

Supply in GST

4.1 Introduction

Any occurrence that is subject to tax is a taxable event. A taxable event is actually the necessary feature without which a tax cannot be levied. For instance, manufacturing goods in India is a taxable event according to Excise law. No excise duty could be levied on goods that are not manufactured in India. The sale of goods is a taxable event under VAT law. VAT cannot be levied if no goods are sold. In GST law, the taxable event is supply. Perhaps the most fundamental change that the GST law has brought is the term supply, replacing all the terms like manufacture, sale, service and purchase. If something is not a supply, then no GST can be levied and collected. This fundamental rule must be kept in mind while studying GST. This chapter will describe the meaning of the term supply, its inclusions, exclusions and other aspects.

4.2 Concept of Supply—Chapter III, the CGST Act

Since no supply means no GST, it becomes necessary to know the meaning of the term supply. Chapter III of the CGST Act, which should be read with Schedules I, II, and III, contains the meaning and scope of supply. Let us see them.

4.2.1 Scope of Supply—Section 7

1. Forms of supply: Section 7(1)(a): Supply includes sale, transfer, exchange, barter, lease, rent, license and disposal made or agreed to be made for consideration by a person in the course or furtherance of business.

Supply in GST	From of supply	Meaning
1.	Sale	Sale refers to the exchange of goods or services for money. The ownership of the goods or services is transferred from the seller to the buyer.
2.	Transfer	Transfer refers to the act of moving or handing over ownership of an asset or property from one person to another. Transfer can be done with or without monetary exchange. For example, the transfer of property ownership through a gift deed or inheritance does not involve monetary exchange.

3.	Exchange	Exchange refers to the mutual transfer of goods or services between two parties. In an exchange, the value of the goods or services exchanged is generally considered to be equal. For example, a person may exchange a used car for a used motorcycle with another person.
4.	Barter	Barter refers to the direct exchange of goods or services between two parties without the use of money. For example, a farmer may trade his crop for a carpenter's furniture.
5.	Lease	A lease is a contractual agreement between a lessor and a lessee, where the lessor grants the right to use a property or asset for a specified period in exchange for rent or payment. A lease typically involves a longer-term commitment and usually refers to real estate or high-value assets such as machinery or vehicles.
6.	Rent	Rent is the periodic payment made by a tenant to a landlord for the use of a property or asset. Rent is typically paid monthly, and it can refer to any type of property, including real estate, vehicles, equipment, or even personal property like clothing.
7.	License	A license is a legal permission granted by a licensor to a licensee to use a particular product, service, or intellectual property. A license usually involves the use of intangible assets such as software, music, or patents. The licensee is granted a non-exclusive right to use the asset, but the ownership and control of the asset remain with the licensor.
8.	Disposal	Disposal refers to the act of getting rid of an asset, either by selling, donating, or discarding it. It can refer to any type of asset, including real estate, vehicles, equipment, or personal property. Disposal may involve a one-time transaction or a series of transactions, and it usually involves transferring ownership or control of the asset.

2. Supply by a person to its members/constituent: Section 7(1) (aa) **[with effect from 1 January 2022]:** Supply includes the activities or transactions by a person, other than an individual, to its members or constituents or vice-versa, for cash, deferred payment or other valuable consideration.

Example 4.1: XYZ Co-operative Society is a registered cooperative society with its members being small dairy farmers. The society procures milk from its members and processes it into dairy products, which are then sold to its members and other consumers for a price. In this case, the society is the person other than an individual, and its members are the constituents. The society carries out activities or transactions with its members for valuable consideration, which is the price paid by the members for the dairy products purchased from the society.

3. Import of services for consideration: Section 7(1)(b): Import of services for a consideration whether or not in the course or furtherance of business is a supply.

4. Activities specified in Schedule I: Section 7(1)(c): Schedule I specifies the activities that are supply-made or agreed to be made without consideration.

5. Supply of goods or Supply of services as referred to in Schedule II: Section 7(1A): Where a transaction or activity is a supply as per section 7(1), then it is important to know whether it is a supply of good or service, then we should refer to Schedule II.

6. Some activities are neither a supply of goods nor a supply of services: Section 7(2): Section 7(2) overrides section 7(1) and specifically says that the following activities or transactions are treated neither as a supply of goods nor a supply of services.

(a) Activities or transactions specified in Schedule III *or*

(b) notified activities or transactions undertaken by the Central Government, a State Government or any local authority in which they are engaged as public authorities.

7. Government may notify the nature of transactions: Section 7(3): As per this section, the government may notify the transactions that are treated as

(a) a supply of goods and not as a supply of services *or*

(b) a supply of services and not as a supply of goods.

4.2.2 Schedules specified under Section 7

Three schedules have been specified under section 7. These are as follows:

Schedule I

Schedule I specifies the activities made or agreed to be made even if made **without** a consideration to be treated as supply.

1. Permanent transfer of business assets

Where business assets (the input tax credit of which has been availed) are transferred or disposed of permanently.

Example 4.2: Mr. Jetha Lal purchases fifty refrigerators for his shop, Jetha Lal Gada Electronics. He has duly availed of the input tax credit on these refrigerators. He gifts one refrigerator to his friend Babita. Is this gift a supply?

Solution

(a) The gift made to Babita is a permanent transfer of a business asset, i.e., a refrigerator.

(b) Input tax credit has been availed on the above refrigerator.

Since all the conditions of para 1 of Schedule I are satisfied, therefore, the transfer is a supply and therefore, Jetha Lal must charge GST.

Example 4.3: ABC Ltd. purchases a 5-seater car for its business purpose. This car is later on permanently transferred free of cost. Is this a supply?

Solution

(a) The car transferred is a permanent transfer of a business asset.

(b) Input tax credit on 5-seater car is blocked under section 17(5); therefore, ABC Ltd. could not avail the input tax credit on it.

Since all the conditions of para 1 of Schedule I are not satisfied, therefore, the transfer is not a supply.

Example 4.4: XYZ Ltd. purchases a bus for its business purpose. This bus is later permanently transferred free of cost. Though the bus is eligible for the input tax credit, XYZ Ltd. did not avail of the credit. Is this a supply?

Solution

(a) The bus transferred is a permanent transfer of a business asset.

(b) Input tax credit has not been availed despite the bus is eligible for credit.

Since all the conditions of para 1 of Schedule I are not satisfied, therefore, the transfer is not a supply.

2. Supply between related or distinct persons

Supply between related persons or distinct persons as specified in section 25, when made in the course or furtherance of business. However, gifts not exceeding ₹50,000 in value in a financial year by an employer to an employee are not a supply.

Example 4.5: Suppose that V Ltd. and T Ltd. are related persons. V Ltd. transfers product X to T Ltd. without consideration in the course of its business. Is it a supply?

Solution

(a) V Ltd. and T Ltd. are related persons.

(b) The transfer of the goods is in the course of business.

Since all the conditions of para 2 of Schedule I are satisfied, therefore, the transfer is a supply and therefore, V Ltd. must charge GST.

3. Outward or inward supply of goods through an agent

Supply of goods by a principal to his agent, where he supplies the goods on behalf of his principal, or by an agent to his principal, where he receives goods on behalf of his principal.

Example 4.6: ABC Ltd. is a manufacturer of industrial machinery. They have appointed PQR Pvt. Ltd. as their agent to sell their machinery to customers. ABC Ltd. supplies the machinery to PQR Pvt. Ltd., who then sells it to customers on behalf of ABC Ltd. Comment on the supply of goods.

Solution

In this case, ABC Ltd. is the principal, and PQR Pvt. Ltd. is the agent; therefore, as per para 3 of Schedule I, the supply of goods by a principal to his agent or vice-versa is a supply.

4. Import of services from related persons or other establishments of the importer

Where services are imported by a person from a related person or any of his other establishments located outside India in the ordinary course of business.

Example 4.7: A has a registered business of Tax consultancy in Delhi. His son B is also a tax expert in London. A has received some tax consultancy from his son without any consideration. Is it a supply?

Solution

Since the service of tax consultancy is imported from London by A from his son B (A and B are related persons as per section 15), therefore, as per para 4 of Schedule I, it is a supply. Moreover, A is liable to pay GST under the reverse charge mechanism.

Schedule II

This schedule lists the cases that are supply, but whether it is supply of goods or services. It is irrelevant whether these supplies are for consideration or without consideration.

1. Transfer

(a)	Transfer of title in goods (or ownership in goods) is a supply of goods.
(b)	Transfer of right in goods or of undivided share in goods without transfer of title is a supply of services. In this scenario, the owner of the goods retains the ownership while granting the lessee or renter the right to use or possess the goods for a specified period.
(c)	If there is an agreement to transfer title in goods at a future date on payment of the agreed consideration, then such transfer is the supply of goods.

Example 4.8: Wizard Mobile Co. sells a mobile phone to a customer for ₹40,000. Is it a supply of goods or services?

Solution

As per clause (a) of para 1 of Schedule II, the transfer of title in goods (i.e., ownership of the mobile phone in the present case) is a supply of goods.

Example 4.9: Shri Ravi Shankar gives Kishan machinery on rent for 3 months. Is it a supply of goods or services?

Solution

As per clause (b) of para 1 of Schedule II, the transfer of right in goods without making the transferee owner is a supply of services. Therefore, renting machinery to Kishan is a supply of services.

Example 4.10: X enters into an agreement with Y on 19 March 2022. Under this agreement, X will sell 5000 bags of white cement to Y on 1 December 2022 at ₹1050 per bag. Title in goods will be transferred to Y at the time of payment of full consideration on 1 December 2022. Is it a case of supply of goods or services?

Solution

As per clause (c) of para 1 of Schedule II, if title in goods is to be transferred, under an agreement, in the future, then it is treated as supply of goods. In the present example, there is an agreement to transfer the title to goods in the future; therefore, this is the supply of goods.

2. Land and building

(a)	any lease, tenancy, easement, licence of occupying land is the supply of services.
(b)	any lease or letting out of the building, including a commercial, industrial or residential complex for business or commerce, either wholly or partly, is the supply of services.

Example 4.11: X gives land on lease/rent to Y for fifty years. Is it a supply of services or goods?

Solution

As per clause (a) of para 2 of Schedule II, giving land on lease or rent is a supply of services. Therefore, the land given on lease to Y is a supply of service.

Example 4.12: A gives a residential or complex building on lease/rent to B. Is it a supply of services or goods?

Solution

As per clause (b) of para 2 of Schedule II, giving a building on lease or rent is a supply of services. Therefore, the residential or commercial building given on lease to Y is a supply of service.

3. Treatment or process or job work

Any treatment or process applied by a person (known as job-worker) on the goods owned by another person (known as principal), then such treatment or process is treated as a supply of services. In short, job work is a supply of services.

Example 4.13: X Ltd. is a shirt manufacturer. It sends 5000 shirts to Y Ltd. for their dying for a consideration of ₹10 lakhs. Is it a supply of services or goods?

Solution

As per para 3 of Schedule II, any treatment or process (dying on the shirts in the present case) applied to the goods of another person is a supply of services. Therefore, Y Ltd. has supplied services.

4. Transfer of business assets

<table>
<tr><td>(a) Transfer or disposal of business assets by the businessman or on his direction: Where a person transfers or disposes his business assets and such assets are no longer business assets, then such transfer or disposal is a supply of goods. The same provision is applied when the person does not do so himself, but directs somebody else to do so.</td></tr>
<tr><td>(b) Business goods are put to personal or other use: Where a person running a business puts the goods (held or used for his business purposes) to personal use or makes such goods available to any person for the use (other than the said business purpose), then such use or making available of such goods is a supply of services. The same provision is applied when the person does not do so himself, but directs somebody else to do so.</td></tr>
<tr><td>(c) A person is no longer a taxable person: Where any person is no longer a taxable person, then any goods that are part of the business assets are deemed to be supplied by him in the course or furtherance of his business immediately before the person is no longer a taxable person. However, in the following cases, this provision is not applied.
(i) There is a transfer of business as a going concern to another person or
(ii) The business is run by a personal representative who is deemed to be a taxable person.
Author's Note:
It simply means that if someone is not a taxable person anymore, then he is required to pay tax on the business assets on hand immediately before he is no longer a taxable person. Here, it is assumed that those goods have been supplied to himself. So, the supplier and recipient are both the same person. The logic behind this principle seems that the Government wants to prevent the situation of tax loss in which those assets may be supplied even after he is no longer a taxable person.</td></tr>
</table>

Example 4.14: Mr. Jetha Lal Champak Lal Gada, the owner of Gada Electronics registered in Mumbai, directs his staff Bagha and Nattu Kaka to sell excess inventory. Is it a supply?

Solution

Yes, it is a supply of goods. As per para 4(a), if the person carrying on business directs someone to transfer or dispose of goods that are business assets, then such transfer or disposal is the supply of goods.

Example 4.15: Atama Ram owns a construction company that specializes in building homes. He also owns a pickup truck that he uses to transport materials and tools to and from his job sites. The truck is registered in the name of his business, and he claims depreciation. However, on the weekends, he uses the truck to go camping and fishing with his family. He also allows his friends to borrow the truck for similar purposes. Is it a supply?

Solution

In this case, the usage of the truck (goods held for business use) for non-business purposes constitutes a supply of services as per para 4(b) of Schedule II. As a result, Atama Ram is liable to pay GST on this supply.

Example 4.16: Ms. Abha runs a small bakery business that is registered in Lucknow. One day, she decides to retire and close down her business. As a result, she informs the tax authorities that she will no longer be a taxable person and deregisters for GST. At the time of closer of her business, there are unsold cakes and breads in her bakery that are valued at ₹10,000 and a counter valued at ₹50,000. Comment on the taxability.

Solution

As per para 4(c) of Schedule II, when she deregisters for GST, she will be required to treat these goods as if she has supplied them to herself for ₹10,000 and ₹50,000 and charge herself GST on these amounts.

5. Supply of services

(a) Renting of immovable property. **Author's Note:** **The Government has notified the cases where the renting of immovable property is exempt. For example, if an immovable property is given on rent to an unregistered person, then this is an exempt supply. In Chapter 6, this exemption has been explained.**
(b) the construction of • a complex (including a complex intended for sale to a buyer), • building (including a building intended for sale to a buyer), • civil structure, or • a part of it. but the following condition must be satisfied: **Condition:** Part or entire consideration is received before earlier of the following: (i) issuance of completion certificate, if required, by a competent authority, or (ii) first occupation.

Notes: (1) Construction includes additions, alterations, replacements, or remodelling of any existing civil structure. (2) Competent authority means the Government or any authority having the power to issue a completion certificate under any law for the time being in force, and in case of non-requirement of such certificate from such authority, then competent authority means the following: o **Architect:** an architect registered with the Council of Architecture constituted under the Architects Act, 1972, o **Chartered engineer:** a chartered engineer registered with the Institution of Engineers (India), or o **Licensed surveyor:** a licensed surveyor of the respective local body of the city or town or village or development or planning authority.
(c) Transferring or permitting, on a temporary basis, the use or enjoyment of any intellectual property right (IPR).
(d) Information Technology Software • developing, • designing, • programming, • customizing, • adapting, • upgrading, • enhancing, • implementing an information technology software. However, the supply of packed or readymade software is a supply of goods.
(e) Agreeing to the obligation • to refrain from an act, or • to tolerate an act or a situation, or • to do an act
(f) Transfer of the right to use any goods for any purpose (whether or not for a specified period) for cash, deferred payment or other valuable consideration.

Example 4.17: A Limited lets out his ground floor to B (a registered person) for placing a vending machine for a consideration of ₹10,00,000. Is it a supply?

Solution

Yes, as per para 5(a) of Schedule II, renting of immovable property is the supply of services.

Example 4.18: Ganesh Builders constructs four residential floors in a building in Ghaziabad. The price of each floor is thirty lakhs. The buyer paid 40% of the amount before the construction completion. Is it a supply of goods or services?

Solution

As per para 5 of Schedule II, construction of a building is a supply of service provided a part or the entire consideration is received before the completion of the construction or the first occupation, whichever is earlier. In the present case, 40% of the consideration is received before completion of the construction; therefore, the construction is a supply of service and subject to GST.

Example 4.19: Ram Baxy Ltd. allows Y Ltd. to use a patent right temporarily. Is it a supply of goods or services?

Solution

As per para 5 of Schedule II, if a person transfers or allows an intellectual property right (i.e., in the present case) on a temporary basis, then it is a supply of services.

Example 4.20: SS (P) Ltd. develops a management information system software for R Ltd. Is it a supply of service or goods?

Solution

As per para 5 of Schedule II, developing IT software is a supply of service.

Example 4.21: Jeevan (registered in Nehru Place, Delhi) sells packed accounting software to a company.

Solution

As per para 5 of Schedule II, if software is developed, designed, programmed, customized, adapted, upgraded, enhanced, implemented, then it is a supply of services. In the present case, Jeevan supplies an already developed software; hence, it is not covered by Schedule II. It is a supply of goods.

Example 4.22: THE BEST CLASSES (a coaching institution in East Delhi) agrees with THE KS TUTORIALS (a coaching institution in Ghaziabad) not to open its branch in Ghaziabad for a consideration of ₹50 lakhs. Is agreeing to not open the branch a supply of services?

Solution

Yes, as per para 5(e), agreeing to not doing some act (not opening the branch in Ghaziabad) is a supply of services.

6. These composite supplies to be treated as supply of services

(a) **Works contract:** As per section 2(119) works contract means a contract of building, construction, fabrication, completion, erection, installation, fitting out, improvement, modification, repair, maintenance, renovation, alternation or commissioning of any immovable property wherein the transfer of property in goods whether as goods or in some other form is involved in the execution of such contract.

Image courtesy–Freepik

(b) **Restaurant services:** Supply of food, beverages (other than alcoholic liquor for human consumption) or other items that people consume, either as part of service or in any other way for cash, deferred payment or other valuable consideration. It simply means that the supply by a restaurant is a composite supply and be treated as a supply of services.

Image courtesy–Freepik

Schedule III: Negative List

Schedule III states the activities which are neither supply of goods nor supply of services. Hence, not liable to GST.

1. Services by an employee to his employer

Services by an employee to the employer in the course of or in relation to his employment. However, gifts in value exceeding ₹50,000 given to employees in a financial year may be subject to GST.

Example 4.23: Mr. A teaches as an employee at Prisha Public School. Is it a supply?

Image courtesy–Freepik

Solution

As per paragraph 1 of Schedule III, the service given by an employee to his employer is not a supply.

Example 4.24: Mr. X teaches as an employee at Dhani International School. He is a registered painter also. The school gets his services as a painter for its annual function for a consideration of ₹10,000. Is it a supply?

Solution

As per paragraph 1 of Schedule III, the service given by an employee to his employer is not a supply. However, if service is given not in the capacity of the employee, then this is supply. Therefore, the painting service is a supply.

2. Services of Justice

Services by any district court, high court, and the Supreme Court or Tribunal.

3. Services by certain persons

(a) The functions performed by the Members of Parliament (MPs), Members of Legislative Assembly (MLAs), Members of Panchayats, Members of Municipalities and members of other local authorities.

(b) The duties performed by a person who holds a constitutional post (e.g., the President of India, the Prime Minister of India, the Chief Justice of India, etc.).

(c) The duties performed by a chairperson or a member or a director in a body established by the Central Government, State Government, or local authority, but such chairperson or member or director is not deemed an employee before the commencement of this clause.

4. **Services in grief**

Services of funeral, crematorium, mortuary, transportation of diseased.

5. **Sale of immovable property**

• Sale of land, and • Sale of building, but subject to paragraph 5(b) of Schedule II.

Example 4.25: Khushi Builders sells a fully constructed building to Vijay for ₹1 crore. The buyer paid 100 percent of the consideration after the construction completion. Is it a supply?

Solution

As per paragraph 5 of Schedule III, the sale of land and building is not a supply, provided it is not covered by paragraph 5(b) of Schedule II. In the present case, since 100% of the consideration is received by the builder after completion of the construction of the building, therefore it is not covered by paragraph 5(b) of Schedule II. Thus, the transaction is not a supply.

6. **Actionable claims**

Actionable claims except

- lottery,
- betting,
- gambling
- horse racing
- casinos
- online money gaming

Image courtesy–Freepik

7. **Out-and-out supply or Merchant trading**

Supply of goods from Non-taxable territory to Non-taxable territory without entering into India. Such a case is known as Out and out supply or merchant trading.

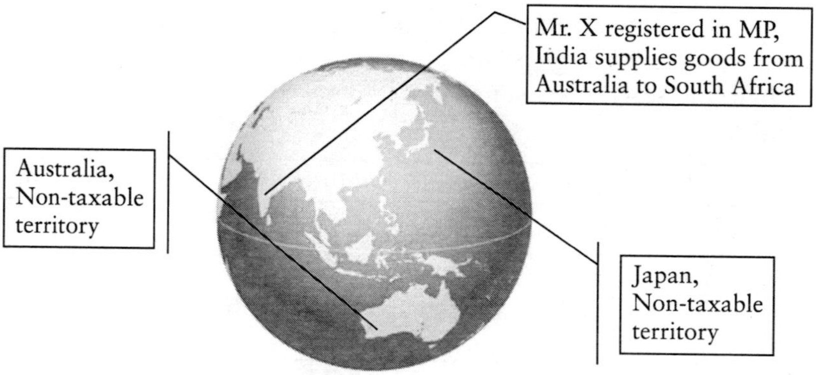

Image courtesy–Freepik

8. **Supply of goods before clearance for home consumption**

(a)	supply of warehoused goods to any person before clearance for home consumption.
(b)	supply of goods by the consignee to any other person by endorsement of title documents after the goods have been dispatched from the port of origin outside India but before clearance for home consumption.

Example 4.26: X imported some goods from the US, but they are lying in the customs bonded warehouse because they have not been cleared for home consumption. After some time, X sold the goods to Y without making the goods cleared from customs. Is it a supply?

Solution

As per paragraph 8(a) of Schedule III, supplying those goods which are not cleared from customs for home consumption is not a supply. Therefore, the goods sold by X to Y are not a supply.

Example 4.27: Suppose that a consignee in India has placed an order for a shipment of electronic equipment from a manufacturer in South Korea. The manufacturer ships the goods from the port of origin in South Korea to the port of destination in India. While the goods are in transit on the high seas, the consignee decides to sell a portion of the shipment to another buyer in India. To do so, the consignee endorses the title documents (e.g., the bill of lading) over to the buyer, effectively transferring ownership of the goods to them. Is it a supply?

Solution

As per para 8(b) of Schedule III, if a consignee transfers the title in goods after they have been dispatched from the port of origin outside India but before the goods are cleared by the Indian Customs for home consumption, such transfer is not a supply. In the present case, the title in goods has been transferred during transit on the high seas; therefore, this is not a supply.

9. Gant of Liquor License—Notification No. 25/2019—Central Tax (Rate) dated 30.09.2019

> If the State Governments (in which they are engaged as public authorities) grant alcoholic liquor licenses against a license fee or application fee or by whatever name called, then it is to be treated as neither a supply of goods nor a supply of services.

4.3 Classification of Supply

Supply can be classified on the basis of bundle, taxability, continuity, and place of supply. The following diagram shows this classification.

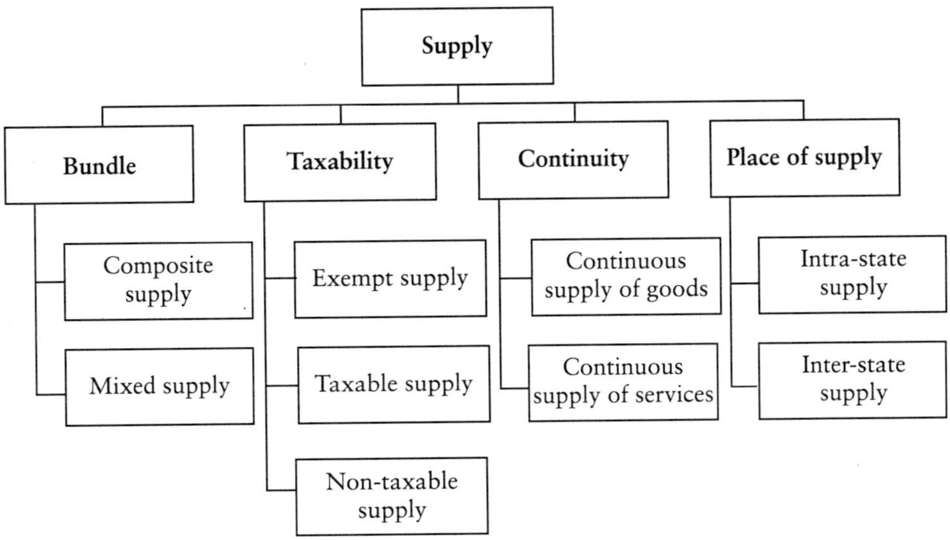

1. Composite Supply: Section 2(30): Composite supply means a supply satisfying the following conditions:

(a) It is a supply made by a taxable person to a recipient.
(b) It consists of two or more taxable supplies of goods or services or both or any combination thereof, which are naturally bundled and supplied in the ordinary course of business. In other words, the bundled supplies are naturally combined and provided together as a single package as a normal business course (it will not be surprising to do so in this type of business).
(c) There is a principal supply or main supply.

Composite supply as a supply of principal supply–Section 8(a): As per section 8(a), a composite supply is treated as the supply of principal supply. Therefore, the tax rate applicable to the principal supply is treated to be the tax rate applicable to the composite supply.

Example 4.28: When we purchase an air-conditioner, we generally get a warranty, too. This is a composite supply, and the principal supply is the supply of air-conditioners, and all other supplies are ancillary.

Example 4.29: When we stay in a hotel, we generally get food services along with accommodation. This is a composite supply, and the principal supply is accommodation in a hotel, and all other supplies are ancillary.

Principal supply

Ancillary Image courtesy–Freepik

Example 4.30: An air travel ticket from Delhi to Hyderabad may include carriage of luggage, providing food on board and free insurance. This is a composite supply, and the principal supply is the **transport of passengers**, and all other supplies are ancillary.

Image courtesy–Freepik

Principal supply Ancillary Supply

2. Mixed supply: Section 2(74): A mixed supply is a supply satisfying the following conditions:

(a) It is a supply made by a taxable person to a recipient.
(b) It consists of two or more individual supplies of goods or services or both or any other combination thereof.
(c) The supply is made for a single price/consolidated price.
(d) The supply is not naturally bundled.
(e) The supply is not in conjunction with each other in the ordinary course of business.

Rate of tax in case of mixed Supply: Section 8(b): According to section 8(b), the tax rate applicable is the highest rate of all the individual supplies rates.

Example 4.31: When we buy a package made of canned foods, sweets, chocolates, cakes, dry fruits, etc., at a single price, then this is a case of mixed supply. Each of these items can be supplied separately and is not dependent on any other.

3. Exempt supply and Taxable Supply: Exempt supply means the supply which

(a) attracts nil rate of tax or
(b) is exempted under section 11 of the CGST Act or section 6 of the IGST Act or
(c) is a non-taxable supply. Non-taxable supply is the supply which is not subject to GST (e.g., petroleum crude, high speed diesel, petrol, natural gas, aviation turbine fuel).

The supply that is not exempt is called **taxable supply**. Taxable supply also includes the zero-rated supply.

4. Zero-Rated Supply: Section 16 of the IGST Act.: Zero-rated supply means

(a) Export of goods or services or both or
(b) Supply of goods or services (for authorized operations) to a SEZ developer or a SEZ unit.

General knowledge (optional)

(1) A Special Economic Zone (SEZ) is a geographical region in a country that is established with the aim of promoting foreign investment, generating employment opportunities,

and boosting exports. SEZs are designated areas that are given certain incentives and benefits by the Government to attract investment, such as tax exemptions, simplified procedures for setting up businesses, and relaxed labour laws.

(2) On the other hand, an SEZ developer is a company or an individual who develops and operates the SEZ. SEZ developers invest in the infrastructure, facilities, and services required to set up businesses in the SEZ, such as roads, water supply, power supply, communication networks, and other basic amenities. The SEZ developer is responsible for obtaining all the necessary approvals and clearances from the Government, as well as for managing and maintaining the SEZ.

(3) A SEZ unit is a company or business that operates within a SEZ.

5. Continuous Supply of Goods: Section 2(32): Section 2(32) states that continuous supply of goods means a supply of goods which is provided, or agreed to be provided, continuously or on a recurrent basis, under a contract, whether or not by means of a wire, cable, pipeline or other conduit, and for which the supplier invoices the recipient on a regular or periodic basis and includes supply of such goods as the Government may, subject to such conditions, as it may, by notification, specify. Thus, the following features of continuous supply can be noted down:

1. Supply may be in present or in future, but on a recurrent basis.
2. Supply is made under a contract.
3. Supplier issues invoices regularly.
4. Means of delivery are irrelevant, i.e., supply is made by way of a wire, cable, pipeline or other conduit or maybe some other way.
5. It includes the supplies notified by the Government.

Example 4.32: Company A agrees, under a contract signed with Company B, to supply a number of cans of water by way of delivery in person at 5 am on a daily basis. The number of cans shall be informed one day before. At the end of each month, Company A will raise an invoice for B. This is a case of continuous supply of goods because the supply is agreed to be made under a contract, and periodical invoicing shall be made.

6. Continuous supply of services: Section 2(33): Section 2(33) states that continuous supply of services means a supply of services which is provided, or agreed to be provided, continuously or on a recurrent basis, under a contract, for a period exceeding three months with periodic payment obligations and including supply of such services as the Government may, subject to such conditions, as it may, by notification, specify. Thus, the following features of continuous supply can be noted down:

1. Supply may be in present or in future, but on a recurrent basis.
2. Supply is made under a contract.
3. Supplier issues invoices regularly.
4. The contract should be valid for more than three months.
5. It includes the supplies notified by the Government.

Example 4.33: Mr. A takes a gym membership. The membership is valid for nine months with periodic payment obligations, and members are entitled to use the facilities during that

time. Since the supply of service is under a contract for a period greater than three months, therefore, it is a continuous supply of services.

Example 4.34: A company signs a contract with an IT services provider to provide ongoing support and maintenance for their computer systems and networks for sixteen months. This would involve regular monitoring, troubleshooting, and maintenance tasks over a period of years with periodic payment obligations. Since the supply of service is under a contract for a period greater than three months, therefore, it is a continuous supply of services.

7. Intra-State and Inter-State Supplies

(a) Intra-state supply: A supply is called intra-state supply if the location of the supplier and the place of supply both fall in the same State or Union territory.

(b) Inter-state supply: A supply is called inter-state supply if the location of the supplier falls in a State X/Union territory X and the place of supply falls in State Y/Union Territory Y. Further, the cases of exports and imports of goods or services are also considered as inter-state supplies. Moreover, the supply from a special economic zone (SEZ) to a non-special economic zone in the same state/UT is also considered an inter-state supply.

The following table illustrates intra-state supply and inter-state supply.

Location of supplier	Place of supply	Inter or Intra State Supply
Delhi	Delhi	Intra-state
Delhi	Uttar Pradesh	Inter-state
Mumbai	Chennai	Inter-state
Bhubaneshwar	Bhubaneshwar	Intra-state
Chandigarh	Haryana	Inter-state
Punjab	Chandigarh	Inter-state
Chandigarh	Chandigarh	Intra-state
New York	Delhi	Inter-state
Bhopal	London	Inter-state
Greater Noida SEZ, UP	Farrukhabad, UP	Inter-state
Meerut, UP	Moradabad SEZ, UP	Inter-state

Theory Questions

1. Define the term supply under GST. Explain its various forms along with their brief meanings.
2. GST is leviable only when there is an existence of consideration in a transaction. Do you agree with this statement? Support your answer.
3. Distinguish between composite supply and mixed supply.
4. What do you mean by exempt supply?
5. Is the exempt supply different from the non-taxable supply?
6. What do you mean by intra-state and inter-state supplies?
7. Explain the cases that are treated neither as the supply of goods nor a supply of services.
8. What is a zero-rated supply? Is it a taxable supply or an exempt supply?
9. Sale of land is subject to GST. Do you agree?
10. The sale of a building is always subject to GST. Explain.
11. Distinguish between continuous supply of goods and services.

Case-based Questions (Unsolved)

1. Vishnu purchased a mobile phone from a shop along with its charger and earphones. Comment whether it is a composite supply or mixed supply.

   Answer: Composite supply
2. Ravi Ltd. entered into a contract with Ram Ltd. to supply readymade shirts packed in designer boxes at the outlets of Ram Ltd. Further, Ravi Ltd. also gets the shirts insured during transit. Is it a composite supply or a mixed supply?

   Answer: Composite supply
3. My friend purchases a washing machine from Maharaja Stores. He received three years warranty also. Is it a composite supply or a mixed supply?

   Answer: Composite supply
4. Yashvi Computers supplies a laptop costing ₹85,000 along with a laptop bag costing ₹5,000 to Dhani for ₹90,000. If the GST rate applicable to laptops is 18%, while the GST rate applicable to laptop bags is 28%, then you are required to answer the following:

   (a) Is it a composite supply or a mixed supply?

   (b) What will be the GST rate applicable to the supply?

   Answer: Composite supply and GST rate applicable is 18%
5. A house (consisting of two floors) is let out under a single rent deed. As per the deed, one floor can be used for residential purposes and the other floor for setting up a printing press at a lump sum rent amount. What type of supply is it?

   Answer: Mixed supply
6. Jyoti, a registered person in Delhi, has made the following supplies in the month of February 2023:

(a) Supply of a laptop along with the laptop bag to a customer of Noida for ₹55,000 exclusive GST.

(b) Supply of 10,000 kits (at ₹50 each) amounting to ₹5 lakhs to Gurpreet Stores in Delhi. Each kit consists of one hair oil, one beauty soap and one hair comb.

(c) 100 kits are given as free gifts to Delhi customers (all unrelated) on the occasion of Devika's birthday. Each kit consists of one hair oil and one beauty soap. The cost of each kit is ₹35. The input tax credit has not been on the goods contained in the kit.

(d) Event management services were provided free of cost to her brother (wholly dependent on her) for his son's marriage function in Rajasthan. The cost of providing said services is ₹80,000.

(e) 1400 chairs and 100 coolers were hired out to function at Pitampura, Delhi, for ₹3,30,000 (exclusive GST), including the cost of transporting the chairs and coolers from Devika's godown. Since Devika is not a goods transport agency, therefore, this service is exempt under notification 12/2017-Central Tax (Rate) dated 28.06.2017.

Assume rates of GST to be as under:

S. No.	Particulars	Rates of GST
1.	Laptop	18%
2.	Laptop bag	28%
3.	Hair oil	18%
4.	Beauty soap	28%
5.	Hair comb	12%
6.	Event Management service	5%
7.	Service of renting of chairs and coolers	12%
8.	Transportation service	5%

From the above information, examine each of the above supplies made by Devika and determine the rate of GST applicable to the same.

Answer: GST rates applicable are 18%, 28%, Nil, 5% and 12%.

7. Sanon Camera Ltd. entered into a contract with an actress, Ms. Diya, to act as a brand ambassador for the cameras produced by Sanon Camera Ltd. The consideration to be paid to Diya is ₹1 crore per year for three years. As per the terms and conditions of the contract, if the contract is terminated by Diya before threeyears, then she will have to pay 50% of the consideration received up to that time. Diya terminated the contract after two years. As a result, she agreed to obey the terms and conditions of the contract. You are required to determine whether the given transaction(s) qualifies(y) as supply(ies).

   Answer: Yes, tolerating an act is a form of supply. Sanon Camera Ltd. is ready to tolerate the termination of the contract by Diya.

5

Levy and Collection of GST

5.1 Introduction

The levy of GST refers to the power of the government to impose a tax. Section 9 of the CGST Act and Section 5 of the IGST Act lay down the provisions of levy and collection of tax. Such a levy is generally known as a regular levy. Apart, there is another levy, i.e., composition levy under section 10 of the CGST Act. Let us see what these levies are and their related aspects.

5.2 Levy and collection of CGST—Section 9

Section 9 provides for regular levy under the CGST Act. The provisions of this section are as follows:

1. **Central tax in case of intra-state supply: Section 9(1):**
   - In the case of all intra-state supplies, a taxable person is required to pay the Central Goods and Services Tax (CGST) calculated on the value of supply, which is calculated as per the provision of section 15.
   - The CGST rate is notified by the Government, but it cannot exceed 20 percent.
   - The CGST shall be collected by the Government in a prescribed manner.
   - However, alcoholic liquor for human consumption is outside the area of GST.

2. **No CGST on supply of the following goods: Section 9(2):** On the recommendation of the GST council, the Government shall notify a date from which CGST on the following goods can be levied:

(a) petroleum crude,
(b) high speed diesel,
(c) motor spirit (or petrol),
(d) natural gas, and
(e) aviation turbine fuel.

3. Government can notify the cases of Reverse Charge Mechanism: Section 9(3): On the recommendation of the GST Council, the Government can notify the cases of reverse charge mechanism.

4. Government can notify the cases of Reverse Charge Mechanism where the supplies are received from an unregistered person: Section 9(4): On the recommendation of the GST Council, the Government can notify the cases of reverse charge mechanism when the goods or services or both are received from unregistered suppliers.

5. Notified services in case of which tax is payable by the e-commerce operator: Section 9(5): On the recommendation of the GST Council, the Government may notify the services in case of which the tax on **intra-state supply** is payable by the e-commerce operator through which such services are provided. In such cases, the e-commerce operator is deemed supplier of such services. Moreover, as per *circular No. 167/23/2021-GST dated 17.12.2021*, the said tax is payable in **cash only** not using the tax credit. The Government has issued *Notification No. 17/2017-Central Tax (Rate), dated 28.06.2017 as amended by Notification No. 23/2017-Central Tax (Rate), dated 22.08.20117 and Notification No. 17/2021-Central Tax (Rate), dated 18.11.2021, to notify such services.*

(a)	Passenger transportation services by a radio-taxi, motor cab, maxi cab, motor cycle, omnibus or any other motor vehicle.
(b)	Accommodation services.
(c)	Housekeeping services.
(d)	Restaurant services (including cloud kitchen). [Effective from 1 January 2022]

(a) Passenger transportation services by a radio-taxi, motor cab, maxi cab, motor cycle, omnibus or any other motor vehicle.

Example: Shri Ravi is a driver who gets passengers booking rides through an e-commerce operator (e.g., OLA, Uber, Meru Cab, etc.). Assuming that Ravi is not liable for registration under section 22(1), then the e-commerce operator (not the driver) is liable to pay tax under section 9(5) and get it registered compulsorily under section 24.

Image courtesy–Freepik

(b) Accommodation services if the supplier is not liable for registration under section 22(1).

Example: ABC Hotels [not liable for registration under section 22(1)] finds its guests through the bookings made on an e-commerce operator, e.g., makemytrip.com. Since the hotel is not liable for registration under section 22(1), therefore, the e-commerce operator is liable (not AB Hotels) to pay tax under section 9(5).

Image courtesy–Freepik

(c) Housekeeping services like plumbing, carpentering, etc., however, the supplier must not be liable for registration under section 22(1).

Example: Mr. Prem [not liable for registration under section 22(1)] is a carpenter and gets his customers through the e-commerce operator, e.g., Urban Company. Since the carpenter is not liable for registration under section 22(1), therefore, the e-commerce operator is liable (not Mr. Prem) to pay tax under section 9(5).

(d) Restaurant services [with effect from 1 January 2022]

Example: Suppose that a restaurant, namely Dilli Darbar, gets food orders booked through e-commerce operators like Swiggy, Zomato, etc. Such e-commerce operators are liable to pay tax and register themselves compulsorily under section 24.

However, if the restaurant services are supplied at premises providing hotel accommodation service having declared tariff ₹7,500 per unit per day or equivalent. Moreover, the restaurant may be registered under section 22(1) or not.

Image courtesy–Freepik

5.3 Levy and Collection of IGST—Section 5 of the IGST Act

Section 5 provides for regular levy under the IGST Act. The provisions of this section are as follows:

1. Integrated tax in case of inter-state supply: Section 5 (1)

- In the case of all inter-state supplies, a taxable person shall pay the Integrated Goods and Services Tax (IGST) calculated on the value of supply (that can be calculated under section 15 of the CGST Act).
- The rate of CGST notified by the Government cannot exceed 40 percent. Apart from that, the IGST is collected by the Government in a prescribed manner. However, alcoholic liquor for human consumption is outside the area of GST.
- Also, the IGST on goods imported into India is levied and collected as per the provisions of section 3 of the Customs Tariff Act, 1975, on the value as calculated under the said Act at the point when duties of customs are levied on the goods under section 12 of the Customs Act, 1962.

2. No IGST on the supply of the following goods: Section 5(2)

On the recommendation of the GST council, the Government shall notify a date from which IGST on the following goods can be levied:

(a) petroleum crude,
(b) high speed diesel,
(c) motor spirit (or petrol),
(d) natural gas, and
(e) aviation turbine fuel.

3. Government may notify the cases of Reverse Charge Mechanism: Section 5(3): On the recommendation of the GST Council, the Government can notify the cases of reverse charge mechanism.

4. Government can notify the cases of Reverse Charge Mechanism where the supplies are received from an unregistered person: Section 5(4): On the recommendation of the GST Council, the Government can notify the cases of reverse charge mechanism when the goods or services or both are received from unregistered suppliers.

5. Notified services in case of which tax is payable by the e-commerce operator: Section 5(5): On the recommendation of the GST Council, the Government may notify the services in case of which the tax on **inter-state supply** is payable by the e-commerce operator through which such services are provided. In such cases, the e-commerce operator is deemed a supplier of such services. Moreover, as per *circular No. 167/23/2021-GST dated 17.12.2021*, the said tax is payable in **cash only,** not using the tax credit. The notified services are the same as notified under section 9(5) of the CGST Act.

5.4 Reverse Charge Mechanism—Section 9 (3) of the CGST Act and Section 5(3) of the IGST Act

There are two types of mechanisms in GST law. These mechanisms are:

1. Forward charge mechanism (FCM): Under this mechanism, the liability to pay GST is on the shoulders of the supplier of goods or services or both.
2. Reverse charge mechanism (RCM): Under this mechanism, the liability to pay GST is on the shoulders of the recipient of goods or services or both. The cases of reverse charge are given below:

Reverse Charge in Case of Goods			
S. No.	**Goods**	**Supplier**	**Recipient**
1.	Cashew nuts, not shelled or peeled	Agriculturist	Any registered person
2.	Bidi wrapper leaves	Agriculturist	Any registered person
3.	Tobacco leaves	Agriculturist	Any registered person
3.A	Following essential oils other than those of citrus fruit namely: (a) Of peppermint (Menthapiperita) (b) Of other mints: Spearmint oil (exmth spicata), Water mint-oil (ex-mentha aquatica), Horsemint oil (ex-mentha-sylvestris), Ber-gamet oild (ex-menta citrate)	Any unregistered person	Any registered person
4.	Silk yarn	Any person who manufactures silk yarn from silk or silkworm cocoons for supply of silk yarn.	Any registered person

5.	Raw cotton	Agriculturist	Any registered person
6.	Supply of lottery	State Government, UT or any local authority	Lottery distributor or selling agent
7.	Used vehicles, seized and confiscated goods, old and used goods, waste and scrap	Central Government, State Government, UT or a local authority	Any registered person
8.	Priority sector lending certificate	Any registered person	Any registered person

Services notified under section 9(3) of reverse charge mechanism

The Central Government has issued Notification No. 13/2017-Central Tax (Rate), dated 28.06.2017 under **section** 9(3) of the CGST Act for notifying services under the reverse charge mechanism. The notification has been amended from time to time. The notified services are as follows:

1. Transportation of goods services by a Goods Transport Agency (GTA)

Supplier	Recipient	Service
Goods Transport Agency (GTA)	(a) **factory** registered under the Factories Act, 1948 or (b) **society** registered under the Societies Registration Act, 1860 or under any other law or (c) **co-operative society** established by or under any law or (d) **person** registered under the GST law or (e) **body corporate** established by or under any law or (f) **partnership firm** (including association of persons) whether registered or not or (g) **casual taxable person** located in taxable territory.	Transportation of goods. Exceptions: (a) GTA opts to pay tax under forward charge mechanism, but the following conditions are to be satisfied: • It is registered under the CGST Act, • It issues a tax invoice and makes a declaration in Annexure III on such invoice issued by it. (b) Specified recipient • Department or establishment of the Central Government or State Government or Union Territory or • a local authority or • Government agencies which have taken GST registration only for deducting tax at source under section 51. Thus, if such agency has taken registration to make taxable supply of goods or services, it is not covered under exception.

Illustration 5.1: Showing the above provision

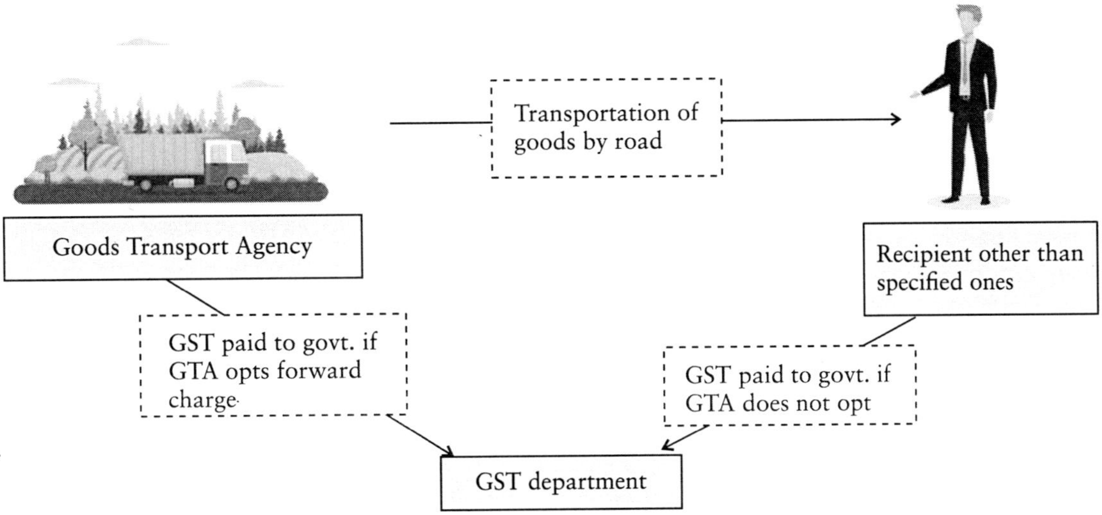

2. Legal services

Supplier	Recipient	Service
(a) Individual advocate or (b) senior advocate or (c) a firm of advocates or	Business entity located in taxable territory.	Legal services, i.e., any service provided in relation to • advice, • consultancy, • assistance in any branch of law, • representing before any court, tribunal or authority.

Illustration 5.2: Showing the above provision

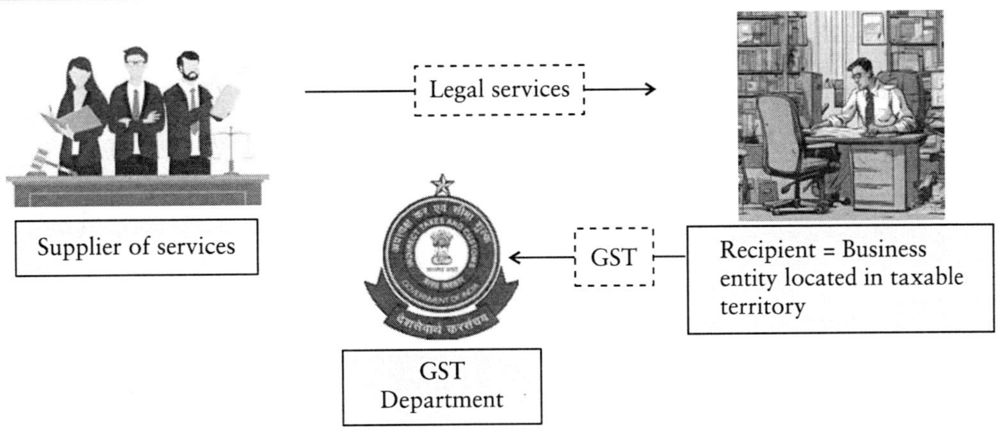

3. Services supplied by an arbitral tribunal

Supplier	Recipient	Service
Arbitral tribunal	Business entity located in taxable territory.	Services by an arbitral tribunal.

4. Sponsorship

Supplier	Recipient	Service
Any person	(a) Any body corporate or (b) Partnership firm, located in taxable territory.	Sponsorship services.

Illustration 5.3: Showing the above provision

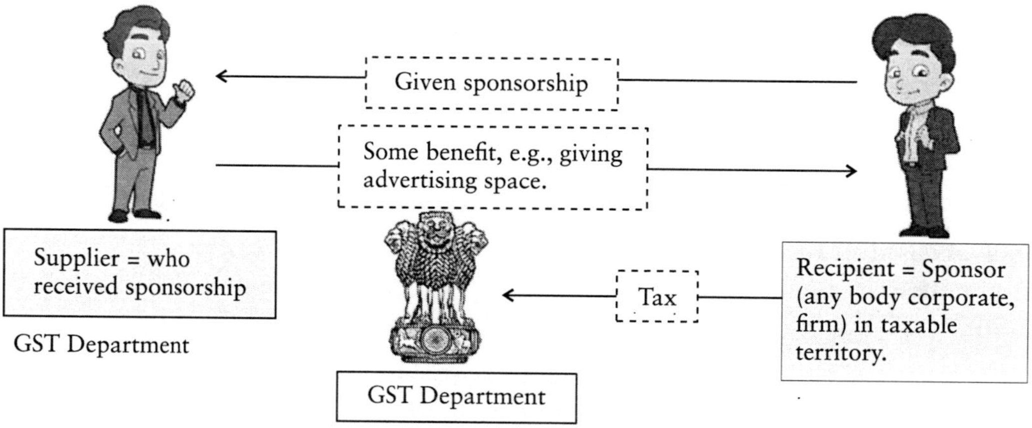

5. Services by government

Supplier	Recipient	Service
(a) Central government, (b) State government, (c) Union Territory, (d) Local authority,	Business entity located in taxable territory.	Services other than the following: (a) Renting of immovable property. (b) Services by the departments of posts. (c) Services in relation to an aircraft or a vessel, inside or outside the precincts of a port or an airport. (d) Transport of goods or passengers.

Illustration 5.4: Showing the above provision

Case (a): Non-exceptional case

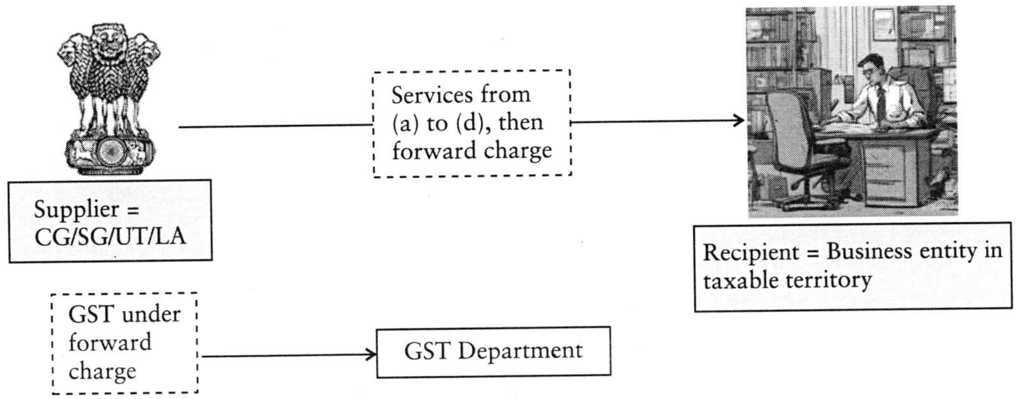

Case (b): Exceptional case

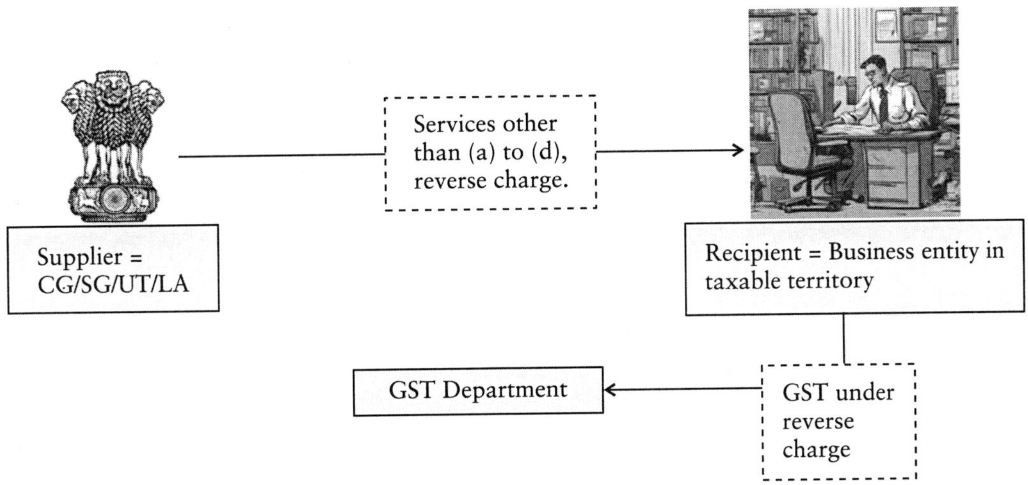

5A. Renting of immovable property

Supplier	Recipient	Service
(a) Central government, (b) State government, (c) Union Territory, (d) Local authority,	Any person who is registered under the CGST Act.	Renting of immovable property.

5AA. Renting of residential dwelling: [Inserted by Notification No. 5/2022-Central Tax (Rate), dated 13.07.2022 and effective from 18.7.2022]

Supplier	Recipient	Service
Any person	Any person who is registered under the CGST Act.	Renting of residential dwelling.

5B. Transfer of specified rights

Supplier	Recipient	Service
Any person	Promotor	Transfer of • development rights, • floor Space Index (FSI), • additional FSI for construction of a project by a promoter. **Notes:** 1. **FSI** is a ratio that defines the total floor area of a building in relation to the size of the land it occupies. For example, if a plot of land has an FSI of 2, it means that the total floor area of the building(s) constructed on that plot can be twice the area of the land. So, if the land is 1,000 square meters, the total floor area that can be constructed would be 2,000 square meters (1,000 square meters multiplied by the FSI of 2). 2. **Project** means a real estate project (REP) or a residential real estate project (RREP). 3. **Promoter** means the promoter as defined in clause (zk) of section 2 of the Real Estate (Regulation and Development) Act, 2016. 4. **REP** means the real estate project as defined under clause (zn) of section 2 of the Real Estate (Regulation and Development) Act, 2016. 5. **RREP** means a REP in which the carpet area of the commercial apartments ≤ 15% of the total carpet area of all the apartments in the REP. 6. **Apartment** means the apartment as defined under clause (e) of section 2 of the Real Estate (Regulation and Development) Act, 2016.

5C. Long-term lease of land

Supplier	Recipient	Service
Any person	Promotor	Lease of land (30 years or more) in the following forms: • Upfront amount (also known as premium, salami, cost, price, development charges, or by any other name) *or/and* • Periodic rent for construction of a project by a promoter.

6. Services by a director of a company/body corporate

Supplier	Recipient	Service
A director of • a company or • a body corporate	• The company or • The body corporate located in taxable territory.	Services of directorship.

7. **Services by an insurance agent**

Supplier	Recipient	Service
Insurance agent	A person running business of insurance located in taxable territory.	Services of insurance agent.

8. **Services by a recovery agent**

Supplier	Recipient	Service
Recovery agent	• A banking company. • A financial institution, • Non-banking financial company located in taxable territory.	Recovery agent services.

9. **Services by a music composer, photographer, etc.**

Supplier	Recipient	Service
• Music composer, • Photographer, • Artist, etc.	• Music company, • Producer, etc., located in taxable territory.	Transferring or permitting the use or enjoyment of a copyright [covered under section 13(1)(a) of the Copyright Act, 1957] relating to *original dramatic, musical or artistic works.*

Illustration 5.5: Showing the above provision

9A. **Services by an author**

Supplier	Recipient	Service
An author	A publisher located in taxable territory.	Transferring or permitting the use or enjoyment of a copyright [covered under section 13(1)(a) of the Copyright Act, 1957] relating to *original literary works.* **Exception:**

Supplier	Recipient	Service
		However, if the author • has taken registration under the GST Act, • declares to the jurisdictional CGST or SGST Commissioner that he wants to pay tax under forward charge for at least one year from the date of exercising forward charge, • and he makes a similar declaration on the invoice issued by him in Form GST Inv–I to the publisher, then the reverse charge is not applicable.

Illustration 5.6: Showing the above provision

10. Services by the member of the Overseeing Committee created by RBI

Supplier	Recipient	Service
Members of the Overseeing Committee	Reserve Bank of India	Services as the members of Overseeing Committee

11. Services by individual Direct Selling Agents (DSA)

Supplier	Recipient	Service
Individual direct-selling agents other than • a body corporate, • partnership firm, • limited liability partnership firm	• Banking company, • Non-banking financial company located in taxable territory	Services by individual direct selling agents. **Note:** Direct selling agents, often referred to as independent representatives, consultants, or distributors, are individuals or entities who engage with direct selling companies to promote and sell their products or services. These agents act as intermediaries between the company and the end consumer. They earn commissions or incentives based on their sales performance.

Illustration 5.7: Showing the above provision

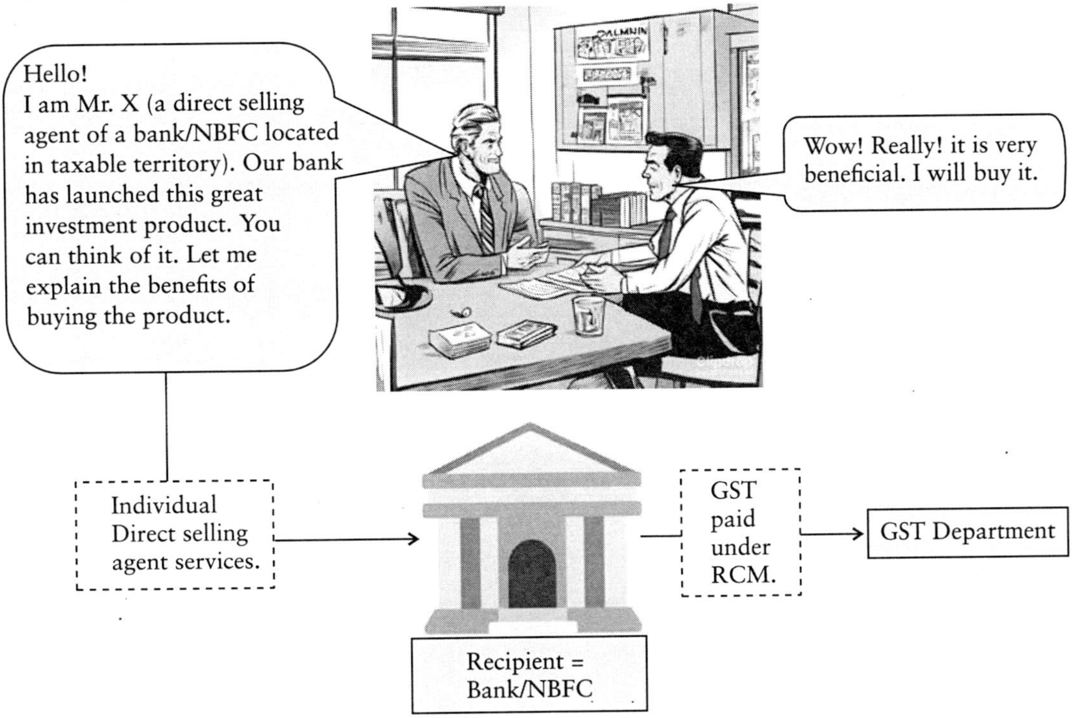

12. Services by a business facilitator to a banking company

Supplier	Recipient	Service
Business facilitator	A banking company located in taxable territory	Services of business facilitator

13. Services by an agent of business correspondent

Supplier	Recipient	Service
Business correspondent	Business correspondent located in taxable territory.	Services as a business correspondent

14. Security services

Supplier	Recipient	Service
Any person other than a body corporate.	A registered person located in taxable territory.	Supply of security personnel. Exceptions: If services are given to the following, then the reverse charge mechanism is not applicable. • Department or establishment of the Central Government or State Government or Union Territory or • A local authority or

Supplier	Recipient	Service
		• Government agencies that have taken GST registration only for deducting tax at source under section 51. Thus, if such an agency has taken registration to make a taxable supply of goods or services, it is not covered under the exception. • A person paying tax under a composition levy.

15. Renting of motor vehicle

Supplier	Recipient	Service
Any person	Any body corporate located in a taxable territory other than a body corporate and does not issue an invoice charging CGST at 6%.	Renting any motor vehicle made for carrying passengers where the cost of fuel is included in the consideration charged from the recipient.

16. Services of lending of securities

Supplier	Recipient	Service
Lender	Borrower	Services of lending of securities under the Securities Lending Scheme, 1997 ("Scheme") of SEBI.

Cases notified under section 9(4) of reverse charge

The Central Government has notified the cases, by Notification No. 7/2019-Central Tax (Rate), dated 29.03.2019, as amended from time to time, where supplies of goods or services or both are received from an unregistered person by a registered person. In simple words, in the following notified cases of reverse charge mechanism, the supplier is unregistered, but the recipient is registered; therefore, the registered person is liable to pay tax.

Services notified under section 5(5) of the IGST Act of reverse charge

The Central Government has issued *Notification No. 10/2017-Integrated Tax (Rate), dated 28.06.2017* under **section** 5(3) of the IGST Act for notifying services under the reverse charge mechanism. The notification has been amended from time to time. The notified services are as follows:

1. Services from non-taxable to territory to taxable territory

Supplier	Recipient	Service
Any person (located in non-taxable territory)	Any person located in taxable territory (other than non-taxable online recipient).	Any service.

2. Services of transportation by a vessel

Supplier	Recipient	Service
Any person (located in non-taxable territory)	An importer located in taxable territory.	Transportation of goods by a vessel from a place outside India up to the customs station of clearance in India.

Notes:

1. No partial reverse charge is applicable under the GST regime as was in Service Tax.
2. Payment of taxes under the reverse charge mechanism cannot be made using input tax credit; therefore, tax is to be paid in cash only.
3. Reverse charge mechanism is applicable in cases where the supplier of goods or services is unregistered, but the recipient is registered.
4. **Body corporate** means body corporate as defined under section 2(11) of the Companies Act, 2013.

5.5 Composition Levy or Composition Scheme

A software developer may write two versions of software: (i) **a heavy** version for the systems with high configuration and (ii) **a lite** version for the systems with low configuration. Of course, the heavy version must be more expensive than the lite version, and every person would not like to buy the heavy version because of various reasons, and the most prominent is low configuration of the system. Similarly, in the GST law, there are two versions of GST, i.e.,

1. **Regular levy** that is comparable to heavy software. This is a relatively complicated system in which there are more compliances and high rates of taxes. Section 9 of the CGST Act, 2017, is the relevant section for it.
2. **Composition levy** that is comparable to a lite software. This is a simple system of taxation in which there are less compliances and lower tax rates. However, this scheme is subject to some conditions and restrictions as imposed by section 10 and rule 5.

5.6 Composition Levy or Composition Scheme—Section 10(1) and 10(2)

5.6.1 According to section 10(1), a supplier can opt composition scheme if he satisfies the following basic conditions:

Section 10(1)	Basic condition
1.	The aggregate turnover [calculated as per explanation 1 of section 10(1)] in the preceding financial year is up to ₹75 lakhs (in case of specified states given below) or ₹1.5 crore (in case of remaining states). **Specified States:** (a) Uttarakhand (b) Sikkim (c) Arunachal Pradesh (d) Nagaland (e) Manipur (f) Mizoram (g) Tripura (h) Meghalaya

Section 10(1)	Basic condition
Second Proviso regarding supply of services along with goods	There is a possibility that a person supplies services (other than restaurant service) in addition to the supply of goods. Now a question arises, i.e., whether or not the person is eligible for the composition scheme because the composition scheme is available in case of **goods only** [as per the first additional condition of section 10(2)]. The second proviso of section 10(1) answers this question. According to this proviso, if the value of service does not exceed higher of the following amounts, he can opt composition scheme. (a) 10% of the turnover in a State or Union Territory in the preceding financial year. (b) ₹5,00,000. **Author's Note:** This is also possible that during the preceding financial year, the person does not make any supply of services, but he wants to make it during the current financial year, then the same proviso is applied, and the limit to supply services can be calculated. For this, refer to example 5.2.

Additional eligibility conditions to opt composition scheme are as follows:

Section 10(2)	Additional Conditions
(a)	He does not make supply of services. (**Author's comment:** This clause is overridden by the second proviso of section 10(1) explained above).
(b)	He does not make any supply of goods or services that are not taxable under the CGST Act, e.g., petrol, diesel, aviation turbine fuel, etc.
(c)	He does not make inter-state outward supply of services. [**Amended by Section 137 of the Finance Act, 2023**]
(d)	He does not make supply of services through an e-commerce operator who is liable to collect tax at source under section 52. [**Amended by Section 137 of the Finance Act, 2023**]
(e)	He does not manufacture notified goods, i.e., ice-cream and other edible ice, pan masala, tobacco and manufactured tobacco substitutes, aerated water, fly ash bricks or fly ash aggregate/blocks, bricks of fossil meals, building bricks, earthen/roofing tiles.
(f)	He should not be a casual taxable person or a non-resident taxable person.
Proviso of section 10(2)	Where there are many registered persons having the same Permanent Account (PAN), the registered person is not eligible to opt composition scheme unless all such registered persons opt to pay tax under the composition scheme. It simply means that if at least two persons have GST Identification Number (GSTIN) under the same PAN, then a composition levy for one of them can be opted only when all remaining persons also opt it.

5.6.2 Aggregate turnover to find eligibility: Section 2(6) read with explanation 1 of Section 10

Particulars	Amount
All taxable supplies (excluding value of inward supplies on which tax is payable on reverse charge basis)	–
Exempt supplies (excluding the interest or discount on extending deposits, loans or advances)	–
Export of goods or services or both	–
Inter-state supplies of persons having the same PAN.	–
Aggregate turnover	–

Notes:

(a) The above supplies are exclusive of CGST, SGST/UTGST, IGST, Cess.

(b) All supplies are from the 1st day of April of a financial year up to the date when he becomes liable for registration.

(c) Although section 2(6) does not specifically exclude the interest or discount on extending deposits, loans or advances, but explanation 1 of section 10 does.

Author's comment: As per section 10(2)(c), making inter-state outward supply of goods or services causes ineligibility for availing composition scheme, then why does it appear in the calculation of aggregate turnover shown above? The answer is that the above definition of aggregate turnover is as per section 2(6), which is a general definition, not specifically created for section 10 but slightly adjusted as per the requirement of section 10. Therefore, where we find that the person is engaged in making an inter-state outward supply of goods or services, then he is ineligible only, and there is no point in calculating the aggregate turnover.

Example 5.1: Mr. Ghosh is a supplier of goods in West Bengal. In the preceding financial year 2021-22, his turnover was ₹80 lakhs. Is he eligible for a composition levy in the current financial year 2022-23? What would be your answer if he also supplied some services, the value of which was ₹6 lakhs? What will happen if the value of the service reaches to ₹10,00,000?

Solution

1. Yes, Mr. Ghosh is eligible for the composition scheme because the aggregate turnover during the preceding turnover was ₹90 lakhs, not exceeding ₹1.5 crore (specified limit in case of West Bengal); therefore, he is eligible for the composition scheme in the current financial year 2022-23.
2. He can opt composition scheme even if he made a supply of services provided the value of the services does not exceed higher of the following amounts:

   (a) 10% × ₹80,00,000 = ₹8,00,000

   (b) ₹5,00,000

Thus, he is still eligible to opt composition scheme because the value of service – ₹6 lakhs does not exceed higher of the above amounts – ₹8 lakhs.

3. He will lose his eligibility for composition levy as the value of services exceeds ₹8,00,000. Thus, for the value of service of ₹10,00,000, he will be ineligible.

Example 5.2: Mr. X is a supplier of goods in Punjab. In the preceding financial year 2021-22, his turnover was ₹90 lakhs. Is he eligible for a composition levy in the current financial year 2022-23? What will be your answer if he is willing to make the supply of services during 2022-23? What will happen if the value of service reaches ₹11,00,000 during 2022-23?

Solution

4. Yes, Mr. X is eligible for the composition scheme because the aggregate turnover during the preceding turnover was ₹90 lakhs, not exceeding ₹1.5 crore (specified limit in case of Punjab); therefore, he is eligible for the composition scheme in the current financial year 2022-23.
5. During the financial year 2022-23, he can supply services to the extent of higher of the following amounts:
   (c) 10% × ₹80,00,000 = ₹8,00,000
   (d) ₹5,00,000

Thus, he can make the supply of services amounting to ₹8,00,000 without losing his eligibility for the composition scheme.

6. He will lose his eligibility for composition levy as the value of services exceeds ₹8,00,000. Thus, for the value of service of ₹10,00,000, he will be ineligible.

5.7 Alternate Composition Scheme—Section 10(2A)

Although section 10(2A) does not use the term alternate composition scheme, the benefit under this section is popular by this term only. According to section 10(2A), an alternate composition scheme can be availed when the following basic and additional conditions are satisfied:

Basic conditions	Conditions
1.	The aggregate turnover [calculated as per explanation 1 of section 10(1)] in the preceding financial year is up to ₹50 lakhs.
2.	The value of supply of services exceeds the amount allowed by the second proviso of section 10(1). In simple words, the value of supply exceeds higher of the following amounts: (a) 10% of the turnover in a State or Union Territory in the preceding financial year. (b) ₹5,00,000

Section 10(2A)	Additional Conditions
(a)	He does not make any supply of goods or services which are not taxable under the CGST Act, e.g., petrol, diesel, aviation turbine fuel, etc.
(b)	He does not make inter-state outward supply of services. **[Amended by Section 137 of the Finance Act, 2023]**
(c)	He does not make supply of services through an e-commerce operator who is liable to collect tax at source under section 52. **[Amended by Section 137 of the Finance Act, 2023]**

Section 10(2A)	Additional Conditions
(d)	He does not manufacture notified goods, i.e., ice-cream and other edible ice, pan masala, tobacco and manufactured tobacco substitutes, aerated water.
(e)	He should not be a casual taxable person or a non-resident taxable person.
Proviso of section 10(2A)	Where there are many registered persons having the same Permanent Account (PAN), the registered person is not eligible to opt alternate composition scheme unless all such registered persons opt to pay tax under composition scheme. It simply means, if at least two persons are having GST Identification Number (GSTIN) under the same PAN, then alternate composition scheme one of them can be opted only when all remaining persons also opt it. [**Author's comment:** This is the same as proviso of section 10(2)].

Example 5.3: RPV Ltd. is registered in Jaipur. The data of turnover during 2022-23 is given below:

Inter-state taxable supply	₹34,00,000
Intra-sate taxable supply	₹4,00,000
Supply of services	₹10,00,000
Exempt supply	₹1,00,000

Is RPV Ltd. eligible for an alternate composition scheme under section 10(2A) during 2023-24?

Solution

Basic conditions to avail alternative composition scheme are:

Basic conditions	Conditions	Amount in the present example
1.	The aggregate turnover [calculated in the same way as in case of section 10(1)] in the preceding financial year is upto ₹50 lakhs.	Aggregate supply during the preceding financial year 2022-23 = ₹49,00,000 < ₹50 lakhs. Thus, condition 1 is satisfied.
2.	The value of supply of services exceeds the amount allowed by the second proviso of section 10(1). In simple words, the value of supply exceeds higher of the following amounts: (a) 10% of the turnover in a State or Union Territory in the preceding financial year. (b) ₹5,00,000	Value of supply services allowed by the second proviso of section 10(1) = Higher of the following amounts: (a) 10% × ₹49 lakhs = ₹4.9 lakhs (b) ₹5 lakhs i.e., higher amount = ₹5 lakhs Value of supply of services = ₹10 lakhs Since value of supply of services > higher amount calculated. Therefore, condition 2 is also satisfied.

Conclusion: Since RPV Ltd. satisfies both the basic conditions and assuming that all the additional conditions are also satisfied, therefore, RPV Ltd. can opt alternate composition scheme during 2023-24.

Example 5.4: RPV Ltd. is registered in Jaipur. The data for turnover during 2022-23 is given below:

Inter-state taxable supply	₹34,00,000
Intra-sate taxable supply	₹4,00,000
Supply of services	₹10,00,000
Exempt supply	₹1,00,000

Is RPV Ltd. is eligible for composition scheme under section 10(1) during 2023-24?

Solution

Basic conditions	Conditions	Amount in the present example
1.	The aggregate turnover in the preceding financial year is up to ₹1.5 crore (in case of Jaipur, Rajasthan).	Aggregate supply during the preceding financial year 2022-23 = ₹49,00,000 < ₹1.5 crore.
2.	The value of supply of services exceeds the amount allowed by the second proviso of section 10(1). In simple words, the value of supply does not exceed higher of the following amounts: (a) 10% of the turnover in a State or Union Territory in the preceding financial year. Or (b) ₹5,00,000	Value of supply services allowed by the second proviso of section 10(1) = Higher of the following amounts: (a) 10% × ₹49 lakhs = ₹4.9 lakhs (b) ₹5 lakhs i.e., higher amount = ₹5 lakhs Value of supply of services = ₹10 lakhs

Conclusion: Since value of supply of services exceeds the higher amount calculated, therefore, RPV Ltd. cannot opt composition scheme under section 10(1).

5.8 Lapse of the composition levy—Section 10(3)

The date on which the supplier exceeds the threshold limit of turnover during a financial year, the option of the composition levy under section 10(1)/(2A) lapses and the supplier is required to pay GST on the invoices issued on the date as per normal tax rates.

5.9 Restriction on collection of tax and input tax credit—Section 10(4)

1. The person opting for the composition levy under section 10(1)/(2A) cannot collect tax. Thus, such a supplier bears the burden of tax.
2. The person opting for the composition levy under section 10(1)/(2A) is not eligible to avail the input tax credit.

5.10 Penalty in case of wrongful availment of composition scheme—Section 10(5)

Where the proper officer has reasons to believe that a taxable person has paid tax under section 10(1)/(2A) despite he was not eligible to do so, such person is liable to penalty and tax as per the provisions of section 73 and section 74.

5.11 Intimation and effective date of composition scheme—Rules 3 and 4

1. Already registered persons: Any person who is already registered and wants to opt composition scheme, whether under section 10(1) or section 10(2), then he is required to furnish FORM GST CMP-02 before 1 April of the financial year for which the composition scheme is to be opted. Apart, he is also required to furnish FORM ITC-03 within 60 days from 1 April of the relevant financial year. These forms can be furnished either on the GST portal or through facilitation centre. Further, 1 April of the relevant financial year is taken as ***effective date*** of composition scheme. Therefore, from this effective date, the supplier can issue bill of supply.

2. Persons seeking registration for the first time: Any person seeking registration for the first time, then he is required to furnish FORM GST REG-01 in which there is item no. 5, which asks for *option for composition: Yes or No*. If the person specifies Yes, then this is considered as intimation. Thus, such a person is not required to furnish FORM GST CMP-02. Further, the date of registration is taken as ***effective date*** of composition scheme. Therefore, from this effective date, the supplier can issue a bill of supply.

5.12 Conditions and Restrictions under Composition Scheme—Rule 5

A supplier under composition scheme OR Alternate composition scheme is required to satisfy the following conditions:

(a) he must not be a casual taxable person or a non-resident taxable person.

(b) the goods held in stock by him on the appointed day have not been purchased in the course of inter-state trade or commerce (including import) or from his branch situated outside the State or from his agent or principal outside the State.

Example 5.5: Suppose Mr. X runs a small stationery shop in Maharashtra, India. He sells various stationary items such as pencils, pens, notebooks, etc. His closing stock on 31.3.2022 includes purchases from a supplier in Delhi. His aggregate turnover during the financial year 2021-22 was ₹60 lakhs. From 1st April 2022, Mr. X wants to opt composition levy. Can he do so?

Solution: Although his aggregate turnover during the previous year 2021-22, does not exceed the threshold limit of ₹1.5 crore in the case of Maharashtra, he cannot opt composition scheme due to rule 5(b). According to this rule, if the closing stock on the appointed day includes the goods purchased in the course of inter-state trade/commerce, then composition levy cannot be adopted. In the present case, the closing stock includes the goods purchased from Delhi (inter-state trade); therefore, X cannot opt composition scheme.

(c) the goods held in stock by him have not been purchased from an unregistered supplier, and if he has purchased, he must pay the tax under section 9(4).

(d) he must pay tax under section 9(3) or section 9 (4) on inward supply of goods or services or both, i.e., he has to pay tax on inward supplies under reverse charge mechanism.

(e) he was not manufacturing the notified goods during the preceding financial year.

(f) the words composition taxable person, not eligible to collect tax on supplies must be written at the top of the bill of supply issued by him, and

(g) the words composition taxable person, not eligible to collect tax on supplies must be written on every notice or signboard displayed at a prominent place at his principal place of business and at every additional place or places of business.

Note: The registered person paying tax under section 10 is not required to intimate every year, and he may continue to pay tax under the said section subject to the provisions of the Act and these rules.

5.13 Validity of composition scheme—Rule 6

1. **Validity period:** Composition scheme under section 10 remains valid so long as the supplier satisfies all the required conditions.
2. **What if any of the required conditions is failed:** Where on any day, the supplier fails to satisfy any of the required conditions for the composition scheme, then the supplier is required to pay tax [under section 9(1)] from the day of such failure. He cannot issue a bill of supply thereafter, and as a result, he is mandated to issue tax invoices for every taxable supply made. Further, he is required to file an intimation for withdrawal from the scheme in FORM GST CMP-04 within seven days of the day of failure.
3. **Voluntary withdrawal from the composition scheme:** If a registered person is willing to opt out of the composition scheme, then he is allowed to do so. For this purpose, he needs to file an application in FORM GST CMP-04 on the common portal.
4. **Consequences of availing composition scheme without being eligible or contravening the provisions:** If the proper officer finds that a registered person has availed composition scheme without being eligible or has contravened the provisions of the CGST Act or provisions of this Chapter II of the CGST rules, then the proper officer has power to issue a show cause notice to such person in FORM GSTCMP-05 and the reply to the notice must be filed within 15 days of the date of receipt of the notice. The reply is furnished in FORM GST CMP-06.
5. **What after receipt of the reply to above show cause notice?:** Upon receipt of the reply to the above show cause notice, the proper officer may accept the reply or deny to continue the composition scheme by issuing an order in FORM GST CMP-07 within a period of 30 days of the receipt of such reply.
6. **Furnishing FORM GST ITC-01:** If a person opts out of the composition scheme (whether voluntarily withdrawn or denied by the GST department), then he is required to furnish a statement in FORM GST ITC-01 containing details of
   (a) the stock of inputs or
   (b) inputs contained in semi-finished or
   (c) inputs contained in finished goods

held in stock by him on the date on which he opts for the composition scheme. This statement is to be furnished within 30 days from the date of opting out of the composition scheme.

7. **Opting out of the composition scheme** in respect of any place of business in any State or Union territory is deemed to be an intimation in respect of all other places of business registered on the same PAN.

5.14 Specified Rates under Composition Scheme—Rule 7

Particulars	CGST	SGST/UTGST
Manufacturers other than notified by the Government.	0.5% of the turnover in the State or UT.	0.5% of the turnover in the State or UT.
Suppliers making supplies under paragraph 6(b) of Schedule II, i.e., restaurant services.	2.5% of turnover in the State or UT.	2.5% of turnover in the State or UT.
Other cases not covered above, i.e., traders.	0.5% of the taxable supplies of goods and services in the State or UT.	0.5% of the taxable supplies of goods and services in the State or UT.
Supplier of services under section 10(2A).	3% of turnover of supplies of goods and services in the State or UT.	3% of turnover of supplies of goods and services in the State or UT.

Turnover in the State or Union territory means Section 2(112) adjusted as per the requirement of Rule 7

Particulars	Amount
All taxable supplies (excluding the value of inward supplies on which tax is payable under reverse charge)	–
Add: Exempt supplies made within the State or UT	–

Note: All the components are exclusive of CGST, SGST/UTGST, IGST or Cess.

Thus, the simple definition of the turnover in the State or UT, for the purpose of Rule 7, is as follows:

Particulars	Amount
Taxable intra-state supply	–
Add: Exempt supplies made within the State or UT	–
Turnover in the State or UT	–

Example 5.6: BIS Ltd. is registered in Delhi. The company is engaged in the supply of services (other than restaurant services). The details of the turnover during the financial year 2022-23 are as follows:

Quarters	Amount (in ₹)
April–June	20 lakhs
July–Sept	30 lakhs
October–December	20 lakhs

Since the turnover exceeds 20 lakhs during the quarter July–September, therefore, the company takes registration effective from 1 July 2022. The company has opted composition scheme. You are required to calculate tax payable during all the quarters of the financial year 2022-23. Assume that normal GST rates are 9% as CGST and 9% as SGST.

Solution

As per the second proviso of section 10(1), the value of services (other than restaurant services) is allowed to the extent of higher of the following amounts:

(a) 10% of the turnover in a State or Union Territory in the preceding financial year.

(b) ₹5,00,000.

In the present case, the aggregate turnover in the preceding financial year 2021-22 was nil; therefore, the value of services is higher of the following:

(a) 10% × 0 = 0

(b) ₹5,00,000.

Thus, during the current year 2022-23, BIS Ltd. can supply services up to ₹5,00,000 under the composition scheme, but the actual value of services exceeds ₹5,00,000; thus, BIS Ltd. is not eligible for composition scheme under section 10(1). However, BIS Ltd. is eligible for an alternate composition scheme under section 10(2A) because its preceding financial year aggregate turnover is nil < ₹50 lakhs.

Further, as per rule 7, the applicable GST rates are 3% of intra-state aggregate supply as CGST and 3% of intra-state aggregate supply as SGST. Thus, GST liability for given quarters are as follows:

Quarters	Amount (in ₹)	Cumulative amount (in ₹)	CGST rate (%)	SGST rate (%)	GST payable (in ₹)
April–June	20 lakhs	20 lakhs (See note 1)	Nil	Nil	0
July–Sept	30 lakhs	50 lakhs (See note 2)	3%	3%	1.8 lakhs
October–December	20 lakhs	70 lakhs	9%	9%	3.6 lakhs

Notes:

1. Up to ₹20 lakhs, BIS Ltd. is not liable to get it registered under section 22(1); therefore, no GST is payable.
2. As per section 10(3), beyond this amount of ₹50 lakhs, the alternate composition scheme lapses; therefore, GST is to be paid as per normal provisions for the quarter October–December.

Theory Questions

1. What is levy of tax under section 9 of the CGST Act?
2. Explain the advantages and disadvantages of the composition levy.
3. Distinguish between the forward charge mechanism and the reverse charge mechanism. List 10 cases of reverse charge mechanism.
4. What is composition levy under section 10?
5. What are the provisions relating to tax payable on a reverse charge basis under section 9(3)? What are the categories of supply of services on which the recipient of services has to pay tax on a reverse charge basis?
6. Explain the provisions with respect to the Reverse Charge Mechanism in the case of services.
7. What is composition levy under section 10(2A)?
8. Who are the persons who cannot pay tax under composition scheme under section 10?

Case-based Questions (Unsolved)

1. Bittoo and Co. (registered in Noida) is engaged in making inter-state supplies of furniture. The aggregate turnover of the company in the preceding financial year is ₹85 lakhs. Therefore, it has opted composition scheme under section 10(1). Consequently, it pays tax under the composition scheme during the current financial year. The proper officer has reasons to believe that Bittoo and Co. is not eligible to pay tax under section 10(1), therefore, he issues a show can notice, and on being dissatisfied with the reply submitted, he imposes a penalty. Is the action taken by the proper officer valid in the eyes of the law?

   Answer: Yes, the action taken by the proper officer is valid because of section ineligibility due to inter-state supplies.
2. Dilli Dawat is a restaurant registered in Ghaziabad. During the financial year 2022-23, its aggregate turnover from restaurant services is ₹100 lakhs, while aggregate turnover from other services is ₹12 lakhs. Determine the eligibility of Dilli Dawat to avail composition scheme under section 10(1) from 1.04.2023. If the restaurant is not eligible for composition scheme under section 10(1), then determine its eligibility for an alternate composition scheme under section 10(2A).

   Answer: He is not eligible for composition scheme under section 10(1)/(2A).
3. LT Ltd. has three registered places of business located in Delhi, UP and Pune. Its aggregate turnover during the previous financial year was ₹98 lakhs. It wants to opt regular scheme of tax for UP and Pune places of business, while a composition scheme for Delhi places of business. Is it possible?

   Answer: No
4. Laxman & Co. (a registered manufacturer of non-notified goods in Madhya Pradesh) has opted composition scheme from 1 April 2022. The details of the turnover achieved during the quarter ending on 30 June 2022 are as follows:

Taxable turnover of goods within the state	₹25 lakhs

Exempted turnover of goods within the state ₹22 lakhs

Calculate tax payable.

Answer: CGST – ₹ 23,500 and SGST – ₹ 23,500

5. Bharat & Co. (a registered trader in Jharkhand) has opted composition scheme from 1 April 2023. The details of the turnover achieved during the quarter ending on 30 June 2023 are as follows:

   Taxable supply of goods within Jharkhand ₹23 lakhs

   Exempted supply of goods within Jharkhand ₹18 lakhs

   Calculate tax payable.

   Answer: CGST – ₹11,500 and SGST – ₹11,500

6

Exemptions

6.1 Introduction

The government may relax some supplies from GST if it is in the public interest to do so, and the GST Council recommends it. Such relaxations are called exemptions. Exemptions are given by way of notifications or a special order.

6.2 Types of Exemption Notifications

As per section 11 of the CGST Act or section 6 of the IGST Act, there are two types of exemptions:

1. **Absolute exemptions (or unconditional exemptions)**
   - (a) These are those exemptions in cases of which there is no condition for exemption. For example, services by way of public conveniences such as the provision of facilities of bathrooms, washrooms, lavatories, urinals or toilets are unconditionally exempt.
   - (b) Absolute exemptions are mandatory to be availed, i.e., the supplier is required to avail the exemption.
   - (c) Such exemptions may be from the whole tax or a part of the tax.
2. **Conditional exemptions**
   - (a) These exemptions can be taken if some specified conditions are satisfied. For example, services by an artist in folk or classical art forms: (a) music, (b) dance, or (c) theatre are exempt, but only when the consideration charged is up to ₹1,50,000, and the artist is not performing in the capacity of a brand ambassador. Such exemptions are optional on the part of the supplier.
   - (b) Conditional exemption is at the option of the supplier. If he does not want to avail the exemption, then he can do so.

6.3 Ways of Exemptions

- (a) As per section 11 of the CGST Act or section 6 of the IGST Act, exemptions are either given by issue of notification or special order under exceptional circumstances, which are mentioned in the order itself.

Example 6.1: The Government has issued *Notification No. 12/2017-Central Tax (Rate) dated 28.06.2017, giving exemption from GST for intra-state supply of services, and Notification No. 9/2017-Integrated Tax (Rate) dated 28.06.2017* under section 6 of the IGST Act giving exemption from IGST for inter-state supply of services.

(b) The government may give explanations or clarifications regarding the scope or applicability of such notification or order but within one year from the date of such notification or order. The effect of such explanations or clarifications shall be taken from the date of the notification or order.

(c) If the explanation is regarding a particular entry in the notification, then its effective date is from the date of inception of the entry, not the date of the notification.

6.4 Goods exempted

Notification No. 2/2017-CT (Rate) dated 28.06.2017 exempts the specified goods from GST for intra-state supply. As per the notification, there are 149 entries, which can be easily accessed on the following link

https://taxinformation.cbic.gov.in/view-pdf/1001007/ENG/Notifications or scan the following QR code:

Some of the goods are:

1. Indian national flag
2. Hearing aids
3. Gandhi topi
4. Rupee notes or coins, when sold to RBI or the Government of India
5. Natural honey (other than pre-packed and labelled)
6. Fresh milk/pasteurised milk/separated milk/milk and cream (not concentrated or containing added sugar or sweetening matter
7. Puja samagri
8. Prasadam (supplied by religious places)
9. Electrical energy
10. Kajal (other than kajal pencil sticks), kumkum, bindi, sindur, alta
11. Live fish
12. Curd, Lassi, Buttermilk
13. Tender coconut water (other than pre-packed and labelled)
14. Plastic bangles
15. Jaggery of all types, including cane jaggery (gur), palmyra jaggery and khandsari sugar, but these must not be pre-packed and labelled).

6.5 Services exempted [Principal Notification No. 12/2017-Central Tax (R)]

1. Services by an entity registered under section 12AA of the Income-tax Act, 1961, by way of charitable activities.
2. Services by way of transfer of a going concern, as a whole or an independent part thereof.

Example 6.2: Sheela runs a small bakery business that is registered in Lucknow. One day, she decides to retire and close down her business. As a result, she informs the tax authorities that she will no longer be a taxable person and deregisters for GST. At the time of closer of her business, she has some unsold cakes and breads in her bakery that are valued at ₹50,000. Since the business ceases not transferred, therefore an exemption is not available.

3. Pure services (excluding works contract service or other composite supplies involving the supply of any goods) given to the
   - Central Government,
   - State Government or
   - Union territory or
   - local authority

by way of any activity in relation to any function entrusted to a Panchayat and Municipality under articles 243G and 243W of the Constitution, respectively.

3A. Composite supply given to the
   - Central Government,
   - State Government or
   - Union territory or
   - local authority

by way of any activity in relation to any function entrusted to a Panchayat and Municipality under articles 243G and 243W of the Constitution, respectively. However, this exemption is available only when the value of the supply of goods ≤ 25% of the value of the composite supply.

4. Services by governmental authority by way of any activity in relation to any function entrusted to a municipality under Article 243W of the Constitution.
5. Services by a governmental authority by way of any activity in relation to any function entrusted to a Panchayat under Article 243G of the Constitution.
6. **Services by Government:** Services given by the Central Government, State Government, Union territory or local authority. However, the following services are not exempt:
   (a) Services by the Department of Posts [partially omitted with effect from 18 July 2022]
   (b) Services in relation to an aircraft or a vessel, inside or outside the precincts of a port or an airport,
   (c) transport of goods or passengers or
   (d) any service, other than specified services, given to business entities.

Note: For the purpose of brevity, the term specified services has been used to represent the services from (a) to (c). This term has been used in entries 7 to 9 also.

7. **Services by Government to a business entity:** Services given by the Central Government, State Government, Union territory or local authority to a business entity with an aggregate turnover of up to such amount [i.e., ₹20 lakhs or 10 lakhs in case of specified states or ₹40 lakhs subject to some conditions] in the preceding financial year as makes

it eligible for exemption from registration under the CGST Act. However, the exemption is not available in the following cases:

(a) Specified services.

(b) Renting of immovable property.

8. **Services by Government to another Government:** Services given by the Central Government, State Government, Union territory or local authority to another Central Government, State Government, Union territory or local authority. However, the exemption is not available to specified services.

9. **Services by Government where consideration is up to ₹5,000:** Services given by Central Government, State Government, Union territory or local authority if the consideration does not exceed ₹5,000. However, the exemption is not available to specified services.

Note: In case of continuous supply of service, the exemption shall apply only where the consideration charged for such service does not exceed ₹5,000 in a financial year.

9A. Services given to and by FIFA and its subsidiaries directly or indirectly related to any of the events under FIFA U-17 World Cup 2017 to be hosted in India.

9AA. Services given to and by FIFA and its subsidiaries directly or indirectly related to any of the events under FIFA U-17 Women's World Cup 2020 to be hosted in India.

9AB. Services provided by and to AFC: Services provided by and to Asian Football Confederation (AFC) and its subsidiaries directly or indirectly related to any of the events under AFC Women's Asia Cup 2022 to be hosted in India.

9B. Supply of services associated with transit cargo both from and to Nepal and Bhutan. This service also includes the movement of empty containers.

9C. Services by a Government entity to Government: Where a government entity provides a service to

- the Central Government or
- the State Government or
- a Union territory or
- any specified person or

for a consideration in the form of grants, then such service is exempt.

9D. Services by Government-run old age home: Services by an old age home to its residents (age least 60 years) are exempt if the following conditions are satisfied:

(a) Such old age home is run by the

- Central Government or
- State Government or
- Charitable institute (which is registered under section 12AA or section 12AB of the Income Tax Act, 1961).

(b) The consideration does not exceed ₹25,000 per month per member.

(c) The above consideration also includes charges for boarding/lodging/maintenance.

10. **Pure labour contract services under specified mission or yojana:** The following services provided under a pure labour contract are exempt.

- construction,
- erection,
- commissioning,
- installation,
- completion,
- fitting out,
- repair,
- maintenance,
- renovation, or
- alteration of a civil structure or

any other original works related to the beneficiary-led individual house construction or enhancement under the

- Housing for All (Urban) Mission or
- Pradhan Mantri Awas Yojana.

10A. Services given by electricity distribution utilities: The following services by electricity distribution utilities are exempt:

- construction,
- erection,
- commissioning,
- installation

of infrastructure for extending electricity distribution network upto the tube well of the farmer or agriculturist for agricultural use.

General knowledge (optional)

An electricity distribution utility, also known as an electric utility or power distribution company, is a company or organization responsible for the delivery of electricity to end-users. Its primary function is to operate, maintain and manage the infrastructure required for the distribution of electrical power within a specific geographic area. In Delhi, BSES Rajdhani Power Limited (BRPL) and BSES Yamuna Power Limited (BYPL) are two electric distribution utilities.

11. Pure labour contract: The following services under a pure contract are exempt:

- construction,
- erection,
- commissioning, or
- installation

of original works related to a single residential unit other than as a part of a residential complex.

General knowledge: Indeed, there are two types of labour contracts: (1) works contract and (2) pure labour contract. In works contract, labour and material both are supplied, but in pure labour contract, only labour is supplied.

11A. Service by Fair Price Shops to Government: Service given by Fair Price Shops to Central Government, State Government or Union territory is exempt if the following conditions are satisfied:

(a) Service is by way of sale of food grains, kerosene, sugar, edible oil, etc., under the Public Distribution System (PDS).
(b) The consideration is in the form of commission or margin.

General knowledge (optional)

The Public Distribution System (PDS) in India is a government-sponsored program that aims to provide essential foodgrains and other commodities to economically disadvantaged sections of society at affordable prices. It is one of the largest food security initiatives in the world and plays an important role in ensuring food security for millions of people in India. The PDS operates through a network of Fair Price Shops (FPS), also known as ration shops or PDS outlets, which are established at various locations across the country. These FPS are responsible for distributing essential commodities like rice, wheat, sugar and kerosene oil to eligible beneficiaries at subsidized rates.

12. Renting of residential dwelling to an unregistered person: Renting of residential dwelling for residence purposes to an unregistered person is an exempted service. However, from 1.1.2023, if the following conditions are satisfied, then the exemption is available even if the renting is made to a registered person.

(a) The registered person is the proprietor of a proprietorship concern and rents the residential dwelling in his personal capacity for use as his own residence; and
(b) such renting is on his own account and not that of the proprietorship concern.

Consider the following example:

Example 6.3: Let us say Mr. Sanjeev Raj runs a proprietorship firm that sells clothes. The firm is registered under GST in Delhi. He rents a residential apartment in Delhi for his personal use as his own residence. He pays the rent from his personal bank account, and the rental agreement is in his name alone, not in the name of his proprietorship firm. In this case, the renting is on his own account and not that of the proprietorship concern. Therefore, he is eligible for exemption.

13. Services by way of

(a) conducting any religious ceremony (e.g., hawan, pooja, mundan, shaadi, etc.),
(b) renting of precincts of a religious place meant for the general public, owned or managed by an
- charitable/religious trust registered under section 12AA of the Income Tax Act, 1961 or
- a trust or an institution registered under sub-clause (v) of clause (23C) of section 10 of the Income Tax Act or
- a body/an authority covered under clause (23BBA) of section 10 of the Income Tax Act.

However, exemption under (b) is not available in the following cases:

- renting of rooms where per day charges are ₹1,000 or more,

- renting of premises, community halls, kalyanmandapam or open area, and the like where per day charges are ₹10,000 or more,
- renting of shops or other spaces for business or commerce where per month charges are ₹10,000 or more.

14. This entry has been omitted with effect from 18 July 2022. This entry was related to accommodation services by a hotel, inn, guest house, campsite, etc., for which the value of supply of a unit was up to ₹1,000 per day.

15. Transport of passengers, with or without belongings, by:

- air in economy class, leaving from or landing at an airport situated in
  - (a) Arunachal Pradesh,
  - (b) Assam, Manipur,
  - (c) Meghalaya, Mizoram,
  - (d) Nagaland,
  - (e) Sikkim,
  - (f) Tripura,
  - (g) Bagdogra located in West Bengal;

Image courtesy–Freepik

- non-airconditioned contract carriage except radio taxi, for transportation of passengers, excluding tourism, conducted tour, charter or hire; or
- stage carriage except air-conditioned stage carriage.

Note: This entry is not applicable to those suppliers (making supply through the e-commerce operators) covered under section 9(5) of the CGST Act.

16. Services provided to the Central Government by way of transport of passengers with or without accompanying belongings, by air, leaving from or landing on a regional connectivity scheme airport, against consideration in the form of viability gap funding (VGF). However, the entry will not be applicable on or after three years from the date of commencement of operations of the regional connectivity scheme airport as notified by the Ministry of Civil Aviation.

Example 6.4: Under the UDAN (Ude Desh Ka Aam Nagrik) scheme launched by the Government of India in 2016, several regional airports in India were identified and selected for the development and enhancement of air connectivity in the country. One such airport is the Jharsuguda Airport in Odisha, which was developed under the UDAN scheme. To ensure the viability of operations at the Jharsuguda Airport, the Central Government provided viability gap funding (VGF) to the airlines operating at the airport. The VGF is financial support provided by the government to make a project commercially viable. Under the UDAN scheme, the VGF is used to subsidize the cost of air travel on regional routes, making air travel affordable for the common people. Airlines operating at the Jharsuguda Airport receive VGF from the Central Government for every seat sold on their flights. This subsidy helps airlines to keep the airfare low and affordable for the passengers. The VGF provided by the Central Government has been instrumental in attracting airlines to operate at the Jharsuguda Airport and improve air connectivity in the region. Thus, the services given by the airlines by way of transport of passengers to the Central Government are exempted services.

17. Passenger transportation services:

Passenger transportation service is exempt if they are by the following modes:

(a) railways (except first class and AC coach);
(b) metro rail, monorail or tramway;
(c) inland waterways;
(d) public transport (except predominantly for tourism purposes) in a vessel between places located in India, e.g., normal public ships that carry passengers from one place to another;
(e) metered cabs or auto rickshaws or e-rickshaws (except in the case under section 9(5) of the CGST Act, i.e., passenger transportation services through the e-commerce operator).

Image courtesy–Freepik

18. Transportation of goods by

(a) Road except in the case of a goods transportation agency and a courier agency.
(b) Inland waterways.

19. Services by way of transportation of goods by an aircraft from a place outside India up to the customs station of clearance in India.

19A and 19B. These entries have been omitted with effect from 1 October 2022. These entries were related to services of transportation of goods by an aircraft/vessel from a customs station of clearance in India to a place outside India.

19C. Launch of satellite by ISRO, ACL, NSIL: Satellite launch services supplied by ISRO, Antrix Corporation Limited or New Space India Limited.

Example 6.5: PSLV-C51 Mission: In February 2021, ISRO launched the PSLV-C51 mission, which carried Amazonia-1, an earth observation satellite for Brazil. The satellite was launched from the Satish Dhawan Space Centre in Sriharikota, Andhra Pradesh, India. The launching of the PSLV-C51 satellite is an exempted service.

20. Transportation of goods by rail or vessel: Services by way of transportation by rail or a vessel from one place in India to another of the following goods:

(a) relief materials meant for victims of natural or man-made disasters, calamities, accidents or mishaps.
(b) defence or military equipment.
(c) newspaper or magazines registered with the Registrar of Newspapers.
(d) Omitted.
(e) agricultural produce.

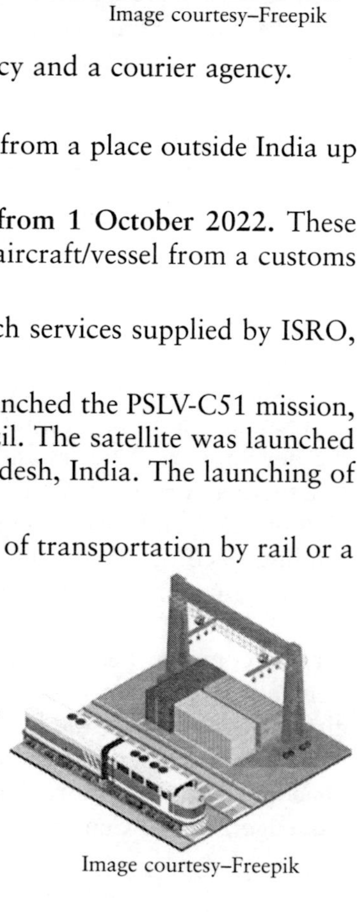

Image courtesy–Freepik

(f) milk, salt and food grains, including flour, pulses and rice.
(g) organic manure.

21. GTA services with regard to some goods: Services provided by a goods transport agency by way of transport in a goods carriage of—

(a) agricultural produce.
(b) omitted.
(c) Omitted.
(d) milk, salt and food grains, including flour, pulses and rice.
(e) organic manure.
(f) newspaper or magazines registered with the Registrar of Newspapers.
(g) relief materials meant for victims of natural or man-made disasters, calamities, accidents or mishaps or
(h) defence or military equipment.

21A. Services provided by a goods transport agency (GTA) to an unregistered person (including an unregistered casual taxable person). However, if the recipient is any of the following persons, then the services are not exempted:

(a) any factory,
(b) any society,
(c) any co-operative society,
(d) anybody corporate,
(e) any partnership firm or Association of Persons (AOP),
(f) any casual taxable person (registered under GST).

21B. Services provided by a goods transport agency (GTA) by way of transportation of goods in a goods carriage to:

A department or establishment of the CG/SG/UT/local authority/government agencies which has taken registration under the CGST Act, 2017 only for the purposes of TDS under section 51, not for making a taxable supply of goods or services.

22. Services by way of giving on hire: (a) to a state transport undertaking, a motor vehicle meant to carry more than 12 passengers; or (aa) to a local authority, an electrically operated vehicle meant to carry more than twelve passengers; or (b) to a goods transport agency, a means of transportation of goods; or (c) motor vehicle for transport of students, faculty and staff, to a person providing services of transportation of students, faculty and staff to an educational institution providing services by way of pre-school education and education upto higher secondary school or equivalent.

Explanation: For the purposes of this entry, "Electrically operated vehicle" means vehicle falling under Chapter 87 in the First Schedule to the Customs Tariff Act, 1975, which is run solely on electrical energy derived from an external source or from one or more electrical batteries fitted to such road vehicle.

23. Tolls: Allowing access to a road or a bridge on payment of toll charges.

23A. This entry has been omitted with effect from 1 January 2023. Up to 31 December 2022, Services in the form of giving access to a road or a bridge on payment of annuity were exempt.

24. Services by way of loading, unloading, packing, storage or warehousing of rice.

24A. Services by way of warehousing of minor forest produce.

General knowledge (optional)

Minor forest produce refers to non-timber forest products (NTFPs) collected from forests, such as fruits, nuts, medicinal plants, honey, bamboo and other products that are of minor economic value but are significant sources of income for forest dwellers and local communities.

24B. Storage and warehousing of specified goods: Services in the form of storage or warehousing of the following items are exempted services:

- Cereals
- Pulses
- Fruits and
- Vegetables

Note: With effect from 18 July 2022, the following goods have been omitted: Nuts, spices, copra, sugarcane, jaggery, raw vegetable fibres, such as cotton, flax, jute, etc. indigo, unmanufactured tobacco, betel leaves, tendu leaves, coffee and tea.

24C. Services by the Department of Post: The following services given by the *Department of Posts* are exempt:

Postcards, inland letters, book post, ordinary post (envelops having weight less than 10 grams).

25. Service given by an electricity transmission or distribution utility in the form of transmission or distribution of electricity.

26. This entry has been omitted with effect from 18 July 2022. Earlier, services by the Reserve Bank of India were exempt.

27. Giving money as

- deposits (e.g., fixed deposits with a bank), loans or advances and the consideration received is in the form of interest or discount (other than interest involved in credit card services);
- sale or purchase of foreign currency between banks or authorised dealers of foreign exchange or between banks and such dealers.

27A. Services provided by a banking company to Basic Saving Bank Deposit account holders under Pradhan Mantri Jan Dhan Yojana.

28. Services of life insurance business given by way of annuity under the National Pension System regulated by the Pension Fund Regulatory and Development Authority of India (PFRDAI) under the Pension Fund Regulatory and Development Authority Act, 2013.

29. Life insurance services by Armed Forces Group Insurance Funds to the members of the armed forces: Services of life insurance business given or agreed to be given by the

- Army Group Insurance Fund,
- Naval Group Insurance Fund and
- Air Force Group Insurance Fund

to the members of the

- Army,
- Navy and
- Air Force, respectively,

under the Group Insurance Schemes of the Central Government.

29A. Life insurance services by the Naval Group Insurance Funds to the personnel of Coast Guard: Making or agreeing to make life insurance to the personnel of Coast Guard (under the Group Insurance Schemes of the Central Government) by the Naval Group Insurance Fund is exempt service.

29B. Life insurance services by the Central Armed Police Forces Funds to their members: Making or agreeing to make life insurance to the members (under the Group Insurance Schemes of the concerned Central Armed Police Force) by the Central Armed Police Forces (under Ministry of Home Affairs) Group Insurance Funds is exempt service.

30. Services by ESIC: Services by the Employees' State Insurance Corporation (ESIC) to persons governed under the Employees' State Insurance Act, 1948.

31. Services by EPFO: Services provided by the Employees Provident Fund Organisation (EPFO) to the persons governed under the Employees Provident Funds and the Miscellaneous Provisions Act, 1952.

31A. Services by Coal Mines Provident Fund Organisation to person government by the Coal Mines Provident Fund and Miscellaneous Provisions Act, 1948.

31B. services by NPS trust to its members against consideration in the form of administrative fees.

32. This entry has been omitted with effect from 18 July 2022. This was related to services by IRDAI to insurers under the IRDAI Act, 1999.

33. This entry has been omitted with effect from 18 July 2022. This was related to services by SEBI by way of protecting the interest of investors, promoting and regulating the securities market.

34. If a banking company/financial institution/NBFC (known as acquiring bank) settles an amount not exceeding ₹2,000 in a single transaction which is being paid through credit card, debit card, charge card or other payment card service, then such service by an acquiring bank is exempt.

Example 6.6: Let us say you are a customer at a local grocery store, and you want to buy some items that cost ₹1,800. You don't have enough cash on hand, so you decide to pay with your debit card. When you swipe your card at the store's card terminal, the transaction is processed by the acquiring bank, say, HDFC Bank, which the store uses to process payments. In this case, since the settlement amount is up to ₹2,000, therefore, the service by HDFC Bank is exempted.

Image courtesy–Freepik

34A. Services supplied by Central Government, State Government, or Union Territory to their undertakings or Public Sector Undertakings by way of guaranteeing the loans taken by such undertakings or PSUs from banking companies and financial institutions.

35. General insurance services under the following schemes:
- Hut Insurance Scheme;
- Cattle Insurance under Swarnajaynti Gram Swarozgar Yojna (earlier known as Integrated Rural Development Programme);
- Scheme for Insurance of Tribals;
- Janata Personal Accident Policy and Gramin Accident Policy;
- Group Personal Accident Policy for Self-Employed Women;
- Agricultural Pumpset and Failed Well Insurance;
- Premia collected on export credit insurance;
- Restructured Weather Based Crop Insurance Scheme;
- Jan Arogya Bima Policy;
- Pradhan Mantri Fasal Bima Yojana;
- Pilot Scheme on Seed Crop Insurance;
- Central Sector Scheme on Cattle Insurance;
- Universal Health Insurance Scheme;
- Rashtriya Swasthya Bima Yojana;
- Coconut Palm Insurance Scheme;
- Pradhan Mantri Suraksha Bima Yojna;
- Niramaya Health Insurance Scheme implemented by the Trust constituted under the provisions of the National Trust for the Welfare of Persons with Autism, Cerebral Palsy, Mental Retardation and Multiple Disabilities Act, 1999.
- Bangla Shasya Bima.

36. Life insurance services under the following schemes:
- Janashree Bima Yojana;
- Aam Aadmi Bima Yojana;
- Life micro-insurance product as approved by the Insurance Regulatory and Development Authority, having maximum amount of cover of ₹2,00,000;
- Varishtha Pension BimaYojana;
- Pradhan Mantri Jeevan JyotiBimaYojana;
- Pradhan Mantri Jan Dhan Yogana;
- Pradhan Mantri Vaya Vandan Yojana.

36A. Reinsurance of the insurance schemes mentioned in Entry 35, 36, or 40.

37. Collecting contributions under the Atal Pension Yojana.

38. Collecting contributions under any pension scheme of the State Governments.

39. Services by the following persons in respective capacities:

(a) business facilitator or a business correspondent to a banking company with respect to accounts in its rural area branch;

(b) any person as an intermediary to a business facilitator or a business correspondent with respect to services mentioned in entry (a) or

(c) business facilitator or a business correspondent to an insurance company in a rural area.

General knowledge (optional)

A business correspondent, also known as a bank correspondent or banking correspondent, is an individual or entity that acts as an agent on behalf of a bank or financial institution to provide banking services in areas where the bank's physical presence is limited or non-existent. Business correspondents play a crucial role in expanding financial inclusion, particularly in rural and underserved areas.

Business facilitators conduct financial literacy programs, explain the benefits of banking, assist in completing documentation for account opening, and guide individuals in availing of credit facilities. BFs do not handle actual financial transactions but refer customers to the nearest bank branch or business correspondent for the same.

39A. Services by an intermediary of financial services located in a multi-services SEZ with International Financial Services Center (IFSC) status to a customer located outside India for International financial services in currencies other than Indian rupees.

40. Services given to the

- Central Government,
- State Government,
- Union Territory

under any insurance scheme, the total premium of which is paid by the Central Government, State Government or Union Territory.

41. Long-term lease of industrial plots: The service by way of a long-term lease is exempt to the extent of an upfront amount if the following conditions are satisfied:

1. Lesser is
   (a) State Government Industrial Development Corporations or Undertakings or
   (b) Other entities in which at least 20% ownership is taken by the Central Government, State Government or Union Territory.
2. Lessee is the industrial units or the developers in any industrial or financial business area.
3. Lease asset is industrial plots or plots for the development of infrastructure for financial business.
4. Lease period must be at least thirty years. Then, only this is called a long-term lease.
5. The leased plots must be used for industrial or financial activity in an industrial or financial business area.
6. Exemption is equal to the upfront amount. *Upfront amount means a sum of money that is paid in advance as a prepayment or initial payment for a purchase/service/agreement. Upfront amount is also known as premium, salami, cost, price, development charges or by any other name.*
7. The State Government concerned is required to monitor and enforce the above condition as per the order issued by the State Government in this regard.
8. If there is any violation or change in land use later on, for any reason, the original lessor, original lessee, subsequent lessee, buyer or owner are liable to pay CGST on the upfront amount as if there were no exemption. Such tax shall be paid with interest and penalty. Moreover, the said persons are jointly and severally liable.

9. In case of any violation or subsequent change of land use, due to any reason whatsoever, the original lessor, original lessee, as well as any subsequent lessee or buyer or owner shall be jointly and severally liable to pay such amount of central tax, as would have been payable on the upfront amount charged for the long-term lease of the plots but for the exemption contained herein, along with the applicable interest and penalty.
10. The lease agreement entered into by the original lessor with the original lessee or subsequent lessee or sub-lessee, as well as any subsequent lease or sale agreements, for the lease or sale of such plots to subsequent lessees or buyers or owners shall incorporate in the terms and conditions, the fact that the central tax was exempted on the long term lease of the plots by the original lessor to the original lessee subject to above condition and that the parties to the said agreements undertake to comply with the same.

41A. Transfer for development rights or floor special index: Service by way of Transfer of Development Rights (TDR) or Floor Special Index (FSI) on or after 1.04.2019 for construction of residential apartments by a promoter in a project intended for sale to a buyer, wholly or partly, except where the entire consideration has been received after issuance of completion certificate, where required, by the competent authority or after its first occupation, whichever is earlier. Exemption under this entry is limited to the GST attributable to the residential apartments; therefore, a proportionate amount of GST is calculated, and the remaining GST is payable to the promoter under the reverse charge mechanism.

Note: If some apartments are unbooked on the date of issuance of the completion certificate or first occupation of the project, then the exemption is reduced by an amount equal to the exemption attributable to unbooked apartments. However, such reduction cannot exceed 0.5% (for CGST) of value of the apartment in case of affordable residential apartments and 1% (for CGST) of value in case of other residential apartments.

Example 6.7: Mr. Khushi Ram owns a land of 4,000 square meters. On 10.10.2020, he transferred TDR to a builder/promoter registered in Delhi for ₹2 crore. The promoter will create residential apartments as well as commercial shops on the land. The carpet areas of the residential apartments and commercial shops are 1600 square meters and 2000 square meters, respectively. The construction completion date as per the certificate issued by a competent authority, is 15.05.2021, and the date when the first person occupied an apartment is 26.03.2021. The GST rate is 18%. If no apartment is un-booked and the entire consideration from the buyers is received on 26.03.2021, calculate the exemption under entry 41A.

Solution

S. No.	Particulars	Amount (in ₹)
(a)	Date of completion of construction	15.05.2021
(b)	Date of occupation of the apartment by the first person	26.03.2021
(c)	Earlier of the above dates	26.03.2021
(d)	Since the entire consideration was received on 26.02.2021, which is, therefore, an exemption under entry 41A is available.	

S. No.	Particulars	Amount (in ₹)
(e)	Total Consideration for the project	2 crores
	GST on total consideration	18% × 2 crores = 36,00,000
(f)	Total carpet area of the project	1,600 + 2,000 = 3,600 sq. meters
(g)	Proportion of the residential apartments out of total carpet area	3,600/4,000= 90%
(h)	Exemption = GST attributable to residential apartments	90% × 36,00,000 = 32,40,000
(I)	GST (payable by the promoter under reverse charge mechanism)	36,00,000 – 32,40,000 = 3,60,000

Example 6.8: Mr. Khushi Ram owns a land of 4,000 square meters. On 10.10.2020, he transferred TDR to a builder/promoter registered in Delhi for ₹2 crore. The promoter will create residential apartments as well as commercial shops on the land. The carpet areas of the residential apartments and commercial shops are 1600 square meters and 2000 square meters, respectively. The construction completion date as per the certificate issued by a competent authority, is 15.05.2021, and the date when the first person occupied an apartment is 26.03.2021. The GST rate is 18%. If one apartment (with a total carpet area 400 square meters) is un-booked on 26.03.2021, calculate the exemption under entry 41A assuming that the value of the apartment is ₹30 lakhs.

Solution

If there were 100% booking, then exemption is ₹32,40,000, as calculated in the previous example. However, one apartment is unbooked; therefore, the exemption should be reduced with regard to this unbooked apartment. As a result, the proportionate amount of exemption based on carpet area = 32,40,000 × 400/1600 = ₹8,10,000. This reduction should not exceed 5% of the value of the unbooked apartment (2.5% CGST and 2.5% SGST) provided the apartment is other than affordable apartment, else this rate is 1% (0.5% CGST and 0.5% SGST) in case of affordable apartments. Now, 5% of the value of the apartment is ₹1,50,000, as a result, the effective exemption = ₹1,50,000.

S. No.	Particulars	Amount (in ₹)
(a)	Total GST	3,60,000
(b)	Less: Effective exemption	1,50,000
(c)	GST payable under reverse charge mechanism	2,10,000

41B. Upfront amount: Upfront amount (called premium, salami, cost, price, development charges or by any other name) payable in respect of service by way of granting of long-term lease of 30 years, or more, on or after 01.04.2019, for construction of residential apartments by a promoter in a project, intended for sale to a buyer, wholly or partly, except where the entire consideration has been received after issuance of completion certificate, where required, by the competent authority or after its first occupation, whichever is earlier. Exemption under this entry is limited to the GST attributable to the residential apartments; therefore, a proportionate amount of GST is calculated, and the remaining GST is payable to the promoter under the reverse charge mechanism.

Note: If some apartments are unbooked on the date of issuance of the completion certificate or first occupation of the project, then the exemption is reduced by an amount equal to the exemption attributable to unbooked apartments. However, such reduction cannot exceed 0.5% (for CGST) of value of the apartment in case of affordable residential apartments and 1% (for CGST) of value in case of other residential apartments.

General knowledge (optional)

An upfront amount is a sum of money paid at the beginning of a transaction or contract as an initial payment or deposit. It is typically a portion of the total amount due and serves as a guarantee of the bu'er's commitment to follow through with the agreement:

42. Issuing Telecomm operator license or Radio Frequency Spectrum license: Where the

- Central Government,
- State Government,
- Union territory or
- local authority

allows a business entity to

- operate as a telecom service provider or
- use radio frequency spectrum

during the period prior to 1 April 2016, on payment of license fee or spectrum user charges, then such service by way of allowing the business entity is exempt.

43. This entry has been omitted with effect from 1 October 2021. This service was related to the leasing of wagons, coaches, etc., by the Indian Railways Finance Corporation to Indian Railways:

44. Services provided by an incubatee: If an incubatee satisfies the following conditions, then it can get an exemption to a total turnover of ₹50,00,000 in a financial year.

(a) total turnover in the previous year ≤ ₹50,00,000

(b) a period of three years has not elapsed from the date of entering into an agreement as an incubatee.

The following diagram explains the above exemption conditions.

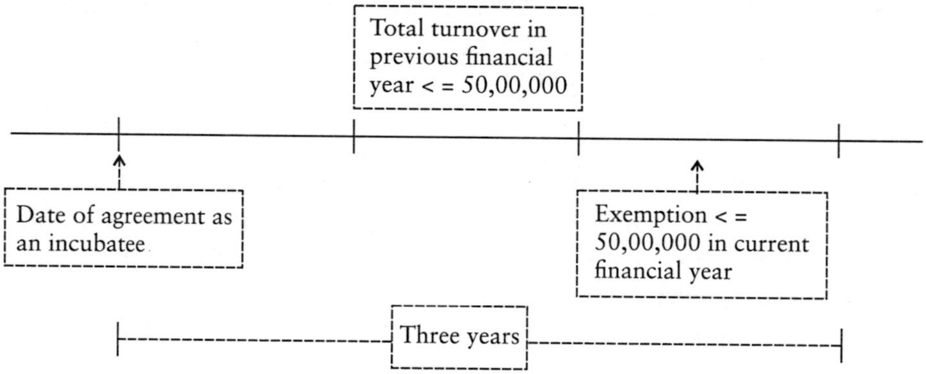

General knowledge (optional)

An incubatee refers to a startup company or entrepreneur that is being supported and nurtured by an incubator or an accelerator program. An incubator is an organization that provides resources and support to early-stage companies, generally in exchange for equity or some other form of compensation. An incubatee is typically given access to office space, mentorship, funding, and other resources to help them develop their business ideas and products. Incubators are often associated with technology startups, but they can also support businesses in other industries. The goal of incubators is to help startups become self-sustaining and successful by providing them with the tools and resources they need to grow and succeed. One such example of an incubatee is Agnikul.

Agnikul is a Chennai-based space start up or incubatee that was incubated at the Indian Institute of Technology (IIT) Madras in 2018. The company aims to build a small satellite launch vehicle to make space accessible to more people.

45. Legal services

Supplier	Recipient
• Arbitral tribunal	• any person except a business entity or
• A partnership firm of advocates or an individual advocate except a senior advocate	• a business entity with an aggregate turnover upto such amount in the previous financial year as makes it eligible for exemption from registration under the CGST Act,
• A senior advocate	• the Central Government, State Government, Union territory, local authority, Governmental Authority or Government Entity;

46. Health care services given by a veterinary clinic.

Note: A veterinary clinic is a specialized medical facility that provides healthcare services for animals and birds. It is a place where veterinarians and veterinary staff diagnose, treat and prevent diseases and injuries in various types of animals, including pets, livestock and wildlife.

Designed by Freepik

47. Services given by the Central Government, State Government, Union territory or local authority in the form of

(a) registration under any law for the time being in force

Example: Registering a company under the Companies Act, 2013, GST law, etc.

(b) testing, calibration, certification or safety check relating to protection or safety of workers, consumers or public at large, including fire license, required under any law for the time being in force.

Examples:

1. Fire safety license issued by the fire department.
2. Food safety and hygiene certification issued by the Food Safety and Standards Authority of India (FSSAI).

3. Building safety certification by local authorities.
4. Environmental safety certification by the Pollution Control Board.
5. Certification of weights and measures by the Department of Legal Metrology.

47A. This entry has been omitted with effect from 18 July 2022. This was related to the licensing, registration, analysis or testing of food samples by the FSSAI.

48. Taxable services, provided or to be provided, by a Technology Business Incubator or a Science and Technology Entrepreneurship Park recognised by the National Science and Technology Entrepreneurship Development Board of the Department of Science and Technology, Government of India or bio incubators recognised by the Biotechnology Industry Research Assistance Council, under the Department of Biotechnology, Government of India.

Example 6.9: Suppose a technology business incubator located in Bangalore, Karnataka, provides office space and facilities such as high-speed Internet, meeting rooms, and printing services to start-up companies working in the field of artificial intelligence. The incubator is recognized by the National Science and Technology Entrepreneurship Development Board of the Department of Science and Technology, Government of India. In this scenario, the services provided by the technology business incubator to the start-up companies are taxable services, but as per the notification, these services are exempt from service tax.

49. Services by PTI, UNI, independent journalist: Services by way of collecting or providing news by an independent journalist, Press Trust of India or United News of India.

Designed by Freepik

General knowledge (optional)

Press Trust of India (PTI) and United News of India (UNI) are two of the largest news agencies in India. They are independent news organizations that collect and distribute news from various sources to media outlets across the country.

For example, if there is a breaking news story about a political development or a major event happening in a particular part of the country, PTI and UNI reporters will be dispatched to the location to collect information and gather quotes from key stakeholders.

Once the reporters have collected the necessary information, they will file their stories with their respective news organizations. These stories will then be edited and packaged for distribution to media outlets, including newspapers, TV channels, and online news portals. Media outlets that subscribe to PTI and UNI services will then receive these stories and can use them to create their own news reports, articles, or broadcasts. This helps to ensure that the news is disseminated quickly and efficiently across the country and that citizens have access to accurate and up-to-date information about important events happening around them.

50. Lending of books, publications or any other knowledge-enhancing content or material by public libraries.

Image courtesy–Freepik

51. This entry has been omitted with effect from 18 July 2022. Earlier, services given by the GST Network (GSTN) to the Central Government, State Governments or Union territories for implementing GST were exempt.

52. Services by an organiser to any person in respect of a business exhibition held outside India.

Image courtesy–Freepik

52A. (Effective from 18.07.2022): This exemption is related to a tour operator service, which is performed partly in India and partly outside India, supplied by a tour operator to a foreign tourist. The amount of exemption is only limited to the value of service that is performed outside India. Therefore, we have the following format to calculate exemption and taxable value.

	Particulars	Amount (in ₹)
(a)	Consideration	A
(b)	Proportionate consideration related to foreign country	(A) × No of days in foreign country/Total days of tour
(c)	Specified amount–Notification no. 4/2022-CT (Rate) causing amendment to Notification no. 12/2017	50,000
(d)	Exemption = (b) or (c), whichever is less	–
	Taxable value of supply = (a) – (d)	–

Notes:

1. If the fractional part of a day is equal to 12 hours or more, then it will be taken one full day, e.g., three days 14 hours will be taken four days.
2. If the fractional part of a day is less than 12 hours or more, then it will be taken a half day, e.g., five days seven hours will be taken 5.5 days.
3. A foreign tourist means a person who is not normally resident in India but enters India for a maximum period of six months for legitimate non-immigrant purposes.

Example 6.10: A tour operator provides a tour operator service to a foreign tourist as follows: eight days in India and two days in Bhutan. Consideration charged is ₹3,00,000. Calculate the exemption.

Solution

	Particulars	Amount (in ₹)
(a)	Consideration	1,00,000
(b)	Proportionate consideration related to tour to Bhutan	3,00,000 × 2/10 = 60,000
(c)	Specified amount	50,000
(d)	Exemption = (b) or (c), whichever is less	50,000
	Taxable value of supply = (a) – (d)	50,000

Example 6.11: Ashish Tour and Travelers (a tour operator) provides a tour package to a foreign tourist as follows: 2.5 days in India and 7.5 days in Nepal. Consideration charged is ₹10,00,000. Calculate the exemption.

Solution

	Particulars	Amount (in ₹)
(a)	Consideration	10,00,000
(b)	Proportionate consideration related to tour to Bhutan (If number of hours in a day is equal to or greater than 12 hours, then it will be taken one full day, therefore, 7.5 days ~ 8 days)	10,00,000 × 8/10 = 8,00,000
(c)	Specified amount	50,000
(d)	Exemption = (b) or (c), whichever is less	50,000
	Taxable value of supply = (a) – (d)	**9,50,000**

53. Sponsoring sports events organised

(a) by a national sports federation or its affiliated federations, where the participating teams or individuals represent any district, State, zone or country; or

(b) by Association of Indian Universities (AIU), Inter-University Sports Board, School Games Federation of India, All India Sports Council for the Deaf, Paralympic Committee of India or Special Olympics Bharat; or

(c) by the Central Civil Services Cultural and Sports Board; or

(d) as part of national games by the Indian Olympic Association; or

(e) under the Panchayat Yuva Kreeda Aur Khel Abhiyaan Scheme.

53A. This entry has been omitted with effect from 18 July 2022. Earlier, fumigation in a warehouse of agricultural produce was exempt.

54. Services relating to cultivation of plants and rearing of all life forms of animals, except the rearing of horses, for food, fibre, fuel, raw material or other similar products or agricultural produce by way of:

(a) agricultural operations directly related to production of any agricultural produce, including cultivation, harvesting, threshing, plant protection or testing;

(b) supply of farm labour;

(c) processes carried out at an agricultural farm including tending, pruning, cutting, harvesting, drying, cleaning, trimming, sun drying, fumigating, curing, sorting, grading, cooling or bulk packaging and such like operations which do not alter the essential characteristics of agricultural produce but make it only marketable for the primary market;

(d) renting or leasing of agro machinery or vacant land with or without a structure incidental to its use;

(e) loading, unloading, packing, storage or warehousing of agricultural produce;

(f) agricultural extension services;

(g) services by any Agricultural Produce Marketing Committee or Board or services provided by a commission agent for sale or purchase of agricultural produce;

(h) **Omitted with effect from 18 July 2022.**

55. Carrying out an intermediate production process as job work in relation to cultivation of plants and rearing of all life forms of animals, except the rearing of horses, for food, fibre, fuel, raw material or other similar products or agricultural produce.

55A. Services by way of artificial insemination of livestock (except horses).

56. This entry has been omitted with effect from 18 July 2022. Before this date, slaughtering of animals was an exempt service.

57. Services in the form of pre-conditioning, pre-cooling, ripening, waxing, retail packing, labelling of fruits and vegetables which do not change the essential characteristics of the said fruits or vegetables.

58. Services given by the National Centre for Cold Chain Development (NCCCD) under the Ministry of Agriculture, Cooperation and Farmer's Welfare by way of cold chain knowledge dissemination.

59. Services by a foreign diplomatic mission situated in India, e.g., Embassy of the United States, High Commission of the United Kingdom, etc.

60. Services provided by a specified organisation in respect of a religious pilgrimage made possible by the Government of India, under a bilateral agreement.

61. Issue of specified documents by the Government: Issue of passport, visa, driving license, birth certificates or death certificates by the Central Government, State Government, Union Territory or Local authority.

61A. Providing a national licence to **a goods carrier** so that they can operate throughout India or the contiguous states.

General knowledge (optional)

Contiguous states in India refer to those states which share a common boundary with each other.

62. Services given by the Central Government, State Government, Union territory or local authority in the form of **tolerating** non-performance of a contract for which fines or liquidated damages are payable to the Central Government, State Government, Union territory or local authority under such contract.

63. Services given by the Central Government, State Government, Union territory or local authority in the form of giving **right to use natural resources** to **an individual farmer** for cultivation of plants and rearing of all life forms of animals, except the rearing of horses, for food, fibre, fuel, raw material or other similar products.

Example 6.12: The government of Tamil Nadu in India has launched a scheme called "Uzhavan (farmer) Card", which provides various benefits to farmers, including the assignment of the right to use land for farming and livestock rearing. Therefore, such services by the Government of Tamil Nadu are exempted from GST.

64. Services given by the Central Government, State Government, Union territory or local authority in the form of giving right to use **any natural resource** where such right was given by the Central Government, State Government, Union territory or local authority before 1 April 2016. However, the exemption is applicable only to tax payable on a one-time charge payable, in full upfront or in installments, for giving right to use such natural resources.

65. 'Services provided by the Central Government, State Government, Union territory by way of deputing officers after office hours or on holidays for inspection or container stuffing or such other duties in relation to import export cargo on payment of Merchant Overtime charges.'

65A. Giving information under the Right to Information Act, 2005.

65B. Services supplied by a State Government to Excess Royalty Collection Contractor (ERCC).

Giving the right to collect royalty (on behalf of the State Government) on the Mineral dispatched by the mining lease holders, is an exempt service. However, the following conditions are to be satisfied:

- **GST deposited by mining lease holders EXCEEDS GST exemption given to ERCC:** At the end of the contract period, ERCC is required to furnish an account to the State Government and certify that the amount of GST deposited by mining lease holders on royalty exceeds than the GST exempted on the service given by the State Government to the ERCC of assignment of right to collect royalty.
- **GST deposited by mining lease holders IS LESS THAN GST exemption given to ERCC:** If GST deposited by mining lease holder is less than GST exemption given to ERCC, the exemption is reduced to the amount of GST paid by the mining lease holders. Further, the difference in tax amount shall be paid by ERCC. Thus,

Exemption	= GST deposited by mining leaseholders
Amount to be paid by ERCC	= GST exemption given to ERCC – GST deposited by mining leaseholders

66. Case I: Services given by an educational institution

(a) The services given by an educational institution to its students, faculty, and staff are exempt.

(b) Conducting an entrance examination (for an entrance fee) by an educational institution is an exempt supply.

Case II: Services given to an educational institution

The following services given to an educational institution are exempt:

(a) Transportation of students, faculty and staff of an educational institution providing preschool education and education up to higher secondary or equivalent.

(b) Catering services (including any mid-day meals scheme sponsored by the Central Government, State Government or Union territory) to an education institution providing preschool education and education up to higher secondary or equivalent.

(c) Security, cleaning and house-keeping services performed to an education institution providing preschool education and education up to higher secondary or equivalent.

(d) Services relating to admission to such institution.

(e) Services relating to conduct of examination by such institution.

(f) Supply of online educational journals or periodicals to educational institutions ***other than*** the institutions providing

- pre-school education and education up to higher secondary school/equivalent or
- education as a part of an approved vocational education course.

If we summarize the above discussion, then we have the following table:

Supplier	Recipient	Service	Exempt or not
Any educational institution	Students, faculty, staff	Educational service and others	Exempt
Any educational institution	Prospective student	Conducting entrance examination taking of entrance fee	Exempt
Transporter	Educational institutions from play-way schools to schools up to 12th class	Transportation of students, faculty and staff	Exempt
Caterer	Educational institutions from play-way schools to schools up to 12th class	Catering services including the services under mid-day meal schemes of a government	Exempt
Security guard, sweeper, house-keeper	Educational institutions from play-way schools to schools up to 12th class	Security, cleaning, housekeeping	Exempt
Any organisation	Any educational institution	Services relating to admission to such educational institution	Exempt
Any organisation	Any educational institution	Services in relation to conducting entrance examinations by such educational institution	Exempt
Supplier of journals, e.g., publisher of journal	Educational institutions other than play-schools, schools up to 12th class and institutions providing education as a part of an approved vocational course	Supply of educational journals	Exempt

Illustration 6.1: Showing the above provision

Case (a): Educational Institution is Recipient of Services

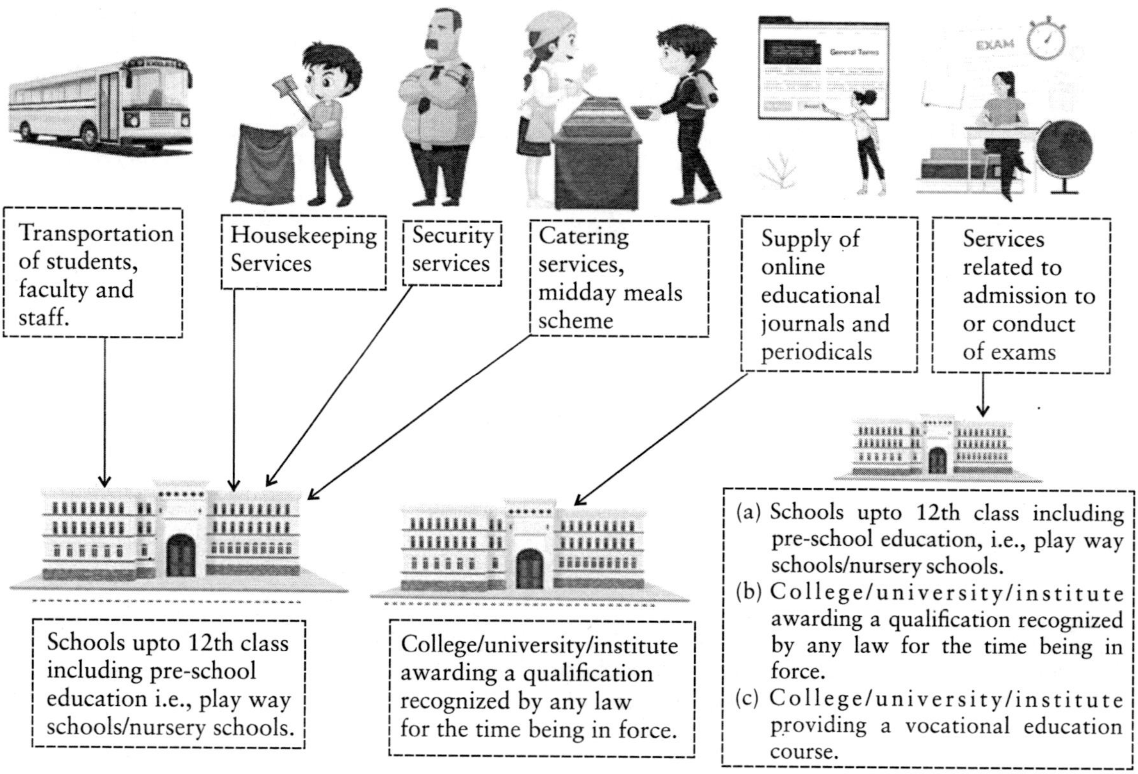

Case (b): Educational Institution is Supplier of Services

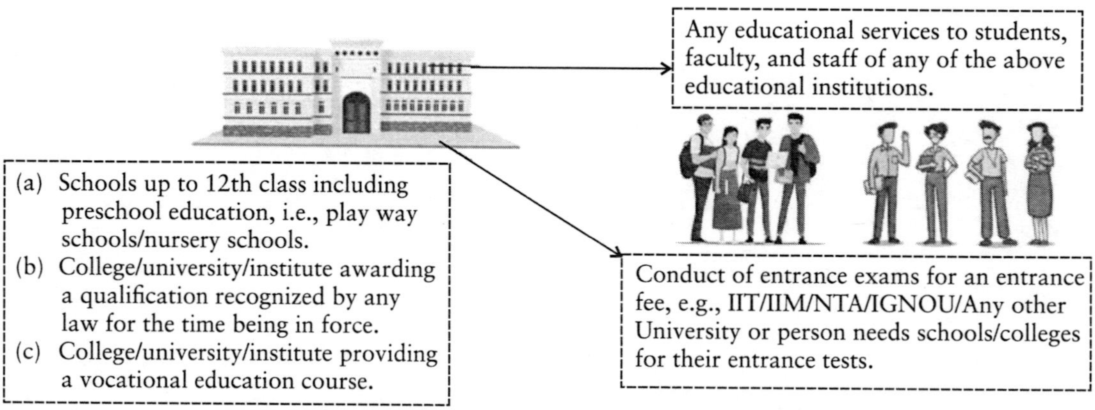

67. This entry has been omitted with effect from 1st September 2019. This entry exempted two-year Post Graduate Diploma in Management (PGDM), fellow programme in management (FPM), and five-year integrated programme in management by Indian Institute of Management (IIM).

68. Services by an umpire, coach, team manager, etc.

Image courtesy–Freepik

(a) Services given by an individual to a recognized sports body as a player, referee, umpire, coach or team manager for taking part in a sports event organised by a recognized sports body.

(b) Services given by a recognised sports body by another recognised sports body.

69. Any services given by

(a) the National Skill Development Corporation (NSDC) set up by the Government of India;

(b) a Sector Skill Council approved by the National Skill Development Corporation;

(c) an assessment agency approved by the Sector Skill Council or the National Skill Development Corporation;

(d) a training partner approved by the National Skill Development Corporation (NSDC) or the Sector Skill Council in relation to

(i) the National Skill Development Programme implemented by the National Skill Development Corporation; or

(ii) a vocational skill development course under the National Skill Certification and Monetary Reward Scheme; or

(iii) Any other Scheme implemented by the National Skill Development Corporation.

70. Services given by the assessing bodies (which are from the panel list prepared by the Directorate General of Training, Ministry of Skill Development and Entrepreneurship) in the form of assessments under the Skill Development Initiative Scheme.

71. 'Services given by training providers (Project implementation agencies) under Deen Dayal Upadhyaya Grameen Kaushalya Yojana of the Ministry of Rural Development, Government of India, in the form of offering skill or vocational training courses certified by the National Council for Vocational Training.'

72. Services given to the Central Government, State Government and Union Territory Administration as part of any training programme for which the Central Government, State Government or Union Territory Administration bears 75% or more of the total cost.

73. This entry has been omitted with effect from 18 July 2022. This entry was related with services in the form of preservation of stem cells.

74. Health care services

(a) Health care services by a clinical establishment, an authorized medical practitioner or para-medics; however, the exemption is not available with respect to giving room [other than Intensive Care Unit (ICU)/Critical Care Unit (CCU)/Intensive Cardiac Care Unit (ICCU)/ Neonatal Intensive Care Unit (NICU)] having room charges exceeding ₹5,000 per day to a person receiving health care services.

Image courtesy–Freepik

(b) Services of transportation of a patient in an ambulance, other than those specified in (a) above.

Notes:

1. Clinical establishment means a hospital, nursing home, clinic, sanatorium, etc., that provides services or facilities requiring diagnosis or treatment or care for illness, injury, deformity, abnormality or pregnancy in any recognised system of medicines in India like allopathy, ayurveda, unani, homoeopathy, etc. It also includes diagnostic centres too.
2. Health care services mean diagnosis or treatment or care for illness, injury, deformity, abnormality or pregnancy in any recognised system of medicines in India like allopathy, ayurveda, unani, homoeopathy, etc. However, hair transplants or cosmetic or plastic surgery are not health care services unless they are performed to restore or reconstruct anatomy or functions of the body affected due to congenital defects, developmental abnormalities, injury or trauma.

74A. Services provided by rehabilitation professionals recognised under the Rehabilitation Council of India Act, 1992 by way of rehabilitation, therapy or counselling and such other activity as covered by the said Act at medical establishments, educational institutions, rehabilitation centres established by the Central Government/State Government/Union Territory or an entity registered under section 12AA/12AB of the Income Tax Act, 1961.

75. This entry has been omitted with effect from 18 July 2022. This entry was related to bio-medical treatment facility.

76. Public convenience services, e.g., public bathrooms, washrooms, lavatories, urinals or toilets.

77. Service by an unincorporated body or a non-profit entity registered under any law for the time being in force to its own members by way of reimbursement of charges or share of contribution

Image courtesy–Freepik

(a) as a trade union.

Example 6.13: If a member of a trade union is facing legal issues related to their employment, the trade union may reimburse the member for the legal fees incurred in hiring a lawyer to represent them. Such service by way of reimbursement of legal fees is exempted from GST.

(b) for the provision of carrying out any activity which is exempt from the levy of Goods and Services Tax.

Example 6.14: Let us say there is a non-profit organization that is registered under the applicable law and is engaged in promoting environmental sustainability. The organization has a group of members who contribute to its activities and events. One of the activities that the organization carries out is a tree-planting drive. The organization purchases saplings, tools, and other equipment required for the tree-planting drive. The organization then reimburses its members for the expenses they incurred while participating in the drive, such as travel expenses, food expenses, etc. Since the activity of tree-planting is exempt from the levy of Goods and Service Tax, the reimbursement of expenses incurred by members is also exempt from GST.

(c) up to an amount of ₹7,500 per month per member for sourcing goods or services from a third person for the common use of its members in a housing society or a residential complex.

Example 6.15: Gokul Dham Housing Society may engage a vendor to provide cleaning and maintenance services for the common areas of the society. The cost of these services may be shared among the members, and as a result, ₹5,000 per member per month is charged. Since the share of contribution is up to ₹7,500 per member per month, therefore, the amount collected is exempted from GST. If the share were ₹8,000 per member per month, then the entire amount would have been taxable.

77A. Services provided by an unincorporated body or a non-profit entity registered under any law for the time being in force, engaged in:

(i) activities relating to the welfare of industrial or agricultural labour or farmers; or

(ii) promotion of trade, commerce, industry, agriculture, art, science, literature, culture, sports, education, social welfare, charitable activities and protection of environment,

to its own members against consideration in the form of membership fees up to an amount of ₹1,000 per member per year.

Example 6.16: Let us say there is an unincorporated body or non-profit entity called the "Farmers Welfare Association" that is registered under a relevant law. The association is engaged in activities relating to the welfare of farmers and agricultural labour in a particular region. The association provides various services to its members, such as providing information on the latest farming techniques, best practices, and new technologies, organizing workshops and training sessions for farmers to improve their skills and knowledge, etc. The membership fee is ₹800 per member per year. There are 200 members of the association. Since the association is a non-profit entity engaged in activities relating to the welfare of farmers and the fee is up to ₹1,000 per member per year, therefore, the entity is eligible for exemption.

78. If an artist performs in folk or classical art forms of:

- music,
- dance,
- theatre,

then the service is exempt if the consideration charged for such performance is not more than ₹1,50,000 and the service provided by such artist is not as a brand ambassador.

Image courtesy–Freepik

Example 6.17: Suppose a folk musician (e.g., Kutle Khan from Rajasthan), who is not a brand ambassador is invited to perform at a private event in Mumbai. The consideration charged for his performance is ₹1,40,000. Since the consideration charged is not more than ₹1,50,000, the musician can avail of the exemption, and the service provided by him will be exempted from GST.

Image courtesy–Freepik

79. Entry to a museum, zoo, national park, etc.: Services by way of admission to a museum, national park, wildlife sanctuary, tiger reserve or zoo.

79A. Entry to protected monuments: Services by way of admission to a protected monument so declared under the Ancient Monuments and Archeological Sites and Remains Act, 1958 or any of the State Acts from the time being in force.

General knowledge (optional)

The Ancient Monuments and Archeological Sites and Remains Act, 1958, is an Indian law that aims to protect and preserve ancient monuments and archaeological sites and remains of national importance. Here are some of the monuments that are protected under the act:

1. Taj Mahal, Agra, Uttar Pradesh
2. Red Fort, Delhi
3. Qutub Minar, Delhi
4. Hampi Monuments, Karnataka
5. Khajuraho Group of Monuments, Madhya Pradesh
6. Konark Sun Temple, Odisha
7. Ajanta Caves, Maharashtra
8. Ellora Caves, Maharashtra
9. Mahabalipuram Group of Monuments, Tamil Nadu
10. Sanchi Stupa, Madhya Pradesh

80. This entry has been amended with effect from 18 July 2022. According to the amended entry, the following service is exempt:

- the training or coaching in recreational activities relating to arts or culture by an individual or
- the training or coaching in recreational activities relating to sports by charitable entities that are registered under section 12AA or 12AB of the Income-tax Act.

81. Admission or entry to

(a) Circus, dance, or theatrical performance, including drama or ballet;

(b) concert, award show, pageant, music show or any sporting event other than a recognised sporting event;

(c) recognised sporting event;

(d) planetarium

where the entry fee or charge does not exceed ₹500 per person.

Image courtesy–Freepik

82. Admission to the events organised under FIFA U-17 World Cup 2017.

82A. Admission to the events organised under FIFA U-17 Women's World Cup 2020 (whenever rescheduled).

82B. Admission to the events organised under AFC Women's Asia Cup 2022.

Theory Questions

1. What do you mean by exemption? What are the different types of exemptions?
2. Write any ten conditional exemptions under the GST law.
3. Can you list any five absolute exemptions under the GST law?
4. Distinguish between absolute and conditional exemptions.
5. Exemption is limited to services only, not goods. Do you agree with this statement?

Case-based Questions (Unsolved)

1. IGNOU approaches VIPS (an educational institution registered in Delhi) for conducting OPENMAT entrance test. They enter into an agreement in which VIPS shall provide a place, invigilators, and other necessary facility for the entrance test to be conducted on 8 January 2023 and in return IGNOU shall pay ₹2,44,000 as consideration. Calculate GST payable.

   Answer: Nil

2. Amazing Food Service Limited (AFSL) is registered in Ghaziabad. It enters the following agreements:

S. No.	Date	Agreement with	Purpose	Monthly payment to school or college (in ₹)
1.	01.04.2022	SK Public School, Ghaziabad (The school is recognised and offers education from 6th class to 12th class.)	Canteen services	2,00,000
2.	15.04.2022	LR College, Delhi (The college is recognised and offers undergraduate courses.)	Canteen services	3,00,000
3.	20.04.2022	KRISIL Pvt. Limited, Noida (This is a company which develops computer software.)	Canteen services	10,00,000

   Calculate the amount of exemption available to AFSL under the GST law.

   Answer: ₹2,00,000

3. Anil Diwakar is registered in GST in Delhi. He charges ₹4,00,000 for umpiring in a cricket match organised by BCCI (Board of Control for Cricket in India). His total value of supplies of services (including above said ₹4,00,000) are ₹18,00,000. If the tax rates are CGST – 9% and SGST – 9%, then calculate the tax payable.

   Answer: CGST–₹1,26,000 and SGST–₹1,26,000

4. Suppose a Bollywood musician, who is not a brand ambassador, is invited to perform at a private event in Delhi. The consideration charged for his performance is ₹1,20,000.

The tax consultant of the musician argues that since the consideration charged does not exceed ₹1,50,000 and the musician is not a brand ambassador; therefore, the musician can avail of the exemption under entry 78. Do you agree with this argument? Explain.

Answer: His argument is not justified under entry 78.

5. Whether or not GST is to be charged in the following cases?
   (a) Vinay visited to National Zoological Park, Delhi and paid for entry ticket.
   (b) Radhika visited to Rajaji National Park, Uttarakhand and paid for entry ticket.
   (c) Sarita visits Hampi monuments, Karnataka and paid for entry ticket.
   (d) A college students group visit Sanchi Stupa, Madhya Pradesh and paid for entry ticket.
   (e) A college students group visit a University Fest, Gurugram and paid for entry ticket.

   Answer: No, No, No, No, Yes. Refer to entries 79 and 79A

6. Laxmi Bank has collected processing fees from its customers on sanction of loans to them. The amount of processing is ₹32,00,000. Is it taxable?

   Answer: Yes. Refer to entry 27

7. Akshay Limited has obtained registered under GST in the preceding financial year 2021-22. During the current financial year 2021-22, it availed legal consultancy services for its business from Anubhav Associates (a partnership firm of advocates). Is the tax consultancy given by Anubha Associates exempt?

   Answer: No. Refer to entry 45

8. Arogya Hospital provides health care services and it is registered under GST in Uttar Pradesh. The details of various services during November 2022 are as follows:

S. No.	Services	Amount (in ₹)
1	Treatment of Cancer patients	12,00,000
2	Treatment of Tuberculosis patients	1,00,000
3	Treatment of Corona patients	2,00,000
4	Diagnosis services (X-ray, Blood test, etc.)	50,000
5	Hair transplant	3,00,000
6	Plastic surgery to correct an injury	5,00,000
7	Provided rooms to 10 patients (charges ₹10,000 per day) for 15 days	15,00,000
8	ICU room charges	4,00,000

   What is the value of exempted services?

   Answer: ₹24,50,000

9. Calculate State whether GST is payable in respect of each of the following services given by the registered persons:

(a) Fees of ₹20,000 are charged from office staff for an in-house personality development course conducted by Agrasen College, providing education as part of a curriculum for obtaining qualifications recognized by Indian law.

(b) Bus service fees of ₹3,500 per month are collected from students by the above college.

(c) Housekeeping service provided by Cleaner Axis Limited to Micky School, a play school, for cleaning its playground and classroom–₹30,000 per month.

(d) Taylor & Co. supplies an online educational journal to the students of KG class of Sydney School–₹4,000.

Answer: (a): Exempt service; (b): Exempt service; (c): Exempt service; (d): Taxable service

7
Time of Supply

7.1 Introduction

Yashvi signs an agreement on 8 August 2021, promising to supply Dhanvi with some goods. On 9 August 2021, she raises an invoice for Dhanvi and delivers the goods. Dhanvi receives them on 3 September 2021. On 7 March 2021, the payment is received. When Yashvi is asked to pay her GST liability by the government, she questions when the GST liability actually arises. She is perplexed since there are several dates associated with a supply, including the date of the agreement, the date of the invoice, the date of delivery, the date of receipt of the goods, and the date of payment, all of which, regrettably, can occur at various periods in time. In light of this, the topic of time of supply is significant. Time of supply is the point in time when the GST liability arises. To determine time of supply, we have the following sections under the CGST Act, 2017.

(a) **Section 12:** Time of supply of goods.

(b) **Section 13:** Time of supply of services.

(c) **Section 14:** Time of supply in case of change in the rate of tax.

7.2 Time of Supply of Goods—Section 12

1. Charging section: Section 12(1): According to this section, the liability to pay GST on goods arises at the time of supply, which shall be determined as per the provisions of this section.

2. General Section: Section 12(2): According to this section, the *earlier* of the following dates is the time of supply:

(a)	Date of issue of invoice or the last date to issue an invoice as per Section 31.
(b)	Date of receipt of payment, which is earlier of the following dates: • Date of entry of receipt of payment in the books of account of the supplier. • Date of credit of receipt in the bank account of the supplier.

The section further provides that if a supplier receives an amount in excess of the invoice issued and such excess amount is up to ₹1,000, then the supplier has a choice between the following two options:

1. Take the date of receipt of such excess amount as the time of supply with regard to the excess amount.
2. Take the date of issue of invoice regarding the excess amount as the time of supply.

Notification No. 66/2017-Central Tax, dated: 15.11.2017: As per this notification the date of receipt of payment is irrelevant to determine the time of supply. However, this notification is not for those who have opted composition levy under section 10 other than registered persons making supply of specified actionable claims. (**As amended by Notification No. 50/2023-Central Tax, dated 29.09.2023**).

Case I: Supply involves movement of goods: Section 31(1)(a): When goods are required to be moved from one place to another so that supply takes place, then this is said that the supply involves the movement of goods. This movement of goods can be undertaken by the supplier or recipient or even a third person. As per section 31(1)(a), a supplier is required to issue a tax invoice **before or at the time of removal of goods** for supply to the recipient.

Case II: Supply DOES NOT involve movement of goods: Section 31(1)(b): When goods are required to be moved from one place to another so that supply takes place, then this is said that the supply involves the movement of goods. This movement of goods can be undertaken by the supplier or recipient or even a third person. As per section 31(1)(b), a supplier is required to issue a tax invoice **before or at the time of delivery of goods or making them available to the recipient** for supply to the recipient.

Example 7.1: Croma Stores sells a mobile phone to B on 12 October 2022 for ₹80,000 and issues the invoice on the same day. B pays the amount due by issuing a cheque which is credited to Croma Stores account on 15 October 2022. Determine the time of supply.

Solution

When you buy a phone, then there is movement in the goods at on the part of the recipient. Therefore, the last date to issue invoice, as per Section 31(1), is before or at the time of removal of goods for the recipient, i.e., 12 October 2022.

As per Section 12(2), the earlier of the following dates is the time of supply:

(a) DOI or the last date to issue invoice as per Section 31
(b) Date of receipt of payment

However, due to notification 66/2017, the date of receipt of payment is irrelevant, hence

Time of supply = DOI or the last date to issue invoice as per Section 31
= 12 October 2022 or 12 October 2022
= 12 October 2022

Example 7.2: Rajiv Bajaj sells some goods (not involving movement) to Rahul Arora on 17 July 2022 for ₹1,18,000, including IGST at 18% and issues the invoice (number 2401) on the same day. Rahul makes an online payment of ₹1,18,800 dated 18 July 2022. Rahul again transacts with Rajiv on 8 September 2022 and got an invoice (number 2596) for ₹40,000, excluding IGST at 18%. On 12 September 2022, he pays ₹46,400 after adjusting the excess amount paid earlier against invoice number 2401. Determine the time of supply.

Solution

	Invoice 2401 Dated 17.07.2022 (in ₹)	Invoice 2596 Dated 08.09.2022 (in ₹)
Value of supply	1,00,000	40,000
Add: IGST at 18%	18,000	7,200
Invoice price	**1,18,000**	**47,200**
Less: Amount paid by Rahul	1,18,800	46,400
Excess amount paid	(800)	0
Excess amount adjusted	–	800
Balance payable by Rahul	0	0

Now, applying the provisions of Section 12(2), we determine the time of supply of the following:

(i) The time of supply with regard to invoice 2401

(ii) The time of supply with regard to the excess amount of ₹800

(iii) The time of supply with regard to invoice 2596.

S. No.	Particulars	Time of Supply
1.	**Invoice 2401** Date of invoice or the last date to issue invoice u/s 31 (**Note:** Date of payment is irrelevant due to notification 66/2017) **Comment:** The liability of IGST of ₹18,000 arises on 17.07.2022, and it must be paid by the next month.	17.07.2022
2.	**Excess amount of ₹800** **Option 1:** Date of receipt of payment of the excess amount (**Note:** This option is not relevant due to notification 66/2017) **Option 2:** Date of invoice against which this excess amount is adjusted, i.e., invoice 2596.	18.07.2022 8.09.2022
3.	**Invoice 2501** Date of invoice or the last date to issue invoice u/s 31 (**Note:** Date of payment is irrelevant due to notification 66/2017) **Comment:** The liability of IGST of ₹7,200 arises on 8.09.2022, and it must be paid by the next month.	8.09.2022

3. Reverse Charge Mechanism (RCM): Section 12(3): This section determines the time of supply in the case of the **Reverse charge mechanism.** As per this section earlier, the following is the time of supply:

(a)	Date of receipt of the goods.
(b)	Date of entry of payment in the books of the recipient or date of debit for the payment in the bank account of the recipient, whichever is earlier.
c)	The date following 30 days from the date of issue of invoice or such other document, i.e., the 31st day from the date of invoice or such other document.

Example 7.3: Akshat Co. supplies a good to D Ltd., which is covered under the reverse charge mechanism. D Ltd. received the goods on 25 September 2022 against an invoice dated 20 September 2022. D Ltd. writes a cheque on HDFC Bank amounting to ₹50 lakhs. The journal entry for the payment was passed on 27 September 2022, and the cheque was cleared by Akshat Co. on 3 October 2022. Determine the time of supply.

Solution

Applying Section 12(3), we determine the time of supply as follows:

(a)	Date of receipt of goods	25.09.2022
(b)	Date of entry for payment in the books of the recipient or date of debit to the account of the recipient, whichever is earlier	27.09.2022
(c)	31st Day from the date of invoice i.e., 20.09.2022 + 31	21.10.2022
	Time of supply = Earlier of the above dates	**25.09.2022**

4. Supply of Vouchers: Section 12(4): This section determines the time of supply in case of supply of **vouchers**. As per this section, there may be two cases:

S. No.	Cases	Time of supply
1.	Supply can be identified at the time of issue of the voucher	Date of issue of voucher
2.	Supply cannot be identified at the time of issue of voucher	Date of redemption of voucher

Example 7.4: Reliance Fresh supplies some goods to a customer on 1.01.2023 for ₹1,00,000 and charges 9% CGST and 9% SGST. At the same time, the customer is issued a voucher worth ₹20,000, redeemable up to 31.02.2023. As per the terms and conditions, the voucher can be redeemed to buy only a product RS, attracting 9% CGST and 9% SGST. Determine the time of supply of the voucher.

Solution

In the question, it is given that the voucher can be redeemed to buy only a product RS, therefore, the supplier can identify the supply at the time of issue of the voucher. Therefore, as per Section 12(4), the time of supply of issue of the voucher is the date of issue of the voucher, i.e., 1.01.2023.

Example 7.5: A grocery store supplies some goods to a customer on 15.02.2023 for ₹1,00,000 and charges 9% CGST and 9% SGST. At the same time, the customer is issued a voucher worth ₹20,000, redeemable up to 31.02.2023. As per the terms and conditions, the voucher can be redeemed to buy any good at the grocery store. The customer used the voucher on 18 March 2023. Determine the time of supply of the voucher.

Solution

In the question, it is given that the voucher can be redeemed to buy only any good; therefore, the suppliers cannot be identified at the time of issue of the voucher. Therefore, as per Section 12(4), the time of supply of issue of the voucher is the date of redemption of the voucher, i.e., 18.03.2023.

5. Residuary: Section 12(5): Where the time of supply cannot be determined as per the provisions of the above sections, then the time of supply of supply is determined as follows:

(a)	Where periodical return is to be filed Time of supply = Date of file of the return
(b)	Other cases Time of supply = Date of payment of GST

6. Interest, late fee, penalty for delayed payment: Section 12(6): As per section 15(2)(d), interest/late fees, penalty, etc., charged by the supplier for delayed or late payment, then such interest or late fee is a part of the value of supply. Therefore, GST is leviable on this interest, late fee and penalty. To determine its time of supply, section 12(6) is applied according to which the time of supply is the time when such interest or late fee is received.

Example 7.6: A sold some goods to B for ₹10,00,000 plus 18% IGST and a credit period of 20 days. The date of issue of invoice (number 1903) is 25.4.2022. B paid on 21.05.2022 with a delay of six days. A is charged ₹100 per day as a late fee, and the same is paid by B on 23.5.2022. Calculate the time of supply.

Solution

Time of supply with regard to invoice number 1903

The time of supply of this invoice can be determined by applying Section 12(2). Therefore,

Time of supply = Date of invoice or the last date to issue invoice as per Section 31.

= 25.4.2022

Therefore, the IGST liability of ₹18,000 arises on 25.4.2022 and must be paid by the next month.

Time of supply with regard to late fee

Section 12(6) is applicable here; therefore, the time of supply is the date when the late fee is received, i.e., 23.5.2022.

Therefore, the liability of GST on this amount arises on 23.5.2022 and must be paid by the next month.

7.3 Time of Supply of Service

1. Charging section: Section 13(1): According to this section, the liability to pay GST on services arises at the time of supply, which shall be determined as per the provisions of this section.

2. General Section: Section 13(2)

S. No.	Cases	Time of supply
1.	Where an invoice is issued within the time specified under section 31	Date of issue of invoice or date of receipt of payment, whichever is earlier
2.	Where an invoice is not issued within the time specified under section 31	Date of provision of service or date of receipt of payment, whichever is earlier

The section further provides that if a supplier receives an amount in excess of the invoice issued and such excess amount is up to ₹1,000, then the supplier has a choice between the following two options:

1. Take the date of receipt of such excess amount as the time of supply with regard to the excess amount.
2. Take the date of issue of invoice regarding the excess amount as the time of supply.

Notes:

1. Date of receipt means the date of entry for payment in the books of the supplier or the date of credit to the account of the supplier, whichever is earlier.
2. Notification No. 66/2017-Central Tax is not applicable in the case of services.

Example 7.7: XYZ Limited supplies a service to PQR Limited on 17.08.2022, and the invoice is raised on 28.08.2022. The payment was received on 03.09.2022. Determine the time of supply.

Solution

Date of service	17.08.2022
Add: Specified time in normal case	+ 30 days
Date up to which invoice is required to be issued u/s 31	16.09.2022
Date of invoice	**28.08.2022**
Date of receipt of payment	**03.09.2022**
Therefore, the invoice is issued within the specified time of 30 days from the date of service, and then, as per Section 13(2), the time of supply is Date of invoice or Date of receipt of payment, whichever is earlier, i.e., 28.08.2022 or 03.09.2022, whichever is earlier.	28.08.2022

Example 7.8: Royal Bank (RBB) supplies a service to TPS Limited on 19.08.2022, and the invoice is raised on 17.10.2022. The payment was received on 03.10.2022. Determine the time of supply.

Solution

Date of service	19.08.2022
Add: Specified time in case of a bank	+ 45 days
Date up to which invoice is required to be issued u/s 31	03.10.2022
Date of invoice	**17.10.2022**
Date of receipt of payment	**03.10.2022**
Therefore, if the invoice is not issued within the specified time of 45 days from the date of service, then as per Section 13(2), the time of supply is Date of provision of service or Date of receipt of payment, whichever is earlier, i.e., 19.08.2022 or 03.10.2022, whichever is earlier.	19.08.2022

Example 7.9: DJ Finance (an NBFC) supplies a service to Mr. B on 20.02.2022, and the invoice was raised on 14.04.2022. The cheque was received on 27.03.2022 but entered in the books on 1.04.2022 and deposited into the bank. It was cleared on 3.04.2022. Determine the time of supply.

Solution

Date of service	20.02.2022
Add: Specified time in case of a NBFC	+ 45 days
Date up to which invoice is required to be issued u/s 31	06.04.2022
Date of invoice	14.04.2022
Date of receipt of the payment (a) date of book entry, i.e., 1.04.2022 (b) date of credit to the bank account, i.e., 3.04.2022, whichever is earlier	1.04.2022
Therefore, if the invoice is not issued within the specified time of 45 days from the date of service, then as per Section 13(2), the time of supply is Date of provision of service or Date of receipt of payment, whichever is earlier, i.e., 20.02.2022 or 01.04.2022, whichever is earlier.	20:02.2022

3. Reverse Charge Mechanism: Section 13(3): This section determines the time of supply in the case of **Reverse charge mechanism.** As per this section earlier, the following is the time of supply:

(a)	Date of entry of payment in the books of the recipient or date of debit for the payment in the bank account of the recipient, whichever is earlier.
(b)	The date following 60 days from the date of issue of invoice or such other document, i.e., the 61st day from the date of invoice or such other document.

Example 7.10: From the following information, calculate the time of supply, assuming that the supply is covered under the reverse charge mechanism.

Date of service rendered	12.06.2022
Date of invoice	28.06.2022
Date of receipt of cheque from the recipient	01.07.2022
Date of entry of payment in the books of the recipient	01.07.2022
Date of debit to the account of the recipient	14.07.2022

Solution

Applying Section 13(3), we can determine the time of supply as follows:

(a)	Date of entry of payment in the books of the recipient or Date of debit to the account of the recipient, whichever is earlier,	01.07.2022
(b)	61st day from the date of invoice, i.e., 28.06.2022+61	28.08.2022
	Time of supply = Earlier of the above dates	**01.07.2022**

4. Supply of Vouchers: Section 13(4): This section determines the time of supply in case of the issue of **vouchers**. As per, there may be two cases:

S. No.	Cases	Time of supply
1.	Supply can be identified at the time of issue of the voucher	Date of issue of voucher
2.	Supply cannot be identified at the time of issue of voucher	Date of redemption of voucher

5. Residuary: Section 13(5): Where the time of supply cannot be determined as per sections 13(2), 13(3) and 13(4), then the time of supply should be calculated as:

(a)	**Where periodical return is to be filed** Time of supply = Date of file of the return
(b)	**Other cases** Time of supply = Date of payment of GST

Example 7.11: An income tax and money laundering case against Mr. Goga, working in a multi-national company, reveals a large volume of undisclosed assets, which he claims as service income. On this basis, the GST authorities investigate the GST liability. Dates of provision of service, whether in the first half or the second half of the financial year being scrutinized by the authorities, are not known. Mr. Goga voluntarily pays GST during the investigation. What is the time of supply?

Solution

Since the GST authorities could not determine the dates of provision of service, therefore, section 13(2) cannot be applied. Moreover, as per the information given, the question does not seem to be the case of reverse charge or voucher. Therefore, sections 13(2) to 13(4) are not applicable here. Consequently, residual section 13(5) is applied according to which the time of supply should be calculated as:

1. **Where periodical return is to be filed**

   Time of supply = Date of file of the return

2. **Other cases**

   Time of supply = Date of payment of GST

Since Mr. Goga is not registered, therefore, the question of periodical return does not arise here. As a result, the time of supply should be the date of payment of GST.

6. Interest, late fee, penalty for delayed payment: Section 13(6): As per section 15(2)(d), interest/late fees, penalty, etc., charged by the supplier for delayed or late payment, then such interest or late fee is a part of the value of supply. Therefore, GST is leviable on this interest, late fee and penalty. To determine its time of supply, section 13(6) is applied, according to which the time of supply is the time when such interest or late fee is received.

7.4 Time of Supply in Case there is Change in Rate of Tax—Section 14

Section 14 has an overriding effect on Section 12 and Section 14. Therefore, in case there is a change in the rate of tax, then the provisions of section 14 shall be applied.

Case I: Where the supply is made BEFORE the change in effective rate of tax

(i) Where the invoice is issued, and the payment is also received **after** the change in the tax rate, the time of supply is earlier of the following:

(a) Date of receipt of payment

(b) Date of issue of invoice

(ii) Where the invoice is issued **before** the change in tax rate, but payment is received **after** the change, then the time of supply is the **date of invoice.**

(iii) Where the payment is received **before** the change in tax rate, but invoice is issued after the change, then the time of supply is the **date of receipt of payment.**

Case II: Where the supply is made AFTER the change in effective rate of tax

(i) Where the invoice is issued and payment is received **before** the change, then earlier of the following is the time of supply:

(a) Date of receipt

(b) Date of issue of invoice

(ii) Where the payment is received **after** the change, but the invoice is issued **before** the change, then the time of supply is the **date of receipt of payment.**

(iii) Where the invoice is issued **after** the change, but the payment is received **before** the change, then the time of supply is the **date of issue of invoice.**

A special note on the date of receipt of payment for Section 14

Date of receipt of payment means earlier of the following:

(a) Date of entry in the books of the supplier

(b) Date of credit to the account of the supplier.

However, if the credit to the bank account occurs after four-working days from the date of change of rate of tax, then the date of credit shall be taken as the date of receipt of payment.

Example 7.11: A supplier received a cheque from a recipient on 18.2.2022, and it was entered in the books of account by the supplier. The cheque was deposited into the bank on 19.02.2022. With effect from 21.02.2022, there is a change in the GST rate. The cheque was cleared on 23.02.2022. What is the date of receipt of payment?

Date of change in tax rate	21.02.2022
Add: 4 working days	+ 4 days
Resulting date	25.02.2022
Date of credit to the bank account	23.02.2022
Since the date of credit to the bank account is not after four working days from the date of change in tax rate, hence, the date of receipt of payment is earlier of the following dates: (a) Date of entry in the books of account = 18.2.2022 (b) Date of credit to the bank account = 23.02.2022 Date of receipt of payment = 18.2.2022	

Example 7.12: A supplier received a cheque from a recipient on 18.2.2022, and it was entered in the books of account by the supplier. The cheque was deposited into the bank on 19.02.2022. With effect from 21.02.2022, there is a change in the GST rate. The cheque was cleared on 28.02.2022. What is the date of receipt of payment?

Date of change in tax rate	21.02.2022
Add: 4 working days	+ 4 days
Resulting date	25.02.2022
Date of credit to the bank account	28.02.2022
Since the date of credit to the bank account is **after** four working days from the date of change in tax rate, hence, the date of receipt of payment is the date of credit to the bank account, i.e., 28.02.2022	

Chart summarising the provisions of Section 14

CASE I: When DOS falls before DOC

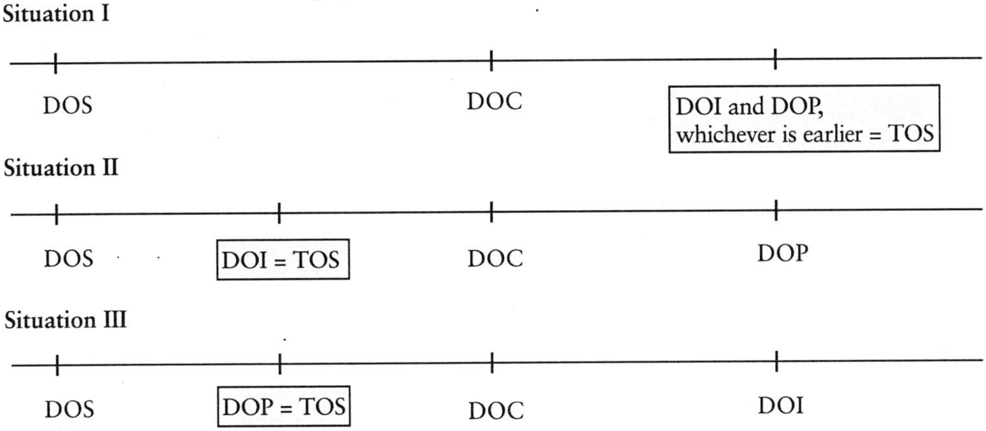

CASE II: When DOS falls after DOC

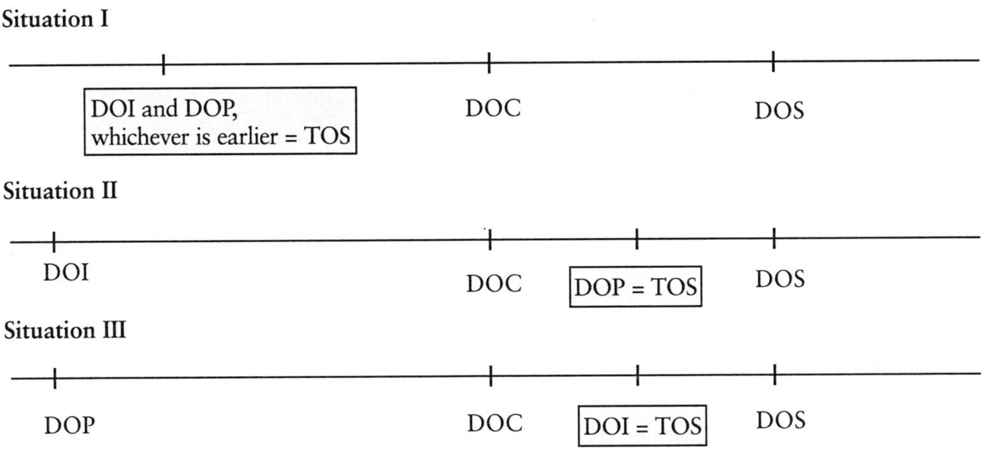

where, DOC = Date of change in tax rate; DOS = Date of service; DOI = Date of invoice; DOP = Date of receipt of payment

Notes:

1. Notification No. 66/2017-Central Tax is applicable in Section 14 also. Therefore, in the case of goods, the time of supply shall be determined on the basis of the date of invoice or the last date to issue the invoice under section 31, whichever is earlier.
2. GST is charged on the basis of the old rate or new rate, depending upon the tax rate applicable at the time of supply.

Example 7.13: Suppose the tax rate was 28% up to 31.08.2022, but from 01.09.2022, it reduced to 18%. Calculate the time of supply in the following independent situations. Also, comment which tax rate is applicable.

Situations	Date of service	Invoice date	Payment received
1.	28.8.2022	03.9.2022	10.9.2022
2.	28.8.2022	30.8.2022	10.9.2022
3.	28.8.2022	31.8.2022	30.8.2022
4.	03.9.2022	28.8.2022	05.9.2022
5.	03.9.2022	28.8.2022	29.8.2022
6.	03.9.2022	05.9.2022	02.9.2022

Solution

Date of Change (DOC) = 1.09.2022

S. No.	DOS	DOI	DOP	TOS	Applicable rate	Relevant section
1.	28.8.2022	03.9.2022	10.9.2022	03.9.2022	New rate	Section 14
2.	28.8.2022	30.8.2022	10.9.2022	30.8.2022	Old rate	Section 14
3.	28.8.2022	31.8.2022	30.8.2022	30.8.2022	Old rate	Section 13(2)
4.	03.9.2022	28.8.2022	05.9.2022	05.9.2022	New rate	Section 14
5.	03.9.2022	28.8.2022	29.8.2022	28.8.2022	Old rate	Section 14
6.	03.9.2022	05.9.2022	02.9.2022	02.9.2022	New rate	Section 13(2)

Example 7.14: Suppose the tax rate was 28% up to 31.8.2022, but from 1.9.2022, it reduced to 18%. Calculate the time of supply in the following independent situations. Also, comment which tax rate is applicable.

Situations	Date of Supply of goods	Invoice date	Payment received
1.	28.8.2022	03.9.2022	10.9.2022
2.	28.8.2022	30.8.2022	10.9.2022
3.	28.8.2022	31.8.2022	30.8.2022
4.	03.9.2022	28.8.2022	05.9.2022
5.	03.9.2022	28.8.2022	29.8.2022
6.	03.9.2022	05.9.2022	02.9.2022

Solution

Date of Change (DOC) = 1.09.2022

After applying Notification No. 66/2017-Central Tax.

S. No.	DOS	DOI	DOP	TOS	Applicable rate	Relevant section
1.	28.8.2022	03.9.2022	10.9.2022	03.9.2022	New rate	Section 14
2.	28.8.2022	30.8.2022	10.9.2022	30.8.2022	Old rate	Section 14
3.	28.8.2022	31.8.2022	30.8.2022	31.8.2022	Old rate	Section 12(2)
4.	03.9.2022	28.8.2022	05.9.2022	28.8.2022	Old rate	Section 14
5.	03.9.2022	28.8.2022	29.8.2022	28.8.2022	Old rate	Section 14
6.	03.9.2022	05.9.2022	02.9.2022	05.9.2022	New rate	Section 13(2)

Theory Questions

1. What do you mean by time of supply?
2. Do a comparative analysis of the provisions relating to the time of supply of goods and services.
3. Determining the time of supply is useless. Do you agree with the statement?
4. If the GST rate is changed, then how will you determine the time of supply?
5. In the case of goods, there is no GST on advance payment. Explain this in the context of time of supply.

Case-based Questions (Unsolved)

1. X supplies certain material to Y on 11.6.2019 and raises the invoice on the same date. The payment was received on 26.6.2019, and it was entered into his books on the same date and credited to his bank account on 28.6.2019.

   (a) What shall be the time of supply?

   (b) What will be your answer if the invoice was issued on 16.6.2019?

   Answer: 11.6.2019 and 11.6.2019

2. Shargun purchases a gift voucher for ₹16,000 on 9.12.2019 from a trader that deals in a variety of products. The voucher is valid for a period of three months. The voucher is exchanged for a product X on 15.1.2020. What is the time of supply?

   Answer: 15.1.2020

3. Anuj Jain, a chartered accountant, provides you with the following details:

   (i) Date of supply of service: 24.11.2021

   (ii) Date of invoice issued: 27.11.2021

   (iii) Date of entry of the payment in the books: 6.12.2021

   (iv) Date of credit of payment in the bank: 5.12.2021

   Determine the time of supply.

   Answer: 27.11.2021

4. Axis Bank provides the following details:

   (i) Date of supply: 15.11.2021

   (ii) Date of issue of invoice: 20.12.2021

   (iii) Date of receipt of payment: 18.11.2021

   Determine the time of supply.

   Answer: 18.11.2021

5. Vodafone Ltd., a registered person, provides the following information with respect to its regular customer Vidya.

Date	Particulars	Amount
1.7.2022	Supply of telephone service for the month of June 2022	₹2,500
1.7.2022	Date of invoice	₹2,500
18.7.2022	Receipt of payment	₹3,000

Determine the time of supply of excess payment of ₹500.

Answer: Option 1: 18.7.2022 and Option 2: The date of the invoice to be issued in 1.8.2022 (assuming that the same cycle of billing is used).

6. MT receives a supply of services from non-taxable territory in respect of tax is liable to be paid on a reverse charge basis by her. Further, she provides the following information:

Date	Particulars
28.6.2019	Date of payment as entered in her books of account
6.7.2019	Date on which payment is debited in her bank account
6.7.2019	Date of issue invoice

Determine the time of supply.

Answer: 28.6.2019

7. X Ltd. is engaged in the supply of two different taxable services, namely Gym services and Hair treatment. It issued a voucher of ₹12,000 to Y on 12.7.2019. The said voucher can be redeemed within two months from the date of such voucher for either of the two aforesaid services or partly for each of the two services. Y redeemed the said voucher on 10.9.2019. Determine the time of supply of voucher.

Answer: 10.9.2019

8. Indore branch of Oriental Insurance Co. Ltd. supplies insurance services to Delhi branch on 29.12.2019. However, the supplier issues the invoices on 27.1.2020 but records the supply on 1.2.2020. The payment is received on 8.3.2020. Determine the time of supply.

Answer: 27.1.2020

9. Rice College rented out its auditorium for a conference to Y for an agreed sum of ₹50,000. Other details are as follows:
   (a) Advance received ₹20,000 on 16.9.2019
   (b) Date of conference 15.10.2019
   (c) Invoice issued by the college for ₹50,000 on 21.11.2019 after deduction of the advance, and balance payable is ₹30,000
   (d) The balance payment received on 26.11.2019.

   Determine the time of supply. If the GST rate is 18%, then also calculate the GST liability.

   Answer: 16.9.2019 for ₹20,000 and 15.10.2019 for ₹30,000

10. Suppose the tax rate was 12% up to 31.8.2021, but from 1.9.2021 it increased to 18%. Calculate the time of supply in the following independent situations. Also, comment which tax rate is applicable.

Situations	Service date	Invoice date	Payment received
1.	28.8.2021	03.9.2021	10.9.2021
2.	28.8.2021	30.8.2021	10.9.2021
3.	28.7.2021	31.8.2021	30.8.2021
4.	03.9.2021	28.8.2021	05.9.2021
5.	03.9.2021	28.8.2021	28.8.2021
6.	23.9.2021	05.9.2021	01.9.2021

11. Bittoo purchases a Samsung LED TV from Croma Store on 10 October 2022, for ₹50,000. This TV is purchased under the Diwali bumper offer. Under the offer, he gets a voucher on an extra payment of ₹2,000 (voucher can be redeemed against Canon Printer at any time within 30 days from Diwali). The voucher is redeemed by him on November 11, 2022. Calculate the time of supply if the date of Diwali was October 24, 2022.

    Answer: 10 October 2021

12. PLC Ltd. sells gift vouchers of ₹10,000. These vouchers can be redeemed at any branch of PLC Ltd. The holder of voucher can purchase any item up to ₹10,000. X Ltd. purchases 10 vouchers on 5 December 5 2019, from PLC Ltd., Mumbai and the same are given to its employees as Bonus gifts. Sunil (one of the employees who gets vouchers) purchases three casual shirts on 3 January 2020, from a branch of PLC Ltd.

    Answer: 3 January 2020

8
Place of Supply

8.1 Introduction

Place of supply (POS) is a very important topic in the GST law to determine whether a supply is an inter-state supply or an intra-state supply. In fact, the location of the supplier of goods or services and the place of supply both determine whether the supply is inter-state supply or intra-state supply. If the location of the supplier and the place of supply both fall in the same state or union territory, then the supply is intra-state, and CGST and SGST/UTGST are charged. However, when a supply is made from a Special Economic Zone (SEZ) to a non-Special Economic Zone (non-SEZ) in the same state, then it is an inter-state supply. In other cases, IGST is charged. Sections 2(15), 10, 11, 12, 13 and 14 of the IGST Act are the relevant sections.

Note: According to Section 5(1) of the IGST Act, all inter-state supplies are subject to IGST. If the place of supply falls outside taxable territory, i.e., India, then no GST is charged. Therefore, it becomes necessary to know the meaning of the term taxable territory.

8.2 Taxable Territory—Section 2(22) of the IGST Act and Section 2(109) of the CGST Act, 2017

As per the relevant sections, taxable territory means the territory to which the provisions of the IGST Act, 2017 and CGST Act, 2017 are applicable. In simple words, the GST Acts cannot be applied to the United States, the United Kingdom, Canada, Japan, or any other country; therefore, they are all non-taxable territories. Hence, taxable territory means India only and the rest of the world is non-taxable territory. In the pre-GST regime, the term taxable territory was more relevant because, at that time, Jammu and Kashmir (J&K) was not a taxable territory but part of India. In the GST regime, the terms taxable territory and India are used interchangeably. Therefore, it is also important to know the definition of India.

8.3 Definition of India—Section 2(56) of the CGST Act, 2017

"India" means the territory of India as referred to in Article 1 of the Constitution, its territorial waters, seabed and sub-soil underlying such waters, continental shelf, exclusive economic zone or any other maritime zone as referred to in the Territorial Waters, Continental Shelf, Exclusive Economic Zone and other Maritime Zones Act, 1976, and the air space above its territory and territorial waters.

Article 1 of the Constitution of India

India, that is Bharat, shall be a Union of States. The States and the territories shall be as specified in the First Schedule. India comprises 28 States and eight Union Territories.

Territorial waters: Every point in the sea which is at the distance of 12 nautical miles (or 22.224 km) from the nearest point of an appropriate base line.

Continental shelf: The continental shelf of India comprises the seabed and subsoil of the submarine areas that extend beyond the limit of its territorial waters throughout the natural prolongation of its land territory to the outer edge of the continental margin or to a distance of 200 nautical miles (or 370.4 km) from the baseline where the outer edge of the continental margin does not extend up to that distance.

Exclusive Economic Zone (EEZ): The exclusive economic zone of India is an area beyond and adjacent to the territorial waters, and the limit of such zone is 200 nautical miles from the baseline.

Illustration 8.1: showing the meaning of India

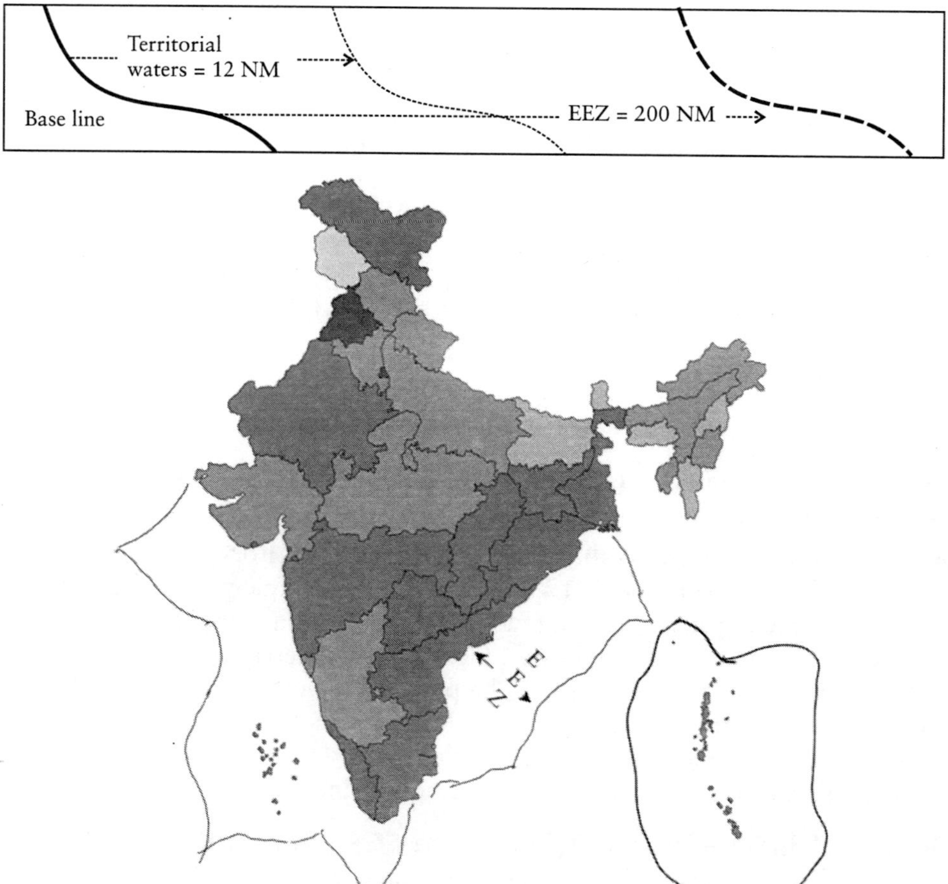

Source: https://upload.wikimedia.org/wikipedia/commons/9/90/Map_of_the_Territorial_Waters_of_the_Atlantic_and_Indian_Ocean.png

8.4 Location of Supplier of Goods or Services

Location of supplier of goods (LOS): Section 2(15) has defined the term "location of supplier of service" but not the term "location of supplier of goods". However, with regard to the location of the supplier of goods, we have the meaning of the word location. Location means the geographical point where the supplier is situated with the goods in his control and ready to supply.

Location of the supplier of service (LOS): Section 2(15): As per section 2(15), the location of the supplier of service shall be determined as follows:

S. No.	Cases	LOS
1.	Where the supply is made from the registered place of business.	The location of the place of business.
2.	Where the supply is not made from the registered place of business but from a fixed establishment.	The location of the fixed establishment.
3.	Where the supply is made from more than one establishment, whether the place of business or fixed establishment.	The location of the establishment most directly concerned with the provision of the supply.
4.	Other cases.	Usual place of residence of the supplier.

Note: As per section 2(50) of the CGST Act, 2017, a fixed establishment is a place that is characterised by a sufficient degree of permanence and suitable structure in terms of human and technical resources to supply services or to receive and use services for its own needs.

Example 8.1: Prof. Ram Avtar has a coaching institution for the preparation of IIT Entrance exams. The institution is situated in Hauz Khas, Delhi, and it has been registered in GST. Determine the location of the supplier.

Solution

Since the service is supplied from the registered place of business, therefore, as per section 2(15), the location of the supplier is the location of the institution, i.e., Delhi.

Example 8.2: Dr. Seema runs a coaching institution in Delhi at two places: (i) Laxmi Nagar and (ii) Patel Nagar. The registered place of business is Laxmi Nagar, not Patel Nagar. Students are taught at Patel Nagar only. All the human and technical resources are arranged at Patel Nagar only.

Solution

Since the institution at Patel Nagar is a fixed establishment because all the human and technical resources are available at Patel Nagar, and it seems the establishment to have a sufficient degree of permanency also; therefore, as per section 2(15), the location of the supplier is the location of the fixed establishment, i.e., Patel Nagar, Delhi.

Example 8.3: CA Mukesh runs a coaching institution in UP at three places: (i) Lucknow, (ii) Noida, and (iii) Ghaziabad. The registered place of business is Ghaziabad, and the remaining two locations are fixed establishments. However, 95% of the students are taught at Noida centre only.

Solution

Since the service is supplied from more than one place, therefore, as per section 2(15), the location of the supplier is the most directly concerned with the provision of the supply, i.e., Noida, Uttar Pradesh.

Example 8.4: CA Tarun Kumar (resident of Mumbai) does not have any place of business, but he gives lectures on Income Tax and Audit at various educational institutions, conferences, etc.

Solution

Since CA Tarun Kumar has no place of business, therefore, as per section 2(15), his residential address is the location of the supplier, i.e., Mumbai, Maharashtra.

8.5 Location of the Recipient of Services (LOR)

As per section 2(14), the location of the recipient of service shall be determined as follows:

S. No.	Cases	LOR
1.	Where the supply is received at the registered place of business.	The location of the place of business
2.	Where the supply is not received at the registered place of business, but at a fixed establishment.	The location of the fixed establishment
3.	Where the supply is received at more than one establishment, whether the place of business or fixed establishment.	The location of the establishment most directly concerned with the provision of the supply
4.	Other cases	Usual place of residence of the recipient

Notes:

Place of business: As per section 2(85) of the CGST Act, place of business means

(a) a place from where the business is generally carried on;

(b) a warehouse, a godown or any other place where goods can be stored by a taxable person;

(c) a place from where a taxable person provides goods or services or both;

(d) a place where a taxable person receives goods or services or both;

(e) a place where books of account are maintained by a taxable person;

(f) a place where a taxable person is engaged in business through an agent.

Fixed establishment: As per section 2(50) of the CGST Act and 2(7) of the IGST Act, the fixed establishment is a place that is characterised by a sufficient degree of permanence and suitable structure in terms of human and technical resources to supply services, or to receive and use services for its own needs. Thus, we can say that for a place to be classified as a fixed establishment, it must meet the following criteria:

(a) **Sufficient degree of permanence:** The location should have a certain level of stability and continuity in its operations. It implies that the establishment is not temporary.

(b) **Suitable structure:** The establishment should have the necessary infrastructure, both in terms of human resources (employees) and technical resources (equipment, other facilities), to either provide services or receive and use services for its own needs.

8.6 POS in case of supplies within India, i.e., other than import and exports of goods—Section 10

1. **Supply involves movement in goods: Section 10(1)(a):** If, in order to make a supply, the goods are needed to be moved, then the place of the supply is the location where the movement of the goods ultimately terminates. The movement may be made by the supplier or the recipient or even a third person.

Example 8.5: Deep Verma is a resident of Himachal Pradesh. He visits a furniture showroom in Chandigarh. He purchases a sleeping bed for ₹30,000. The showroom owner agrees to deliver the bed at Verma's house in Himachal. What is the place of supply?

Solution

Location of supply (LOS)	Chandigarh
As per section 10(1)(a), in the case of supply of goods involving the movement of goods, then the place of supply is the place where the movement of the goods ends. Therefore, the place of supply	Himachal Pradesh

Since LOS is in Chandigarh and POS is in Himachal Pradesh, therefore, it is a case of inter-state supply. Thus, the showroom owner is required to charge IGST in the invoice.

Note: Since the responsibility for the movement of the goods is taken by the supplier, therefore, the movement is by the supplier.

Example 8.6: Devika is a resident of Delhi. She visits a mobile showroom at Dwarka, Delhi. She purchases an iPhone for ₹1,10,000. She receives the invoice and takes the delivery of the phone after paying the amount due. What is the place of supply?

Solution

Location of supply (LOS)	Delhi
As per section 10(1)(a), in the case of supply of goods involving the movement of goods, the place of supply is the place where the movement of the goods ends. Therefore, the place of supply	Delhi

Since LOS and POS are both in Delhi, therefore, it is an intra-state supply. Thus, the supplier must charge CGST and SGST in the invoice.

Note: The responsibility for the movement of the goods is on the recipient, so the movement is by the recipient.

2. **Bill-to-Ship-to Model: Section 10(1)(b):** When a supplier (say A) supplies goods to a recipient (say B) on the instruction of a third person (say C), then it is deemed that C has received the goods, and his principal place of business is the place of supply. It is irrelevant whether the instruction is given during the movement of the goods or before the movement. This type of situation is called **bill-to-ship-to** model.

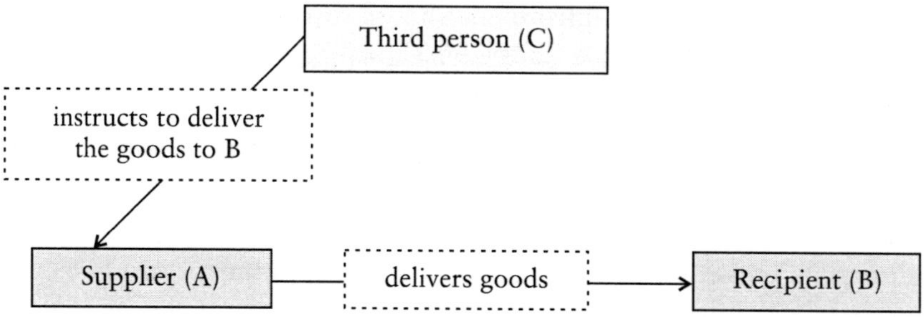

Example 8.7: X (a supplier registered in UP having a principal place of business at Kanpur) asks Y of Udaipur to deliver 100 refrigerators to Z of Delhi. What is the place of supply?

Solution

Diagrammatic presentation of the information given.

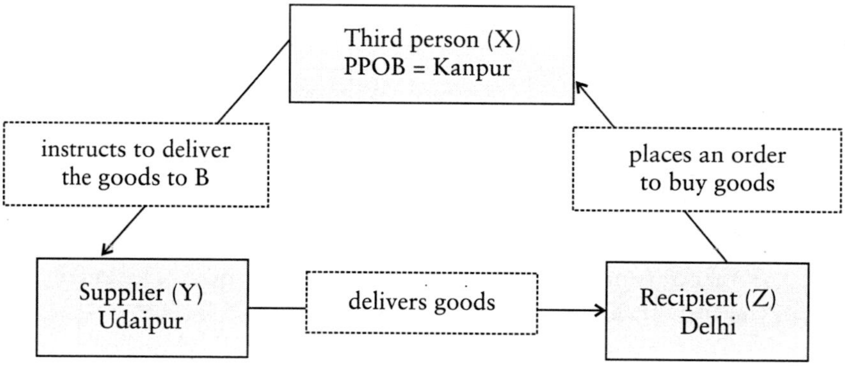

Name of the third person	X
Principal place of business of X	Kanpur, Uttar Pradesh
Name of the supplier	Y
Location of supplier (LOS)	Udaipur, Rajasthan
Name of the actual recipient	Z
Location of recipient (LOR)	Delhi
Relevant section for the supply between X and Z	Section 10(1)(a) POS = Delhi
Relevant section for the supply between X and Y	Section 10(1)(b) POS = Uttar Pradesh

3. Supply does not involve movement of goods: Section 10(1)(c): Where the supply does not involve the movement of goods, whether by the supplier or the recipient, the place of supply shall be the location of such goods at the time of the delivery to the recipient.

Example 8.8: HG Ltd. (New Delhi) has leased its machine to HT Ltd. (Gurugram) for the production of goods. The lease rent is ₹50,000 per month. After five months, HG Ltd. agreed to sell the machine leased for a stipulated amount of money. What is the place of supply?

Solution

Location of supplier (LOS)	New Delhi
In the present case, since the machine is already lying with HT Ltd., therefore, no movement is required to deliver the machine. As per section 10(1)(c), in the case of supply of goods where no movement of goods is required, then the place of supply is the place at the time of delivery to the recipient. Therefore,	POS = Gurugram, Haryana
Nature of supply	Inter-state

Since LOS and POS both fall in different states, therefore, it is a case of inter-state supply. Thus, HG Ltd. is required to charge IGST in the invoice.

Example 8.9: Richa purchased a house from a builder, say, Khushi Builders Pvt. Ltd. (registered in Mathura, Uttar Pradesh). The house was fully furnished. What is the place of supply if there was a separate agreement for the purchase of the furniture?

Solution

Location of supplier (LOS)	Mathura, Uttar Pradesh
In the present case, since the furniture is already available in the house, therefore, no movement is required to deliver the furniture. As per section 10(1)(c), in the case of supply of goods where no movement of goods is required, then the place of supply is the place at the time of delivery to the recipient. Therefore,	POS = Mathura, Uttar Pradesh
Nature of supply	Intra-state

Since LOS and POS both fall in the same state, therefore, it is a case of intra-state supply. Thus, Khushi Builders Pvt. Ltd. is required to charge CGST and SGST in the invoice. As far as the sale of house is concerned, there will be no GST on its sale because the sale of a house (i.e., building) is not a supply as per Schedule III.

4. Assembly or Installation of goods: Section 10(1)(d): Where the goods are assembled or installed at the site, the place of supply shall be the place of such installation or assembly.

Example 8.10: A is an engineer registered in GST in Delhi. B Ltd. registered in GST in Uttar Pradesh, approaches A for the assembly of some machines at his factory in Jaipur. What is the place of supply?

Solution

Location of supplier (LOS)	Delhi
As per section 10(1)(d), in the case of assembly of goods, the place of supply is the place where the goods are assembled. Therefore,	POS = Rajasthan
Nature of supply	Inter-state

Since LOS and POS both fall in different states, therefore, it is a case of inter-state supply. Thus, A is required to charge IGST in the invoice.

5. Supplying goods on board a conveyance: Section 10(1)(e): Where the goods are supplied on board a conveyance, including a vessel, an aircraft, a train or a motor vehicle, the place of supply shall be the location at which such goods are taken on board.

Example 8.11: Mr. A (Delhi) boards the Delhi-Mumbai train at Delhi. He sells the goods taken on board by him at Agra during the journey. What is the place of supply?

Solution

Location of supplier (LOS)	Delhi
As per section 10(1)(e), where the goods are taken on board a conveyance, then the place of supply is the location where such goods are taken on board. Therefore, the place of supply is Delhi	

Since LOS and POS both fall in the same state, therefore, it is a case of intra-state supply. Thus, the supplier is required to charge CGST and SGST in the invoice.

8.7 POS in case of import and export of goods—Section 11

Section	Different situations	Place of supply
11(a)	Import to India from a place outside India	Location of importer
11(b)	Export of goods from India to a place outside India	Location outside India

Example 8.12: Mr. A (registered in Delhi) imports goods from Italy. What is the place of supply? Comment on the tax liability.

Solution

As per section 11(a), the location of the importer is the place of supply, i.e., Delhi. Moreover, the import of goods always attracts IGST. Since POS falls in the taxable territory, therefore, Mr. A is required to pay IGST under the reverse charge mechanism.

Example 8.13: BAC Ltd. (registered in Punjab) exports some goods to the Netherlands. What is the place of supply?

Solution

As per section 11(b), the location where goods are exported is the place of supply, i.e., the Netherlands. Since POS falls outside taxable territory, therefore, no GST will arise here.

8.8 POS where LOS and LOR of services are in India—Section 12

1. Charging section: Section 12(1): As per this section, the place of supply of services shall be determined as per the provisions of section 12, given the location of the supplier and recipient is in India.

2. General Section: Section 12(2): If the place of supply cannot be determined as per the provisions of sections 13(3) to 13(14), then it is determined as per the provision of this section.

S. No.	Case Cases	Place of supply
(a)	Recipient is registered	The Location of the recipient
(b)	Recipient is unregistered (i) Address is available in the records of the supplier (ii) Remaining cases	The Location of the recipient The Location of the supplier

Example 8.14: Mr. Harish (a practising CA in Patparganj, Delhi). Amazing Ltd. (registered in GST in Haryana) is his audit client. What is the place of supply?

Solution

Since the recipient is a registered person, therefore, as per section 12(2), the place of supply is the location of the recipient, i.e., Haryana. Also, Mr. Harish should charge IGST in his invoice because the LOS and POS fall in different states, making it an inter-state supply.

Example 8.15: CA Anuj Jain (registered in GST in Sahibabad, Uttar Pradesh) files the income tax return of Shri M. Sharma (an unregistered person). The address of Shri M. Sharma is not available in the records of Anuj. What is the place of supply?

Solution

Since the recipient is an unregistered person and his address is also not available in the records of the supplier, therefore, as per section 12(2), the place of supply is the location of the supplier, i.e., Sahibabad. Also, CA Anuj should charge CGST and SGST in his invoice because the LOS and POS fall in the same state, making it an intra-state supply.

3. Services in relation to immovable property or by way of accommodation in such property: Section 12(3)

S. No.	Case Cases	Place of supply
(a)	Services directly in relation to immovable property, including services provided by architects, interior decorates, surveyors, engineers and other related experts or estate agents, any service by way of grant of rights to use immovable property or for carrying out or coordination of construction work or	The place where such immovable property is located or intended to be located.
(b)	Services by way of **lodging accommodation** by a hotel, inn, guest house, homestay, club or campsite, by whatever name called, and including a house boat or any other vessel or	The place where such immovable property or boat or vessel is located or intended to be located.
(c)	Services by way of **accommodation** in any immovable property for organizing any marriage or reception or matters related thereto, official, social, cultural, religious or business function, including services provided in relation to such function at such property or	The place where such immovable property is located or intended to be located.
(d)	Any service ancillary to the service referred to in (a), (b) and (c).	The place where such immovable property or boat or vessel is located or intended to be located.

Notes:

(i) If the location of the immovable property or boat or vessel is located or intended to be located outside India, the place of supply is the location of the recipient.

(ii) Where the immovable property or boat or vessel is located in more than one State or Union territory, the supply of services shall be treated as made in each of the respective States or Union territories, in proportion to the value for services separately collected or determined in terms of the contract or agreement entered into in this regard or, in the absence of such contract or agreement, on such other basis as may be prescribed.

Example 8.16: XYZ Limited is a real estate company registered in GST in Haryana. It is planning to create a housing society in Rohtak; therefore, it takes the services of Mr. A (a renowned architect registered in Delhi). What is the place of supply? If the value of supply is ₹10 00,000 and the GST rate is 18%, then what is his tax liability?

Solution

Immovable property	**Housing Society, Rohtak**
Supplier	Mr. A, Delhi
Location of supplier (LOS)	Delhi
As per section 12(3)(a), POS = the place where the immovable property is to be located.	Haryana
Value of supply	10,00,000
Add: IGST at 18%	1,80,000
Invoice price	11,80,000

Example 8.17: Shri Khushi Ram is a private builder registered in GST in Delhi. He has created a 4-storey building in Laxmi Nagar of Delhi, and for its interior decoration, he appointed Ms. Usha (a famous interior decorator registered in GST in Noida). What is the place of supply?

Solution

Immovable property	**4-storey building, Delhi**
Supplier	Ms. Usha, Noida
Location of supplier (LOS)	Uttar Pradesh
As per section 12(3)(a), POS = the place where the immovable property is located.	Laxmi Nagar, Delhi

Since LOS is in UP and POS is in Delhi, therefore, Ms. Usha will charge IGST in the invoice.

Example 8.18: Mr. Harish Bali is a YouTube Channel owner, namely, Visa2Travel. To create a content video, he travels to Panna, MP and stays in a hotel there. What is the place of supply?

Solution

Name of service	**Lodging accommodation in a hotel**
Supplier	Hotel, Madhya Pradesh
Location of supplier (LOS)	Madhya Pradesh
As per section 12(3)(b), POS = the place where the immovable property is located.	Madhya Pradesh

Since LOS and POS fall in the same state, therefore, the supplier will charge CGST and SGST in the invoice.

Example 8.19: VK and KK got married at Six Senses Fort Barwara, Rajasthan. What is the place of supply?

Solution

Name of service	Accommodation in a hotel for marriage
Supplier	Six Senses Fort Barwara
Location of supplier (LOS)	Rajasthan
As per section 12(3)(c), POS = the place where the immovable property is located	Rajasthan

Since LOS and POS fall in the same state, therefore, the supplier will charge CGST and SGST in the invoice.

Example 8.20: For the session 2022-23, a college booked a banquet hall for a painting competition for the students. The banquet hall is registered in GST in Pune. What is the place of supply?

Solution

Name of service	Accommodation in a banquet hall for fresher party
Supplier	Banquet hall
Location of supplier (LOS)	Pune, Maharashtra
As per section 12(3)(c), POS = the place where the immovable property is located	Maharashtra

Since LOS and POS fall in the same state, therefore, the supplier will charge CGST and SGST in the invoice.

4. Specified services: Section 12(4)

Specified services	Place of supply
(a) restaurant and catering services	The location where the service is actually performed.
(b) personal grooming services	
(c) fitness services	
(d) beauty treatment services	
(e) health services, including cosmetic and plastic surgery	

Example 8.21: Classy Saloon (registered in GST in Delhi) gives a haircut and facial service to Sailesh of Delhi. What is the place of supply?

Solution

Name of service	Haircut and facial service
Supplier	Classy Saloon
Location of supplier (LOS)	Delhi
As per section 12(4), POS = the place where the service is actually performed.	Delhi

Since LOS and POS fall in the same state, therefore, the supplier will charge CGST and SGST in the invoice.

5. Training and Performance Appraisal Services: Section 12(5)

Cases	Place of Supply
Recipient is registered	The location of the recipient
Recipient is unregistered	The location where the service is actually performed

Example 8.22: CA Rajender Kumar (registered in Gujarat) agrees to train the employees of Bajaj Limited (registered in Delhi) on Income Tax Laws. What is the place of supply?

Solution

Supplier	CA Rajender Kumar
Recipient (a registered person)	Bajaj Limited
Location of supplier (LOS)	Gujarat
Location of recipient (LOR)	Delhi
Place of supply (POS), as per section 12(5), in case of registered recipient = The location of the recipient	Delhi

Since LOS is in Gujarat and POS is in Delhi, therefore, it is an inter-state supply. Thus, CA Rajender Kumar must charge IGST in his invoice.

Example 8.23: Suppose that Mr. K.C. Singh (registered in Mumbai) signs an agreement to train Mr. SSS (an unregistered person from Mohali, Punjab) in classical music. The training is held at the house of Mr. SSS. What is the place of supply?

Solution

Supplier	Mr. K.C. Singh
Recipient (an unregistered person)	Mr. SSS
Location of supplier (LOS)	Mumbai
Location of recipient (LOR)	Punjab
Place of supply (POS), as per section 12(5), in case of an unregistered recipient = The location where the service is actually performed.	Punjab

Since LOS is in Mumbai and POS is in Punjab, therefore, it is an inter-state supply. Thus, Singh should charge IGST while raising the invoice.

6. Entry to an event or amusement park: Section 12(6): Admission to any of the events given below:

Cases	Place of Supply
(a) a cultural, (b) artistic, (c) sporting, (d) scientific, (e) educational, (f) entertainment event or (g) amusement park or any other place and (h) service ancillary thereto,	Where the event is actually held or where the park or such other place is situated.

Example 8.24: A company (registered in Faridabad) organizes a singing show at Major Dhyan Chand Stadium, Delhi. It sells entry tickets to 2,000 people. What is the place of supply? Is it inter-state or intra-state supply?

Solution

Name of service	Admission to entertainment event
Supplier	The company
Location of supplier (LOS)	Haryana
Place of supply (POS) as per section 12(6) = the location where the event is actually held	Delhi

Since LOS and POS are both in different states, therefore, it is an inter-state supply. Thus, the supplier should charge IGST.

7. Organisation of an event: Section 12(7)

Services	Place of Supply	
	Registered recipient	Unregistered recipient
(a) Organisation of an event or (b) Services in relation to a conference, fair, exhibition, celebration or similar events (c) Services ancillary to such events (d) Assigning sponsorships to such events. **Note:** Events may be a cultural, artistic, sporting, scientific, educational or entertainment event, including a conference, fair, exhibition, celebration or similar events.	The location of the recipient.	The location where the event is actually held.
Event is held outside of India	The location of the recipient	The location of the recipient

Explanation: Where the event is held in more than one state or UT and a consolidated amount is charged for the supply of services relating to such event, the place of supply of such services shall be taken as being in each of the respective states or UT in proportion to the value for services separately collected or determined in terms of the contract or agreement entered into in this regard or in the absence of such contract or agreement, on such other basis as may be prescribed.

8. Transportation of Goods, including by mail or courier: Section 12(8)

Cases	Place of Supply
(a) Recipient is registered	The location of the recipient.
(b) Recipient is unregistered	The location at which such goods are handed over for their transportation is a place of supply.
Proviso to Section 12(8): [Omitted by Section 161 of the Finance Act, 2023]	

Example 8.25: Ankita, a resident of Delhi, approaches her local area courier service. She gets her some journals booked for courier with destination Uttarakhand. What is the place of supply?

Solution

Name of service	Transportation of goods using courier service
Supplier	The courier service
Location of supplier (LOS)	Delhi
Place of supply (POS), as per section 12(8), in case of an unregistered recipient = the place where goods are handed over for transportation.	Delhi

Since LOS and POS are both in the same state, therefore, it is an intra-state supply. Thus, the supplier should charge CGST and SGST.

9. Transportation of Passenger Services: Section 12(9)

Cases	Place of Supply
(a) Recipient is registered	The location of the recipient.
(b) Recipient is unregistered	The place where the passenger embarks on the conveyance for a continuous journey is a place of supply.
Note: (i) Section 2(3) of the IGST Act defines a continuous journey as continuous journey means a journey for which a single or more than one ticket or invoice is issued at the same time, either by a single supplier of service or through an agent acting on behalf of more than one supplier of service, and which involves no stopover between any of the legs of the journey for which one or more separate tickets or invoices are issued. The term stopover means a place where a passenger can disembark either to transfer to another conveyance or break his journey for a certain period in order to resume it at a later point of time.	

Author's note

A continuous journey refers to a trip where a single or multiple tickets or invoices are issued at the same time, either by a single service provider or through an agent representing multiple service providers. In this type of journey, all the legs of the trip are planned and booked together, without any stopovers in between. A stopover is a designated place where a passenger can disembark during their journey to either transfer to another mode of transportation or take a break for a certain period before resuming their journey.

Example: Imagine you are planning a vacation from New Delhi to Mumbai. You book a flight ticket that includes a connection in Jaipur but without any stopover. In this case, the journey from New Delhi to Mumbai is considered a continuous journey, as you receive a single ticket for the entire trip.

Example: Let us continue with the previous example. Suppose your flight from Delhi to Mumbai includes a layover in Jaipur for six hours. During this layover, you have the option to leave the airport, explore the city, and then continue your journey to Mumbai. In this case, Jaipur acts as a stopover since you have the opportunity to disembark and explore the city before continuing your journey.

(ii) Where the right to passage is given for future use, and the point of embarkation is not known at the time of issue of the right to passage, the place of supply of such service shall be determined in accordance with the provisions of section 12(2).

(iii) The return journey shall be treated as a separate journey, even if the right to passage for onward and return journey is issued at the same time.

10. Services on board a conveyance: Section 12(10): If some services are given to a passenger while travelling on a conveyance, including a vessel, an aircraft, a train or a motor vehicle, then the place of supply is the first scheduled point of departure of that conveyance.

Example 8.26: Let us say there is a cruise ship that embarks on a journey from Mumbai, Maharashtra. If services like catering, entertainment, or spa treatments are provided on board the ship during the journey, the place of supply for those services would be considered Mumbai, Maharashtra. This is because Mumbai is the location of the first scheduled point of departure for the cruise.

Example 8.27: Consider a flight departing from New Delhi to Chennai. During the flight, the airline offers in-flight meals, entertainment systems, and other services. In this case, the place of supply for those services would be New Delhi, as it is the first scheduled point of departure for the aircraft journey.

Example 8.28: Let us say there is a bus service that operates regular trips from Delhi to Jammu. It embarks on a journey to Vaishno Devi from Delhi ISBT. The bus offers amenities such as Wi-Fi, refreshments, and onboard restrooms. In this case, the place of supply for these services would be Delhi, as it is the first scheduled point of departure for the bus journey.

11. Telecommunication Services, data transfer (or Internet services), DTH, etc.: Section 12(11)

(a) Services through fixed telecommunication line, leased circuits, Internet-leased circuits, cable or dish antenna: To take a fixed landline phone, we require a cable network and a telephone device; to take a cable Internet service, we need a cable network and a modem device; to receive Direct to Home (DTH) service we require a dish antenna and a set-top box. Therefore, in all these cases, some kinds of installations are done. In such cases, the place of supply is the place where the installation is done.

Example 8.29: Mr. A (Delhi) gets a landline phone installed at his home from MTNL. Here, the place of supply is the place where the phone is installed, i.e., Delhi.

Example 8.30: Mr. Y (Bengaluru) gets DTH Connection installed at his home from Tata Play. Here, the place of supply is the place where the phone is installed, i.e., Bengaluru, Karnataka.

(b) Services on a post-paid basis: In case of

(i) post-paid mobile services or

(ii) post-paid internet services,

the place of supply is the billing address, but if the billing address is not available, the place of supply is the location of the supplier.

Example 8.31: Mr. Z (Surat) takes a mobile connection from Vodafone on a post-paid basis. While taking the connection, he submits various documents, e.g., his Aadhaar card. Here, the place of supply is the billing address.

(c) Services on pre-paid services: prepaid mobile services, internet services, and direct-to-home television (DTH) services may be provided in the following ways:

- through an intermediary, e.g., selling agent/re-seller/distributor of Subscriber Identity Module (SIM) card or recharge voucher.

  In such case, the place of supply = The address of such selling agent/re-seller/distributor of SIM card or recharge voucher in the records of the supplier at the time of supply.

- through any person to the final subscriber (e.g., a grocery shop)

  In such cases, the place of supply = the location where such pre-payment is received or such vouchers are sold is the place of supply.

(d) In other cases, the address of the recipient as per the records of the supplier of services and where such address is not available, the place of supply shall be the location of the supplier of services.

Note: If such pre-paid service is availed or the recharge is made through Internet banking or other online mode of payment, the place of supply is the location of the recipient in the records of the supplier of services. If the location of the recipient in the records of the supplier is not available, then the place of supply is the location of the supplier.

12. Banking and financial services, including stock broking services: Section 12(12)

Cases	Place of Supply
(a) Address of the recipient is available in the records of the supplier	The location of the recipient of services as per the records of the supplier.
(b) Address of the recipient is NOT available in the records of the supplier	The location of supplier.

Example 8.32: Y maintains his bank account with Axis Bank, East Delhi Branch. Y withdraws some money from the ATM of Axis Bank, Noida. What is the place of supply assuming that Y has crossed his free limits of withdrawal from the ATM?

Solution

Name of service	Banking service
Supplier	Axis Bank
Location of supplier (LOS)	Noida, Uttar Pradesh
Place of supply (POS) as per section 12(12) = If the location of the recipient is available on the records of the supplier, then the location of the recipient.	Delhi

Since LOS and POS are both in different states, therefore, it is an inter-state supply. Thus, the supplier should charge IGST.

Example 8.33: Y maintains his bank account with Axis Bank, East Delhi Branch. Y withdraws some money from an HDFC ATM in Faridabad. What is the place of supply assuming that Y has crossed his free limits of withdrawal from the ATM?

Solution

Name of service	Banking service
Supplier	HDFC Bank
Location of supplier (LOS)	Faridabad, Haryana
Place of supply (POS) as per section 12(12) = If the location of the recipient is not available on the records of the supplier, then the location of the supplier is the place of supply.	Haryana

Since LOS and POS are both in the same state, therefore, it is an intra-state supply. Thus, the supplier should charge CGST and SGST.

Example 8.34: Mr. Raju (Delhi) buys shares listed on NSE (Mumbai) from a broker in Delhi. What is the place of supply?

Solution

Name of service	Broking
Supplier	Broker
Location of supplier (LOS)	Delhi
Place of supply (POS) as per section 12(12) = If the location of the recipient is available in the records of the supplier, then the location of the recipient is the place of supply.	Delhi

Since LOS and POS are both in the same state, therefore, it is an intra-state supply. Thus, the supplier should charge CGST and SGST.

13. Insurance services: Section 12(13)

Cases	Place of Supply
Recipient is registered	The location of the recipient.
Recipient is unregistered	The location of the recipient on the records of the supplier.

14. Advertising services to the Government: Section 12(14): Where advertising services are supplied to the

- Central Government,
- State Government,
- Local authority

meant for the state or Union territory identified in the contract, then each of such States/UT where the service is intended for.

Author's note: The readers are suggested to refer Notification No. 12/2017-Integrated Tax, dated: 15.11.2017. This notification describes the place of apportionment of IGST with respect to advertising services.

8.9 POS where either of LOS or LOR of services is outside India—Section 13

1. Charging section: Section 13(1): If either the location of the supplier or the location of the recipient of services is outside India, then the place of supply shall be determined as per the provisions of this section.

2. General section: Section 13(2): If sections 13(3) to 13(13) are not applicable, then the place of supply shall be determined as per the provisions of this section. According to this section, the location of the recipient of services is the place of supply.

Note: The location of the recipient of services. If the location of the recipient is not available in the ordinary course of business, the place of supply shall be the location of the supplier.

Cases	Place of Supply
(a) The location of the recipient is available in the ordinary course of business.	The location of the recipient.
(b) The location of the recipient is not available in the ordinary course of business.	The location of the supplier.

3. Where physical presence is necessary to perform service: Section 13(3)

Cases	Place of Supply
(a) Services are in relation to goods: Where it is necessary to make the goods physically available to the supplier of services or a person acting on his behalf so that concerned services on the goods can be performed. However, if the services are performed remotely by taking remote access using electronic means, then the place of supply shall be the location where the goods are available at the time of service. **Exception:** This clause is not applicable in the case of services supplied in respect of goods which are temporarily imported into India for repairs or for any other treatment or process and are exported after repairs, or treatment or process without being put to any other use in India other than which is required for such repairs or treatment or process.	The location where the services are actually performed.

(b) Services are in relation to individuals: Where a service is given to an individual (whether he is himself a recipient or working on behalf of the recipient) and the physical presence of the recipient or the person acting on his behalf is necessary.	The location where the services are actually performed.

Example 8.35: A (from Delhi) purchased a computer from B, Germany, and it gets out of order. B asks him to deliver the computer to Germany so that it can be repaired. A does accordingly. What is the place of supply? Also, comment on the GST liability.

Solution

Since the computer is required to be made physically available to B so that he can repair it, as per section 13(3)(a), the place of supply is the location where the services are actually performed. Therefore,

POS = Germany

Comment on GST liability: Since POS falls in non-taxable territory, i.e., outside India, therefore, no GST liability will arise here.

Example 8.36: X Ltd. (registered in GST in Delhi) purchased an expensive laptop from Z (from Japan), and it got out of order. As per the terms and conditions, in case any problem arises, the computer can be delivered to a service centre of Z available in Noida. Therefore, X Ltd. sends the laptop to the service centre to get it repaired. What is the place of supply? Also, comment on the GST liability.

Solution

Since the laptop is required to make physically available to the service centre so that repairs can be made, then as per section 13(3)(a), the place of supply is the location where the services are actually performed. Therefore,

POS = Noida, Uttar Pradesh

Comment on GST liability: Since POS falls in taxable territory, i.e., Noida, Uttar Pradesh, therefore, the supply is subject to GST. Also, the LOS is also in Uttar Pradesh; hence, the service centre is required to charge CGST and SGST in the invoice.

Example 8.36: A Ltd. (registered in GST in Pune) purchased a computer from C (from London), but the software of the computer is not working well. C accesses the computer from London only using the TeamViewer Remote Access Tool. What is the place of supply? Also, comment on the GST liability.

Solution

Since the computer is accessed remotely, as per section 13(3)(a), the place of supply is the location where the goods are available at the time of service. Therefore,

POS = Pune, Maharashtra

Comment on GST liability: Since POS falls in taxable territory, i.e., outside India, therefore, GST liability will arise here under the reverse charge mechanism.

Example 8.38: Suppose that VFA Studio (registered in GST in Mumbai) is going to start the shooting of an upcoming movie, and for this purpose, it needs a particular make-up style, and for this, it calls a known makeup artist Mr. Harrod from Hollywood to the studio situated. What is the place of supply? Also, comment on the GST liability.

Solution

If the concerned actor (the person working on behalf of the recipient VFA Studio) is not physically available for makeup, then Mr. Harrod (the supplier) would not be able to perform his service; therefore, section 13(3)(b) is applicable here. According to this section, the place of supply is the location where the service is performed. Therefore,

POS = Mumbai, Maharashtra

Comment on GST liability: Since POS falls in taxable territory, i.e., Maharashtra, therefore, GST liability will arise under the reverse charge mechanism.

4. Services in relation to immovable property: Section 13(4)

Cases	Place of Supply
(a) The services supplied directly in relation to immovable property, including services supplied in this regard by experts and estate agents, architects or interior decorators	The location where the immovable property is located or intended to be located.
(b) supply of accommodation by a hotel, inn, guest house, club or campsite, by whatever name called,	
(c) grant of rights to use immovable property, services for carrying out or coordination of construction work, including that of architects or interior decorates	

5. Admission to/Organisation of an event: Section 13(5)

Cases	Place of Supply
Admission to or organisation of a cultural, artistic, sporting, scientific, educational or entertainment event, or a celebration, conference fair, exhibition or similar services ancillary to such admission or organisation.	The place where the event is actually held.

Example 8.39: A circus company from Ohio, the United States, organizes a circus in Lucknow. What is the place of supply?

Solution

As per section 13(5), in the case of the organisation of an entertainment event, the place of supply is the place where the event is actually held; therefore,

POS = Lucknow, Uttar Pradesh

Example 8.40: Suppose Harvard University organizes an international education fair at Pragati Maidan, New Delhi. What is the place of supply?

Solution

As per section 13(5), in the case of the organisation of an educational event, the place of supply is the place where the event is actually held; therefore,

POS = New Delhi

6. Specified services at more than one location and one location is in taxable territory: Section 13(6)

Cases	Place of Supply
Where any services given in sections 13(3) to 13(5) is supplied at more than one location, including a location in the taxable territory.	The location in taxable territory.

Example 8.41: An event management company registered in New Delhi organizes an art exhibition displaying the works of international painters based in Canada. The exhibition is organised in four places in the world, i.e., Singapore, Nepal, China and New Delhi in India. What is the place of supply?

Solution:

Since the organisation of an art exhibition is an item of section 13(3) and the event is organised at more than one location, out of which one location is New Delhi (i.e., taxable territory), therefore, section 13(6) is applicable here. According to section 13(6), the place of supply is the location in the taxable territory, i.e., New Delhi.

7. Specified services supplied at more than one state/UT in taxable territory: Section 13(7)

Cases	Place of Supply
Where any services referred to sections 13(3) to 13(5) is supplied at more than one state or Union Territory	Each of the respective state or Union Territory

8. Banking, Financial, Intermediary services and hiring of means of transport: Section 13(8)

Cases	Place of Supply
(a) services supplied by a banking company, financial institution or a NBFC to account holders	The location of the supplier.
(b) intermediary services	
(c) services consisting of hiring of means of transport (including yachts but excluding aircraft and vessels) for up to a period of one month,	

Notes:

1. **Account** means an account bearing interest to the depositor and includes a non-resident external (NRE) account and a non-resident ordinary (NRO) account.

   General Knowledge (Optional)

   - **NRE (Non-Resident External) Account:** This type of account is used to manage the income earned by NRIs outside India. In other words, this account is used to transfer foreign income to India. The account can be in the form of salary, business income, or any other income earned outside India. The account can be opened only in the name of the NRI, and the funds deposited in this account are freely repatriable (i.e., can be transferred back to the country of residence without any restrictions). The interest earned on NRE accounts is tax-free in India.
   - **NRO (Non-Resident Ordinary) Account:** This type of account is used to manage the income earned by NRIs in India. It can be in the form of rent, dividends, pensions,

or any other income that is earned within India. The account can be opened in the name of the NRI or jointly with a resident Indian. The interest earned on NRO accounts is subject to income tax in India.

2. **Intermediary** means a broker, an agent or any other person, by whatever name called, who arranges or facilitates the supply of goods or services or both, or securities, between two or more persons but does not include a person who supplies such goods or services or both or securities on his own account. The following points of *Circular No. 159/15/2021, GST, dated: 21.09.2021* are noteworthy:
   - Sub-contracting for a service is not an intermediary service.
   - There are two different supplies in the case of intermediary service. These supplies are:
     - **Main supply:** the supply between the two principals.
     - **Ancillary supply:** this is the service of facilitating or arranging the main supply between the two principals.

3. Since aircraft and vessels are excluded from section 13(8), therefore, they are covered under section 13(2).

Example 8.42: Shri Vivek Chaudhary, a non-resident, has an NRE account with the State Bank of India, Delhi. The SBI gives some banking services to him. What is the place of supply?

Solution

As per section 13(8), in the case of services supplied by a banking company, the place of supply is the location of the supplier. Therefore,

POS = Delhi

Example 8.43: Brar & Bros., Chandigarh, is an agent who facilitates the supply of goods between Steve (a foreign customer) and Ramesh (an Indian supplier). What is the place of supply?

Solution

As per section 13(8), in the case of intermediary services, the place of supply is the location of the supplier. Therefore,

POS = Chandigarh

Example 8.44: Mr. Brad (a foreigner from Los Angeles) visits Rishikesh, Uttarakhand. He takes a bike on rent for 10 days from a local company, Bisht Bikes for Rent Pvt Ltd. What is the place of supply?

Solution

As per section 13(8), in the case of hiring means of transport (bike in the present case) for up to one month, the place of supply is the location of the supplier. Therefore,

POS = Uttarakhand

Example 8.45: Mr. Brad (a foreigner from Los Angeles) visits Rishikesh, Uttarakhand. He takes a bike on rent for 40 days from a local company, Bisht Bikes for Rent Pvt Ltd. What is the place of supply?

Solution

Section 13(8), in the case of hiring means of transport (bike in the present case), is applicable only if hiring period is up to one month, but in the present case, it is 40 days; therefore, Section 13(8) cannot be applied here. Consequently, Section 13(2) is applied, according to which the place of supply is the location of the recipient.

POS = Los Angeles

Comment: Since the POS falls outside taxable territory, therefore, no GST liability will arise here.

Example 8.46: Mr. Y (an unregistered person from Delhi). He takes an aircraft from a company based in Canada. What is the place of supply?

Solution

Since hiring of aircraft is excluded from Section 13(8), therefore, Section 13(2) is applied, according to which the place of supply is the location of the supplier. Thus,

POS = Canada

Comment: Since the POS falls outside taxable territory, therefore, no GST liability will arise here.

Example 8.47: Mr. Z (an unregistered person from Gujarat). He takes a yacht from a company based in Dubai for 18 days. What is the place of supply?

Solution

As per section 13(8), in the case of hiring means of transport (yacht in the present case) for up to one month, the place of supply is the location of the supplier. Therefore,

POS = Dubai

Comment: Since the POS falls outside taxable territory, therefore, no GST liability will arise here.

9. Transportation of Goods except mail or courier: Section 13(9): [Omitted by Section 162 of the Finance Act, 2023]

10. Transportation of Passengers: Section 13(10)

Cases	Place of Supply
Transportation of passengers	The place where the passenger embarks on the conveyance for a continuous journey.

Example 8.48: Mr. Michael (a foreigner) books a ticket for a New Delhi-London flight from an airline registered in New Delhi. What is the place of supply? Assume that it is a continuous journey without any stopover.

Solution

As per section 13(10), in the case of the transportation of passengers, the place of supply is the place of embark on the conveyance for a continuous journey.

POS = New Delhi

Comment: Since the POS falls in taxable territory, therefore, GST liability will arise here. The airline, being the supplier of service, will charge IGST.

Example 8.49: Asuka (a Japanese) books a ticket for a Tokyo-New Delhi flight from an airline registered in New Delhi. What is the place of supply? Assume that it is a continuous journey without any stopover.

Solution

As per section 13(10), in the case of the transportation of passengers, the place of supply is the place of embark on the conveyance for a continuous journey.

POS = Tokyo

Comment: Since the POS falls outside taxable territory, therefore, no GST liability will arise here.

11. Services on board of a conveyance: Section 13(11)

Cases	Place of Supply
Services provided on board a conveyance during the course of a passenger transport operation, including services intended to be wholly or substantially consumed while on board	the first scheduled point of departure of that conveyance for the journey

Example 8.50: Atsushi (a foreigner) was travelling on an Air India Flight from Mumbai to Tokyo. Air India makes a movie available on demand, for which it charges some money not included in the ticket. What is the place of supply?

Solution

As per section 13(11), where a service is supplied on board a conveyance, then the first scheduled point of departure of the conveyance is the place of supply. Therefore,

POS = Mumbai

Comment: Since the POS falls in taxable territory, therefore, GST liability will arise in the hands of the airline. The airline is required to charge IGST.

12. OIDAR: Section 13(12): OIDAR stands for Online Information Database Access and Retrieval services is a category of services provided through the Internet and received by the recipient online without having any physical interface with the supplier of such services. For example, downloading an e-book for a payment would amount to receipt of OIDAR services by the consumer downloading the e-book and making payment. It also includes the following:

(a) advertising on the Internet, e.g., Facebook/Meta, YouTube, Instagram, etc.

(b) providing cloud services, e.g., the vMware vCloud Suite from Lenovo, Google workspace, etc.

(c) provision of e-books, movies, music, software and other intangibles through telecommunication networks or the Internet, e.g., Jstore.org. Gaana.com, kukufm.com, Amazon Kindle, Movavi.com, etc.

(d) providing data or information, retrievable or otherwise, to any person in electronic form through a computer network, e.g., Shaadi.com, Jeevansathi.com, etc.

(e) online supplies of digital content (movies, television shows, music and the like), e.g., Netflix, Amazon Prime, Zee5, YouTube, etc.

(f) digital data storage, e.g., Google Drive, Microsoft OneDrive, etc.

In the case of online information and database access or retrieval services (OIDAR), the place of supply is the location of the recipient, but here, finding the location of the recipient is not easy because the recipient generally does not allow his location while accessing online information. Therefore, the government has framed some rules in this regard.

Section 13(12) lays down seven conditions, and if any two non-contradicting conditions are satisfied, then the location of the recipient is in India. These two conditions are as follows:

(1) the address presented by the recipient of services through internet is in India.
(2) the credit card or debit card or store value card or charge card or smart card or any other card by which the recipient of services settles payment has been issued in India.
(3) the billing address of the recipient of services is in India.
(4) the IP address of the device used by the recipient of services is in India.
(5) the bank of the recipient of services in which the account used for payment is maintained is in India;
(6) the country code of the SIM card used by the recipient of services is of India;
(7) the location of the fixed landline through which the service is received by the recipient is in India.

Notes:

1. Online courses consisting of pre-recorded videos and downloadable PDFs plus support from a live tutor are not OIDAR.
2. Individually commissioned content sent in digital form, e.g., photographs, reports, medical reports, etc., is not OIDAR.
3. PDF document automatically emailed by provider's system OR PDF document automatically downloaded from the website is OIDAR.
4. PDF document automatically downloaded from the site is OIDAR.
5. Stock of photographs/themes/wallpapers, etc., available for automatic download is OIDAR.

Example 8.52: Vivekananda Institute of Professional Studies (registered in Delhi) downloads 100 research papers on its library system from JStor.Org based in New York. It makes an online payment using an international debit card.

Solution

Since the debit card used has been issued in India, and the device used in India (i.e., IP address should be of India), therefore, as per section 13(12),

POS = Delhi

Comment: Since the POS falls in taxable territory, therefore, it is subject to GST on a reverse charge basis.

Example 8.53: Mr. Rahul (living in London) joins Jeevanthi.com from London only for his marriage purposes. He takes a three-month plan by paying ₹3,500 using an International Debit card issued by a bank in Jaipur. Moreover, he has made available his billing address of Jaipur, Rajasthan. What is the place of supply?

Solution

S. No.	Conditions	Satisfied or not
1.	the address presented by the recipient of services through Internet is in India.	No
2.	the credit card or debit card or store value card or charge card or smart card or any other card by which the recipient of services settles payment has been issued in the taxable territory.	Yes
3.	the billing address of the recipient of services is in India.	Yes
4.	the IP address of the device used by the recipient of services is in India.	No
5.	the bank of the recipient of services in which the account used for payment is maintained is in India.	No
6.	the country code of the SIM card used by the recipient of services is of India.	No
7.	the location of the fixed landline through which the service is received by the recipient is in India.	No

Since two conditions out of seven are satisfied, therefore, as per section 13(12),

POS = Jaipur

Comment: Since the POS falls in taxable territory, therefore, it is subject to GST payable by Jeevansthi.com.

13. Notified services: Section 13(13): To avoid double taxation or no taxation of the supply of a service or for the uniform application of rules, the government shall have the power to notify any service or circumstances in which the place of supply shall be the place of effective use and enjoyment of a service. As of now, the following services have been notified:

A. R&D services related to the pharma sector
   1. Integrated discovery and development.
   2. Integrated development.
   3. Evaluation of the efficacy of new chemical/biological entities in animal models of disease.
   4. Evaluation of biological activity of novel chemical/biological entities in in-vitro assays.
   5. Drug metabolism and pharmacokinetics of new chemical entities.
   6. Safety assessment/toxicology.
   7. Stability studies.
   8. Bio-equivalence and bioavailability.
   9. Clinical trials.
   10. Bioanalytical studies.

B. Repair and overhaul services of aircraft or aircraft engines/components/parts.

Theory Questions

1. What do you mean by Place of Supply?
2. What is the location of the supplier of goods?
3. What is the location of the supplier or the recipient?
4. What is the location of the recipient of goods and services?
5. How will you determine if some supply is an inter-state or intra-state?
6. How is the place of supply determined in the case of goods?
7. How will you determine the place of supply if the location of the recipient is in India but the location of the supplier is outside India?
8. How would you find out the place of supply of services where the location of both supplier and recipient is in India?

9

Value of Taxable Supply

9.1 Introduction

GST is calculated on ad-valorem basis. Where a tax is calculated by taking some percentage of a given value, then this is called ad-valorem basis. For example, if the GST rate is 18% and the value of supply is ₹20,000, then GST is 18% × ₹20,000 = ₹3,600. Therefore, if we are given a GST rate, then what do we need to calculate the tax? The answer is the value of supply. If the value of supply is manipulated, then tax is also manipulated; therefore, the law has tried to frame legal provisions so that the value of supply is determined in such a way that the chance of tax evasion is reduced. Section 15 of the CGST Act deals with the issue of the value of the supply of goods and services.

9.2 Value of Taxable Supply—Section 15

1. Entire consideration is in money terms: Section 15(1): The value of supply is the transaction value if the following two conditions are satisfied:

(a) the supply is made to an unrelated person, and
(b) the price is the sole consideration for the supply, i.e., the entire consideration is received in money terms.

Note: Transaction value means the price paid or payable for the supply of goods or services or both. Thus, the price still outstanding is also included in the transaction value.

Example 9.1: A (Delhi) sells one LED television set to B (Delhi), who is not related to A. The price payable B is ₹65,000 plus applicable GST. What is the value of supply?

Solution

Since A and B are not related and price is the only consideration, therefore, two conditions of section 15(1) are satisfied. As a result, the value of supply is the transaction value, i.e., the price payable ₹65,000.

Note: Persons are said to be related persons in any of the following cases:

(a) *Such persons are officers or directors of one another's businesses;*

Example 9.2: The CEO of Company A is also a board member of Company B, while the CEO of Company B is also a board member of Company A. So, both companies are related persons.

(b) *Such persons are legally recognised partners in business;*

Example 9.3: Two individuals establish a law firm together and become partners in the business, sharing profits and losses equally. So, both individuals are related persons.

(c) *Such persons are employer and employee;*

Example 9.4: An individual, Rahul, owns a chain of retail stores and employs his friend Ishu as a store manager. These persons are related persons.

(d) *Any person directly or indirectly owns, controls or holds twenty-five percent or more of the outstanding voting stock or shares of both of them;*

Example 9.5: An investment firm owns 30% of the outstanding voting stock of Company A and 40% of the outstanding voting stock of Company B.

(e) *One of them directly or indirectly controls the other;*

Example 9.6: Company A acquires a controlling interest in Company B, enabling it to make key decisions and exert significant influence over the operations of Company B.

(f) *Both of them are directly or indirectly controlled by a third person;*

Example 9.7: Two subsidiary companies are both controlled by a parent company that holds a majority stake in each of them.

(g) *Together, they directly or indirectly control a third person;*

Example 9.8: Two companies join forces to create a joint venture, with each company contributing resources and expertise to the new entity.

(h) *They are members of the same family. Family here means*

(i) Spouse and children of the person and

(ii) Parents, grandparents, brothers and sisters of the person if they are wholly or mainly dependent on the said person.

Example 9.9: PK supplies some goods to his brother DK (mainly dependent on PK). Since DK is dependent on PK, therefore, they are members of the same family and, hence, related persons.

2. Additions to be made to the transaction value: Section 15(2): According to this section, if the above transaction value does not include the following items, then they shall be added:

(a) Any taxes other than GST Any taxes, duties, cesses, fees and charges levied under any law for the time being in force other than CGST, SGST/UTGST and GST (Compensation to States), IGST if charged separately by the supplier. "Thus, all those taxes/duties/cesses/fees/charges other than GST must be added, however, tax collected at source (TCS) under the Income Tax Act, 1961 must not be added because TCS is way of collection of tax not a tax in reality."
(b) Payment by the supplier to a third party on behalf of the recipient Payments made by the recipient to a third person for a liability of the supplier related to the supply.

(c) Incidental expenses Incidental expenses, including commission and packing, charged by the supplier to the recipient of a supply and any amount charged for anything done by the supplier in respect of the supply of goods or services or both at the time of or before delivery of goods or supply of services. **Note:** Incidental expenses may include commission paid to an agent, packing, inspection or certification charges, installation and testing charges, weighing charges, loading charges, designing charges, etc.
(d) Interest for late payment Interest or late fee or penalty for late payment of any consideration for any supply.
(e) Subsidies directly linked to the price Subsidies directly linked to the price, excluding the subsidies provided by the Central Government and Statement Governments. **Note:** Blanket subsidy/donations received are not included.

Example 9.10: A (Delhi) takes an auditorium on rent from B (Hyderabad). Rent is ₹1,00,000 plus local municipality taxes at 5%. What is the value of supply assuming that A and B are not related?

Solution

Since A and B are not related and price is the only consideration, therefore, two conditions of section 15(1) are satisfied. As a result, the transaction value is the value, but it should be increased by all those items specified under section 15(2) to arrive at the value of supply.

Particulars	Amount (in ₹)
Transaction value	1,00,000
Add: Local municipality taxes at 5% by virtue of section 15(2)(a)	5,000
Value of supply	1,05,000

Example 9.11: A TV Channel (registered in Noida, UP) is going to organize an award show at a hotel located in Delhi. The hotel is charging ₹10,00,000 plus tax. The hotel contracts with Mr. B to supply various items like a mic, camera, podium, etc., on the date of the show. B charges ₹1,00,000. After the show is over, the TV Channel is ready to pay Mr. B the amount payable by the hotel. What is the value of supply?

Solution

Since the TV Channel and hotel are not related and the price is the only consideration, therefore, two conditions of section 15(1) are satisfied. As a result, the transaction value is the value of supply, but it should be increased by all those items specified under section 15(2) to arrive at the value of supply. In the present case, the hotel is liable to pay B, but this liability is paid by the channel in relation to the supply by the hotel to the channel; therefore, as per section 15(2), it should be added to the transaction value.

Particulars	Amount (in ₹)
Transaction value	10,00,000
Add: Payment made by the TV channel to Mr. B (a third party)—Section 15(2)(b)	1,00,000
Value of supply	11,00,000

Example 9.12: A supplier registered in Chennai supplies a machine to a recipient. The supplier charges the following items:

Price of the machine	₹5,00,000
Weighing charges	₹1,000
Commission to an agent	₹20,000

What is the value of supply?

Solution

Assuming that the supplier and recipient are not related, then as per section 15(1), the transaction value is the value of supply. However, due to section 15(2), the incidental expenses at or before delivery of the goods are included in the transaction value to arrive at the value of supply. Weighing charges and commission to an agent are the incidental expenses in the present case. Therefore,

Particulars	Amount (in ₹)
Transaction value	5,00,000
Add: Incidental expenses—Section 15(2)(c) (a) Weighing charges (b) Commission to an agent	 1,000 20,000
Value of supply	**5,21,000**

Example 9.13: A company X Ltd. sells a set of books for ₹500. An NGO gives a subsidy of ₹400 per set so that the books can be supplied in rural areas or underdeveloped areas at a price of ₹100.

What is the value of supply?

Solution

Particulars	Amount (in ₹)
Transaction value	100
Add: Subsidy received from NGO is a part of the value of supply—Section 15(2)(e)	400
Value of supply	500

Example 9.14: A company X Ltd. sells a set of books for ₹500. The State Government gives a subsidy of ₹400 per set so that the books can be supplied in rural areas or underdeveloped areas at a price of ₹100. What is the value of supply?

Solution

Particulars	Amount (in ₹)
Transaction value	100
Add: Subsidy received from the State Government is not a part of the value of supply—Section 15(2)(e)	–
Value of supply	100

3. Subtractions to be made from the transaction value: Section 15(3): According to this section, the following items should be subtracted from the transaction value.

(a) any discount allowed before or at the time of supply if such discount has been duly shown in the invoice.

(b) any discount allowed after the supply if the following two conditions are satisfied:

   (i) such discount is given because of the terms of the agreement entered into at or before the time of such supply and specifically linked to relevant invoices, and

   (ii) input tax credit attributable to the discount component has been reversed.

Illustration 9.1: Showing the above provision

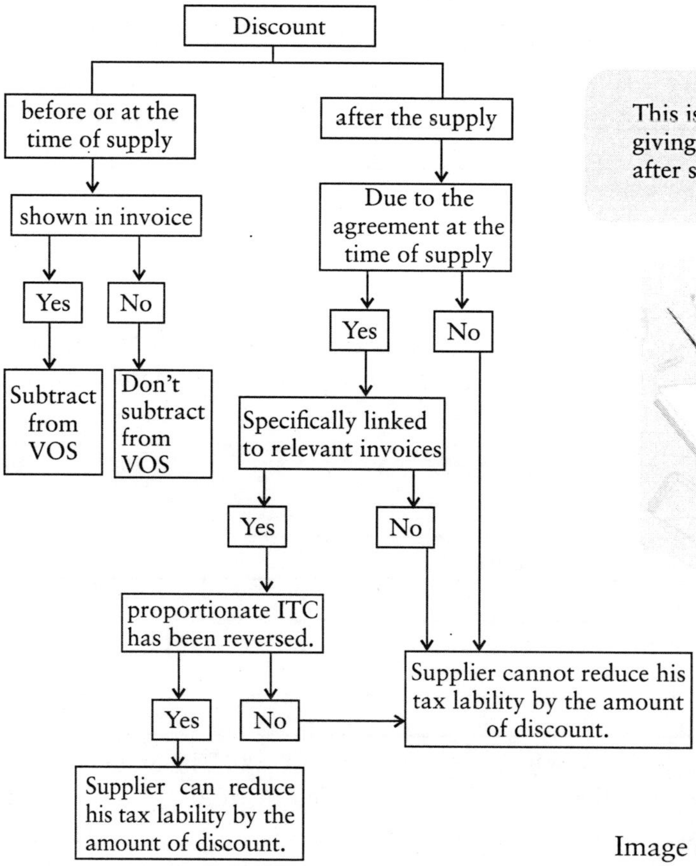

Image courtesy–Freepik

Example 9.15: Goyal G & Co. (registered in GST in Meerut, UP) supplies 1000 units of a good at a price of ₹100 per unit. It allows a 15% discount on the list price to the recipient. The discount is shown in the invoice. Determine the value of supply.

Solution

Since the discount is given at the time of supply and shown in the invoice, therefore, as per section 15(3), it can be subtracted to arrive at the value of the supply. Therefore,

Particulars	Amount (in ₹)
Transaction value (1000 × 100 per unit)	1,00,000
Less: Discount at 15% – Section 15(3)	15,000
Value of supply	85,000

Example 9.16: The agreement of Mittal Electronics with its dealers is that the purchase of rice cookers over 1,000 pieces in the Diwali month will entitle them to a discount of 10% per cooker. The demand for the cookers was 1200 cookers, and the entire demand was met by Ramesh (a registered dealer in Delhi). Therefore, Ramesh got the discount, and the same was shown in the invoice. What is the value of supply if the price of a cooker is ₹100?

Solution

Since the discount is given at the time of supply and shown in the invoice, therefore, as per section 15(3), it can be subtracted to arrive at the value of the supply. Therefore,

Particulars	Amount (in ₹)
Transaction value (1200 × 100 per unit)	1,20,000
Less: Discount at 10% – Section 15(3)	12,000
Value of supply	1,02,000

Example 9.17: Yashvi Ltd. sold goods to Dhani Ltd. on 17th February 2022 at ₹50,000 (exclusive of taxes and discounts) and charged ₹9,000 as IGST at 18%. The terms of supply stipulated that a discount of 2% would be given to Dhani Ltd. if it made the payment within one month of the supply. Dhani Ltd. avails the input tax credit of ₹9,000 and makes the payment for the goods on 10 March 2022. As a result, Dhani Ltd. receives a 2% discount as decided earlier after receiving a credit note issued by the supplier, and it has reversed the proportionate credit.

Determine the amount of discount that can be subtracted by Yashvi Ltd. from the tax liability for March 2022.

Solution

Since a discount has been given after the supply, therefore, some conditions are required to be satisfied first.

1. **Condition 1:** The discount should be because of the terms of the agreement entered into at the time of the supply, and it can be specifically linked to the invoice. This condition is satisfied.
2. **Condition 2:** The proportionate amount of ITC is reversed by the recipient. This condition is also satisfied.

Therefore, as per section 15(3), the post-supply discount can be adjusted now by subtracting the GST liability of the month concerned.

Invoice value at the time of supply

Particulars	Amount (in ₹)
Transaction value	50,000
Add: IGST at 18%	9,000
Invoice value	59,000

Now, Dhani Ltd. is eligible for the discount of 2%; therefore, Yashvi Ltd. issues a credit note for ₹1,180 (see working note) to Dhani Ltd. As Dhani Ltd. receives the credit note, it reverses the input tax credit equal to ₹180. Yashvi Ltd. can reduce its GST liability for the month of March by ₹180.

Working Note

If the discount were given at the time of supply only, then the invoice value would have been ₹57,820 calculated as follows:

Particulars	Amount (in ₹)
Transaction value	50,000
Les: 2% Discount	1,000
After discount value	49,000
Add: IGST at 18%	8,820
Invoice value	57,820

However, the reality is that the invoice value was ₹59,000. Moreover, that invoice cannot be revised; therefore, Yashvi Ltd. should issue a credit note of ₹1,180 (= ₹59,000 – ₹57,820). Another way to calculate this amount is

Discount on transaction value = ₹1,000

Add: IGST at 18% = ₹180

Credit note amount = ₹1,180

9.3 Value of Supply cannot be determined under Section 15(1)—Section 15(4)

According to this section, if the value of supply cannot be determined under section 15(1), then it shall be determined in the manner prescribed in Chapter IV of the CGST Rules, 2017.

9.4 The Government can notify goods or services the value of which shall be determined in such manner as may be prescribed—Section 15(5)

Irrespective of section 15(1) or section15(4), on the recommendation of the GST Council, the Central Government reserves the power to notify the supplies the value of which shall be determined as per the CGST Rules, 2017. As of now, the following supplies have been notified.

(a) Purchase or sale of foreign currency including money changing.
(b) Booking air tickets by an air travel agent.
(c) Life insurance service.

(d) Buying and selling of second-hand goods.
(e) Vouchers, token, coupons or stamps (other than postage stamps) redeemable against goods or services.
(f) Services provided without consideration between distinct persons under GST law that are different units of the same legal entity.
(g) Lottery, betting, gambling, and horse racing.
(h) Supply of online money gaming. **[With effect from 1.10.2023]**
(i) Supply of online gaming, other than online money gaming. **[With effect from 1.10.2023]**
(j) Supply of actionable claims in casinos. **[With effect from 1.10.2023]**

9.5 Determination of Value of Supply—CGST Rules, 2017

Before we proceed further, it is important to know the meaning of the following terms:

Open Market Value (OMV)	Open Market Value of a supply means the full value of money which is payable by an unrelated recipient to get such supply at the time of valuation of such supply, provided the price is only the consideration. We can say that open market value is an unbiased price (also known as an arm's length price).
Supply of like kind and quality	Supply of like kind and quality means any other supply having the following features: (a) It is made under similar circumstances, (b) It is the same or closely or substantially resembling in respect of characteristics, quality, quantity, functionality and reputation to the supply being valued.

1. Where the consideration is not in 100% money form: Rule 27

(a) Open market value, at the time of supply, is known

Value of supply = Open market value	–

(b) Open market value is not known

Consideration in money	–
Add: Money value of the consideration in kind, if known at the time of supply	–
Value of supply	–

(c) When money value of the consideration in kind is not known

Value of supply = Value of supply of like kind and quality	–

(d) When the value of supply of like kind and quality is also not known

Consideration in money	–
Add: Money value of the consideration in kind as determined under Rule 30 or Rule 31 in that order.	–
Value of supply	–

Note: In the case of services, rule 31 can be applied directly at the choice of the supplier.

Example 9.18: Rajiv Bajaj (registered in Uttarakhand) supplies a Scooty under two options for a buyer:

1. Exchange any old Scooty or bike and take a new Scooty plus ₹85,000.
2. Non-exchange offer, in which the price of the Scooty is ₹1,02,000 excluding GST.

A buyer purchases a new Scooty under the exchange offer. Determine the value of supply.

Solution

Since the consideration is not 100% in money, therefore, rule 27 is applied here. The open market value of the new Scooty is ₹1,02,000. As per rule 27, if the open market value is available, then the value of supply is the open market value. Thus, the value of supply = ₹1,02,000.

Example 9.19: Where a laptop is supplied for ₹50,000 along with the barter of a printer that is manufactured by the recipient, and the value of the printer known at the time of supply is ₹10,000, but the open market value of the laptop is not known. What is the value of supply?

Solution

Since the consideration is not 100% in money, therefore, rule 27 is applied here. The open market value of the laptop is not known, but the value of the printer is known. Then, as per Rule 27

Particulars	Amount (in ₹)
Consideration in money	50,000
Add: Money value of the printer known at the time of supply	10,000
Value of supply	60,000

Example 9.20: A laptop is supplied for ₹50,000 along with the barter of a printer that is manufactured by the recipient, and the value of the printer is not known at the time of supply. The same model of laptop is sold by a nearby dealer for ₹65,000. What is the value of supply?

Solution

Since the consideration is not 100% in money, therefore, rule 27 is applied here. The open market value of the laptop and the value of the printer is not known. As per rule 27, if the money value of the consideration in kind is not known, then

Particulars	Amount (in ₹)
Value of supply of like kind and quality	65,000
Value of supply	65,000

Example 9.21: A laptop is supplied for ₹50,000 along with the barter of a printer that is manufactured by the recipient, and the value of the printer is not known at the time of supply. What is the value of supply if the value of the printer, as determined under Rule 30, is ₹10,000?

Solution

Since the consideration is not 100% in money, therefore, Rule 27 is applied here. The open market value of the laptop and the value of the printer is not known. As per Rule 27, if the value of supply of like kind and quality is also not available, then the value of the printer can be determined as per Rule 30 or 31 in that order.

Particulars	Amount (in ₹)
Consideration in money	50,000
Add: Money value of the printer as determined under Rule 30	10,000
Value of supply	60,000

2. Value of supply between distinct or related persons other than through an agent: Rule 28

1. Open market value, at the time of valuation, is known

Value of supply = Open market value	–

Note: If the recipient is eligible for full input tax credit, then the value declared in the invoice is taken as the open market value.

2. Open market value is not available

Value of supply = Value of supply of like kind and quality	–

3. When the value of supply of like kind and quality is not known

Value of supply = Value determined as per Rule 30 or Rule 31 in that order	–

Note: In the case of services, Rule 31 can be applied directly at the choice of the supplier.

4. *Another option (other than above) in case of goods only:* Where the recipient has received the goods for making further supply, the supplier has the option to accept the value of supply equal to 90% of the price charged for the supply of goods of like kind and quality by the recipient from his unrelated customer.

3. Value of supply of goods where supply is made or received through an agent: Rule 29

Case I: Open market value is known

If the open market value of such supply is known, then the value of supply is the open market value.

Or

Where the recipient has received the goods for making further supply, the supplier has the option to accept the value of supply equal to 90% of the price charged for the supply of goods of like kind and quality by the recipient from his unrelated related customer.

Example 9.22: XYZ Ltd. supplies a product MN to its agent, and the agent is supplying of like kind and quality in subsequent supplies at a price of ₹3,000 on the day of the supply. XYZ Ltd. also supplies the same product to an unrelated customer at a price of ₹3,200. What is the value of supply?

Solution:

As per rule 29, the supplier has two options:

1. Take open market value as the value of supply, therefore,
   Value of supply = ₹3,200

2. Take 90% of the price charged by the agent from his unrelated customers for the supply of goods of like kind and quality, as the value of supply, therefore,

   Value of supply = 90% × ₹3,000

   = ₹2,700

Case II: When open market value is not available

If the open market value is not available, the value shall be determined as per Rule 30 or Rule 31 in that order.

4. Value of supply based on cost: Rule 30

If the value of supply of goods or services or both cannot be determined as per the above methods, then the value can be determined as follows:

Cost of production/manufacture/acquisition of such goods or cost of provision of such services	–
Add: 10% of the above cost	–
Value of supply	–

Example 9.23: Suppose that the value of a good supplied cannot be determined as Rules 27 to 29. The cost of acquisition of the goods is 1,00,000. Determine the value of the supply of the goods.

Solution

Particulars	Amount (in ₹)
Cost of acquisition	1,00,000
Add: 10% of the above cost	10,000
Value of supply	1,10,000

5. Residual method: Rule 31: This a method of best judgement. If the value cannot be determined as per Rule 30, then Rule 31 is applied. However, valuation under Rule 30 shall be done using reasonable means consistent with the principles and general provisions of section 15 and the provisions of Chapter IV of the CGST Rules, 2017.

6. Value of supply of lottery, betting, gambling and horse racing: Rule 31A

(a) Supply of lottery

Value of supply = Higher of the following:

(a) 100/128 × the face value of the lottery ticket or
(b) 100/128 × the price notified in the Official Gazette by the Organising State

(b) Betting, gambling, horse racing

Value of supply = 100% × the face value of the bet or the amount paid into the totalisator

Note: General knowledge (optional)

1. In India, lottery play is legal in the following states: Arunachal Pradesh, Punjab, Kerala, Goa, Mizoram, Nagaland, Sikkim, West Bengal, and Maharashtra.

2. A totalisator, also known as a "tote," is a system used for betting on horse racing or other forms of pari-mutuel betting. It is a computerized system that calculates the total amount of money bet on each horse or other outcome and then divides that money among the winners after the race or event has finished.

Example 9.24: The Kerala Government runs a lottery where the face value of the lottery ticket is ₹400, and the price notified in the Official Gazette is ₹380.

Solution

Particulars	Amount (in ₹)
100/128 × the face value of the ticket	312.5
100/128 × the price notified in the Official Gazette	296.8
As per rule 31A, the higher of the above two amounts is the value of supply.	312.5

7. Services of purchase or sale of foreign currency including money changing: Rule 32(2)

Option 1:

Case I: Where one of the currencies exchanged is Indian rupees: Rule 32(2)(a)

RBI reference rate	A
Buying/Selling rate	B
Value of supply	= (A – B) × units of foreign currency

Note: If the RBI reference rate is not available, then the value is 1% of the gross amount of Indian rupees provided or received by the person changing the money.

Example 9.25: Mr. Shuja got USD $80 converted through the State Bank of India at the exchange rate of ₹75/$. RBI reference rate at that time was ₹76.30/$. Calculate the value of supply.

Solution

Particulars	Amount
RBI reference rate	₹76.30/$
Buying rate	₹75/$
Value of supply	= (76.30 – 75) × $80 = ₹1.30/$ × $80 = ₹104

Example 9.26: Dr. Raman got ₹74,100 converted into US $1000 through an authorized dealer at ₹74.1/$. RBI reference rate at that time was ₹75.2/$. Calculate the value of supply.

Solution

Particulars	Amount
RBI reference rate	₹75.2/$
Buying rate	₹74.1/$
Value of supply	= (75.2 – 74.1) × $1000 = ₹1.1/$ × $1000 = ₹1,100

Example 9.27: Ms. Deepika got US$700 converted through a registered dealer at the exchange rate of ₹75/$. RBI reference rate was not available at that time. Calculate the value of supply.

Solution

Particulars	Amount (in ₹)
Gross money received	52,500
Value of supply = 1% of the above amount	525

Case II: Where neither of the currencies exchanged is Indian rupees

Value of supply = 1% of the lesser of the two amounts:

(a) Indian rupee value of foreign currency 1

(b) Indian rupee value of foreign currency 2

Example 9.28: A company got US $9,000 converted into UK £4,500. RBI reference rates at that time were ₹76/$ and ₹95/£. Calculate the value of supply.

Solution

Particulars	Amount (in ₹)
USD $9,000	6,84,000
UK £4,500	4,27,500
Value of supply = 1% × lower of the above two amounts	4,275

Option 2

A person supplying the services may exercise the option to ascertain the value as given below for a financial year, and such option shall not be withdrawn during the remaining part of that financial year.

Amount exchanged	Value of Supply
Gross amount ≤ ₹1,00,000	1% of the gross amount of currency exchanged Or ₹250, whichever is higher.
₹1,00,000 < Gross Amount ≤ ₹10,00,000	₹1,000 + 0.5% × ₹ (Gross Amount – 1,00,000)
Gross Amount > ₹10,00,000	₹5,500 + 0.1% × ₹ (Gross Amount – 10,00,000) Or ₹60,000, whichever is lower.

Example 9.29: Thomas (a money changer) has exchanged US $11,000 for INR at ₹75.4 per US $. What will be the value of supply if option 2 given in Rule 32(2)(b), is chosen by him?

Solution

Particulars	Amount (in ₹)
Gross amount exchanged	US $11,000 × ₹75.4/$= ₹8,29,400
Since, ₹1,00,000 < ₹8,29,400 ≤ ₹10,00,000, therefore, value of supply = ₹1,000 + 0.5% × ₹(Gross Amount – 1,00,000)	₹1,000 + 0.5% × ₹(8,29,400 – 1,00,000) = ₹1,000 + 0.5% × ₹7,29,400 = ₹1,000 + ₹3,647 = ₹4,647

8. Value of supply in case of online gaming including online money gaming: Rule 31B (Notification No. 45/2023 Central Tax, dated: 06.09.2023 and Notification No. 49-Central Tax, dated: 29.09.2023)

As per Rule 31B, the value of online gaming services, including those involving real money, is the total amount paid or deposited by players. This includes actual money, virtual assets, or anything else of value. Any refunds or returns by the gaming platform to the player, for whatever reason, should not be subtracted from the total value of the gaming service.

Note: If a player wins an amount in one event (including game, scheme, competition or any other activity or process) and decides to use those winnings to participate in another event without withdrawing the money, the winnings are not considered as if the player has paid or deposited that amount with the supplier.

Example 9.30: Imagine Mr. Gambler deposits ₹50 to an online gaming platform to participate in a virtual poker game. The total value of the supply of online gaming, according to this rule, is the entire ₹50 you deposited. Even if the platform later refunds ₹10 for some reason (like if you decide not to play), the initial value for the gaming service remains ₹50. The ₹10 refund does not reduce the overall value considered for the gaming transaction.

9. Value of supply of actionable claims in case of casino: Rule 31C (Notification No. 45/2023-Central Tax, dated: 06.09.2023 and Notification No. 49-Central Tax, dated: 29.09.2023)

The value of supply of actionable claims in casino is the total amount paid or payable by or on behalf of the player for:

(i) purchase of the tokens, chips, coins or tickets, by whatever name called, for use in casino; or

(ii) participating in any event, including game, scheme, competition or any other activity or process, in the casino, in cases where the token, chips, coins or tickets, by whatever name called, are not required:

However, any amount returned or refunded by the casino to the player on return of token, coins, chips, or tickets, as the case may be, or otherwise, is not deductible from the value of the supply of actionable claims in casino.

Note: If a player wins an amount in one event (including game, scheme, competition or any other activity or process) and decides to use those winnings to participate in another event without withdrawing the money, the winnings are not considered as if the player has paid or deposited that amount with the supplier.

Example 9.31: Suppose a player goes to a casino and purchases ₹ 100 worth of casino chips to use at the gaming tables. In this case, the value of the supply of actionable claims in the casino would be ₹100, as this is the total amount paid by the player for the purchase of chips for use in the casino.

Alternatively, if the casino hosts a special event or competition, and the player pays ₹ 50 to participate without the need to purchase any additional tokens or chips, then the value of the supply of actionable claims in the casino would be ₹ 50 in this scenario.

It is important to note that any amount refunded or returned to the player upon the return of tokens, coins, chips, or tickets, or for any other reason, would not be subtracted from the total value of the supply of actionable claims in the casino, as per Rule 31C.

Example 9.32: Suppose a player visits a casino and participates in a high-stakes poker tournament that does not require the purchase of specific tokens, chips, coins, or tickets. The entry fee for the tournament is ₹ 200. In this case, the value of the supply of actionable claims in the casino would be ₹ 200, representing the total amount paid by the player for participating in the poker tournament.

If the player later decides to withdraw from the tournament before it begins and the casino refunds ₹ 50 as a withdrawal or cancellation fee, the value of the supply of actionable claims would still be ₹ 200, as the refund is not deductible according to Rule 31C.

10. Air ticket booking by a travel agent: Rule 32(3)

Cases	Value of Supply
Domestic ticket	5% × Basic fare
International ticket	10% × Basic fare

Note: Basic fare means the part of the fare on which the travel agent receives commission from the airline.

Example 9.33: Sachin runs a travel agency. He books national as well as international flights for his customers. During the month of January 2023, he has given the following information:

Cases	Basic fare	Other charges
Domestic ticket	₹3,25,000	10,000
International ticket	₹5,26,000	25,000

Find the value of supply made by Sachin during January 2023.

Solution

Cases	Basic fare	Amount (in ₹)
Domestic ticket	₹3,25,000	5% × 3,25,000 = 16,250
International ticket	₹5,26,000	10% × 5,26,000 =52,600
Total value of supply as per rule 32(3)		68,850

11. Life insurance business: Rule 32(4)

(a) **Insurance policy with risk cover as well as investment benefit:** If an insurance policy carries risk cover as well as investment benefits and the amount allocated for investment or saving is intimated to the policyholder at the time of supply of service, then

Particulars	Amount (in ₹)
Gross premium charged from the policyholder	–
Less: amount allocated for investment or savings	–
Value of supply	–

(b) **Single premium annuity policy:** Value of supply = 10% × single premium charged

(c) **Remaining cases not covered above**

Years	Value of Supply
First-year	25% × premium in the first year
Subsequent year	12.5% × premium in the subsequent year

(d) **Entire premium covers risk only:** Value of supply is equal to the entire premium.

Example 9.34: JC Insurance Ltd. has received a gross premium of ₹200 lakhs from its policyholders for the life insurance policies in 2021-22. Out of this amount of premium, ₹120 lakhs have been allocated for investment on behalf of the policyholders. Calculate the value of the supply of life insurance services provided by JC Insurance Ltd. if the amount allocated for investment has been intimated to the policyholders at the time of supply of service.

Solution

If an insurance policy covers risk premiums and investment benefits and the investment amount is intimated to the policyholder at the time of supply of service, then as per rule 32(4), the value of supply is calculated as follows:

Particulars	Amount (in ₹ lakhs)
Gross premium charged from the policyholder	200
Less: amount allocated for investment or savings	120
Value of supply	80

Example 9.35: What would be your answer if the amount allocated for investment were not intimated to the policyholder?

Solution

If an insurance policy covers risk premiums and investment benefits and the investment amount is not intimated to the policyholder at the time of supply of service, then as per rule 32(4), the value of supply is calculated as follows:

Particulars	Value of supply Amount (in ₹ lakhs)
First year (2021-22) = 25% × premium charged	50

Example 9.36: What will be your answer if the insurance policy covers risk only?

Solution

If a life insurance policy covers risk only, then as per rule 32(4), the value of supply is the entire premium charged. Therefore, the value of supply is ₹200 lakhs.

12. Value of second-hand goods: Rule 32(5)

Where we find that a person supplies a second-hand good, then rule 32(5) is applicable. There are two cases in this regard, i.e., (i) a person dealing in second-hand goods and (ii) a person who repossesses a good from a defaulter.

Case I: *Dealer in second-hand goods*

(a) **If input tax credit is not availed by the dealer:** If a dealer does not avail of the input tax credit, then the valuation shall be done as follows:

Particulars	Amount
Selling price	A
Less: Purchase price	B
Margin (if positive) = Value of supply	A – B

(b) If input tax credit is availed by the dealer: If the dealer avails the input tax credit, then the value of the supply of the second-hand goods is determined as per other provisions of the CGST Act.

Case II: *Repossession of goods by a lender*

If goods are repossessed by a lender in case of default of the loan, then the value of supply is determined as follows:

(a) **If defaulter is unregistered:** If the defaulter is unregistered, then the margin is calculated by taking the purchase price as follows:

Particulars	Amount
Selling price	A
Less: Purchase value	E
Margin (if positive) = Value of supply	A – E

Where purchase value is calculated as follows:

Particulars	Amount
Purchase price for the defaulter	C
Less: 5% per quarter or part of it	D
Purchase value	C – D = E

Note: Number of quarters is calculated from the date of purchase to the date of re-supply of the repossessed goods.

(b) **If defaulter is registered:** If the defaulter is registered, then the value of supply is the selling price.

Example 9.37: Jaggi is a dealer in second-hand goods. He purchases a second-hand television from an unregistered person for ₹22,000. After some repairing, the television is sold by him for ₹35,000. Determine the value of supply.

Solution

As per rule 32(5), the value of supply is calculated as follows:

Particulars	Amount (in ₹)
Selling price	35,000
Less: Purchase price	22,000
Margin (if positive) = Value of supply	13,000

Example 9.38: What will be your answer if the television is sold for ₹18,000 because of massive demand for the model of the TV?

Solution

Particulars	Amount (in ₹)
Selling price	18,000
Less: Purchase price	22,000
Margin (if positive) = Value of supply	0

Example 9.39: AB Ltd. supplied a machine to Mr. C (unregistered person) on loan on 1.1.2022 for ₹1,00,000. Mr. C paid two instalments and was unable to pay the remaining six instalments. Consequently, AB Ltd. the machine was repossessed on 5.04.2022. The company resold the machine for 90,000 on 17.07.2022. What is the value of supply?

Solution

Particulars	Amount (in ₹)
Selling price	90,000
Less: Purchase value	→ 85,000
Margin (if positive) = Value of supply	5,000

where,

Particulars	Amount (in ₹)
Purchase price for the defaulter	1,00,000
Less: 5% per quarter or part of it, i.e., 5% × 3 quarters (see note)	15% × 1,00,000 = 15,000
Purchase value	85,000

Note: Number of quarters has been calculated from the date of purchase to the date of resale, i.e., from 1.1.2022 to 17.07.2022.

13. Value of a token, or a voucher or a coupon or a stamp (other than postage stamp) which is redeemable against a supply of goods or services or both: Rule 32(6)

Value of supply = Money value of the goods or service or both redeemable against such token, voucher, coupon or stamp.

Example 9.40: A company supplies ₹2,000 worth of coupons to Mr. B. What is the value?

Solution

As per rule 32(6), the value of supply is the value of the goods against which such coupon will be used. Therefore, the value is ₹2,000.

14. Value of taxable services provided by such class or service providers as may be notified by the government as referred in paragraph 2 of Schedule I: Rule 32(7)

Value of supply = Nil

15. Expenditure incurred by a Pure agent: Rule 33

Where a supplier works as a pure agent of the recipient, and he incurs some expenditure or cost on behalf of the recipient, a question arises, i.e., is such expenditure or cost incurred a part of the value of supply? Rule 33 answers it. It states that if the following conditions are satisfied, then such expenditure must not be taken into account to calculate the value of supply.

(a) The expenditure is incurred in the capacity of the pure agent with authority from the recipient: The supplier makes a payment to a third party in the capacity of a pure agent with authority from the recipient.
(b) The expenditure shown clearly in the invoice issued by the pure agent: the payment made by the pure agent on behalf of the recipient of supply has been separately indicated in the invoice issued by the pure agent to the recipient of service.

(c) The supplies received as pure agent are not the supplies given by the pure agent: the supplies procured by the pure agent from the third party as a pure agent of the recipient of supply are in addition to the services he supplies on his own account.

Note: For the purposes of this rule, the expression *pure agent* means a person who

(a) Enters into a contractual agreement with the recipient of supply to act as his pure agent to incur expenditure or costs in the course of the supply of goods or services or both,

(b) neither intends to hold nor holds any title to the goods or services or both so procured or supplied as a pure agent of the recipient of the supply,

(c) does not use for his own interest such goods or services so procured, and

(d) receives only the actual amount incurred to procure such goods or services in addition to the amount received for supply, which he provides on his own account.

Example 9.41: Corporate services firm A is engaged to handle the legal work pertaining to the incorporation of Company B. Other than its service fees, A also recovers from B the registration fee and approval fee for the name of the company paid to the Registrar of Companies. The fees charged by the Registrar of Companies for the registration and approval of the name are compulsorily levied on B. A is merely acting as a pure agent in the payment of those fees. Therefore, A's recovery of such expenses is a disbursement and not part of the value of supply made by A to B.

16. Rate of exchange of currency, other than Indian rupee, for determination of value: Rule 34

To covert the value of supply expressed in foreign currency into Indian currency, the following rule shall be applicable:

Cases	Rate of exchange
Goods	Exchange rate notified by the CBIC under section 14 of the Customs Act, 1962, for the date of time of supply of such goods as per section 12 of the CGST Act. In other words, first, calculate the date of time of supply as per section 12 of the CGST Act, and then find the exchange rate notified by the CBIC for this date.
Services	Exchange rate as determined by Generally Accepted Accounting Principles (GAAP) for the date of time of supply of such services as per section 13 of the CGST Act.

17. Tax determination in case value of supply is inclusive of GST: Rule 35

Where the value of supply is inclusive of IGST or CGST or SGST/UTGST, then the tax amount shall be determined using the formula:

$$\text{Tax} = \text{Value of supply} \times \left(\frac{\text{Tax rate}}{100 + \text{Tax rate}}\right)$$

Therefore, if ₹354 is the value of supply inclusive IGST of 18%, then the IGST is

$$\text{IGST} = 354 \times \left(\frac{18}{100+18}\right) = \frac{6372}{118}$$

$$\text{IGST} = ₹54$$

Theory Questions

1. If parties are related, then how will you determine the value of taxable supply?
2. What are the items to be added to the transaction value if the parties are not related and the price is the only consideration?
3. What is family in the context of Section 15 of the CGST Act?
4. When are persons related?
5. How will you value the supplies in case of exchange of currencies?
6. Who is a pure agent? What are the conditions to be met if the expenditure incurred by him is not added to arrive at the value of supply?
7. How is valuation made if the persons are related?
8. How is the value of supply determined in the case of second-hand goods?

Case-based Questions (Unsolved)

1. Yashvi Limited, registered in Punjab, is a manufacturer of product X. It imports a machine from New Zealand. Yashvi Manufacturers Limited enters into a contract with Yashasvi Logistics, a licensed customs broker with its office in Chennai, to meet all the legal formalities in getting the said machine cleared from the customs station.

   Yashvi Manufactures Limited authorises Yashasvi Logistics to incur, on its behalf, the expenses in relation to the clearance of the imported machine from the customs station and bringing the same to the warehouse of Yashvi Limited, which shall be reimbursed by Yashvi Manufacturers Limited to Yashasvi Logistics on the actual basis in addition to agency charges.

   Yashasvi Logistics provided the following details in the invoice issued by it to Yashvi Limited:

Particulars	Amount (in ₹)
Agency charges	7,00,000
Unloading of machine at the port	50,000
Charges for transportation of machine from the port to the godown of Yashasvi Logistics	25,000
Charges for transportation of machine from the above godown to the warehouse of Yashvi Limited in Punjab	28,000
Prepared and submitted Bill of Entry and paid customs duty	3,00,000
Dock dues paid	50,000
Port charges paid	50,000
Weight expenses	60,000
Travelling expenses	10,000
Other expenses	2,000

   Calculate the value of supply made by Yashasvi Logistics.

   Answer: ₹7,72,000

2. Kinshuk of Delhi sells goods to Rishabh of Ghaziabad for Rs. 1,00,000 and charges CGST and SGST at 9% each. Find the value of the supply if this is known that Kinshuk and Rishabh are not related parties.

   Answer: ₹1,00,000

3. Shreya, a trader has agreed to supply certain imported goods for ₹16,00,000 + Basic Customs Duty of ₹1,00,000. Calculate the value of supply if the supplier and the recipient are not related parties.

   Answer: ₹17,00,00

4. Surbhi Pvt. Limited supplied some goods to Raghuveer with the following terms and conditions:

Value of supply of goods if payment is made by 20.5.2022	₹3,00,000
Interest if payment is made after 20.5.2022 but before 25.7.2023	₹10,000

   Compute the time of supply and value of taxable supply if payment is made on 10.10.2022.

5. Manohar is the owner of a tour and traveller. During the month of February 2023, he has given the following information:

Bookings	Basic fare (in ₹)	Other charges (in ₹)
Tickets for three flights:		
(a) Delhi to Mumbai	75,000	10,000
(b) Jaipur to Mumbai	1,25,000	20,000
(c) Delhi to Jaipur	2,00,000	35,000
International flight from Delhi to Germany	2,50,000	50,000

   Find the value of supply made by him during February 2023.

   Answer: ₹45,000

6. Tarun Singh & Co. is a CA firm and the concurrent auditor of Raju & Co. For the audit, it receives ₹50,000 per month. Apart, a car is provided to the auditor, the cost of which is paid by Raju & Co. If the cost is ₹5,000 per month. Compute the GST if the rate of tax is 18%.

   Answer: ₹9,900

7. During April 2019, Arunachal Pradesh Government issues 900 lottery tickets to a distributor. The face value per ticket is ₹6,000, whereas the price notified by the official Gazette is ₹5,000. This lottery cannot be sold by the distributor outside Arunachal Pradesh. The location of the recipient of the supply is in Kerala only. Calculate the value of supply.

   Answer: ₹42,18,750

8. The US $10,000 is converted into UK £5000. The RBI reference rate at that time is 1$ = ₹65 and 1£ = ₹100. Calculate the value of supply.

   Answer: ₹5,000

9. What is GST payable by Mr. Raj, who holds 15% equity shares in × Ltd? He supplies some goods to × Ltd for ₹98,000, whereas the open market value is ₹1,02,000.

   Answer: ₹98,000

10. CK supplied a good to PK (unregistered person) on 1.7.2022 for ₹5,00,000. PK is required to pay 20% as a down payment and the remaining 80% in ten monthly instalments. PK paid four instalments but was unable to pay the remaining instalments. As a result, CK took the goods back on 3.12.2022. CK resold the goods for ₹4,75,000 on 21.01.2023. What is the value of supply in this case?

    Answer: ₹50,000

11. SK supplied a good to PK (a registered person) on 1.7.2022 for ₹5,00,000. PK is required to pay 10% as a down payment and the remaining 90% in ten monthly instalments. PK paid four instalments but was unable to pay the remaining instalments. As a result, SK took the goods back on 13.02.2022. SK resold the goods for ₹4,69,000 on 28.03.2023. What is the value of supply in this case?

    Answer: ₹4,69,000

12. On 10 October 2022, Ajeeb Limited (registered in Delhi) sells a certain quantity of some goods to Gareeb Limited (registered in Delhi). The goods are to be transported by Ajeeb Limited to the Godown of Gareeb Limited situated in Lucknow. The quoted price of the goods is ₹2,50,000 (exclusive GST of 28%). Ajeeb Limited allows a 5% discount on this quoted price and recovers the following additional expenses:
    (a) Pre delivery testing expenses: ₹5,000
    (b) weighing expenses: ₹1,000

Gareeb Limited agrees to pay ₹14,000 to the transporter of the goods (which are actually payable by Ajeeb Limited). Apart, the above-quoted price is after the subsidy of ₹1,00,000 given by the Central Government but before the subsidy of ₹50,000 given by a non-government organisation based in Delhi.

Additional information:

(a) A particular material was purchased by Ajeeb Limited from Kangal Limited (registered in Delhi) to manufacture the above goods. The cost of the material was ₹50,000 plus 18% GST. Date of invoice was 18 October 2022.
(b) The workers had to work two hours extra daily for which they were served food purchased from "Swadisth Food Chain" (registered in Delhi) for ₹10,000 plus 5% GST.
(c) A car (for business use) was purchased for ₹5,00,000 plus 18% IGST.
(d) Some inputs purchased earlier were used for personal consumption. Input tax paid on these inputs were CGST ₹3,000 and SGST ₹3,000.
(e) Other CGST and SGST liabilities for the month of October 2022 are ₹4,800 and ₹3,000, respectively.

Calculate the CGST, SGST and IGST liabilities to be settled in cash for the month of October 2022.

Answer: Value of taxable supply = ₹2,57,500; CGST liability = ₹300; SGST = Nil; IGST liability = ₹70,600

10
Input Tax Credit (ITC)

10.1 Introduction

The backbone of the GST is the concept of input tax credit (popularly known as ITC or just tax credit). When a supplier collects GST on an outward supply, then this GST can be paid to the government after subtracting the GST paid on the inputs, services, and capital goods used in effecting the outward supply. This subtraction of the GST paid from the GST collected is called taking **input tax credit**; however, input tax credit can be taken if thc supplier satisfies various conditions laid down under sections 16, 17, 18, 19, 20 of the CGST Act, 2017 and various rules of the CGST Rules, 2017.

10.2 Input Tax Credit (ITC)

To understand the concept of input tax credit, we take an example in which we consider three suppliers, A, B and C from Delhi, UP and Haryana, respectively. The supply chain starts from A to B to C to D. The other details are as follows:

Particulars	A to B	B to C	C to D
Value of supply	20,000	25,000	40,000
GST at 18%	3,600	4,500	7,200
Invoice price	23,600	29,500	47,200

If **no input tax credit** is availed, A, B, and C are required to pay the GST collected ₹3,600, ₹4,500 and ₹7,200, respectively, to the concerned governments. If input tax credit is taken, then the liability of each supplier is calculated as follows:

Particulars	A	B	C
GST collected	3,600	4,500	7,200
(–) Input tax credit = GST paid on purchases	–	3,600	4,500
Tax payable to government	3,600	9,00	2,700

10.3 Calculation of GST liability

The following format can be used to calculate the GST liability.

Particulars	Amount
Output tax (i.e., GST Collected by supplier from recipient)	–
Less: Eligible Input Tax Credit available in electronic credit ledger (ITC, i.e., the tax paid on inward supply)	–
GST liability to be paid through electronic cash ledger	–

10.4 Utilization and order of utilization of Input Tax Credit—Section 49(5) read with Rule 88A

1. Way of utilisation of the input tax credit: Section 49(5): This section is all about the way of utilization of input tax credit available in electronic credit ledger. The provisions of this section are as follows:

(a) IGST credit is first used for payment of IGST, and the balance credit, if any, may be used for payment of CGST and SGST/UTGST in that order. **Note:** However, Rule 88A overrides the point of "that order".
(b) CGST can be first used for payment of CGST, and the balance, if any, may be used for the payment of IGST.
(c) SGST can be first used for payment of SGST, and the balance, if any, may be used for the payment of IGST. However, the SGST credit can be utilised for payment of IGST tax only when the CGST credit is not available.
(d) UTGST can be first used for payment of UTGST, and the balance, if any, may be used for the payment of IGST. However, the UTGST credit can be utilised for payment of IGST tax only when the CGST credit is not available.
(e) CGST cannot be used for payment of SGST/UTGST.
(f) SGST/UTGST cannot be used for payment of CGST.

2. Zero balance of IGST credit is necessary to use other credits: Section 49A [Effective from 1 February 2019]: Irrespective of section 49, the CGST, SGST or UTGST credit can be utilized for payment of IGST, CGST, SGST or UTGST tax, as the case may be, only after the IGST credit has first been utilized fully towards such payment.

3. Power to prescribe order and the manner of utilization of input tax credit: Section 49B [Effective from 1 February 2019]: On the recommendations of the GST Council, the Government has the power to prescribe the order and manner of utilization of the IGST, CGST, SGST/UTGST credit for payment of any such tax. This section has an overriding effect on Chapter X of the CGST Act, but is subject to section 49(5)(e) and section 49(5)(f). Using the power under this section, the Government has notified Rule 88A, which is explained below.

4. Rule 88A [inserted by Notification No. 16/2017-Central Tax dated 29 March 2019]

- This rule is about the order of utilization of input tax credit. It states that input tax credit on account of integrated tax (IGST) can be first used to pay IGST, and the balance, if any, may be used to pay CGST and SGST/UTGST, as the case may be, in any order. It has been clarified by the CBIC that IGST can be used to pay CGST and SGST in any order and in any proportion.

- The CGST, SGST/UTGST credit can be utilised to pay IGST, CGST, SGST/UTGST, as the case may be, only after the IGST credit is zero.

Illustration 10.1: Showing the summary of Section 49(5), Section 49A, Section 49B and Rule 88A

I must use IGST credit first to pay IGST and remaining IGST credit can be used to pay either CGST or SGST/UTGST whatever preference I want and whatever ratio I want.

↓

Unless, my IGST credit is zero, till then, I cannot use CGST or SGST/UTGST credit.

↓

Once my IGST credit is zero, then CGST can be used to pay CGST and remaining to pay IGST, but not SGST/UTGST.

↓

Once my IGST credit is zero, then SGST can be used to pay SGST and remaining to pay IGST, but not CGST. However, SGST can be used to pay IGST if the CGST credit is zero.

Image courtesy–Freepik

Thus,

Step 1

Input tax credit	Output tax	Order of utilization
IGST →	IGST	1st
CGST	→ CGST	May be CGST or SGST or both in any ratio.
SGST	→ SGST	May be CGST or SGST or both in any ratio

Step 2

Input tax credit	Output tax	Order of utilization
IGST = Zero	→ CGST	2nd
IGST →	CGST	1st
SGST	✕→ SGST	Not allowed

Step 3

Input tax credit	Output tax	Order of utilization
IGST = Zero	IGST	2nd
CGST= Zero	CGST	Not allowed
SGST	SGST	1st

Example 10.1: From the following information, calculate the GST payable through electronic credit ledger (or input tax credit) and electronic cash ledger.

GST	Output tax	Input tax
IGST	50,000	40,000
CGST	30,000	25,000
SGST	30,000	25,000

Solution

Input Tax (in ₹)	IGST	CGST	SGST
Output tax	50,000	30,000	30,000
Less: Input tax credit (IGST) – Rule 88A	40,000	–	–
Balance	**10,000**	**30,000**	**30,000**
Less: Input tax credit (CGST) – Rule 88A	–	25,000	–
Balance	**10,000**	**5,000**	**30,000**
Less: Input tax credit (SGST) – Rule 88A	–	–	25,000
Tax payable through electronic cash ledger	**10,000**	**5,000**	**5,000**

Example 10.2: From the following information, calculate the GST payable through electronic credit ledger (or input tax credit) and electronic cash ledger.

GST	Output tax	Input tax
IGST	50,000	60,000
CGST	30,000	25,000
SGST	30,000	25,000

Solution

Input Tax (in ₹)	IGST	CGST	SGST
Output tax	50,000	30,000	30,000
Less: Input tax credit (IGST) – Rule 88A	50,000	10,000	–
Balance	**Nil**	**20,000**	**30,000**
Less: Input tax credit (CGST) – Rule 88A	–	20,000	–
Balance	**Nil**	**Nil**	**30,000**
Less: Input tax credit (SGST) – Rule 88A	–	–	25,000
Tax payable through electronic cash ledger	**Nil**	**Nil**	**5,000**

Balance in electronic credit ledger

IGST	CGST	SGST
60,000 – 50,000 – 10,000 = 0	25,000 – 20,000 = 5,000	25,000 – 25,000 = 0

Example 10.3: From the following information, calculate the GST payable through electronic credit ledger (or input tax credit) and electronic cash ledger.

GST	Output tax	Input tax
IGST	50,000	90,000
CGST	28,000	25,000
SGST	28,000	25,000

Solution

Input Tax (in ₹)	IGST	CGST	SGST
Output tax	50,000	28,000	28,000
Less: Input tax credit (IGST) – Rule 88A	50,000	28,000	12,000
Balance	**Nil**	**Nil**	**16,000**
Less: Input tax credit (SGST) – Rule 88A	–	–	16,000
Tax payable through electronic cash ledger	**Nil**	**Nil**	**Nil**

Balance in electronic credit ledger

IGST	CGST	SGST
90,000 – 50,000 – 28,000 – 12,000 = 0	25,000	25,000 – 16,000 = 9,000

Example 10.4: From the following information, calculate the GST payable through electronic credit ledger (or input tax credit) and electronic cash ledger.

GST	Output tax	Input tax
IGST	50,000	Nil
CGST	28,000	45,000
SGST	28,000	25,000

Solution

Input Tax (in ₹)	IGST	CGST	SGST
Output tax	50,000	28,000	28,000
Less: Input tax credit (CGST) – Rule 88A	–	28,000	–
Balance	**50,000**	**Nil**	**28,000**
Less: Input tax credit (CGST) – Rule 88A	17,000	–	–
Balance	**33,000**	**Nil**	**28,000**
Less: Input tax credit (SGST) – Rule 88A			25,000
Tax payable through electronic cash ledger	**33,000**	**Nil**	**3,000**

Balance in electronic credit ledger

IGST	CGST	SGST
Nil	45,000 – 28,000 – 17,000 = 0	25,000 – 25,000 = 0

Example 10.5: From the following information, calculate the GST payable through electronic credit ledger (or input tax credit) and electronic cash ledger.

GST	Output tax	Input tax
IGST	95,000	Nil
CGST	30,000	Nil
SGST	30,000	1,20,000

Solution

Input Tax (in ₹)	IGST	CGST	SGST
Output tax	95,000	30,000	30,000
Less: Input tax credit (SGST)	90,000	–	30,000
Tax payable through electronic cash ledger	5,000	30,000	Nil

Balance in electronic credit ledger

IGST	CGST	SGST
Nil	Nil	1,20,000 – 30,000 – 90,000 = 0

10.5 Restriction on use of balance in the Electronic Credit Ledger—Rule 86B

With effect from 1 January 2021, a new rule 86B has been inserted which states that if the value of taxable supply (excluding exempt supply and zero-rated supply) in a month exceeds ₹50 lakhs, then the amount used from electronic credit ledger to pay output tax cannot exceed 99% of the output tax. In other words, an input tax credit cannot be used in excess of 99% of the output tax if the value of taxable supply in a month is greater than ₹50 lakhs. While calculating the value of taxable supply, exempt supply and zero-rated supply shall not be taken into account. Thus, the maximum amount of credit which can be used is lower than of the following:

(a) 99% of output tax
(b) Input tax credit

Exceptions to Rule 86B

Exceptions to Rule 86B are as follows:

1. Payment of income tax > ₹1,00,000: If the following persons have deposited income tax exceeding ₹1 lakh in each of the last two financial years for which the last date to file the return under section 139(1) has passed.

(a)	The registered person,
(b)	The karta or proprietor or the managing director of the registered person,
(c)	Any of the two partners, whole time directors, members of Managing Committee of Associations or Board of Trustees of the registered person as the case may be.

2. Receipt of refund of input tax credit > ₹1,00,000: If the registered person has received, in the previous financial year, a refund of more than ₹1 lakh on account of unutilised input tax credit under section 54(3)(i) and section 54(3)(ii). As per section 54(3)(i) and section 54(3)(ii), a registered person can claim a refund of utilized input tax credit in the following cases:

1.	zero-rated supply made without payment of tax.
2.	where the tax rate on inputs was higher than the tax rate on output supplies and due to this input tax credit has accumulated.

3. Liability paid through electronic cash ledger > 1% of tax liability: The registered person has paid tax liability through the electronic cash ledger for an amount that is greater than 1% of the total output tax liability, applied cumulatively, up to the said month in the current financial year.

Example 10.6: The total output tax liability up to September 2022 is ₹35 lakhs. The registered person paid ₹3,00,000 through electronic cash ledger and the balance using the electronic credit ledger. The turnover during October 2022 is ₹70 lakhs. Is Rule 86B applicable here to pay GST liability for October 2022?

Solution

GST output liability up to September 2022 = ₹35,00,000

1% of the output liability = ₹35,000

Payment made through electronic cash ledger = ₹3,00,000 > 1% of the total output tax liability. Therefore, Rule 86B is not applicable to pay GST liability for October even if the turnover in October 2022 exceeds ₹50 lakhs.

4. Specified registered person:

(a) a Government department
(b) a Public Sector Undertaking (PSU)
(c) a local authority
(d) a statutory body

Example 10.7: The turnover of DFL Ltd. in November 2022 is ₹80 lakhs. Its input and output tax details are given below. Calculate the amount of tax payable through electronic cash ledger.

GST	Output tax	Input tax
CGST	7,20,000	5,00,000
SGST	7,20,000	1,00,000

Solution

Since the value of taxable turnover in November 2022 exceeds ₹50 lakhs, therefore, Rule 86B is applicable here. Therefore, the maximum liability that can be paid through the electronic credit ledger is 99% of output tax liability, i.e., 99% of CGST = ₹7,12,800 and 99% of SGST = ₹7,12,800. Therefore, tax payable through electronic cash ledger can be calculated as follows:

Input Tax (in ₹)	CGST	SGST
Output tax	7,20,000	7,20,000
Less: Input tax credit (CGST, SGST)–Rule 88A	5,00,000	1,00,000
Tax payable through electronic cash ledger	**2,20,000**	**6,20,000**

Example 10.8: The turnover of Ajeet Ltd. in February 2022 is ₹100 lakhs. Its input and output tax details are given below. Calculate the amount of tax payable through electronic cash ledger.

GST	Output tax	Input tax
CGST	7,20,000	8,00,000
SGST	7,20,000	7,35,000

Solution

Since the value of taxable turnover in February 2022 exceeds ₹50 lakhs, therefore, Rule 86B is applicable here. Therefore, the maximum liability that can be paid through the electronic credit ledger is 99% of output tax liability, i.e., 99% of CGST = ₹7,12,800 and 99% of SGST = ₹7,12,800. Therefore, tax payable through electronic cash ledger can be calculated as follows:

Input Tax (in ₹)	CGST	SGST
Output tax	7,20,000	7,20,000
Less: Input tax credit (CGST, SGST) – Rule 88A	7,12,800	7,12,800
Tax payable through electronic cash ledger	7,200	7,200

10.6 Conditions and Eligibility of Input Tax Credit (ITC)—Section 16

Section 16 lays down the conditions and eligibility of availing input tax credit.

1. Credit is available to a registered person only: Section 16(1): As per this section, a registered person shall be entitled to the credit for the GST paid on the goods or services or both provided that such inputs are used for business or furtherance of business. Such input tax credit is credited to the electronic credit ledger. However, this section is subject to such conditions and restrictions as may be prescribed and, in the manner, specified in section 49 related to payment of tax, interest, penalty and other amounts.

2. Additional conditions: Section 16(2): If the following conditions are not satisfied, then even a registered person cannot avail of input tax credit.

1. *Possession of the specified documents*: Section 16(2)(a): The recipient must have a tax invoice or debit note issued by the registered supplier or such documents as specified in Rule 36.
2. *Details of the tax invoice or debit note has been communicated to the recipient*: Section 16(2)(aa)—[Inserted by the Finance Act, 2021 and effective from 1 January 2022]: The supplier has furnished the details of the above tax invoice or debit note in the statement of outward supplies, i.e., GSTR-1, and these details have been communicated to the recipient. It simply means as soon as GSTR-2B is generated on the basis of the information given in GSTR-1, then this condition is satisfied.
3. *Receipt of goods or services or both*: Section 16(2)(b): The goods or services or both have been received by the registered person. In this regard, an understanding of the bill to ship to the model is also necessary.

   (i) **Bill to ship to model in case of goods:** If a registered person (say *x*) gives a direction to a supplier (say *y*) to deliver goods to a recipient or some other person (say *z*), then it is deemed that the person (x) has received the goods. The following points should be noted here:

- The direction may be given during or before the movement of the goods.
- If there is a transfer of documents of title to goods or otherwise, it will be sufficient to assume that goods have been delivered.

(ii) **Bill to ship to model in case of services:** It shall be deemed that the taxable person has received the service where the services are provided by the supplier to any person on the direction of and on account of such registered person.

4. Credit is not restricted under section 38: Section 16(2)(ba)—[Inserted by the Finance Act, 2022 and effective from 1 October 2022]: The details of input tax credit in respect of the said supply communicated to such registered person under Section 38 have not been restricted. It simply means that the input tax credit must not be ineligible as per FORM GSTR 2B.

5. Tax has been paid: Section 16(2)(c): Subject to section 41, the tax charged has been actually paid to either in cash or through utilisation of tax credit admissible.

6. Furnishing return: Section 16(2)(d): The return under section 39 has been furnished by the registered person.

Notes:

(a) **Input tax credit where goods are received in lots: the first proviso of section 16(2)**

Where the goods against an invoice are received in lots or instalments, the registered taxable person can avail of the credit upon receipt of the last lot or instalment.

(b) **Reversal of input tax credit in case of non-payment of consideration within 180 days: the second proviso of section 16(2) read with Rule 37**

- The recipient is required to pay the supplier the amount due (including tax) for the supply of goods or services or both [excluding the supplies covered under reverse charge mechanism, supplies covered under schedule I, and the amount to be added to the transaction value under section 15(2)(b)] within 180 days from the date of invoice.
- If he fails to pay such amount (whether completely or partly), then the proportionate input tax credit availed by him (the recipient) shall be reversed or treated as his output tax liability, which is to be reversed or paid with interest (under section 50) in such manner as prescribed under Rule 37.
- Such input tax shall be reversed or paid while furnishing GSTR-3B for the tax period immediately following 180 days from the date of invoice. However, the recipient can re-avail the credit reversed once he pays the sum due to the supplier.

Example 10.9: White Ltd. supplies a product RT to Black Ltd. for ₹2,00,000 plus 18%. The supplier issues the invoice on 1.09.2022, and Black Ltd. pays the amount due. White Ltd. has paid the tax, and Black Ltd. has filed the return under section 39. Is Black Ltd. eligible to avail of the credit for the month of September 2022?

Solution

Yes, all of the conditions of Sections 16(1) and 16(2) are found to be satisfied; therefore, Black Ltd. is eligible to avail of the credit for the month of September 2022.

Example 10.10: Raju (from Chandigarh) places an order of 100 kg of good with Brijesh (a registered person in Delhi). The quoted price is ₹500 per kg, excluding GST. Brijesh finds that the stock of the good is nil; therefore, he asks Deepak (a registered person in Delhi) to deliver 100 kg of the good directly to Raju. Deepak raises a tax invoice (dated 27 October 2022) on Brijesh for ₹48,000 excluding tax. Brijesh raises a tax invoice on Raju on 24 October 2022. The goods are delivered to Raju on 30 October 2022. Calculate the GST payable by Brijesh and Deepak. Assume that CGST and SGST rates are 9% each and IGST rate is 18%.

Solution

This is a case of the bill-to-ship-to model in which Brijesh directs Deepak to deliver goods directly to Raju.

Transaction between Deepak and Brijesh (intra-state supply)

Particulars	Amount (in ₹)
Value of supply	100 × 480 = 48,000
Add: CGST at 9%	4,320
Add: SGST at 9%	4,320
Invoice price	**56,640**

CGST and SGST liability of Deepak

Particulars	Amount (in ₹)
CGST collected	4,320
Less: Credit for CGST	Nil
CGST payable	**4,320**
SGST collected	4,320
Less: Credit for SGST	Nil
SGST payable	**4,320**

Transaction between Brijesh and Raju (inter-state supply)

Particulars	Amount (in ₹)
Value of supply	100 × 500 = 50,000
Add: IGST at 18%	9,000
Invoice price	**59,000**

IGST liability of Brijesh

Particulars	Amount (in ₹)
IGST collected at 18%	9,000
Less: Credit for CGST (refer note)	4,320
Less: Credit for SGST (refer note)	4,320
IGST payable	**360**

Note: As per section 16(2), in the case of a bill-to-ship-to model, Brijesh is eligible to avail of tax credit for CGST and SGST even if the goods have been delivered directly to Raju. Moreover, it has been assumed that the other conditions of Section 16(2) are also satisfied.

Example 10.11: On 18 January 2023, Ajeet (a registered dealer in Rajasthan) agrees to supply some goods to Sham (a registered person in Jaipur) in four lots. The first two lots were received in January 2022 only, but the last lot will be received by Sham in October 2023. Total GST paid by Sham is ₹1,50,000. Is Sham eligible to avail the credit of ₹1,50,000 for the month of January 2023?

Solution

No, Sham is not eligible to avail the credit for the month of January 2023 by virtue of Section 16(2). He will be eligible when the last lot will be received, i.e., October 2023.

Example 10.12: Bahubali (a registered dealer in Tamil Nadu) supplies some goods to Kattappa (a registered person in Tamil Nadu) for ₹1,00,000 plus 18% tax. The date of the invoice is 1.05.2022. Kattappa avails the tax credit on 7.6.2022. Kattappa paid the due amount on 17.11.2022. Comment.

Solution

The period from the date of invoice to the date of payment

= 1.05.2022 to 17.11.2022

= 200 days > 180 days

Since the payment has been made after 180 days, therefore, Kattappa is required to reverse the tax credit availed along with 18% p.a. interest.

Example 10.13: Prisha (Pvt.) Ltd. is a registered person in Punjab. The following information is provided by the company pertaining to February 2023.

Inward supply	The company has received 50 invoices from a supplier, SR (registered in Punjab). The accounts department of the company reports that out of these 50 invoices, 40 invoices are eligible for an input tax credit of ₹2,70,000, and the remaining 10 contain items of ineligible credit of ₹1,30,000.
Outward supply	The company has issued 80 invoices containing IGST liability of ₹5,50,000.
Information as per Form GSTR-2B	SR has uploaded 30 invoices in his GSTR-1, and therefore, only 30 invoices are reflected in GSTR-2B. These invoices show eligible credit of ₹1,20,000.

You are required to find out the GST liability for February 2023 to be settled using an electronic cash ledger.

Solution

Particulars	Amount (in ₹)
IGST collected	5,50,000
Less: Input tax credit available in electronic credit ledger (see working note)	1,20,000
IGST payable through electronic cash ledger	**4,30,000**

Working Note

Particulars	Amount (in ₹)
Eligible credit as per the records of Prisha (Pvt.) Ltd.	2,70,000
Eligible credit as per Form GSTR-2B	1,20,000
Input tax credit that can be used as per section 16(2) (aa) and 16(2) (ba)	1,20,000
Ineligible input tax credit	2,70,000 – 1,20,000 = 1,50,000

3. Non-availability of ITC on capital goods and plant & machinery on which depreciation has been claimed under the Income Tax Act, 1961: Section 16(3): If a registered person claims depreciation on the GST paid on a capital good and plant and machinery under the Income Tax Act, 1961, then the credit of the input tax paid cannot be taken. However, if the depreciation is not claimed on the GST component, then the credit can be taken.

Example 10.14: ABC Ltd. purchases a machine costing ₹1,00,000 plus 18% GST. The useful life of the asset is 10 years. The company claims depreciation of ₹11,800 as per the provisions of the Income Tax Act, 1961. Is the input tax of ₹18,000 paid eligible for tax credit under the GST law?

Solution

Particulars	Amount (in ₹)
Cost of machine	1,00,000
Add: GST paid	18,000
Invoice price	1,18,000
Depreciation claimed under the IT Act, 1961	1,18,000/10 = 11,800

Since the depreciation has been claimed under the IT Act, 1961 on the GST component, therefore, ABC Ltd. cannot claim the tax credit under the GST law.

4. Time limit to claim input tax credit: Section 16(4): This section states that the credit for a particular invoice can be claimed up to the date, whichever is earlier of the following two dates:

(a) 30 November from the end of the financial year to which such invoice or debit note belongs to
(b) Date of filing annual return (beware *not the due date to file annual return*).

Example 10.15: There is an invoice (dated 17 November 2021 and numbered 2501). The GST paid is ₹10,000. The annual return is filed on 14 October 2022. What is the time limit to vail the tax credit of this invoice?

Solution

As per Section 16(4), tax credit can be taken up to earlier of the following dates:

(1) 30 November 2022

(2) Date of annual return filed: 14 October, 2022

Thus, the credit can be taken up to 14 October 2022.

Example 10.16: There is an invoice (dated 17 November 2021 and numbered 2501). The GST paid is ₹10,000. The annual return is filed on 18 December 2022. What is the time limit to vail the tax credit of this invoice?

Solution

As per Section 16(4), tax credit can be taken up to earlier of the following dates:

(1) 30 November 2022

(2) Date of annual return filed: 18 December 2022

Thus, the credit can be taken up to 30 November 2022.

10.7 Apportionment of Input Tax Credit

Sometimes, an input or input service or a capital good is used to do exempt supply as well as taxable supply. Also, the input may be used for business purposes as well as non-business purposes. The law [through sections 17(1), 17(2)] is very clear that it wants to allow input tax credit for those inputs/input services/capital goods that are used for business purposes and for effecting taxable supply.

1. Input Tax Credit Limited to Business Purpose: Section 17(1): Where the goods or services or both are used by the registered person partly for the purpose of any business and partly for other purposes, the amount of credit shall be restricted to so much of the input tax credit as is attributable to the purposes of his business. Simply put, if an input is used for business purposes as well as for non-business purposes, then only that portion of the input tax credit shall be allowed, which is related to business purposes.

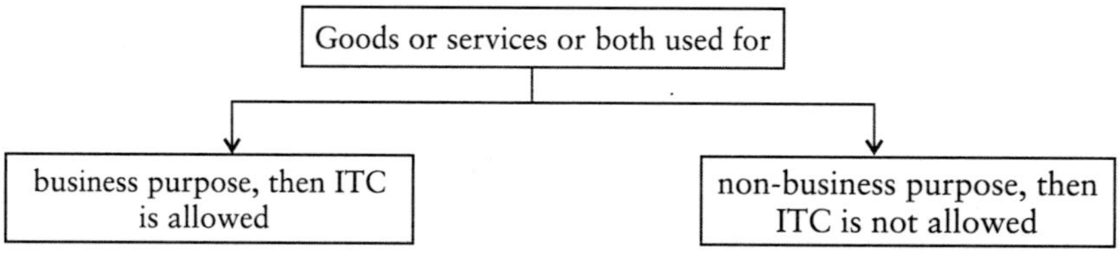

2. Input Tax Credit Limited to Taxable Supply: Section 17(2): Where the goods or services or both are used by the registered person partly for effecting taxable supply, including zero-rated supplies and partly for effecting exempt supplies, then the amount of credit shall be restricted to so much of the input tax as attributable to the said taxable supplies including zero rated supplies. Simply put, if an input (being good or service or both) is used for taxable supply (including zero-rated supply) as well as exempt supply, then only that portion of the input tax credit shall be allowed, which is related to taxable supply.

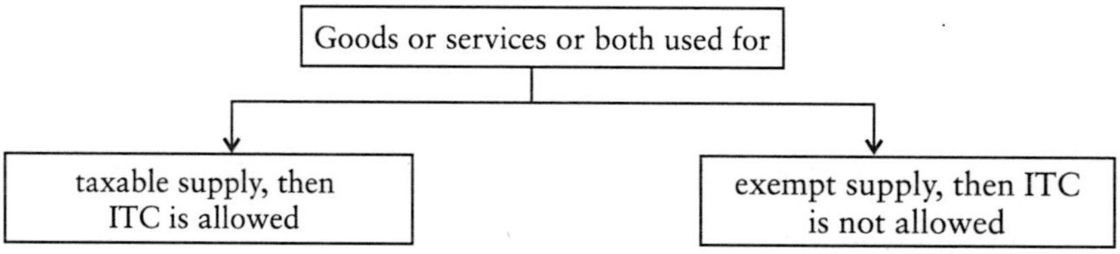

3. What is included in exempt supply: Section 17(3): The value of exempt supply shall be determined as prescribed under Rule 42 and includes

(a) supply under reverse charge mechanism.
(b) transactions in securities equal to 1% of the sale of securities.
(c) Sale of land and sale of building but subject to paragraph 5(b) of Schedule II. According to the paragraph, the construction of a complex, building, civil structure or a part thereof, including a complex or building intended for sale to a buyer, wholly or partly, is a supply of services. However, where the entire consideration has been received after the issuance of the completion certificate, where required, by the competent authority or after its first occupation, whichever is earlier, then this is not a supply; therefore, no GST is applicable.

Note: The expression "value of exempt supply" does not include the value of activities or transactions specified in Schedule III, except the value of activities or transactions specified in paragraph 5 of the said Schedule and the value of such activities or transactions as may be prescribed in respect of clause (a) of paragraph 8 of the said Schedule. [As amended by section 139 of the Finance Act, 2023].

4. Manner of Determination of Input Tax Credit in case of inputs or input services: Rule 42(1): Rule 42 states the manner in which the tax credit under section 17(1) and section 17(2) in respect of inputs or input services used to be apportioned. As per the rule, the following calculations should be done.

Notation	Description	Amount	Credit allowed or not
T	Total input tax credited to electronic credit ledger.	–	
T1	Input tax on the inputs exclusively used or to be used for non-business purposes.	–	Disallowed u/s 17(1)
T2	Input tax on the inputs exclusively used or to be used for exempt supply purposes.	–	Disallowed u/s 17(2)
T3	Input tax blocked, i.e., blocked credits under section 17(5).	–	Disallowed u/s 17(5)
C1	T = T1 – T2 – T3. This credit is further classified as T4 and C2.	–	
T4	Input tax on the inputs exclusively used or to be used for a taxable supply and zero-rated supply.	–	**Allowed u/s 17(2)**
C2	Common credit = C1 – T4	–	
D1	C2 × (E/F) = This is the credit which is related to exempt supply. where, E = the aggregate value of exempt supplies during the current tax period F = the total turnover in the state during the current tax period.	–	Disallowed u/s 17(2)

D2	5% of C2, if required. In fact, this is an assumed ratio, which is attributable to non-business purposes.	–	Disallowed u/s 17(1)
C3	C2 – D1 – D2	–	**Allowed u/s 17(1)/(2)**
Total credit allowed	T4+C3	–	
Total credit to be reversed or payable	T – (T4+C3) = T1 + T2 + T3 + D1+D2	–	

Note: *Rule 42(1) should be applied in respect of CGST, SGST, and IGST separately.*

Chart explaining Rule 42(1)

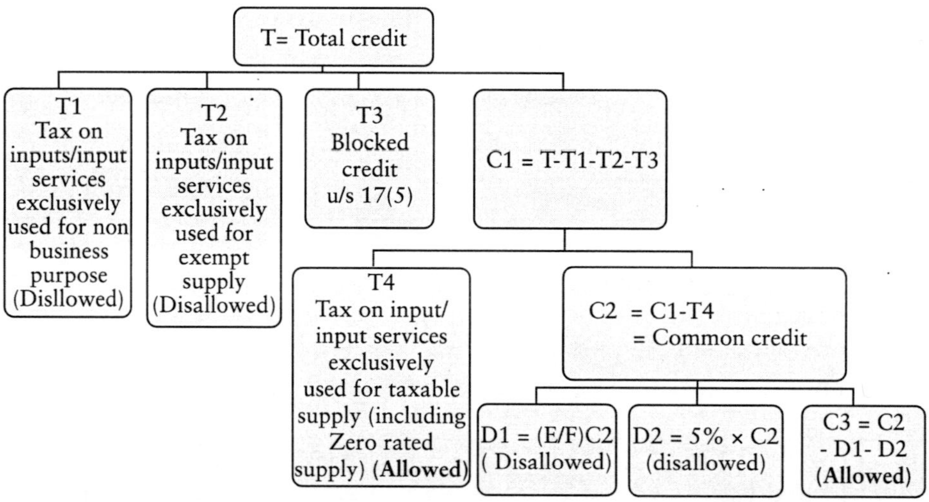

Example 10.17: ABC, a taxable person, supplies goods and services during January 20XX as per the following particulars: (a) Product A–taxable under GST–turnover within India–₹15 lakhs, (b) Product A–taxable under GST–exports without payment of GST–₹20 lakhs, (c) Product B–exempt under GST–turnover ₹10 lakhs. His input tax details are as follows:

(a) Total input tax credit in the taxable period: ₹4,20,000.

(b) Tax on inputs and input services intended to be used exclusively for product B: ₹1,10,000.

(c) Tax on inputs and input services intended to be used exclusively for product A: ₹1,20,000.

Calculate the input tax credit available to ABC.

Solution

Particulars	Amount (₹)
Taxable supply (supply within India) – Product A	15,00,000
Zero-rated supply (exports) – Product A	20,00,000
Exempt supply – Product B	10,00,000
Total turnover (F)	**45,00,000**
T = Total credit	4,20,000
T2 = Tax on inputs and input services intended to be used exclusively for product B	1,10,000
C1 = T – T2	3,10,000
T4 = Tax on inputs and input services intended to be used exclusively for product A (including zero rated supplies)	1,20,000
C2 = C1 – T4 = Common credit	**1,90,000**
D1 = (Exempt supply/Total turnover) × C2	42,222
D2 (Assuming that no common inputs are used for non-business purposes)	Nil
C3 = C2 – D1 – D2	1,47,778
Available credit = T4 + C3	**2,67,778**

Example 10.18: XYZ Ltd., a taxable person, supplies goods and services during December 2022 as per the following particulars:

(1) Product A–taxable under GST–turnover within India–₹20 lakhs Product A–taxable under GST–exports without payment of GST–₹5 lakhs.

(2) Product B–exempt from GST–turnover ₹10 lakhs.

(3) Product C–subject to central excise duty–₹25 lakhs.

(4) Service D–taxable under GST–₹5 lakhs.

His input tax details are as follows:

(a) Total input credit in the taxable period: ₹4 lakhs.

(b) Tax on inputs and input services attributable exclusively for non-business purposes: ₹50,000 (no common inputs/input services were used for non-business purposes).

(c) Tax on inputs and input services intended to be used exclusively for effecting exempt supply: ₹1 lakh.

(d) Tax on inputs and input services intended to be used exclusively for effecting taxable supply: ₹1,20,000.

(e) Input tax credit ineligible under section 17(5) of CGST Act: ₹30,000.

You are required to calculate the amount of credit available to XYZ Ltd.

Solution

Particulars	Amount (₹)
Taxable supply (supply within India) – Product A	20,00,000
Zero-rated supply (exports) – Product A	5,00,000
Exempt supply – Product B	10,00,000
Service D (taxable supply)	5,00,000
Total turnover (F)	**40,00,000**
T = Total credit	4,00,000
T1 = Tax on inputs and input services attributable exclusively for non-business purposes	50,000
T2 = Tax on inputs and input services intended to be used exclusively for effecting exempt supply	1,00,000
T3 = Blocked credit under section 17(5)	30,000
C1 = T-T1-T2-T3	2,20,000
T4 = Tax on inputs and input services intended to be used exclusively for taxable supply	1,20,000
C2 = C1 – T4 = Common credit	**1,00,000**
D1 = (Exempt supply/Total turnover) × C2	25,000
D2 = Zero because no common inputs/input services were used for non-business purposes)	Nil
C3 = C2 – D1 – D2	75,000
Available credit = T4 + C3	**1,95,000**

Example 10.19: XYZ, a taxable person, supplies goods and services during December 2022 as per the following particulars: (a) Product A–taxable under GST–turnover within India–₹20 lakhs, (b) Product A–taxable under GST–exports without payment of GST–₹5 lakhs, (c) Product B–exempt from GST–turnover ₹10 lakhs, (d) Product C–subject to excise duty but not to GST–₹25 lakhs, (e) Service D–taxable under GST–₹5 lakhs. His input tax details are as follows:

(a) Total input credit in the taxable period: ₹4 lakhs.

(b) Tax on inputs and input services attributable exclusively for non-business purposes: ₹50,000 (common input services were used for non-business purposes).

(c) Tax on inputs and input services intended to be used exclusively for effecting exempt supply: ₹1 lakh.

(d) Tax on inputs and input services intended to be used exclusively for effecting taxable supply: ₹1,20,000.

(e) Input tax credit ineligible under section 17(5) of CGST Act: ₹30,000.

You are required to calculate the available amount of credit.

Solution

Particulars	Amount (₹)
Taxable supply (supply within India) – Product A	20,00,000
Zero-rated supply (exports) – Product A	5,00,000
Exempt supply – Product B	10,00,000
Service D (taxable supply)	5,00,000
Total turnover (F)	40,00,000
T = Total credit	**4,00,000**
T1 = Tax on inputs and input services attributable exclusively to non-business purposes	50,000
T2 = Tax on inputs and input services intended to be used exclusively for effecting exempt supply	1,00,000
T3 = Blocked credit under section 17(5)	30,000
C1 = T-T1-T2-T3	2,20,000
T4 = Tax on inputs and input services intended to be used exclusively for a taxable supply	1,20,000
C2 = C1 – T4 = Common credit	**1,00,000**
D1 = (Exempt supply/Total turnover) × C2	25,000
D2 = 5% of C2 because common input services were used for non-business purposes	5,000
C3 = C2 – D1 – D2	70,000
Available credit = T4 + C3	**1,90,000**

Rule 42(2): After applying rule 42(1), the final calculations shall be done before September, after the concerned financial year is over. When final calculations are done, then take the decision as follows:

Case 1: Aggregate of all months D1 and D2 as per rule 42(1) < D1+D2 in the final calculation, then the difference amount is added to the output tax liability of the registered person in the month not later than the month of September following the end of the financial year to which such credit relates.

Case 2: Aggregate of all months D1 and D2 as per rule 42(1) > D1+D2 in the final calculation, then the difference amount is claimed as credit by the registered person in his return for a month not later than the month of September following the end of the financial year to which such credit relates.

10.8 Option for A Financial Institution—Section 17(4)

According to this section, a financial institution, including non-banking financial companies (NBFC), has *two* options:

1. Take input tax credit in a month as per normal provisions.
Or
2. Take an input tax credit in a month equal to 50% of the eligible input tax credit + 100% of the input tax on the inward supplies from the registered entities having the same PAN.

Note:

(a) How to find eligible credit under section 17(4)?

Total input tax	–
Less: Blocked credits under section 17(5)	–
Less: Input tax exclusively attributable to non-business purpose	–
Less: Input tax on inward supplies from the entities having the same PAN	–
Less: Input tax attributable to other ineligibility	–
Eligible credit	–

(b) Once an option is taken, it cannot be changed during the remaining part of the financial year.

(c) The restriction of 50% shall not apply to the tax paid on supplies made by one registered person to another registered person having the same Permanent Account Number (PAN).

Example 10.20: Rigid Bank gives you the following information for the month of November 2022.

Particulars	CGST (in ₹)	SGST (in ₹)
Food and beverages	5,000	5,000
Life insurance premium of the employees paid	20,000	20,000
Input service from Kim Bank (having different PAN)	10,000	10,000
Input service from Sim Bank (having same PAN)	4,000	4,000
Goods purchased from a supplier	18,000	18,000
Inputs used for non-business purpose	2,000	2,000
Inputs used for exempt supply	9,000	9,000
Total	**68,000**	**68,000**

Note: Assume that no common inputs are used for exempt supply or non-business purposes.

Solution

Applying the provisions of section 17(4), we have the following solution.

Option 1: Tax input tax as per the normal provisions

Particulars	CGST (in ₹)	SGST (in ₹)
T = Total input tax	68,000	68,000
T1 = Tax related to inputs exclusively used for non-business purposes not eligible under section 17(1)	2,000	2,000

Particulars	CGST (in ₹)	SGST (in ₹)
T2 = Tax related to inputs exclusively used for exempt supply not eligible under section 17(2)	9,000	9,000
T3 = Blocked credit under section 17(5)	25,000	25,000
C1 = T – T1 – T2 – T3	**32,000**	**32,000**
T4 = Tax related to inputs exclusively used for a taxable supply	0	0
C2 = C1 – T4 = Common credit	32,000	32,000
D1 (no common inputs are used for exempt supply as given)	0	0
D2 (no common inputs are used for non-business purposes as given)	0	0
C3 = C2 – D1 – D1	32,000	32,000
Available credit = C3 + T4	**32,000**	**32,000**

Option 2: Take input tax credit in a month equal to 50% of the eligible input tax credit + 100% of the input tax on the inward supplies from the entities having the same PAN.

Particulars	CGST (in ₹)	SGST (in ₹)
Total input tax	68,000	68,000
Less:		
Input service from Sim Bank (having same PAN)	4,000	4,000
Food and beverages blocked under section 17(5)	5,000	5,000
Life insurance premium of the employees paid blocked under section 17(5)	20,000	20,000
Inputs used for non-business purposes not eligible under section 17(1)	2,000	2,000
Eligible input tax credit	37,000	37,000
50% of the eligible input tax credit	**18,500**	**18,500**
Add:		
Input service from Sim Bank (having same PAN)	4,000	4,000
Available credit	**22,500**	**22,500**

Example 10.21: CBK Bank gives you the following information for the month of December 2022.

Particulars	Amount (in ₹)
Commission, fee, etc., i.e., taxable supply.	15,00,000
Acceptance of deposits and advancing of loans, i.e., exempt supply.	35,00,000
Total supply	**50,00,000**
Total input tax credit, out of which	12,00,000

Particulars	Amount (in ₹)
Blocked credit u/s 17(5)	2,00,000
Tax on inputs exclusively used for effect exempt supply	50,000
Tax on inputs exclusively used for non-business use	30,000
Tax on inputs exclusively used for taxable supply	20,000

Solution

Applying the provisions of section 17(4), we have the following solution.

Option 1: Tax input tax as per the normal provisions

Particulars	Amount (in ₹)
T = Total input tax	12,00,000
T1 = Tax on inputs exclusively used for non-business use	30,000
T2 = Tax on inputs exclusively used for effect exempt supply	50,000
T3 = Blocked credit under section 17(5)	2,00,000
C1 = T – T1 – T2 – T3	**9,20,000**
T4 = Tax on inputs exclusively used for taxable supply	20,000
C2 = C1 – T4 = Common credit	**9,00,000**
D1 = (Exempt supply/Total supply) × C2 = (35,00,000/50,00,000) × 9,00,000	6,30,000
D2 = 5% × C2 (It has been assumed that common inputs have been used for non-business purposes because no contrary information is given)	45,000
C3 = C2 – D1 – D2	2,25,000
Available credit = C3 + T4	**2,45,000**

Option 2: Take input tax credit in a month equal to 50% of the eligible input tax credit + 100% of the input tax credit on the inward supplies from the entities having the same PAN.

Particulars	Amount (in ₹)
Total input tax	12,00,000
Less:	
Tax on inputs exclusively used for non-business use	30,000
Blocked credit under section 17(5)	2,00,000
Eligible credit	**9,70,000**
50% of the eligible credit	4,85,000
Add:	
Input tax credit on the inward supplies from the entities having the same PAN	–
Available credit	**4,85,000**

10.9 Blocked Credits—Section 17(5)

Whatever section 16(1) and section 18(1) say, no input tax credit is allowed if the registered person is covered by any of the following cases:

Section 17(5)(a): Motor vehicles: In the case of motor vehicles (with approved seating capacity less than or equal to 13, including driver) for transportation of persons, then the input tax credit is not available. However, there are three exceptions to this, i.e., if such a motor vehicle is for making

(a) further supply, e.g., car dealers.
(b) transportation of passengers, e.g., taxi, tour and travellers.
(c) imparting training on driving such motor vehicle, e.g., driving schools.

Motor vehicle dealers (Credit allowed)

Transportation of passengers (Credit allowed)

Driving schools (Credit allowed)

(Image courtesy–Freepik)

Note

As per the Motor Vehicles Act, 1988, motor vehicles and conveyances do not include vehicles running on fixed rails, special purpose vehicles for use in a factory or any enclosed premises, vehicles having less than four wheels and engine capacity not greater than 25 cc, therefore, railways, bicycle, etc. are not motor vehicles.

Example 10.22: X Ltd. (registered in Ghaziabad) purchases a seven-seater car for transportation of its employees. IGST paid is ₹3,50,000. The company is not eligible for an input tax credit under section 17(5)(a) because the approved seating capacity is up to 13.

Example 10.23: Vihar Cars (a car showroom registered in Delhi). It purchases 50 cars from a car manufacturer for further sale. Tax paid on purchase of the cars is ₹5 crore. Vihar Cars is eligible for input tax credit because it is covered under the exceptional case of section 17(5)(a), i.e., the cars purchased are for making further supply.

Example 10.24: ABC Ltd. (registered in Pune) purchases a truck for its business use. The company is eligible for input tax credit because trucks are not covered by section 17(5)(a).

Example 10.25: Mintu Motors (a driving school) purchases an Alto Car being used to impart training in driving of car. Mintu Motors is eligible for input tax credit because it is covered under the exceptional case of section 17(5)(a), i.e., the motor vehicle is used to impart training to drive such motor vehicle.

Section 17(5) (aa): Vessels and Aircraft: In the case of vessels and aircraft, the input tax credit is not available. However, in the following cases, the input tax credit is available if such vessel or aircraft is for

(a) further supply of such vessels/aircraft.
(b) transportation of passengers, e.g., airlines.
(c) imparting training on navigating such vessels or imparting training on flying such aircraft.
(d) transportation of goods.

Vessels (Credit blocked)

Aircraft (Credit blocked)

Note: Input tax credit is also available on dumpers, works-trucks, fork-lift trucks, etc.

Section 17(5) (ab): If a motor car or vessel or aircraft is not eligible for input tax credit, then the tax paid on its general insurance, servicing, and repair and maintenance is also not eligible. However, input tax credit is available if the service is received by a taxable person engaged

1. in the manufacture of such motor vehicles, vessels and aircraft or
2. in the supply of general insurance services in respect of such motor vehicles and aircraft insured by him.

Example 10.26: Suppose that a company purchased a motor vehicle (with approved seating capacity 5) for ₹10 lakhs and paid 28% GST. After one year, the company got it serviced for ₹20,000 and paid 18% GST. Since the credit for a motor vehicle with an approved seating capacity up to 13 is blocked under section 17(5) (aa), therefore, as per section 17(5) (ab), the credit for GST paid on servicing of the motor vehicle is also blocked.

Example 10.27: R Ltd. is a car manufacturer company, and it has a stock of 20 cars. It has taken the services of an outside agency for repairing five of the cars. It paid GST of ₹1,20,000. The company is eligible for input tax credit because section 17(5) (ab) states that if a manufacturer of a motor vehicle receives the motor vehicle insured, serviced, repaired and maintained, then the credit is not blocked.

Example 10.28: Bikaner Insurance Ltd. insured a car purchased by Taken Ltd. The car met an accident, and as a result, the insurance amount was paid, including the GST paid on repairing the car. Bikaner Insurance Ltd. is eligible for an input tax credit for the GST paid on repairing the car under section 17(5) (ab).

Section 17(5)(b): Input tax credit is not available on the following supply of goods or services or both:

(i)	Food and beverages, outdoor catering, beauty treatment, health services, cosmetic and plastic surgery, hiring or lease or renting of the motor vehicle, vessel or aircraft, the credit of which is blocked, life insurance, and health insurance. **Exception:** If the above goods or services or both are used by a registered person as an inward supply for outward taxable supply of the same category of goods or services or both or as an element of a taxable composite or mixed supply, then input tax credit is available. It simply means that if the above supplies are inward supplies for making outward supplies (including composite or mixed supplies), then the credit is available to the registered person (i.e., recipient).
(ii)	Membership of a club, health and fitness centre.
(iii)	Travel benefits extended to employees on vacation like leave or home travel concession.
	Exception (applicable to i, ii, iii): If the above supplies are made to the employees by an employer due to any law for the time being in force, then the input tax credit is available.

Example 10.29: Vivekananda Institute conducted a seminar on Global Warming. Two hundred guests attended the seminar; therefore, the institute purchased food and beverages for the guests for ₹1,00,000 plus GST. The institute is not eligible for input tax credit under section 17(5)(b) because food and beverages are blocked.

Example 10.30: A company avails a tour package from a Travel Agency for its employees. The company is not eligible under section 17(5)(b) for the credit for GST paid to the travel agency.

Example 10.31: A factory has 340 employees. Therefore, as per section 46 of the Factories Act, 1948 if a factory employs more than 250 workers, it is mandatory for the factory to provide a canteen facility for its workers. Consequently, the factory arranges catering services at the factory campus. The credit on catering services is available to the factory under section 17(5)(b).

Section 17(5) (c): Works contract services when supplied for construction of an immovable property (other than plant and machinery) except where it is an input service for further supply of works contract service. It simply means that if a person gets an immovable property (except plant and machinery) constructed by a builder/developer/engineer/ contractor, etc., then the input tax credit is blocked.

However, a builder/developer/contractor can avail input tax credit for the tax paid to another builder/developer/contractor for the construction of an immovable property.

Notes:

1. Construction includes re-construction, renovation, additions or alterations or repairs, to the extent of capitalisation to the said immovable property.
2. Plant and machinery mean apparatus, equipment, and machinery fixed to earth by foundation or structural supports that are used for making outward supply of goods

or services or both and includes such foundation or structural support but excludes the following:

(a) Land and building

(b) Other civil structures

(c) Telecommunication towers and pipelines laid outside the factory premises.

Section 17(5)(d): Goods or services or both received by a taxable person for construction of an immovable property (other than plant or machinery) on his own account, including when such goods or services or both are used in the course or furtherance of business. It simply means that if a person constructs an immovable property on his own, nevertheless, the input tax credit is blocked.

Notes:

1. Construction includes re-construction, renovation, additions or alterations or repairs, to the extent of **capitalisation** to the said immovable property.
2. Plant and machinery mean apparatus, equipment, and machinery fixed to earth by foundation or structural supports that are used for making outward supply of goods or services or both and includes such foundation or structural support but excludes the following:

   (a) Land and building

   (b) Other civil structures

   (c) Telecommunication towers and pipelines laid outside the factory premises.

Section 17(5)(e): Tax paid under the composition scheme under section 10. It means a tax paid under a composition scheme cannot be claimed as an input tax credit.

Section 17(5)(f): Tax paid on goods and services received by a non-resident taxable person except goods imported by him.

Note: When goods are imported, then IGST is also payable. Under section 17(5)(f), the non-resident taxable person can claim input tax credit for this IGST.

Section 17(5)(fa): Goods or services or both received by a taxable person, which are used or intended to be used for activities relating to his obligations under corporate social responsibility (CSR) referred to in section 135 of the Companies Act, 2013. **[Inserted by section 139 of the Finance Act, 2023.]**

Section 17(5)(g): Tax paid on goods and services used for personal consumption (may be of employees, directors or even others).

Section 17(5)(h): Tax paid on goods lost, stolen, destroyed, written off or given as gifts or free samples.

Section 17(5)(i): Any tax paid under sections 74, 129 and 130.

10.10 Special Cases of Claiming Input Tax Credit

A supplier being unregistered is not eligible for tax credit due to Section 16(1); therefore, whatever inputs, input services and capital goods he purchased do not qualify for an input tax credit. After sometimes, he gets registered himself, then has a question, i.e., whether or not he is eligible to get a tax credit on those inputs, input services and capital goods purchased/acquired when he was unregistered. To answer this question, we study sections 18(1)(a) and 18(1)(b). The same question arises when a supplier opts out a composition scheme, or an exempt supply becomes a taxable supply. To answer this question, we have sections 18(1)(c) and 18(1)(d). Let us see these sections one by one.

1. First Time Compulsory Registration: Section 18(1)(a): A person who has applied for registration under the Act within 30 days from the date on which he becomes liable to registration has been granted such registration shall be entitled to take credit of input tax attributable to the inputs contained in

(a) stock,
(b) semi-finished goods,
(c) finished goods

on the day immediately preceding the date from which he becomes liable to pay tax under the CGST Act.

Note: Tax credit on input services and capital goods is not allowed.

Example 10.32: Laxman (from Delhi) finds that during 2021-22, his aggregate turnover exceeds ₹25 lakhs on 19 March 2022. He applies for registration on 22 March 2022. The department grants him a registration certificate on 27 March 2022. The following information is available as of 18 March 2022.

Input taxes paid	Amount (in ₹)
Tax paid on inputs contained in stock on 18 March 2022	25,000
Tax paid on inputs contained in semi-finished goods on 18 March 2022	75,000
Tax paid on inputs contained in finished goods on 18 March 2022	50,000
Tax paid on input services	20,000
Tax paid on purchase of capital goods	1,00,000

What is the amount of eligible ITC under section 18(1)(a)?

Solution

Relevant date = The date just before the date when the aggregate turnover exceeds the threshold limit = 18 March 2022.

Input taxes paid	Amount (in ₹)
Tax paid on inputs contained in stock on 18 March 2022	25,000
Tax paid on inputs contained in semi-finished goods on 18 March 2022	75,000
Tax paid on inputs contained in finished goods on 18 March 2022	50,000
Tax paid on input services (ineligible under section 18(1)(a))	–
Tax paid on purchase of capital goods (ineligible under section 18(1)(a))	–
Total eligible credit	**1,50,000**

2. First Time Voluntary Registration: Section 18(1)(b): As per section 18(1)(b), a person who has voluntarily taken GST registration, then he shall be entitled to take credit of input tax for the inputs held in

(a) stock,
(b) semi-finished goods,
(c) finished goods

on the day immediately preceding *the date of registration is granted.*

Note: Tax credit on **input services** and **capital goods** is not allowed.

Example 10.33: KS Ltd. is not required to register under the CGST Act, 2017, but it wanted to obtain voluntary registration; therefore, it applied for voluntary registration on 17 September 2021, and the registration was granted on 25 September 2021. The CGST and SGST liability for the month of September 2021 is ₹24,000 each. X Ltd. provides the following information on inputs and capital goods held in stock on 24 September 2021. It is not engaged in making inter-state outward taxable supplies:

1. Input procured on 02-09-2021 lying in stock: CGST ₹5500 and SGST ₹5500.
2. Input received on 21-02-2021 contained in semi-finished goods held in stock: CGST at 6% ₹7500 and SGST at 6% ₹ 7500.
3. Value of inputs contained in finished goods held in stock: ₹2,00,000 were procured on 19-09-2020-IGST at 18%.
4. Inputs valued at ₹50,000 procured on 13-09-2021 lying stock: IGST at 18%.
5. Capital goods procured on 12-09-2021: CGST at 6% ₹12000 and SGST at 6% ₹12,000.

You are required to compute the amount of tax to be paid in cash by KS Ltd. for the month of September 2021.

Solution

Relevant date = The date before the date of registration = 24 September 2021.

S. No.	Particulars	CGST	SGST	IGST	Reference
1.	Input procured on 02-09-2021 lying in stock on relevant date.	5,500	5,500		Section 18(1)(b)
2.	Input received on 21-02-2021 contained in semi-finished goods held in stock lying on relevant date.	7,500	7,500		Section 18(1)(b)
3.	Value of inputs contained in finished goods held in stock: Ineligible.	-	-	-	Section 18(2)
4.	Inputs valued at ₹50,000 procured on 13-09-2021 lying in stock on relevant date – IGST at 18%.			9,000	Section 18(1)(b)
5.	Capital goods procured on 12.09.2021: Ineligible.	-	–	-	Section 18(1)(b)
	Total eligible credit	13,000	13,000	9,000	

3. Opting Out of Composition Scheme: Section 18(1)(c): Where any registered taxable person ceases to pay tax under the composition scheme under section 10 and opts into the regular scheme under section 9, the person shall be entitled to take credit of input tax credit for the inputs contained in

(a) stock
(b) semi-finished goods
(c) finished goods
(d) capital goods

on the day immediately preceding the date from which the person is liable to pay tax under section 9. Further, tax credit on capital goods shall be reduced by 5% *per quarter or part thereof.*

Note: The number of quarters is calculated from the date of invoice to the date immediately preceding the date from which the person is liable to pay tax under section 9. Any incomplete quarter is taken as one full quarter.

Example 10.34: Ashok Enterprises opts out of the composition levy on 17 September 2022. We have the following information:

Available inputs/capital goods on 16.09.2022	Date of invoice	Input tax (in ₹)
Inputs held in stock	12.03.2022	10,000
Inputs held in semi-finished goods	13.12.2021	25,000
Inputs held in semi-finished goods	18.08.2021	30,000
Input services	10.01.2022	18,000
Capital good – M	21.09.2021	1,00,000
Capital good – Q	11.07.2021	80,000
Inputs held in finished goods	23.04.2022	50,000

The enterprise approaches its CA to consult regarding the input tax credit available to it. If you are that CA, then what is your view?

Solution

Since Ashok Enterprise opts out of the composition scheme and opts in the regular scheme, therefore, it is a case of Section 18(1)(c), and the date preceding the date of opting in the regular scheme is 16.09.2022.

Available inputs/capital goods on 16.09.2022	Date of invoice	ITC available or not	Amt. (in ₹)
Inputs held in stock	12.03.2022	Yes	10,000
Inputs held in semi-finished goods	13.12.2021	Yes	25,000
Inputs held in semi-finished goods	18.08.2021	No (see note 1)	-
Input services	10.01.2022	No (see note 2)	-
Capital good – M	21.09.2021	Yes (see note 3)	75,000
Capital good – Q	11.07.2021	No (see note 4)	-
Inputs held in finished goods	23.04.2022	Yes	50,000
ITC available to Ashok Enterprise			**1,60,000**

Notes

(a) Inputs held in semi-finished goods are eligible for input tax credit u/s 18(1)(c) but subject to Section 18(2), i.e., the invoice must not be older than one year. In this case, the invoice date is 18.08.2021, and if we calculate its duration from 18.08.2021 to 16.09.2022, then it is greater than one year. So, no ITC is available on this invoice.

(b) Input service is not eligible for ITC u/s 18(1)(c).

(c) Capital good is eligible for input tax credit u/s 18(1) (c), but its credit is calculated by the formula:

ITC available = Input tax credit – 5% per quarter or part of it

Quarter months			Number Quarters
–	–	21 Sept, 2021	1
October, 2021	Nov., 2021	Dec, 2021	1
Jan., 2021	Feb., 2022	March, 2022	1
April, 2022	May 2022	June, 2022	1
July, 2022	August 2022	16 Sept, 2022	1
Number of quarters from 21.9.2021 to 16.09.2022			5

Therefore, ITC available = ₹1,00,000 – (5% × 5) × ₹1,00,000 = ₹1,00,000 – ₹25,000
= ₹75,000

(d) Capital good is eligible for input tax credit u/s 18(1)(c) but subject to Section 18(2), i.e., the invoice must not be older than one year. In this case, the invoice date is 17.07.2021, and if we calculate its duration from 11.07.2021 to 16.09.2022, then it is greater than one year. So, no ITC available on this invoice.

4.Exemption is withdrawn by the Government: Section 18(1)(d): Where an exempt supply of goods or services or both by a registered taxable person becomes a taxable supply, such person shall be entitled to take credit of input tax credit for the inputs held in

(a) stock
(b) semi-finished goods
(c) finished goods related to such exempt supply and
(d) capital goods exclusively used for such exempt supply

on the day immediately preceding the day on which the person becomes liable to pay tax. Further, tax credit on capital goods shall be reduced by *5% per quarter or part thereof*.

Note: The number of quarters is calculated from the date of invoice to the date immediately preceding the date from which the exemption is withdrawn. Any incomplete quarter is taken as one full quarter.

Example 10.35: Gaurav Traders (a registered person) receives information that from 14 June 2022, the government has withdrawn the exemption on the goods that were being supplied by Gaurav Traders; hence from 14 June 2022, it is a taxable supply. We have the following information:

Available inputs/capital goods on 13.06.2022	Date of invoice	Input tax (in ₹)
Inputs held in stock	12.03.2022	10,000
Inputs held in semi-finished goods	13.12.2021	25,000
Inputs held in semi-finished goods	Invoice not available (but date of invoice is 2.01.2022)	30,000
Input services	10.01.2022	18,000
A machine	21.09.2021	1,00,000
Inputs held in finished goods	23.04.2022	50,000

Gaurav Traders approaches you for a tax consultancy. Give your consultancy.

Solution

Since an exemption is withdrawn by the government, therefore, it is a case of Section 18(1)(d), and the date preceding the date of becoming taxable supply is 13.06.2022.

Available inputs/capital goods on 13.06.2022	Date of invoice	ITC available or not	Amt. (in ₹)
Inputs held in stock	12.03.2022	Yes	10,000
Inputs held in semi-finished goods	13.12.2021	Yes	25,000
Inputs held in semi-finished goods	02.01.2022	No (see note 1)	-
Input services	10.01.2022	No (see note 2)	-
A machine	21.09.2021	Yes (see note 3)	80,000
Inputs held in finished goods	23.04.2022	Yes	50,000
ITC available to Gaurav Traders			**1,65,000**

Notes:

1. Inputs held in semi-finished goods are eligible for input tax credit u/s 18(1)(d), but as per Section 16(2), if the invoice is not available, the tax credit cannot be availed.
2. Input service is not eligible for ITC u/s 18(1)(d).
3. Capital good is eligible for input tax credit u/s 18(1) (d), but its credit is calculated by the formula:

ITC available = Input tax credit – 5% per quarter or part of it

Quarter months			Number Quarters
–	–	21 September 2021	1
October 2021	November 2021	December 2021	1
January 2021	February 2022	March 2022	1
April 2022	May 2022	13 June 2022	1
Number of quarters from 21.9.2021 to 13.06.2022			**4**

Therefore, ITC available = ₹1,00,000 – (5% × 4) × ₹1,00,000 = ₹1,00,000 – ₹20,000
= ₹80,000

4. Capital good is eligible for input tax credit u/s 18(1)(c) but subject to Section 18(2), i.e., the invoice must not be older than one year. In this case, the invoice date is 17.07.2021, and if we calculate its duration from 11.07.2021 to 16.09.2022, then it is greater than one year. So, no ITC is available on this invoice.

10.11 Change in the constitution of a registered person—Section 18(3) read with Rule 41

If the following conditions are satisfied, then the registered person is allowed to transfer the unutilized credit available in his electronic credit ledger to the transferee business in the manner specified by Rule 41.

Conditions

(a)	There is sale, merger, demerger, amalgamation, lease or transfer of the business of the registered person. The details of such change shall be furnished in FORM GST ITC-02 on common portal as per Rule 41(1).
(b)	There are specific provisions for transfer of liabilities under the above change. For this purpose, a certificate is required to be submitted. This certificate shall be issued by a practicing Chartered Accountant or Cost Accountant as per Rule 41(2).
(c)	Transferee business means the business so sold, demerged, amalgamated, leased or transferred business.

Manner specified in Rule 41

1.	The transferer is required to furnish the details of the above change in FORM GST ITC-02. This form shall be furnished on common portal. This form contains various details like details of the input tax credit to be transferred, details of the certificate issued by a practicing Chartered Accountant or Cost Accountant, etc. Further, in the case of demerger and other forms business re-organisation, the input tax credit is to be apportioned in the ratio of the value of assets of the new units as given in the demerger scheme. Value of assets, here, means the value of the entire assets of the business, irrespective input tax credit availment.
2.	A copy of the certificate issued by a practicing Chartered Accountant or Cost Accountant shall also be submitted. This certificate certifies that the above change is with the provision of transfer of liabilities.
3.	The transferee is also required to accept the details furnished by the transferor and then only the unutilized credit shall be credited to the electronic credit ledger of the transferee.
4.	The inputs and capital goods so transferred must be duly recorded by the transferee in his books of account.

Notes: While calculating the amount of input tax credit that can be transferred to the transferee, the following points must be kept in mind:

1. As said in Rule 41, the transfer of the input tax must be in the ratio of the value of the assets transferred. The value of assets must be taken on appointed date of the demerger scheme or other such change.

2. The ratio of value of assets must be taken on State wise, i.e., the required ratio is the value of assets transferred from a unit in a State *divided by* the value of total assets of that unit.
3. The credit to be transferred must be on aggregate basis, i.e., the ratio calculated above must be applied to the sum total of CGST, SGST/UTGST, IGST.
4. Once the sum total of CGST, SGST/UTGST, IGST is transferred, then the transferred credit can be bifurcated as CGST, SGST/UTGST, IGST in any ratio at the option of the transferor.

Example 10.36: YYD (P) Ltd. is registered in Delhi and Rajasthan with total value of assets ₹250 crore in both the States. It transfers of its assets worth ₹25 crore from Delhi unit and ₹150 crore from Rajasthan unit to BYD Ltd. in a scheme of demerger. From the following details calculate the amount of ITC that can be transferred by the transferor to the transferee.

States where the transferor is registered in GST	Assets on appointed date of demerger (₹)	GST(₹)	ITC Balance of transferor as on the date of filing of FORM GST ITC-02 (₹)
Delhi	50 crores	IGST	5,00,000
		CGST	6,00,000
		SGST	6,00,000
Rajasthan	200 crores	IGST	10,00,000
		CGST	4,00,000
		SGST	4,00,000

Solution

States where the transferor is registered in GST	Asset ratio on State basis	GST(₹)	ITC Balance of transferor as on the date of filing of FORM GST ITC-02 (₹)	ITC Balance that can be transferred as per Section 18(3) and Rule 41
Delhi	25/50 = 0.5	IGST	1,00,000	1,00,000
		CGST	6,00,000	5,50,000
		SGST	6,00,000	–
		Total	13,00,000	13,00,000 × 0.5 = 6,50,000
Rajasthan	150/200 = 0.75	IGST	10,00,000	10,00,000
		CGST	4,00,000	3,50,000
		SGST	4,00,000	–
		Total	18,00,000	18,00,000 × 0.75 = 13,50,000

1 Assets transferred from Delhi/Total assets in Delhi

1 Assets transferred from Rajasthan / Total assets in Rajasthan

2

3 This amount has been bifurcated as ₹1,00,000 as IGST and remaining amount as CGST. This is the freedom of the transferor. He can break it into various combinations. However, such amount bifurcated cannot exceed the balance available, e.g., we cannot allocate ₹2,00,000 out 650000 as IGST because in that case it will exceed IGST balance of ₹1,00,000.

10.12 Special Cases of Reversal of ITC

It may happen that a taxable supply is declared an exempt supply by the government, or it may also happen that a taxable person shifts from a regular scheme to a composition scheme or a registered person becomes unregistered, then a question arises here, i.e., Should the input tax credit availed on the inputs, input services, capital goods before such event be taken back (or reversed) by the government? The law says yes (except in the case of input service). Sections 18(4), 18(6), 29(5) deal in this regard.

1.Taxable supply becomes wholly exempt supply or taxable person opts in composition scheme: Section 18(4) read with Rule 44: According to Section 18(4), the registered person is required to reverse the input tax paid on the inputs held or contained in

(a) stock,
(b) work in progress/semi-finished goods,
(c) finished goods,
(d) Capital goods.

on the date preceding the date from which the taxable supply becomes exempt supply, or the assessee opts into the composition scheme.

Notes:

(a) This reversal will be done by way of debit in the electronic credit ledger or electronic cash ledger.

(b) After payment of such payment, the balance of input tax credit, if any, in the electronic credit ledger shall lapse.

(c) With regard to capital goods, only proportionate credit of remaining useful life is reversed. To calculate the remaining useful life of the capital good, the total life is always taken 60 months, and any fractional month is ignored. Consider the following two situations:

Situation 1	
Total useful life	60 months
Used life	3 years 4 months 12 days = 40 months 12 days
Remaining life (actual)	60 months – 40 months 12 days = 19 months 18 days
Remaining life (for reversal purposes)	19 months
ITC on the capital good	₹30,000
Proportionate credit	₹30,000 × (19/60) = ₹9,500

Situation 2	
Total useful life	60 months
Used life	4 years 6 months 7days = 54 months 7 days
Remaining life (actual)	60 months – 54 months 7 days = 5 months 23 days

Situation 2	
Remaining life (reversal purpose)	5 months
ITC on the capital goods	₹1,20,000
Proportionate credit	₹1,20,000 × (5/60) = 10,000

2. Removal of Capital Good/Plant & Machinery: Section 18(6) read with Rules 40(2) and 44(6): Suppose that a registered person avails the tax credit for the tax paid on a capital good or plant & machinery and thereafter, the said capital goods/plant & machinery is supplied (e.g., sold), then according to section 18(6), the registered person is required to pay the *higher* of the following amounts:

(a) Tax on transaction value (as per section 15) of such capital goods/plant & machinery
(b) Input tax credit – 5% per quarter or part of it.

Note: If *refractory bricks, moulds, dies, jigs and fixtures* are supplied as scrap, then the registered person may pay tax on the transaction value.

Example 10.37: RK (registered in Delhi) purchases a capital good on 8.10.2021 for ₹5,00,000 plus CGST 9% and SGST 9%. He avails the tax credit in the month of November. On 17.8.2022, RK sold the capital goods to AK for ₹3,50,000 plus IGST 18%.

Solution

	Particulars	Amount (in ₹)
	CGST at 9%	45,000
	SGST at 9%	45,000
	Input tax credit availed	90,000
	Less: 5% per quarter or part of it, i.e., 5% × 4 (see working note)	**18,000**
(a)	Input tax credit – 5% per quarter or part of it.	72,000
(b)	18% × Transaction value = 18% × ₹3,50,000	63,000
(c)	ITC to be reversed = (a) or (b), whichever is higher	72,000

Working Note

Quarter months			Number Quarters
8 October 2021	November 2021	December 2021	1
January 2021	February 2022	March 2022	1
April 2022	May 2022	June 2022	1
July 2022	17 August 2022	–	1
Number of quarters from 8.10.2021 to 17.08.2022			4

Example 10.38: On 25 August 2021, M/s Sharma, a registered supplier in Uttar Pradesh, purchased a machine for ₹12,39,000, including IGST, from one supplier of Surat, Gujarat, who issued a tax invoice on the same date. The machine was put to use on the same date, and the credit was also availed. This machine was sold for ₹7,80,000, excluding GST, to Mr. Ravi of

Andhra Pradesh on 20 August 2022. IGST rate is 18%. Is M/s Sharma required to pay GST? If yes, calculate the amount of tax payable at the time of removal of the machine.

Solution

	Particulars	Amount (in ₹)
	IGST at 18%	1,89,000
	Input tax credit availed	**1,89,000**
	Less: 5% per quarter or part of it, i.e., 5% × 5 (see working note)	47,250
(a)	Input tax credit – 5% per quarter or part of it.	1,41,750
(b)	18% × Transaction value = 18% × ₹7,80,000	1,40,400
(c)	**ITC to be reversed = (a) or (b), whichever is higher**	1,41,750

Working Note

Quarter months			Number Quarters
–	25 August 2021	September 2021	1
October 2021	November 2021	December 2021	1
January 2022	February 2022	March 2022	1
April 2022	May 2022	June 2022	1
July 2022	20 August 2022	–	1
Number of quarters from 25.08.2021 to 20.08.2022			5

3. Reversal of tax credit if registration is cancelled: Section 29(5): If the registration of a taxable person is cancelled, then the input tax credit attributable to the inputs contained in

(a) stock,
(b) work in progress/semi-finished goods,
(c) finished goods,
(d) Capital goods.

on the date preceding the date of cancellation.

Notes:

1. This reversal will be done by way of debit in the electronic credit ledger or electronic cash ledger.
2. After payment of such payment, the balance of input tax credit, if any, in the electronic credit ledger shall lapse.
3. With regard to capital goods, only proportionate credit of remaining useful life is reversed. To calculate the remaining useful life of the capital good, the total life is always taken 60 months, and any fractional month is ignored. Refer to Section 18(4) for this.

10.13 Manner of Determination of ITC in case of goods and its reversal—Rule 43

S. No.	Description	Amount
1.	**Exclusive non-business purpose or exempt supplies:** The tax paid on a capital good (purchased during the current tax period), which is used or to be used for 100% non-business purposes or 100% exempt supplies, then its input tax cannot be credited to the electronic credit ledger.	–
2.	**Exclusive taxable supplies, including zero-rated supplies:** The tax paid on capital goods (purchased during the current tax period) which is used or to be used for 100% *taxable supplies* and *zero-rated supply*, then its input tax can be credited to the electronic credit ledger.	–
3.	**Components of common credit**	
	(a) The tax paid on a capital good (purchased during the current tax period) which is for common use, i.e., not covered above, then its input tax be credited to the electronic credit ledger, and the useful life of the capital good is taken to be five years. This amount is denoted by A.	–
	(b) The tax paid on a capital good (*we will call it previous capital good-exempt supply*) that was purchased before the current tax period and its purpose was 100% exempt supply, but now, during the current tax period, this good is being used to be used for common purposes. Moreover, its input tax can also be credited to the electronic credit ledger during the current tax period.	–
	(c) The tax paid on a capital good (*we will call it previous capital good-taxable supply*) that was purchased before the current tax period and its purpose was 100% taxable supply, but now, during the current tax period, this good is being used or to be used for a common purpose. Moreover, its input tax cannot be credited to the electronic credit ledger during the current tax period.	–
4.	Tc, i.e., total common credit = (a) + (b) + (c)	Tc
5.	This step is to calculate the total monthly credit denoted by Tm. In fact, this monthly credit is nothing but the tax credited to the electronic credit ledger, which is related to the current tax period. As per Rule 43(1)(c), the useful life is taken to be 5 years = 60 months; therefore, Tc is divided by 60 to find Tm.	Tm = Tc/60

S. No.	Description	Amount
6.	Tm, being a common credit, contains the credit related to exempt supply, which is not eligible under section 17(2); therefore, the Government wants its proportionate reversal. For this purpose, Rule 43(1)(g) helps us to calculate how much of Tm is related to exempt supply and such portion is denoted by Te, which is calculated by dividing E by F where E is the total exempt supply during the current tax period and F is total supply in the State during the same period.	Te = Tm × E/F
7.	Tie = Input tax related to previous capital asset-exempt supply for the period before the current tax period	5% per quarter or part of it
8.	Amount to be added to the output tax liability of the current tax period	Te + Tie

The summary chart of Rule 43

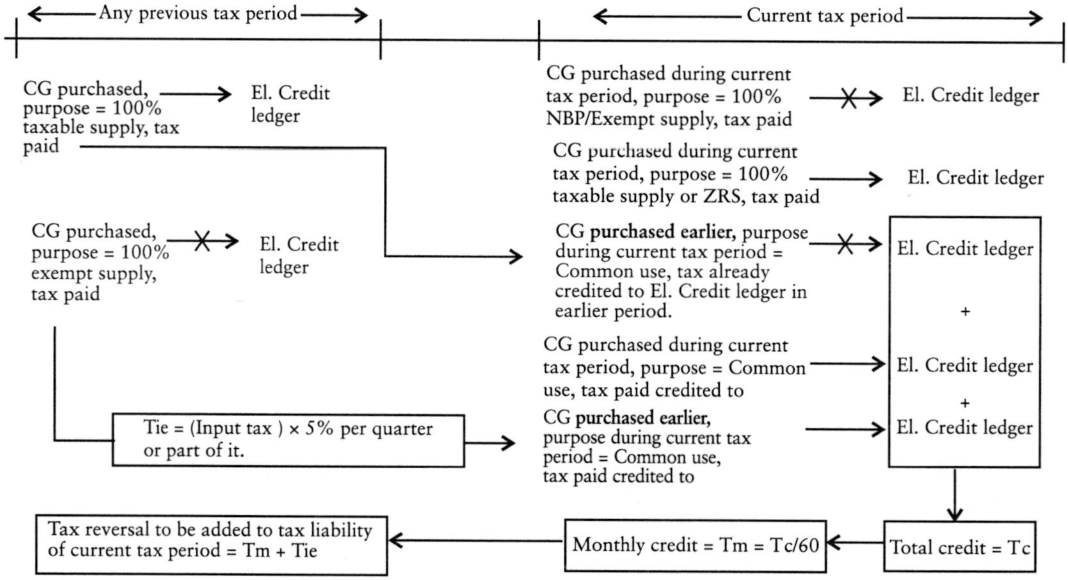

Note:

CG = Capital good, **X** = tax cannot be credited to the electronic credit ledger during the respective tax period.

Example 10.39: SR Enterprises is in possession of certain capital goods and purchases more of them as per the following particulars:

(a) Capital good A–Input tax ₹12,000–Exclusively used for non-business purpose

(b) Capital good B–Input tax ₹24,000–Exclusively used for zero-rated supplies

(c) Capital goods C–Input tax ₹60,000–used both for taxable and exempt supplies

(d) Capital good D–has been exclusively used for two years for exempt supplies–input tax ₹1,20,000, but now there is a change in use, both for taxable and exempt supplies.

(e) Capital good E–has been exclusively used for three years for taxable supplies–₹1,80,000–but now there is a change in use, both for taxable and exempt supplies.

(f) Aggregate value of exempt supplies during the tax period is ₹6,00,000, and the total turnover during the tax period is ₹12,00,000.

Compute the following:

(a) The input tax credit is to be added to the output tax liability of the current tax period.

(b) Amount that is credited to the electronic credit ledger during the current tax period.

Solution

S. No.	Description	Amount
1.	Tax paid on capital good A [100% non-business purpose and its input tax credit is ineligible]	12,000
2.	Tax paid on capital good B [100% zero-rated supply purpose and its input tax can be credited to electronic credit ledger]	24,000
3.	**(a) Tax paid on capital good C** [For common use and its input tax can be credited to electronic credit ledger]	60,000
	(b) Tax paid on capital good D [Earlier 100% exempt supply purpose, but now, for common use and its input tax can be credited to electronic credit ledger]	1,20,000
	(c) Tax paid on capital good E [Earlier 100% taxable supply purpose, but not for common use. Also, its input tax cannot be credited to the electronic credit ledger]	1,80,000
4.	Tc = (a) + (b) + (c)	3,60,000
5.	Tm = 3,60,000/60	6,000
6.	Te = 6,000 × 6,00,000/12,00,000	3,000
7.	Tie = Input tax paid on capital good D × 5% per quarter or part of it = 1,20,000 × 5% × 8	48,000
8.	Amount to be added to the output tax liability of the current tax period = Te + Tie	51,000
9.	Amount credited to the electronic credit ledger = ₹24,000 + ₹60,000 + ₹1,20,000	2,04,000

10.14 Input Tax Credit in the case of Job Work—Section 19

This topic will be discussed in detail in the next chapter.

10.15 Manner of Distribution of Credit by Input Service Distributor (ISD)—Section 20

Suppose there is a company X Ltd. (headquartered in Delhi) receives two types of services from A and B from Gurugram and Delhi, respectively. These services are used by the branches of X Ltd. A and B raise the invoices in the name of X Ltd. only. Now, X Ltd. has two questions:

1. Can it transfer (or distribute) its input tax credit on the above services to its branches? If yes, then what will be the ratio of distribution?
2. If it can be distributed, then the nomenclature of CGST and SGST or IGST will remain the same? This question arises because of the locations of the branches.

To answer the above questions, section 20 has been inserted. The provisions of this section are explained as follows:

Section 20(1): The input service distributor (ISD) is allowed to distribute the credit CGST as CGST or IGST and IGST as IGST or CGST. Also, respective State GST Acts also allow to distribute the credit of SGST as SGST or IGST and IGST as IGST or SGST. However, *Rule 39 states that IGST is distributed as IGST. So, a student should apply rule 39 while solving practical problems.*

Section 20(2): This section lays down the following conditions of distribution:

(a) The credit can be distributed against a document specified.
(b) The amount of credit cannot exceed of credit available.
(c) The credit can be distributed only to a recipient of credit only.
(d) The credit of tax paid on input services attributable to **more than one recipient of credit** shall be distributed amongst such recipients to whom the input service is attributable, and such distribution shall be pro rata on the basis of the turnover in a State or turnover in a Union territory of such recipient, during the relevant period, to the aggregate of the turnover of all such recipients to whom such input service is attributable and which are operational in the current year, during the said relevant period;
(e) The credit of tax paid on input services attributable to **all recipients of credit** shall be distributed amongst such recipients, and such distribution shall be pro rata on the basis of the turnover in a State or turnover in a Union territory of such recipient during the relevant period, to the aggregate of the turnover of all recipients and which are operational in the current year, during the said relevant period.

Procedure for distribution of input tax credit by Input Service Distribution: Rule 39

As per this rule, the following points should be kept in mind:

1. ITC available in a month shall be distributed in the same month, and its details shall be given in FORM GSTR-6.
2. Amount of eligible and ineligible ITC shall be distributed separately.
3. IGST shall be distributed as IGST.
4. CGST and SGST/UTGST shall be distributed as IGST if the branch/unit/depot is located in a State or Union Territory other than that of ISD.
5. CGST and SGST/UTGST shall be distributed as CGST and SGST/UTGST, respectively, if the branch/unit/depot is in the same State or Union Territory as that of ISD.
6. ISD shall issue an input service distributor invoice as per rule 54(1).

Example 10.40: A Limited (registered in Delhi) has three branches/depots located in Delhi, Bhopal, and Noida. A Ltd. received computer maintenance services from X and Y registered in Ghaziabad and Delhi, respectively. The details of the invoices raised by X and Y are as follows:

Supplier of services	Transaction value	Date of invoice	GST
X	₹2,00,000	5 January, 2022	18% IGST
Y	₹1,00,000	17 January, 2022	9% CGST 9% SGST

The details of the turnover in the state achieved by each branch during the financial year 2020-21 are as follows:

Turnover	Branch 1	Branch 2	Branch 3
Taxable supply within state	12,00,000	10,00,000	–
Exempt supply within state	2,00,000	5,00,000	3,00,000
Inter-state supply made from respective branch state	5,00,000	–	8,00,000
Exports of goods	1,00,000	–	29,00,000
Total	**20,00,000**	**15,00,000**	**40,00,000**

How will A Limited distribute the input tax credit to its three branches if it is given that A Limited is registered as ISD?

Solution

Ratio of distribution = 20:15:40

Credit to be distributed	Branch 1 Delhi (Amount in ₹)	Branch 2 Bhopal (Amount in ₹)	Branch 3 Noida (Amount in ₹)
X's invoice IGST credit is distributed as IGST	36,000 × 20/75 = 9,600	36,000 × 15/75 = 7,200	36,000 × 40/75 = 19,200
Y's invoice CGST credit is distributed as CGST	9,000 × 20/75 = 2,400	–	–
SGST credit is distributed as SGST	9,000 × 20/75 = 2,400	–	–
CGST + SGST credit distributed as IGST	–	18,000 × 15/75 = 3,600	18,000 × 40/75 = 9,600
IGST credit balance CGST credit balance SGST credit balance	9,600 2,400 2,400	10,800 0 0	28,800 0 0

Example 10.41: ABC Ltd., having its head office in Mumbai, is registered as ISD. It has three branches in different cities situated in different states namely 'Mumbai', 'Jabalpur' and 'Delhi', which are operational in the current year.

ABC Ltd. furnishes the following information for the month of July:

(a) IGST paid on services used only for the Mumbai branch: ₹3,00,000.

(b) CGST and SGST paid on services used for all branches: ₹12,00,000

Total turnover of the branches for the previous financial year is as follows:

Branches	Turnover (in ₹)
Total turnover of all the branches	10,00,00,000
Turnover of Mumbai branch	5,00,00,000
Turnover of Jabalpur branch	3,00,00,000

Determine the credit to be distributed by ABC Ltd. to each of its three units.

Solution

Credit distributed	Branch 1 Mumbai (Amount in ₹)	Branch 2 Jabalpur (Amount in ₹)	Branch 3 Delhi (Amount in ₹)
IGST credit is distributed as IGST	3,00,000	–	–
CGST credit is distributed as CGST	6,00,000 × 5/10 = 3,00,000	–	–
SGST credit is distributed as SGST	6,00,000 × 5/10 = 3,00,000	–	–
CGST + SGST credit distributed as IGST		12,00,000 × 3/10 = 3,60,000	12,00,000 × 2/10=2,40,000

Theory Questions

1. What is blocked credit? Enumerate the cases, with suitable examples, where the credit is blocked despite the assessee being eligible otherwise under section 16.
2. What are the provisions of availing input tax credit on capital goods under the GST law?
3. How will you apportion input tax credit if you find that common inputs are used for taxable supply, zero-rated supply, exempt supply, non-taxable supply and non-business purposes?
4. Peeyush (a registered dealer in Uttarakhand) thinks that registration and having an invoice are the only conditions to avail of the input tax credit. You are required to give him suitable advice with reference to Section 17(5) of the CGST Act, 2017.
5. What do you mean by input service distributor? How will an ISD distribute its input tax credit over its branches?
6. What are the conditions of availing input tax credit?
7. Is there any special provision with respect to input tax credit in the case of banking companies or financial institutions?

Case-based Questions (Unsolved)

1. Uttar Kumar Traders supplied goods at ₹11,500 plus GST. He purchased inputs for ₹10,000. The supplier has charged GST in his invoice. State tax and central tax rate on supply of goods is 9% each. Calculate the tax payable by him.

   Answer: CGST and SGST ₹135 each.
2. Sarita supplied goods at ₹7500. She received inputs valued at ₹10,000. The supplier has charged GST in her invoice. They sold 60% of the inputs procured, and the balance of 40% was in stock. SGST and CGST rate on supply and purchase of goods is 9% each. Calculate the balance in the electronic credit ledger.

   Answer: Balance in electronic credit ledger: ₹225 each
3. Aakash is a manufacturer of drugs. SGST and CGST rate is 2.5% each. The sold the good at ₹10,000. They purchased inputs at ₹6500. SGST and CGST rate on inputs is 6% each. All the inputs were used in the manufacture of final products. There was no opening or closing stock of inputs or final products. Calculate the balance in the electronic credit ledger.

   Answer: Balance in electronic credit ledger: ₹140 each
4. Anuj Jain is a manufacturer of printing machinery. SGST and CGST rate on the supply of goods is 9% each. He sold the goods within India at ₹4,00,000. They exported goods for ₹6,50,000. They purchased inputs at ₹5,00,000. SGST and CGST rate on inputs is 9% each. All these inputs were used in the manufacture of final products. There was no opening or closing stock of inputs or final products. Calculate the balance in the electronic credit ledger.

   Answer: Balance in electronic credit ledger: ₹9,000 each.
5. A manufacturer procures input goods and services within the state ₹1000, SGST and CGST rate on receipts is 9% each. He manufactured two products out of inputs.

One product of the value of ₹800 was subject to SGST and CGST at 9% each. Other product of the value of ₹800 was exempt from SGST and CGST. Calculate the tax payable.

Answer: ₹27 each

6. Value of supply of goods of a trader in the inter-state is ₹1200. IGST rate on supply of goods is 18%. Value of receipt of goods and services within state is ₹1000. SGST and CGST rate on receipts is 9% each. Calculate the tax payable.

   Answer: Tax to be paid through electronic cash ledger: ₹36

7. Value of supply of goods and services of a manufacturer in the inter-state is ₹100. Value of supply of goods and services of the manufacturer within state is ₹1100. IGST rate on supply of goods and services is 18%. Value of receipts of inputs within state is ₹1000. SGST and CGST rate on receipt is 9% each.

   Answer: SGST: ₹9, CGST: ₹9 and IGST: ₹18

8. Pratap of Delhi supplied some goods to Kavita of Delhi for ₹50,000 exclusive GST. She supplied those goods to Rajender of Uttar Pradesh for ₹1,25,000 exclusive of GST applicable. He sold the same goods to Vallabh of Uttar Pradesh by doing a value addition of 40%. CGST and SGST rate is 9% each, while the IGST rate is 18%. You are required to calculate the SGST, CGST and IGST payable by each supplier. Further calculate the revenue collected by the Central government, Delhi government and UP Government.

   Answer: CGST and SGST payable by Pratap: ₹ 4,500 and ₹ 4,500 respectively.

   IGST payable by Kavita: ₹ 13,500

   CGST and SGST payable by Rajender: Nil and ₹ 9,000 respectively.

   Revenue collected by the Central Government: ₹15,750

   Revenue collected by the Delhi Government: Nil

   Revenue collected by the Uttar Pradesh Government: ₹ 15,750.

   [**Hint:** While calculating the revenue collected by each Government, one should keep in mind that a State Government transfers the deficient amount (arising due to input tax credit) to the Central Government or vice-versa.]

9. Mukesh Ltd. forgot to claim the tax credit for an invoice dated 12/10/2021 (invoice number 252: amount: ₹5,25,000 including GST of ₹25,000). You are required to suggest the tax manager of Mukesh Ltd. about the credit availment of this invoice.

   Answer: Refer to Section 16(3).

10. A supplied goods worth ₹50,00,000 to B by charging GST of 18%. A raised an invoice on 11/01/2022. B paid the due amount on 17/07/2022. Comment on the consequences of the same.

    Answer: Refer to Section 16(2).

11. Prisha (a GST registered supplier) is engaged in the manufacture of taxable goods. The company provides the following information pertaining to GST paid on the purchases made/input services availed of it during the month of July 2022:

    (a) Raw material (to be received in September 2022): ₹2.5 lakhs.

(b) Membership of a club availed for employees working in the factory: ₹1,45,000
(c) Inputs to be received in 5 lots out of which 3rd lot is received during the month: ₹80,000.
(d) Trucks used for transport of raw material: ₹40,000.
(e) Capital goods (out of three items, the invoice for two items is missing, and GST paid on that item is ₹80,000): ₹1,50,000.

Determine the amount of ITC available for the month of July 2022.

Answer: ₹1,10,000

12. From the following information, compute the GST payable for the month of January 2023.

Tax	GST on outward supply	ITC balance in credit ledger
CGST	2,000	NIL
SGST	15,000	1000
IGST	24,000	37,000

Answer: IGST, CGST, SGST payable: Nil.

13. KL Ltd., a registered supplier, is engaged in the manufacture of tanks. The company provides the following information pertaining to GST paid on the purchases made/ input services availed by it during the month of January 2023:
(a) Purchase of machinery (a debit note was issued): ₹1,15,000
(b) Input purchased was directly delivered to KRK, a job worker and a registered supplier: ₹80,000.
(c) Computers purchased (depreciation was claimed on the said GST portion under the income tax act): ₹50,000.
(d) Works contract services availed for construction of staff quarters within the company premises: ₹4,25,000.

Determine the amount of ITC for the month of January 2023.

Answer: ₹1,95,000

14. Durgesh of Delhi supplied a product to Deepak of Delhi for ₹35,400, including GST. Deepak supplied the product to Hari of Mumbai for ₹45,000, excluding GST applicable. Hari supplied the product to Rajesh of Pune after a value addition of 20%. Rajesh supplied the goods to Bittoo of Orissa after a 30% value addition. Assuming that the CGST rate is 9%; SGST rate is 9%, and IGST rate is 18%, you are required to calculate
(a) the SGST, CGST and IGST payable by each supplier, and
(b) the revenue collected by the Central, Delhi, Maharashtra and Orissa Governments.

Answer: CGST and SGST payable by Durgesh : ₹ 2,700 and ₹ 2,700 respectively

IGST payable by Deeapk: ₹ 2,700

CGST and SGST payable by Hari : ₹ 1,620

IGST payable by Rajesh: ₹ 2,916

Revenue collected by the Central Government : ₹ 12,636

Revenue collected by the Delhi Government: Nil

Revenue collected by the Maharshtra Government: Nil

Revenue collected by the Orissa Government: Nil

15. Answer the following independent cases.
    (a) A company purchased a luxury car for its directors. The car cost ₹100,000, and the GST rate is 18%. How much input tax credit will the company be blocked from claiming?
    (b) A company purchased a large quantity of food and drinks for its employees during an office party. The total cost of the food and drinks was ₹5,000 and the GST rate is 18%. How much input tax credit will the company be blocked from claiming?
    (c) A business owner purchased a gift card worth ₹1,000 for their spouse's birthday. The gift card has a GST component of 10%. Since the gift card was used for personal purposes, the business owner cannot claim an input tax credit for the GST paid. Comment on the availability of the credit.

Answer: (a) ₹ **18,000;** (b) ₹ **763;** (c) **Refer to Section 17(5).**

16. ABC Pvt. Ltd. is registered in Delhi. It manufactures two taxable products, P and Q, and one exempt product, R. On 1 October, product Q was exempted through an exemption notification, while the exemption on R was withdrawn on the same date. The turnover (exclusive of taxes) of P, Q and R in October was ₹9,00,000, ₹10,00,000 and ₹6,00,000. ABC Pvt. Ltd. has given the following details:

Particulars	Price (₹)	GST (₹)
Machinery *U* purchased on 1 October for being used in manufacturing all the three products.	2,00,000	36,000
Machinery *V* purchased on 1 October for being used in manufacturing product P.	1,00,000	18,000
Machinery *W* purchased on 1 October for being exclusively used in manufacturing product Q.	3,00,000	54,000
Machinery Y purchased on 1 October four years ago for being exclusively used in manufacturing product Q. From 1 October; such machinery will also be used for manufacturing product R.	4,00,000	72,000
Machinery Z purchased on 1 October two years ago to be used in manufacturing all three products.	3,00,000	54,000
Raw material used for manufacturing P purchased on 6 October.	1,50,000	27,000
Raw material used for manufacturing Q purchased on 11 October.	2,00,000	36,000
Raw material used for manufacturing R purchased on 16 October.	1,00,000	18,000

Calculate the following:

(a) Amount of input tax to be credited to electronic credit ledger for October.

(b) Amount of aggregate value of common credit.

(c) Common credit attributable to exempt supplies for October.

(d) GST liability of the company is payable through the Electronic Cash Ledger for October if the opening balance of input tax credit is nil.

Note: Assume that all the inward and outward supplies are inter-state.

Answer: ₹99,000; ₹1,62,000; ₹1080; ₹1,72,080

11
Job Work

11.1 Introduction

Suppose that Mr. A manufactures fancy shirts, but for the embroidery, the manufactured shirts are sent to another person, say, Sunder Design Ltd. After the embroidery, the shirts are sent back to Mr. A. Such a situation is known as **job work** in which Sunder Design Ltd. is called a **job worker** and the person who sends the goods (i.e., Mr. A) is called **principal**. This chapter discusses the provisions of sections 19, 143 and rule 45 which are related to job work.

11.2 Meaning of Job Work—Section 2(68)

According to section 2(68), job work means any treatment or process undertaken by a person on goods belonging to another registered person.

11.3 Input Tax Credit on Inputs/Capital Goods sent for Job Work—Section 19

Section 19 deals with the aspects of input tax credit related to job work.

1. Credit on inputs sent for job work is allowed: Section 19(1) read with Rule 45: The principal is allowed to take input tax credit on the inputs sent for job work. However, the credit is subject to some conditions and restrictions prescribed under rule 45.

2. Credit is allowed even if the inputs are directly sent to the job worker: Section 19(2): The credit is allowed even if the inputs are directly sent to the job worker. This section has been inserted because of section 16(2), which states that the credit is disallowed if goods are not received.

3. Condition to avail credit in case of inputs sent for job work: Section 19(3): If the inputs sent for job work are not received back or not supplied from the place of business of the job worker as per section 143(1)(a) or section 143(1)(b) *within 1 year*, then this is treated as supply of inputs by the principal to the job worker on the date when such inputs were sent for job work. Further, where the inputs are sent directly to the job worker, the period of 1 year is counted from the date of receipt of inputs by the job worker.

4. Credit on capital goods sent for job work is allowed: Section 19(4): The principal is allowed input tax credit on capital goods sent to a job worker for job work. This section is subject to Rule 45.

5. Credit is allowed even the capital goods are directly sent to the job worker: Section 19(5): The credit is allowed even though the capital goods are directly sent to the job worker. This section has been inserted because of section 16(2), which states that the credit is disallowed if goods are not received. Thus, section 19(5) overrides section 16(2).

6. Condition to avail credit in case of capital goods sent for job work: Section 19(6): If the inputs sent for job work are not received back or not supplied from the place of business of the job worker as per section 143(1)(a) or section 143(1)(b) *within 3 years*, then this is treated as supply of inputs by the principal to the job worker on the date when such inputs were sent for job work.

Further, where the inputs are sent directly to the job worker, the period of 1 year is counted from the date of receipt of inputs by the job worker.

7. Condition of returning inputs/capital goods within 1 year or 3 years is not applicable in certain cases: Section 19(7)

Section 19(3) and section 19(6) are not applicable to **moulds and dies, jigs and fixtures or tools** sent for job work.

11.4 Job Work Procedure—Section 143 read with Rule 45

Section 143 does not talk about the aspects of input tax credit related to job work, but it talks about the compliances to be accomplished in the case of job work.

1. Goods can be sent for job work without payment of tax: Section 143 (1): A registered principal is allowed to send inputs or capital goods (without paying tax) to a job worker, and he may send goods therefrom to another job worker. However, he is required to intimate a proper officer and satisfy the conditions of **Rule 45**. The section further states that

(a) The principal is required to bring back those inputs (within 1 year) or capital goods (within 3 years) once the job work is done. The 1-year or 3-year time is counted from the date when they were sent to the job worker. Moreover, no tax is payable when bringing the goods back.

Notes:

1. The above periods of 1 year and 3 years can be extended by the commissioner if he is given reasonable grounds to do so. However, the extension cannot exceed 1 year in the case of inputs and 2 years in the case of capital goods.
2. The provision of return of goods is not applicable on **moulds, dies, jigs and fixtures, or tools.**

(b) **Registered job worker:** If the job worker is registered and the job work is completed, then the principal is allowed to supply those inputs or capital goods (directly from the place of the job worker) on payment of tax within India or with or without payment of tax for exports. The same rule is applicable when the principal is engaged in the supply of notified goods.

Unregistered job worker: If the job worker is not registered, then the principal can supply those inputs or capital goods from the place of the job worker only when he declares the place of business of the job worker as an additional place of business in his registration.

3. **Responsibility of keeping proper accounts of inputs and capital goods: Section 143(2):** The principal has been given the responsibility to maintain proper accounts of the inputs and capital goods.

4. **What will happen if the inputs and capital goods are brought back within 1 year and 3 years or not supplied from the place of the job worker?: Section 143(3)/(4):** In such a case, this is deemed that the principal had made supply of those inputs or capital goods to the job worker on the date when they were sent to the job worker. Therefore, he would be liable to pay GST along with interest. As per Rule 45, such supply shall be furnished in FORM GSTR-1.

5. **Waste and Scrap generated during job work: Section 143(5):** Irrespective of section 143(1) or section 143(2), a *registered* job worker may supply the waste and scrap generated during the job work on payment of tax. If the job worker is not registered, then the principal may supply the waste and scrap.

11.5 Conditions and restrictions in respect of inputs and capital goods sent to the job worker—Rule 45

1. The goods shall be sent by the principal to the job worker under the cover of a **delivery challan.** If the goods are further sent to another job worker, then the challan may be issued by the principal or the job worker sending those goods.

2. The details of the challan will be as per Rule 55. As per Rule 55, the challan shall be prepared in triplicate (the original copy is for consignee, the duplicate copy is for transporter and the triplicate copy is for consigner).

3. The details of challans in respect of goods sent to a job worker or received back from a job worker during the *specified period* be included in **FORM GST ITC-04** furnished for that period on or before the 25th day of the month succeeding the said period or within such further period as may be extended by the Commissioner by notification in this behalf.

Note: Meaning of specified period

(a) **Principal whose aggregate turnover in the previous financial year > ₹5 crore:** The specified period means the period of 6 consecutive months starting from 1 April and 1 October.

(b) **Principal whose aggregate turnover in the previous financial year ≤ ₹5 crore:** The specified period means a financial year.

4. If the goods are not brought back within 1 year and 3 years, as the case may be, then it will be deemed that the principal had made a supply to the job worker on the date when they were sent to the job worker. Therefore, he would be liable to pay GST along with interest. Such supply shall be declared in **FORM GSTR-1.**

11.6 Registration Requirement for Job Worker

Although this topic has been discussed in detail in the next chapter, here we can say that due to Notification No. 10/2017 IT dated 13.10.2017, a job worker is required to take registration only when his aggregate turnover exceeds ₹20 lakhs or ₹10 lakhs in case of *Mizoram, Tripura, Manipur,* and *Nagaland*. This rule is applicable even in the case of inter-state supply.

Illustration 11.1: Showing the provisions of Job work

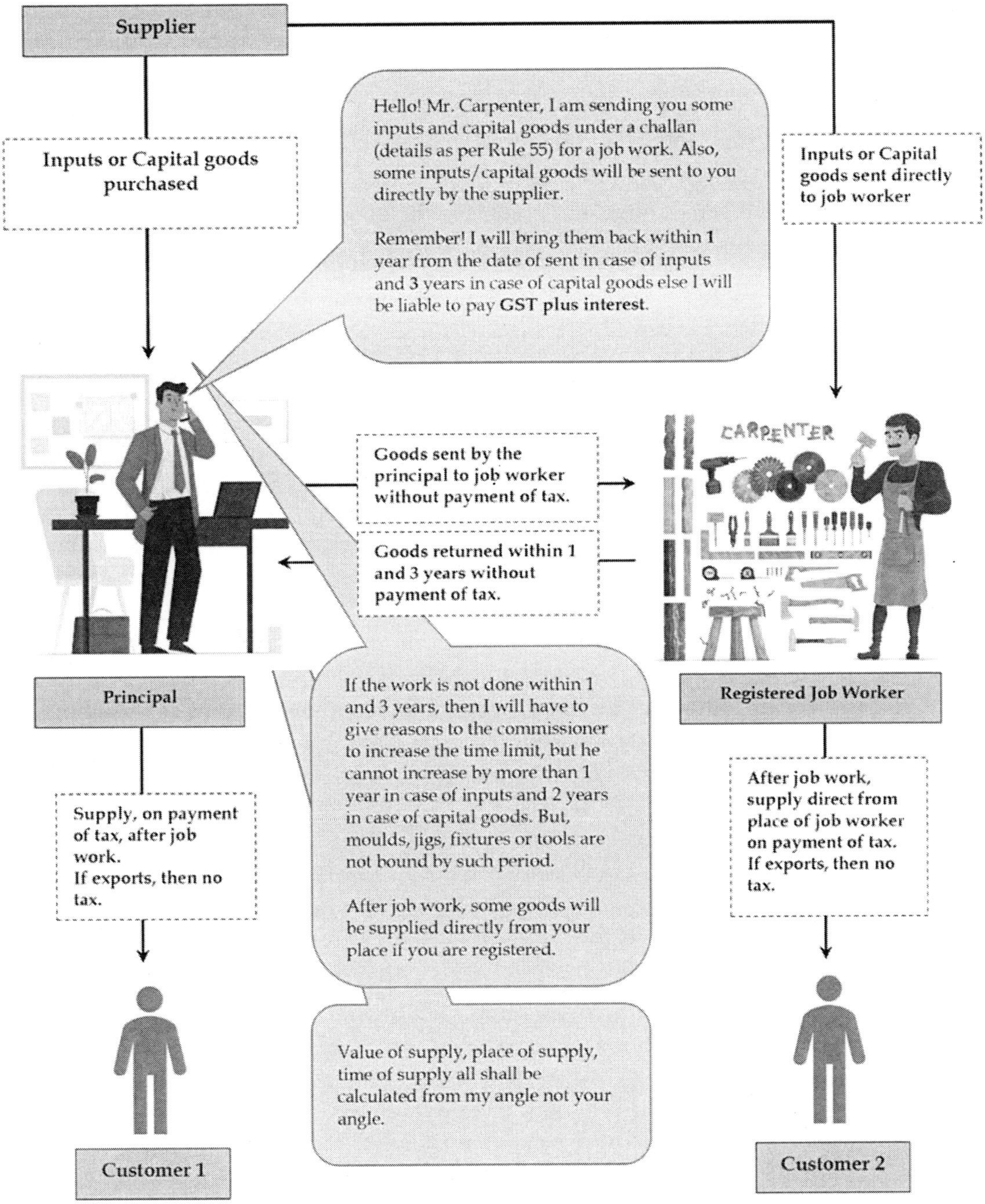

Image courtesy–Freepik

Theory Questions

1. Who is a principal and job worker?
2. What are the provisions of job work under the CGST Act, 2017?
3. Under what cases can the principal directly supply goods from the place of the job worker without declaring the premises of the job worker as his additional place of business?
4. What happens if the goods sent for the job are not returned within 1 year and 3 years in the case of inputs and capital goods, respectively?
5. Is job work a supply by a job worker?
6. Can a principal get an input tax credit for the goods sent for job work?

Case-based Questions (Unsolved)

1. Ram Industries Ltd., registered in Punjab, manufactures plastic pipes for other supplies on a work basis. On 18 January 2022, Amazing Ltd. (registered in the State of Himachal Pradesh) sent plastic worth ₹7,00,000 and moulds worth ₹100,000, free of cost, to Ram Industries Ltd. to make plastic pipes. Ram Industries Ltd. also used its own material—a special type of lamination material for coating the pipes—worth ₹1 lakh in the manufacture of pipes. It raised an invoice of ₹3 lakhs as job charges for making pipes and returned the manufactured pipes through delivery challan to Amazing Ltd. on 22 October 2022. The same quality and quantity of plastic pipes, as was made for Plasto manufacturers, were made by Sudama Industries Ltd. from its own raw material and sold to Solid Pipes (registered in Jammu and Kashmir) for ₹10.5 lakhs on 25 October 2022.

   Examine the scenario and offer your views on the following issues with reference to the provisions relating to job work under the GST laws.

   (a) Is there any difference between the manufacture of plastic pipes by Ram Industries Ltd. for Amazing Ltd. and Solid Pipes?

   (b) Whether Ram Industries Ltd. can use its own material even when it is manufacturing the plastic pipes on a work basis?

   (c) Whether sending the plastic and moulds to Ram Industries Ltd. by Amazing Ltd. a supply, and does a taxable invoice need to be issued for the same?

   (d) Should Ram Industries include the value of free-of-cost plastic and moulds supplied by Amazing Ltd. in its job charges?

   (Adapted from the ICAI Study Material)

   Answer: (a) Yes—Refer to the meaning of Job-work under section 2(68); (b) Yes, it can—Refer to Circular No. 38/12/2018 GST dated 26 March 2018 available on CBIC portal; (c) No, it is not supply—Refer to section 143 and it is not required to issue taxable invoice—Refer to Rule 45; (d) No, it should not—Refer to section 15(2)(b).

2. Suppose that some goods were sent by a principal for job work on 19 March 2021. The job work was completed on 1 April 2022 and returned back the principal on the same date. What is your view in this case?

Answer: This shall be treated as supply—Refer to section 143

3. Mr. A is a manufacturer of furniture, and he sends raw materials to Mr. B, who is a job worker. Mr. B processes the raw materials and returns the finished furniture to Mr. A. Mr. A is registered under GST, and he wants to know how GST applies to this job work arrangement. Can you advise Mr. A on the GST implications of the job work of goods under GST and the compliance requirements he needs to fulfil?

   Answer: Refer to sections 19, 143 and relevant Rules.

4. A Ltd., a registered manufacturer, sent some goods, say, x, worth ₹10 lakhs under a challan to B Ltd., a registered job worker, for job work on 22 February 2022. B Ltd. is required to paste a product y on top of x. Product y is to be supplied by B Ltd. only. As a consideration, it charges ₹4,00,000 for the pasting activity, including the supply of y. During the job work, waste and scrap are generated, which is sold by B Ltd. for ₹50,000. The job work is completed on 17 July 2022 and returned on the same date. If the GST rate for y is 28%, for waste and scrap is 12%, and for services is 18%, you are required to calculate the GST liability of B Ltd.

   Answer: ₹78,000

12

Registration

12.1 Introduction

The functioning of GST cannot be imagined unless the Government is able to track the taxable persons. For implementation of the GST law, registration of taxable persons is necessary. Registration under the GST law falls into the following categories:

1. Registration based on aggregate turnover—Section 22
2. Registration is not required at all—Section 23
3. Compulsory registration—Section 24

12.2 Registration based on Aggregate Turnover—Section 22

According to section 22(1), if the aggregate turnover of a supplier in a financial year exceeds **₹20 lakhs,** he is liable to get registered under the CGST Act, 2017 in that State or Union Territory from where he makes a taxable supply of goods or services or both. However, if the supply is made from a special category state, as per explanation iii of section 22, then the limit is **₹10 lakhs.**

Now a question arises, i.e., **what are the special category states?** The answer is found in **Article 279A(4)(g)** of the Constitution of India and **explanation iii** of **section 22** of the CGST Act. In fact, Article 279A(4)(g) says that the GST council shall make recommendations to the Union and the States on special provisions with respect to the following States:

S. No.	Special category states as per Article 279A(4)(g)	Special category states as per explanation iii of section 22
1.	Arunachal Pradesh	-
2.	Assam	-
3.	Jammu and Kashmir	-
4.	Manipur	Manipur
5.	Meghalaya	-
6.	Mizoram	Mizoram

S. No.	Special category states as per Article 279A(4)(g)	Special category states as per explanation iii of section 22
7.	Nagaland	Nagaland
8.	Sikkim	-
9.	Tripura	Tripura
10.	Himachal Pradesh	-
11.	Uttarakhand	-

Thus, the aggregate turnover limit for registration is as follows:

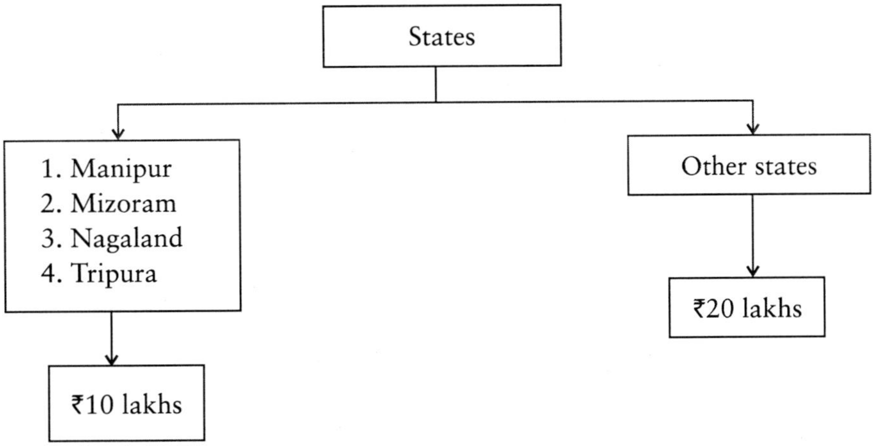

Special case of a supplier exclusively engaged in the supply of goods

As per section 22(1), if a supplier makes the supply of goods only (i.e., not services), then the Government may increase (at the request of a State and on the recommendation of the GST Council) the limit of ₹20 lakhs to ₹40 lakhs. Consequently, *Notification No. 10/2019 CT dated 07.03.2019 as amended by Notification No. 03/2022 CT dated 31.03.2022 and Notification No. 15/2022 CT dated 13.07.2022* have been issued, which say that if a supplier makes the supply of goods only, then he is not required to take registration if his aggregate turnover does not exceed ₹40 lakhs. However, he is required to satisfy the following conditions:

1. He is not covered under section 24.
2. He does not make supply of the following goods:

(a)	Ice cream (whether containing cocoa or not) or
(b)	Pan masala or
(c)	Tobacco and manufactured tobacco substitutes or
(d)	[1]Fly ash bricks, Fly ash aggregates, Fly ash blocks, bricks of fossil meals or similar siliceous earths, building bricks, or earthen/roofing tiles.

1 With effect from 18.07.2022, Fly ash bricks, Fly ash aggregates, Fly ash blocks are included. While bricks of fossil means or similar siliceous earths, building bricks, or earthen/roofing tiles are included with effect from 1.04.2022.

3. He does not make **intra-state** supplies in the following states:

S. No.	States
1.	Arunachal Pradesh
2.	Manipur
3.	Meghalaya
4.	Mizoram
5.	Nagaland
6.	Sikkim
7.	Tripura
8.	Uttarakhand
9.	Telangana
10.	Puducherry

4. He has not taken voluntary registration under section 25(3).

Summary chart of the above discussion

Aggregate Turnover Limit for Registration		
₹10 lakhs	**₹20 lakhs**	**₹20 lakhs for goods or services or both; ₹40 lakhs for goods**
Manipur	Arunachal Pradesh	Jammu and Kashmir
Mizoram	Meghalaya	Assam
Nagaland	Sikkim	Himachal Pradesh
Tripura	Uttarakhand	Other states
	Puducherry	
	Telangana	

Example 12.1: Monu makes an intra-state supply of services from Delhi. His aggregate turnover during the financial year 2021-22 is ₹19,00,000. Is he required to register under section 22?

Solution

Monu is not required to take registration under section 22 because his aggregate turnover does not exceed the specified limit, i.e., ₹20,00,000 in the case of Delhi.

Example 12.2: Neha (from Noida, Uttar Pradesh) is exclusively engaged in intra-state supply of Computer Accessories. Her aggregate turnover during the financial year 2021-22 is ₹32,00,000. Is she required to take registration under section 22?

Solution

She is not required to take registration under section 22 because she is exclusively engaged intra-state supply of goods, and her aggregate turnover does not exceed the specified limit, i.e., ₹40,00,000 in the case of Uttar Pradesh.

Example 12.3: Swati (from Meerut, Uttar Pradesh) is engaged exclusively in inter-state supply of Laptop Bags. Her aggregate turnover during the financial year 2021-22 is ₹28,00,000. Is she required to take registration under section 22?

Solution

Swati is engaged in the inter-state supply of goods; therefore, she cannot take advantage of Notification No. 10/2019. As a result, the aggregate turnover limit is ₹20,00,000 in the case of Uttar Pradesh. Her aggregate turnover exceeds the specified limit; therefore, she is required to take registration.

Example 12.4: Siddhi is engaged exclusively in **intra-state** supply of Laptop Bags from **Mizoram.** Her aggregate turnover during the financial year 2021-22 is ₹12,00,000. Is she required to take registration under section 22?

Solution

She is engaged in the intra-state supply of goods from **Mizoram, where** Notification No. 10/2019 is not applicable here. As a result, the aggregate turnover limit is ₹10,00,000 in Mizoram. Her aggregate turnover exceeds the specified limit; therefore, she is required to take registration.

Example 12.5: Dinesh is engaged exclusively in **intra-state** supply of **Ice cream** from Ahmedabad, Gujarat. His aggregate turnover during the financial year 2021-22 is ₹12,00,000. Is he required to register under section 22?

Solution

He is engaged in the intra-state supply of Ice cream in case of which Notification No. 10/2019 is not applicable here. As a result, the aggregate turnover limit is ₹20,00,000 in Gujarat. His aggregate turnover does not exceed the specified limit; therefore, he is not required to take registration.

Note:

Aggregate Turnover means the total of all the supplies (given in the table below) made by all the persons who have the same PAN in India. Therefore, if A Limited has 2 branches, one in Delhi and the other in Noida, then to calculate the aggregate turnover of A Limited, we will consider the turnover of both branches.

Particulars	Amount
Taxable supplies	–
Exempt supplies	–
Exports, i.e., zero-rated supplies	–
Inter-state supplies	–

The following points are worthy to note:

1. Aggregate turnover does not include any type of GST, i.e., CGST, SGST/UTGST, IGST, GST Compensation cess.
2. If a supplier makes an outward supply that is covered under the reverse charge mechanism, then it shall be taken into account in the aggregate turnover of the supplier but not into the aggregate turnover of the recipient.
3. Aggregate turnover to include all supplies made by the taxable person, whether on his own account or made on behalf of all his principals.

4. Value of goods, after completion of job work, supplied directly from the premises of the registered job worker is not to be included in the aggregate turnover of the job worker.

12.3 Persons not liable for registration—Section 23

As per section 23, the following persons are not required to take registration.

1. Section 23(1)(a): A supplier of an exempt supply: A supplier engaged exclusively in the supply of goods or services or both not liable to GST (such as petrol) or wholly exempt from tax.

Image courtesy–Freepik

Example 12.6: Mr. Amrit is an owner of a petrol pump located in Rohtak, Haryana. Does he need to take GST registration?

Solution

No, he is not required to get registered under GST by virtue of section 23. According to this section, a supplier who is exclusively engaged in making exempt supply is not liable for registration.

Example 12.7: Mr. Maan is the owner of a petrol pump located in Punjab. He also trades in fabric. Is he required to take registration?

Solution

Yes, he is required to get registered under GST by virtue of section 23. According to this section, a supplier who is engaged exclusively in making an exempt supply is not liable for registration, but in the present case, Mr. Maan is not engaged exclusively in making an exempt supply (i.e., he supplies petrol—an exempt supply and fabric—a taxable supply), therefore, he is required to take registration depending upon his aggregate turnover.

2. Section 23(1)(b): An agriculturist: An agriculturist, if they only supply produce out of cultivation of land, is not required to take GST registration. It simply means that if an agriculturist supplies only the output produced out of the farming of his land, then he is not liable for registration, but if he is not engaged exclusively in the supply of the output of cultivation of land, then he is liable for registration under section 22.

Note: An agriculturist means an individual or Hindu Undivided Family (HUF) cultivating land

(a) by own labour
(b) by the labour of family, or
(c) by servants on wages payable in cash or kind or by hired labour under the supervision of him or his family member.

Example 12.8: Chaudhary Virender Singh is a farmer in Baghpat District of Uttar Pradesh. He cultivates his fields of wheat with the help of his family members. The wheat is supplied to a buyer. Is he required to get registered under GST?

Solution

No, he is not required to get registered under GST by virtue of section 23. According to this section, an agriculturist supplying the produce or output out of cultivation of land is not liable for registration.

Example 12.9: Suppose that in the previous example, he decides to supply grapes apart from farming of land. What will be your answer now?

Solution

Yes, he is required to get registered under GST because, as per section 23, exemption from registration is available only when the agriculturist supplies the output out of the cultivation of land. In the present case, the agriculturist is engaged in the supply of wheat (output out of cultivation) as well as grapes (not the supply out of cultivation of his land). Consequently, by virtue of section 22, depending upon the aggregate turnover, he is required to take GST registration.

3. **Persons notified by the Government: Section 23(2)**

(a) **Persons making ONLY supply under reverse charge mechanism:** If a person makes only the supply of goods or services or both which is covered under reverse charge mechanism, then he is not liable for registration. For example, a senior advocate supplying legal services to a corporate body is covered under the reverse charge mechanism; therefore, he does not need to take GST registration.

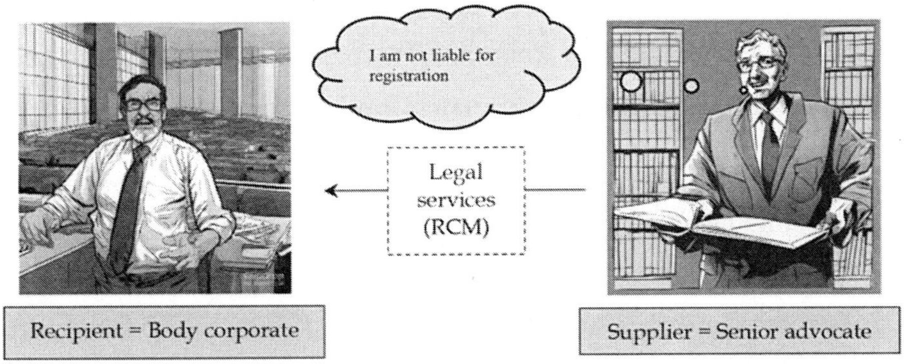

(b) **Job worker making inter-state supply:** A job worker making inter-state supply up to ₹20 lakhs or ₹10 lakhs—Notification No. 7/2017—IT dated 14.09.2017.

(c) Persons making inter-state supplies of *taxable services* up to ₹20 lakhs/₹10 lakhs as the case may be—Notification No. 10/2017—IT dated 13.10.2017.

(d) Persons making inter-state supply of *taxable goods* up to ₹40 lakhs—Notification No. 10/2019—CT dated 07.03.2019.

(e) Persons (including casual taxable persons) making inter-state taxable supplies of notified handicraft goods and notified handmade goods up to ₹20 lakhs/₹10 lakhs as the case may be—Notification No. 3/2018—IT dated 22.10.2018.

(f) Suppliers covered under section 9(5)—Notification No. 65/2017—CT dated 15.11.2017.

(g) **According to Notification No. 34/2023-Central Tax, dated:** 31.07.2023, the persons making supplies of goods through an electronic commerce operator who is required to collect tax at source under section 52 of the CGST Act and having an aggregate turnover in the preceding financial year and in the current financial year not exceeding the amount of aggregate turnover above which a supplier is liable to be registered in the State or Union territory under section 22(1) of the said Act, are exempted from registration. However, they are required to satisfy the following conditions:

(i) they are not allowed to make inter-state supply of goods.

(ii) the supply of goods through e-commerce operator is not allowed in more than one State or Union Territory.

(iii) they must have Permanent Account Number (PAN) issued under the Income Tax Act, 1961.

(iv) before they make any supply of goods through e-commerce operator, they are required to declare on the common portal (i.e., GST Portal) their PAN, address of their place of business and the State or Union territory in which they seek to make such supply, which shall be subjected to validation on the common portal.

(v) they have been granted an enrolment number on the common portal on successful validation of the Permanent Account Number declared and no supply can be made without this enrolment number.

(vi) they shall not be granted more than one enrolment number in a State or Union territory.

(vii) where they are subsequently granted voluntary registration, the enrolment number shall be treated as invalid from the effective date of such voluntary registration.

12.4 Persons mandatorily liable for registration—Section 24

As per section 24, whatever is written in section 22(1), the following persons are required to take GST registration compulsorily, irrespective of their aggregate turnover.

1. Persons making inter-state taxable supply: In the case of inter-state taxable supply, the supplier is required to take registration compulsorily. However, if he makes inter-state supply of services and notified handicraft goods and notified handmade goods, then he can take exemption from registration if his aggregate turnover does not exceed ₹20 lakhs/₹10 lakhs as the case may be and he has obtained PAN.

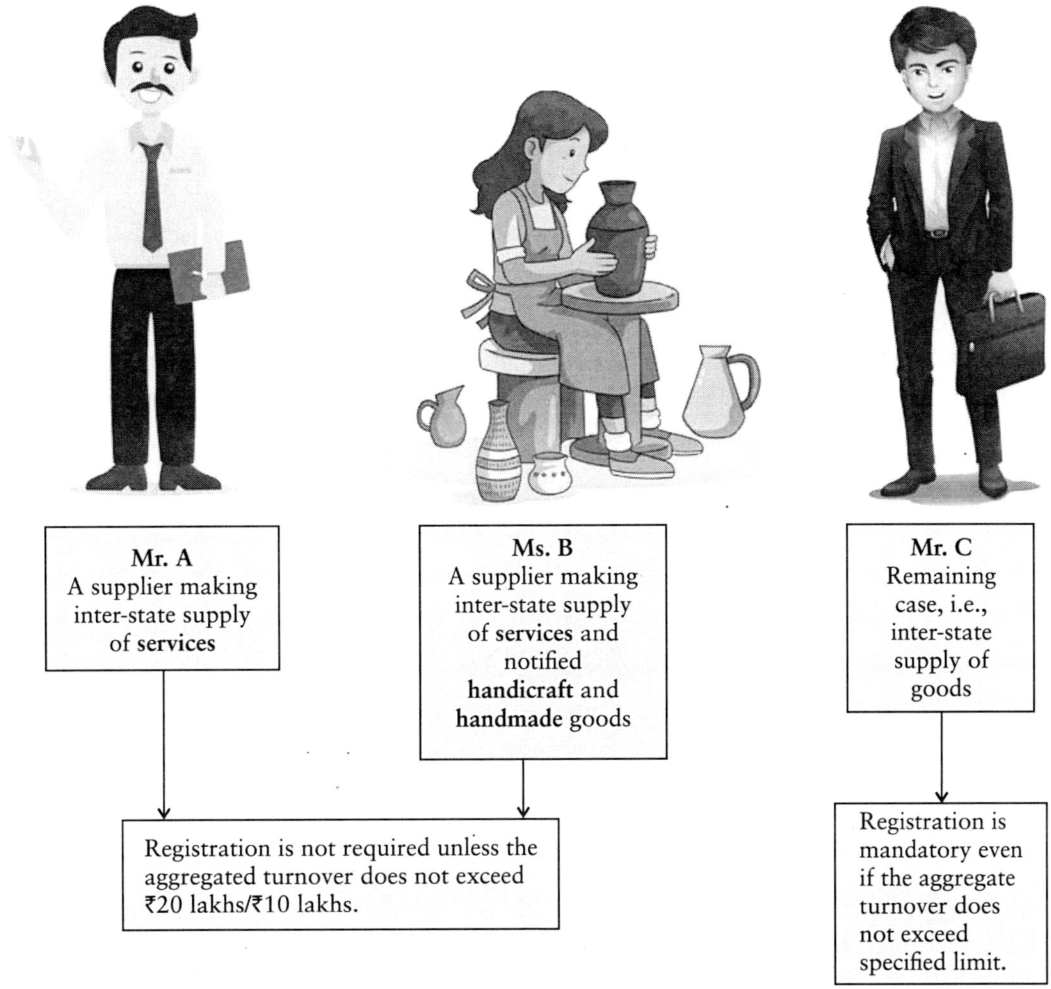

Example 12.10: Mr. A from Delhi supplies a good to Mr. B (registered in Himachal Pradesh). The aggregate turnover of Mr. A is 12 lakhs only during the current year 2021-22. Is he legally liable for registration?

Solution

The location of the supplier is Delhi, and the movement of the goods terminates in Himachal Pradesh; therefore, as per section 10(1)(a), the place of supply is Himachal Pradesh. So, this is a case of inter-state supply of goods. As per section 24, A is mandatorily required to register under GST even if his aggregate turnover does not exceed the specified limit in the case of Delhi, i.e., ₹20 lakhs.

Example 12.11: Suppose that in the previous example Mr. A supplies services to Mr. B. What will be your conclusion now?

Solution

If the services are supplied to a registered recipient, then as per section 12(2), the place of supply is the location of the recipient. Therefore, in the present case, the place of supply is

Himachal Pradesh. The location of the supplier is Delhi, and the place of supply is Himachal Pradesh; therefore, this is a case of inter-state supply of services. Although, under section 24, the supplier of taxable supply is required to take registration compulsorily, in the case of services and notified handicrafts and handmade goods, the exemption from registration can be taken if his aggregate turnover does not exceed a specified limit. In case of Delhi, the specified limit is ₹20 lakhs, and the aggregate turnover of Mr. A is ₹12 lakhs only. Therefore, A is not required to take compulsory registration.

2. A Casual Taxable Person (CTP) making taxable supply: If a casual taxable person makes taxable supply, then he is required to register mandatorily. For example, Mr. A has a place of business in Mumbai only, and he is willing to display and supply goods at the Trade Fair to be held in Delhi. Therefore, he is a casual taxable person and will need registration compulsorily. However, if a casual taxable person supplies notified handicraft and handmade goods, then he can take exemption from registration subject to the following conditions:

(a) He is availing the benefit of Notification No. 3/2018—IT dated 22.10.2018.

(b) His aggregate turnover does not exceed the specified limit of ₹20 lakhs or ₹10 lakhs (in the case of Meghalaya, Manipur, Nagaland and Tripura).

(c) He has a PAN and generated an E-way bill.

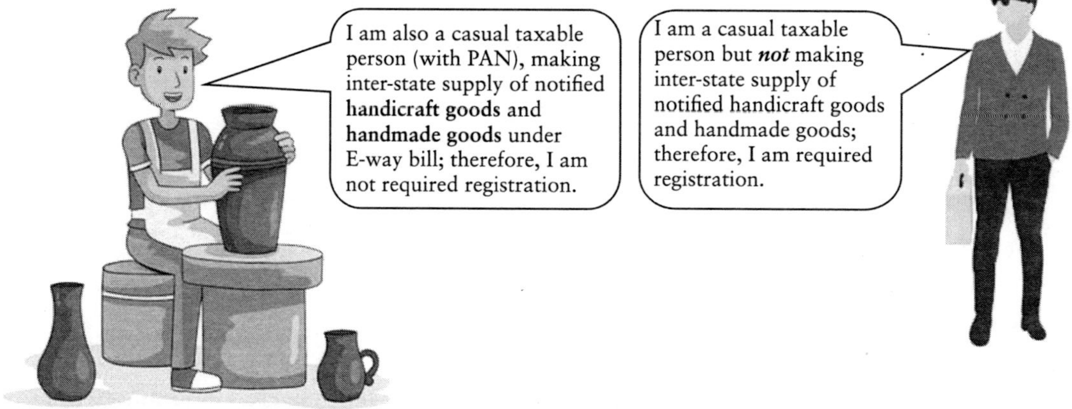

3. The recipient covered under reverse charge mechanism: Persons who are required to pay tax under reverse charge mechanism. For example, a senior advocate supplying legal services to a body corporate is covered under reverse charge mechanism; therefore, he does not need to take GST registration, but the recipient, i.e., body corporate, is required to take registration.

4. Persons who are required to pay tax under section 9(5): According to section 9(5), in case of notified services supplied through an e-commerce operator (ECO), the ECO is liable to pay tax on intra-state supplies as if the ECO is the supplier of those services. The Government has issued *Notification No. 17/2017-Central Tax (Rate), dated 28.06.2017 as amended by Notification No. 23/2017-Central Tax (Rate), dated 22.08.2017 and Notification No. 17/2021-Central Tax (Rate), dated 18.11.2021, to notify the following services:*

(a) Passenger transportation services.
(b) Accommodation services.
(c) Housekeeping services.
(d) Restaurant services (including cloud kitchen). [Effective from 1 January 2022]

Note: This topic has been discussed in detail with examples in Chapter 5.

5. Non-resident taxable persons making taxable supply.

6. Specified persons under section 51: Specified persons who are required to deduct tax under section 51, whether or not separately registered under the CGST Act.

Specified persons:

(a) A department or establishment of the Central Government or State Government.
(b) Local authority.
(c) Government agencies.
(d) Other notified persons.

7. An agent making taxable supply on behalf of others: A person who makes a taxable supply of goods or services or both on behalf of other taxable persons, whether as an agent or otherwise.

8. Input Service Distributor (ISD): Input Service Distributor, whether or not separately registered under the CGST Act.

9. Persons supplying goods or services or both through an e-commerce operator: Those who supply goods or services or both, except notified cases under section 9(5), through such electronic commerce operator who is required to collect tax at source under section 52, are required to take registration compulsorily.

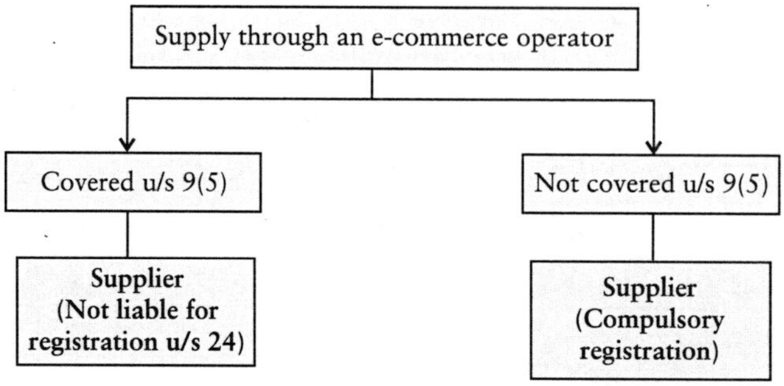

10. E-commerce operator covered under section 52: Every electronic commerce operator who is required to collect tax at source under section 52 is required to take registration mandatorily.

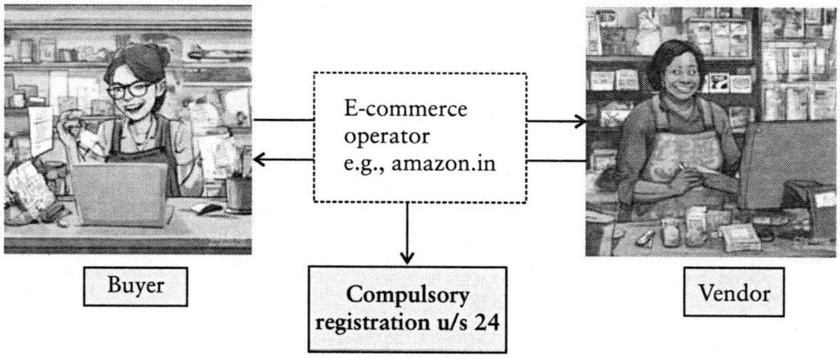

11. Supplier of OIDAR services from outside India to an unregistered person in India: Where a supplier supplies online information and database access or retrieval services (OIDAR) from outside India to an unregistered person in India, the supplier is required to take registration compulsorily.

12. Notified cases: On the recommendation of the GST council, the Government may notify other cases too.

12.5 Procedure for registration—Section 25

1. Time period to apply for registration: Section 25(1): According to this section, every person who is liable for registration under section 22 or section 24 is required to apply for registration (as per rule 10) within the prescribed time limit. There are four cases:

Cases	Time limit	Where to apply
Casual taxable person and non-resident taxable person.	At least 5 days before starting the business.	He shall apply for registration in each such State/UT in which he is liable for registration.
Person covered under section. 22 or 24 except above.	Within 30 days from the date when he becomes liable for registration.	He shall apply for registration in each such State/UT in which he is liable for registration.
A person having an SEZ unit in a SEZ or is an SEZ developer in a state.		He shall apply for separate registration for the unit located outside SEZ in the same State/UT.
Person making supply from territorial waters of India.		He shall obtain registration in the State or UT where the nearest point of the appropriate baseline is located.

Note: SEZ stands for Economic Zone as defined in the SEZ Act, 2005.

2. Number of registrations in a State or UT: Section 25(2) read with Rule 13: This section prescribes the number of registrations in a State/UT. One registration for one State/UT is given. However, if a supplier has multiple places of business/units/branches in a State/UT, then subject to some conditions given in Rule 13, he has the option to apply for multiple registrations in the same State/UT under the same PAN; otherwise he can obtain a single registration for all the places of businesses in the same State/UT. In such case, he will declare one place of business as Principal Place of Business (PPOB) and the remaining places of business as Additional Place of Business (APOB).

Example 12.12: ABC Ltd. supplies some services from Punjab. Its aggregate turnover during the current year is ₹45 lakhs. Comment on the registration requirement of ABC Ltd.

Solution

1. Since the aggregate turnover exceeds the specified limit of ₹20 lakhs (for Punjab), therefore, ABC Ltd. is liable for registration under section 22(1).
2. As per section 25(1), it needs to apply for registration within 30 days from the date when the aggregate turnover exceeds ₹20 lakhs. Further, since taxable supply is made from Punjab, therefore, it is required to take GST registration in Punjab.
3. As per section 25(2), only one registration shall be granted.

Example 12.13: Suppose that in the previous example, ABC Ltd. has two places of business in Punjab, i.e., the head office in Mohali and a branch in Patiala. Can it obtain two separate registrations for the branches?

Solution

Yes, if ABC Ltd. wants two separate registrations for the head office and branch, then this is possible under section 23(2), but some conditions are to be satisfied. The head office may be declared as PPOB and the branch as APOB, or the head office may be declared as APOB and the branch as PPOB.

3. Voluntary Registration: Section 25(3): Although a person is not liable for registration under section 22 or 24, if they want to get registered, then they can apply for registration on voluntary basis. Such a registration is called voluntary registration. Once a voluntary registration is taken, then a specified limit of ₹20 lakhs or ₹10 lakhs is over, and all the provisions of the GST law shall be applicable from the date of registration.

Example 12.14: Shri RK was running a coaching center from 1.01.2019 in East Delhi. The fee per student was ₹500 per month. 100 new students were admitted till 31.03.2020. He voluntarily applied for GST registration and received the registration certificate effective from 01.04.2019. Shri RK was not charging GST from the students because he thought that aggregate turnover did not cross ₹20 lakhs. All the students left the centre after their syllabus was over on 28.02.2020. Was Shri RK doing the right treatment?

Solution

No, he was not legally right. Indeed, he was liable to pay GST from the date of registration, i.e., 01.04.2019 even if the aggregate turnover did not exceed ₹20 lakhs. Specified limit of ₹20 lakhs/₹10 lakhs is for registration, not for deciding tax liability. Therefore, he should have charged GST in the fees for the month of April 2019 and onwards. He collected ₹6,00,000 as coaching fees during the financial year 2019-20.

4. Distinct persons: Section 25(4): A person who has obtained or is required to obtain more than one registration, whether in one State or Union Territory or more than one State or Union Territory shall, in respect of each such registration, be treated as distinct persons for the purposes of the CGST Act.

5. Establishment of distinct persons: Section 25(5): Where a person who has obtained or is required to obtain registration in a State or Union Territory in respect of an establishment has an establishment in another State or Union Territory, then such establishments shall be treated as establishments of distinct persons for the purposes of the CGST Act.

6. PAN is compulsory for registration: Section 25(6): GST registration is PAN-based. Therefore, unless a person does not have a PAN (Permanent Account Number), then he is not eligible for registration. However, the persons liable to deduct at tax at source under section 51 can use the Tax Deduction and Collection Account Number issued under the Income Tax Act.

7. Authentication of Aadhaar: Aadhaar authentication for an already registered person: Section 25(6A):

(a) Every registered person is required to get his Aadhaar card authenticated on the GST portal or furnish proof of possession of the Aadhaar card in a specified manner and time.

(b) If a registered person does not have Aadhaar, then the Government may give other options for authentication.

(c) If an Aadhaar is not authenticated or, proof of its possession is not furnished, or other means of identification (e.g., driver's license) is not furnished, then the registration becomes invalid, and the person is deemed to be an unregistered person.

Aadhaar authentication for every individual as eligibility for registration: Section 25(6B)

To become eligible for registration, every individual is required to

- undergo Aadhaar authentication, or
- furnish proof of possession of Aadhaar in the manner specified by the Government on the recommendations of the GST council.

Note: If an Aadhaar number is not assigned to an individual, such individual shall be offered alternate and viable means of identification in the manner specified by the Government on the recommendation of the GST council.

Aadhaar authentication for every person (except individual) as eligibility for registration: Section 25(6C)

To become eligible for registration, every person, other than individual, is required to

- undergo Aadhaar authentication, or
- furnish proof of possession of Aadhaar number of the
  - Karta,
  - Managing Director,
  - whole time Director,

– such number of partners,
– Members of Managing Committee of Association,
– Board of Trustees,
– authorised representative,
– authorised signatory and
– such other class of persons

in the manner specified by the Government on the recommendation of the GST council.

Note: If an Aadhaar number is not assigned to any of the above persons, then such person shall be offered alternate and viable means of identification in the manner specified by the Government on the recommendation of the GST council.

Non-applicability of section 25(6A) or 25(6B) or 25(6C): Section 25(6D)

The section 25(6A) or 25(6B) or 25(6C) shall not apply to such person or class of persons or any State or Union territory or part thereof specified by the Government on the recommendation of the GST council.

8. PAN is not required in case of registration of non-resident taxable person: Section 25(7) read with Rule 13: Whatever is written in section 25(6), in case of registration of a non-resident taxable person, PAN is not required. Registration to him can be granted as per Rule 13.

9. Suo-motu registration by the proper officer: Section 25(8) and Rule 16: If the proper officer finds that a person is liable for registration but has failed to submit an application for registration, he may temporarily register the said person and issue an order in Form GST REG-12 as per Rule 16(1).

As per rule 16(3), every person who is registered under section 25(8) is required to submit an application for registration in the prescribed form within 90 days from the date of grant of temporary registration. Further, such a person may file an appeal against such temporary registration. If an appeal is filed and the Appellate Authority upholds the liability to registration, an application for registration can be submitted within 30 days from the date of issuance of such order of the Appellate Authority.

10. Specialized Agency: Section 25(9): According to this section, the following agencies are required to take Unique Identity Number (UIN).

(a) any specialized agency of the UNO,
(b) any Multilateral Financial Institution and Organisation notified under the United Nations (Privileges and Immunities) Act, 1947,
(c) consulate or Embassy of foreign countries, and
(d) other persons notified by the commissioner.

11. Rejection after verification only: Section 25(10) read with Rule 9: The application for registration or UIN can be rejected after the verification and within such time as prescribed by Rule 9.

12. Certificate of registration: Section 25(11), Section 25(12), Rule 10: The certificate of registration is granted in FORM GST REG-06, and its effective date is prescribed by Rule 10. If no communication (within 7 working days) is received from the department regarding the deficiency in the application, then the registration or UIN is deemed to have been granted.

12.6 Deemed Registration and Rejection—Section 26

(a) **Section 26(1):** The registration or Unique Identity Number given under an SGST Act/ UTGST Act is deemed to be the registration under the CGST Act.

(b) **Section 26(2):** Any rejection of an application for registration or UIN under the SGST Act/UTGST Act is deemed to be the rejection under the CGST Act.

12.7 Special provisions relating to casual taxable person and non-resident taxable person—Section 27

1. Validity period of registration: Certificate of Registration issued to a casual taxable person (CTP) or a non-resident taxable person (NRTP) is valid for earlier of the following:

(a) the period mentioned in application or

(b) 90 days from the effective date of registration

2. Extension of validity period: If sufficient reasons are given to the proper officer, then he can further extend the above period by a maximum of 90 days.

3. Payment of advance tax: The CTP or NRTP is required to pay advance tax, which is nothing but an estimated tax liability for the period of validity of registration. Such advance tax is increased if an extension is granted by the commissioner. Moreover, this amount of advance tax is credited to the electronic cash ledger of the CTP/NRTP.

12.8 Amendment of Registration—Section 28 and Rule 19

1. The registered person is required to inform about the change: Section 28(1): If there is a change in the information furnished (by a registration person or a person to whom a Unique Identity Number has been given) at the time of registration or subsequent, he must inform the proper officer within 15 days of such change as per Rule 19. For this purpose, application FORM GST REG-14 is furnished either on a common portal or through a facilitation centre.

2. Approval of the proper officer is necessary for change in core information: Section 28(2) read with Rule 29(1): In case of change in core information, i.e., approval of the proper officer is required. The proper officer may accept or reject the application for change, but he is required to give the registered person an opportunity to hear before rejection. If the proper officer, after due verification, approves the changes, then an order in FORM GST REG-15 is issued. If the proper officer thinks that the amendments demanded are not required, or the documents submitted are not correct, then he may issue a show cause notice in FORM GST REG-03 within 15 days of receipt of the application in FORM GST REG-14.

(a) legal name of business,
(b) change in address of principal place of business,
(c) addition, deletion or retirement of partners or directors, Karta, Managing Committee, Board of Trustees, CEO or equivalent, responsible for the day-to-day affairs of the business.

3. Any rejection or approval of amendments under the SGST Act or UTGST Act shall be deemed as rejection or approval under the CGST Act.

4. Change in non-core information: Rule 19(1)(c): If there is a change in non-core information (i.e., information other than mentioned at serial number 2), then such information is deemed to be changed once FORM GST REG-14 is submitted.

5. If there is a change in PAN, then fresh registration is required: Rule 19(1)(d): If a change in the constitution of the business causes the PAN to change, then a fresh registration is required.

Illustration 12.1: Showing the provisions of section 28 and rule 19

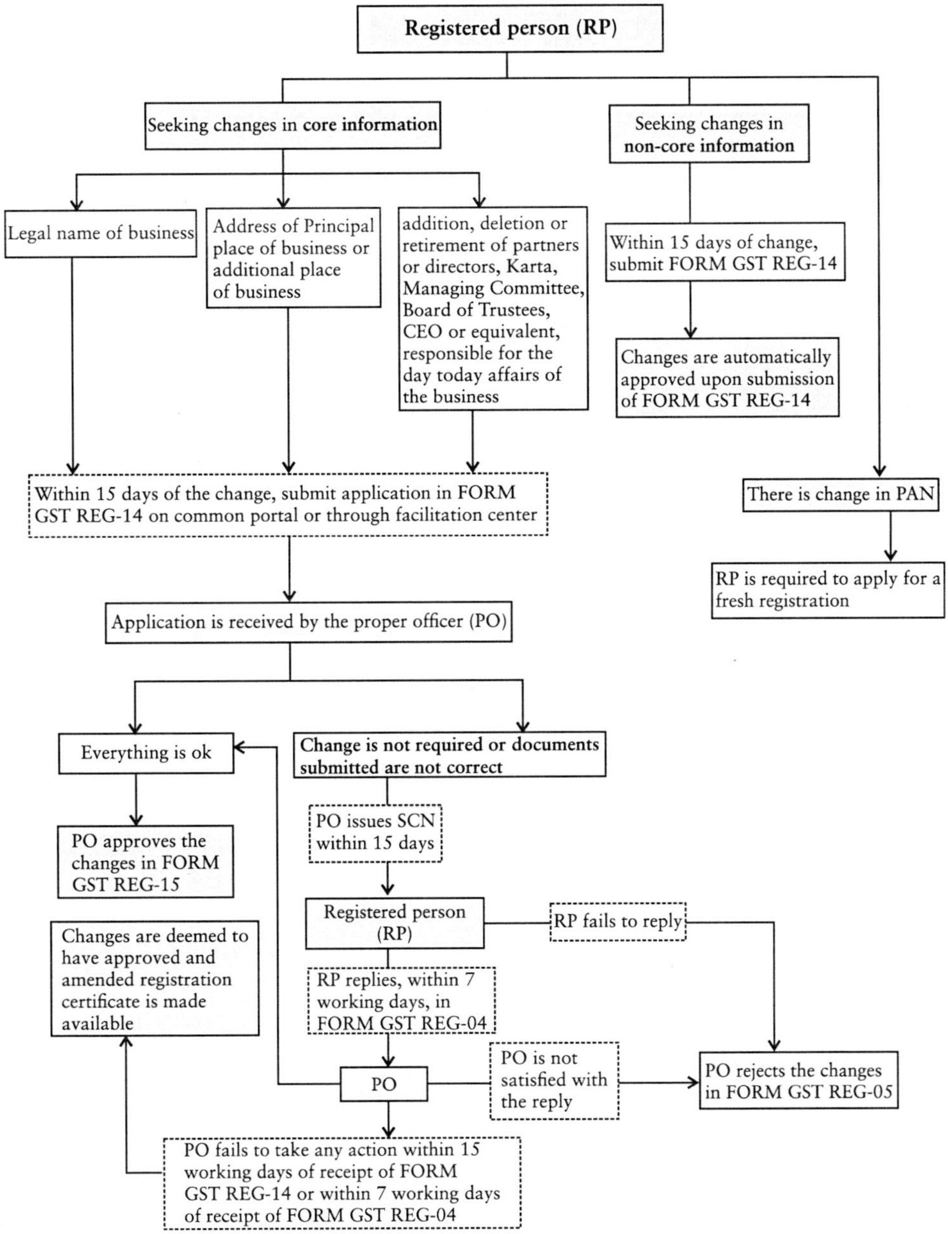

12.9 Cancellation or Suspension of Registration—Section 29

1. Circumstances of registration on application or Suo-motu cancellation: Section 29(1): There are circumstances in which the proper officer has the power to cancel the registration of a person either on his own or if an application for cancellation of registration is submitted by

(a) the registered person

(b) the legal heirs in case of the death of such a person,

Such circumstances are as follows:

1. The business has been discontinued, transferred fully, amalgamated with other entity, demerged or otherwise disposed of;
2. There is any change in the constitution of business;
3. The taxable person is no longer liable to be registered under section 22 or section 24, or he wants to opt out of voluntary registration made under section 25(3).

2. Circumstances of Suo-motu cancellation by the proper officer: Section 29(2): In the following circumstances, the proper officer has the power to cancel the registration on his own motion. Such cancellation is effective from such date as he thinks fit, and even cancellation may be from retrospective effect also.

(a) A registered person contravenes specified provisions of the CGST Act, or rules made thereunder. Rule 21 specifies such provisions, which are as follows:
(i) The said person does not conduct business from the declared place of business. (ii) He issues invoices/bills of supply without the actual supply of goods or services or both. (iii) He violates section 171 of the CGST Act, or rules made thereunder. (iv) He violates rule 10A. (v) He avails input tax credit which is against section 16 of the CGST Act or rules made thereunder. (vi) He furnishes the details of outward supplies in FORM GSTR-1 under section 37 for one or more tax periods, which is in excess of the outward supplies declared by him in his valid return under section 39 for the said tax periods. (vii) He violates rule 86B. (viii) Being a registered person required to file a return under section 39(1) for each month or part thereof, has not furnished returns for a continuous period of 6 months; (ix) being a registered person required to file a return under proviso to section 39(1) for each quarter or part thereof, has not furnished returns for a continuous period of 2 tax periods.
(b) A person who has adopted composition levy under section 10, but have not filed the return for a financial year beyond 3 months from the due date.
(c) A person (other than the composition levy one) has not filed the returns for a specified continuous tax period.
(d) Any registered person who has taken voluntarily registration, but has not commenced business within 6 months from the date of registration.
(e) Registration has been taken by means of fraud, willful misstatement or suppression of facts.

Note: The proper officer shall give an opportunity to be heard before cancellation of the registration.

3. Cancellation of registration shall not affect any liability under the CGST Act/Rules: Section 29(3): The cancellation of registration does not relieve the person from their responsibility to pay taxes and other dues or fulfil any obligations under this Act or its rules for any period before the cancellation. This applies regardless of whether the taxes and dues have been determined before or after the cancellation.

4. Deemed cancellation: Section 29(4): Cancellation of registration under the SGST/UTGST Act is deemed to be the cancellation of registration under the CGST Act.

5. Effect of cancellation on input tax credit: Section 29(5) read with Rule 44: When registration is cancelled, the person whose registration has been cancelled, is required to reverse the input tax credit availed on inputs held in stock,

- inputs contained in semi-finished goods or
- inputs contained in finished goods or
- capital goods or plant and machinery

Note: This topic has been discussed in detail in the Chapter on Input Tax Credit.

12.10 Revocation of cancellation of registration—Section 30 and Rule 23

1. Time period to apply for revocation: Section 30(1): In case of Suo-motu cancellation by a proper officer, the registered person may apply within such time and manner and such conditions and restrictions as may be specified [**Amended by Section 141(a) of the Finance Act, 2023**]. Such application shall be filed in FORM GST REG-21.

Also, the readers are advised to refer Notification 03/2023-Central Tax: Dated: 31 March 2023 in this regard. This notification is available on the CBIC website.

2. Acceptance or Rejection of the above said application: Section 30(2)

(a) If the proper officer has reasons for revocation of cancellation, then he shall pass an order of revocation of cancellation in FORM GST REG-22 within 30 days of receipt of the application and communicate about the same to the applicant.

(b) If the proper officer is not satisfied with the application, then he may reject it after giving the applicant an opportunity to be heard. For this purpose, the proper officer shall issue a Show Cause Notice in FORM GST REG-23 to the applicant, who shall reply to the notice in FORM GST REG-24 within 7 working days of service of the notice. Moreover, the proper officer has to decide about acceptance or rejection within 30 days from the date of application.

(c) No application for revocation shall be filed if the registration has been cancelled for the failure of the registered person to furnish returns unless such returns are furnished and any amount due as tax, in terms of such returns, has been paid along with any amount payable towards interest, penalty and late fee in respect of the said returns.

3. Deemed revocation for cancellation: Section 30(3): Revocation of registration cancellation under the SGST/UTGST Act shall be deemed to be cancellation of registration under the CGST Act.

12.11 Application to generation of acknowledgement—Rule 8

1. Application for registration: Rule 8(1): A person who is required to take registration under section 25(1) or who is willing to take voluntary registration is required to apply in FORM GST REG-01 on the common portal or through a facilitation centre. FORM GST REG-01 consists of two parts: Part A and Part B. The applicant shall declare his PAN and his State or Union territory in Part A before proceeding further.

Note: In the case of an input service distributor (ISD), a separate application for registration as ISD shall be filed even if he is already registered.

2. Verification of PAN, Mobile number and email address: Rule 8(2): The PAN is verified from the database maintained by the CBDT. It is further validated by sending OTPs on the mobile number and email address linked to the PAN. *Notification No. 26/2022-Central Tax, dated 26.12.2022,* has omitted the requirement of verification of the mobile number and email address provided in Part A because they are verified indirectly through the PAN.

3. Generation of Temporary Reference Number (TRN): Rule 8(3): Once the PAN, mobile number, and email address are verified, a *TRN* is generated which is sent to the mobile and email address verified.

4. Furnishing application in Part B of FORM GST REG-01: Rule 8(4): The above-generated TRN is used to furnish part B of FORM GST REG-01. This application must be duly signed or verified using an electronic verification code (EVC). Further, the documents specified in the form are also required to be submitted on the common portal or through the facilitation centre.

5. Biometric-based Aadhaar Authentication for high-risk applicant: Rule 8(4A): [Inserted by Notification No. 26/2022-Central Tax (Rate), dated 26.12.2022]

(a) A person who has opted to undergo the Aadhaar authentication and the common portal shows the person a high-risk applicant; then the application shall go under a biometric-based Aadhaar authentication process.

(b) Apart, the photograph of the following persons shall be taken
  (i) if the applicant is an individual, then the individual and
  (ii) in the case of other applicants, such persons who are notified under section 25(6C).

(c) This process shall be conducted at a facilitation centre notified by the Commissioner.

(d) Verification of the original copy of the documents submitted with the application shall also be done at the facilitation centre.

(e) Only after completing this process the application shall be considered complete.

(f) This rule is applicable in Gujarat only as of now.

(g) The person who is covered under section 25(6D) is not covered by this rule of biometric authentication.

Also, the readers are advised to refer *Notification No. 04/2023-Central Tax, dated 31 March 2023,* in this regard. This notification is available on the CBIC website.

6. The Government may notify the States/UTs where biometric authentication is not required: Rule 8(4B): On the recommendation of the GST council, the Government may notify the State/UT that biometric authentication is not required—Rule 8(4B).

7. **Generation of acknowledgement—Rule 8(5) and Rule 8(6):** Once the application for registration is submitted, an acknowledgement is generated and made available to the applicant in FORM GST REG-02. However, in the case of a casual taxable person, the acknowledgement is generated after he pays the advance tax.

12.12 Verification of the application and its approval—Rule 9

1. **Verification of the application by the proper officer: Rule 9(1)**
   - **Forward of the application to the proper officer:** The application submitted as per Rule 8 is forwarded to the proper officer who is required to examine the same and the documents attached.
   - **Approval for registration if everything is in order:** If everything is found in order, then the proper officer approves the registration within 7 working days from the date of submission of the application.
   - **Need of physical verification of the place of business:** After taking permission from the assistant commissioner or above rank, the proper officer carries out physical verification of the place of business if the applicant [except those mentioned under section 25(6D)]

(a) fails to undergo Aadhaar number authentication or
(b) does not opt for Aadhaar authentication
(c) who has undergone Aadhaar authentication and the common portal system alerts for the need of physical verification.

   - Approval of registration after physical verification: Once the physical verification of the place of business in the presence of the applicant is carried out, the proper officer approves registration within 30 days of the submission of the application.
2. **The proper officer wants some clarification from the applicant: Rule 9(2)**
   - **Issue of notice in FORM GST REG-03:** If the proper officer, while examining the application, finds that the application is deficient due to some information or document, then he may ask for clarification from the applicant. Such clarification is asked by issuing a notice in FORM GST REG-03 within 7 working days. The applicant is required to reply to the notice in FORM GST REG-04 within 7 working days from the date of receipt of the notice. Further, FORM GST REG-03 may also be issued (within 30 days from the date of submission of the application) to carry out the physical verification of the place of business, but prior approval from the assistant commissioner or above rank is necessary. Cases of the need for physical verification are the same as discussed in rule 9(1).

     Note: The term clarification includes modification or correction of particulars declared in the application for registration other than the Permanent Account Number, State, mobile number and e-mail address declared in Part A of FORM GST REG-01.
   - **Approval for the registration:** Where the proper officer is satisfied with the clarification, information or documents furnished by the applicant, he may approve the grant of registration to the applicant within a period of 7 working days from the date of the receipt of such clarification or information or documents.

- **No reply submitted by the applicant:** Where no reply is submitted by the applicant in response to the notice served above, or where the proper officer is not satisfied with the response submitted, then the proper officer can reject the registration application in FORM GST REG-05. However, the reasons for rejection must be recorded in writing.

3. **Deemed approval: Rule 9(5):** The registration is deemed to have been approved if the proper officer does not take any action

(a) within 7 working days from the date of submission of the application in cases where physical verification is not required under Rule 9(1).
(b) within 30 days from the date of submission of the application in cases where physical verification is required under Rule 9(1).
(c) within 7 working days from the date of the receipt of the clarification, information or documents furnished by the applicant under Rule 9(2).

12.13 Issue of Registration Certificate—Rule 10

1. **Registration certificate in FORM GST REG-06: Rule 10(1):** Subject to the provisions of section 25(12), where the registration has been approved under rule 9, a registration certificate in FORM GST REG-06 is made available to the applicant on the common portal. The registration form contains various details, including the Goods and Service Tax Identification Number (GSTIN) or UIN.

2. **GSTIN: Rule 10(1):** GSTIN is PAN based number, which consists of 15 characters, the explanation of which are as follows:

(a) the first two characters represent the State code,
(b) the next ten characters represent the PAN or the Tax Deduction and Collection Account Number,
(c) the next two characters represent the entity code, and
(d) the last character is the checksum character.

For example, suppose that a hypothetical GSTIN is 07ATIHK1453D1ZF, then

07	ATIHK1453D	1Z	F
State code	PAN of the registered person	Entity code	Checksum character

3. **Effective date of registration**

(a) **Application for registration submitted within 30 days: Rule 10(2):** If the application for registration is submitted within 30 days from the date when the person becomes liable for registration, then such date is the effective date of registration.

(b) **Application for registration not submitted within 30 days: Rule 10(3):** In such case, the effective date of registration shall be the date of the grant of registration under Rule 9(1) or Rule 9(3) or Rule 9(5).

4. **Registration certification must be signed or verified by the proper officer: Rule 10(4):** Every certificate of registration shall be duly signed or verified through an electronic verification code by the proper officer under the CGST Act.

5. **Communication and making the registration certificate available: Rule 10(5):** The registration certificate shall be made available to the applicant on the common portal within 3 days after the expiry of the period specified in Rule 9(5).

12.14 Furnishing of Bank Account Details—Rule 10A

A person who has been granted a registration certificate (except those who are covered under Rule 12) is required to furnish bank account details or any other information as may be required on the common portal to comply with any other provision. Such bank details or the information must be furnished as soon as possible, but the time limit is *earlier* of the following:

(i) 45 days from the date of registration

(ii) Due date to furnish return under section 39

12.15 Aadhaar Authentication for Registered Person—Rule 10B

The registered person, except the person notified under section 25(6D), who has been issued a certificate of registration under Rule 10 is required to go under the Aadhaar number authentication of the following persons (given below in the table) in order to be eligible for the following purposes:

1. for filing of application for revocation of cancellation of registration in FORM GST REG-21 under Rule 23.
2. for filing of refund application in FORM RFD-01 under Rule 89.
3. for refund under Rule 96 of the IGST paid on goods exported out of India.

Cases	Persons whose Aadhaar is to be authenticated
proprietorship firm	the proprietor
partnership firm	any partner
Hindu undivided family	the karta
company	the Managing Director or any full-time Director
Any managing committee member	the Association of persons or body of individuals or a Society
Trust	the Trustee in the Board of Trustees
–	the authorised signatory

If the Aadhaar number is not assigned, then the following documents can be furnished, but the Aadhaar authentication is still required within 30 days of the allotment of the Aadhaar number.

1. The Aadhaar Enrolment ID slip; and
2. Bank passbook with photograph; or
3. Voter identity card issued by the Election Commission of India; or
4. Passport; or
5. Driving license issued by the Licensing Authority under the Motor Vehicles Act, 1988)

Illustration 12.2: Showing the provisions of Rules 8, 9 and 10

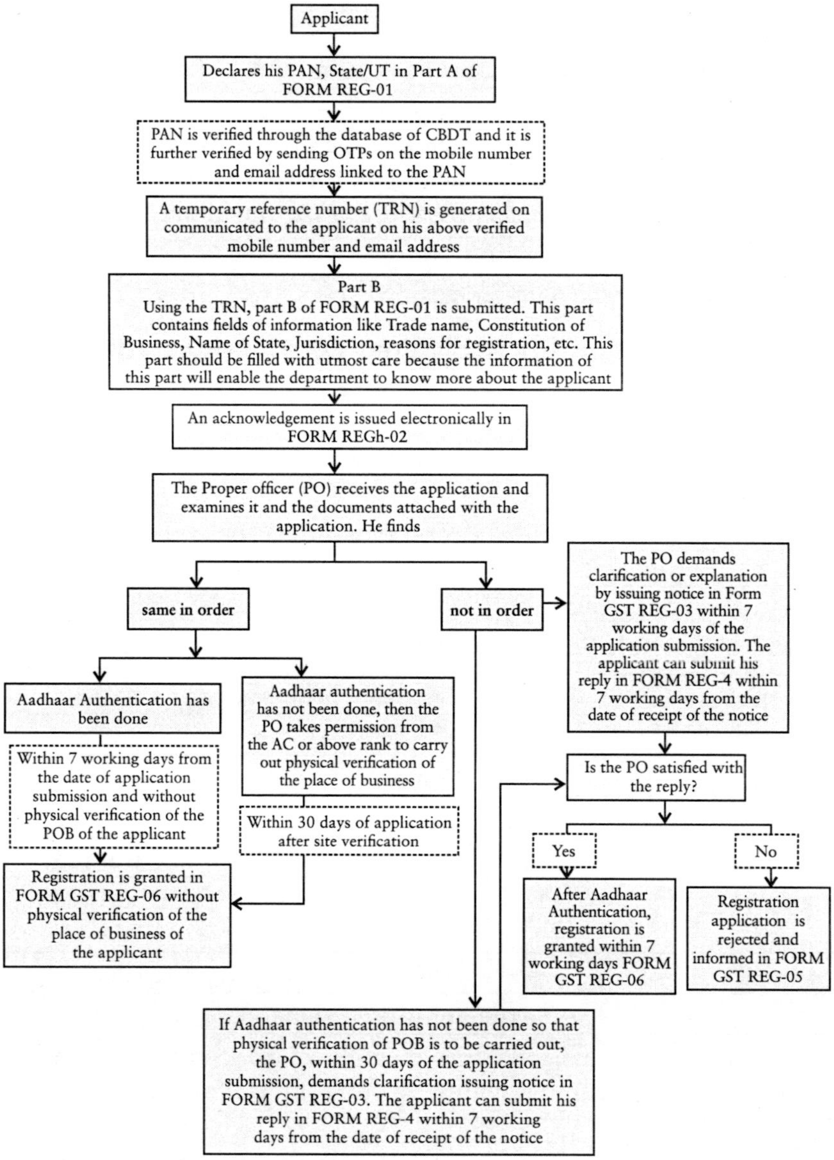

12.16 Separate registration for multiple places of business within a State or a Union territory—Rule 11

1. **Conditions to take registration for multiple places of businesses in a State or UT: Rule 11(1):** If a person has multiple places of business in a State or Union territory and wants to register each place of business separately, then he may be granted separate registrations for each place of business under section 25(2) if he satisfies the following conditions:

(a) such person has more than one place of business as defined in section 2(85).
(b) he cannot opt composition levy (under section 10) for one place of business and regular levy (under section 9) for some other place of business. Moreover, if a place of business loses its eligibility for composition levy, then all other places of businesses shall also lose their eligibility for composition levy.
(c) Such the registered places of businesses shall be treated as district persons.

2. Separate application is required for each place of business: Rule 11(2): A registered person willing to take separate registration for each place of business in a State or Union territory, then he is required to submit a separate application in FORM GST REG-01 for each such place of business.

3. Applicability of Rules 9 and 10: Rule 11(3): Rules 9 and 10 of verification and the grant of registration, respectively, are also, with necessary changes and adjustments, applicable here.

12.17 Grant of registration to persons required to deduct tax at source or to collect tax at source—Rule 12

1. Application for those who are covered under section 51 and section 52: Rule 12(1) and Rule 13(1A)

- Any person (who is liable to deduct tax at source under section 51 or to collect tax at source under section 52) is required to submit the registration application in FORM GST REG-07. Such application shall be furnished on the common portal or through the facilitation centre, and the same must be signed or verified through an electronic verification code.
- If the above person wants to apply for registration in a State or UT where he does not have a physical presence, then he is required to mention the name of the State or UT in PART A of FORM GST REG-07 and mention the name of the State or UT in PART B in which the principal place of business is located which may be different from the State or UT in PART A.

2. Grant of registration: Rule 13(2): After due verification, the proper officer grants registration and issues a registration certificate in FORM GST REG-06 within 3 working days from the date of application submission.

3. Registration cancellation by the proper officer: Rule 13(3): On giving a written request by the person [to whom registration has been granted under Rule 13(2)] or due to an enquiry or pursuant to any other proceeding under the CGST Act, if the proper officer is satisfied that the person is no longer liable to deduct tax at source or collect at source, the proper officer has power to cancel the registration and the person is communicated about the cancellation in FORM GST REG-08. However, the proper officer is required to follow Rule 22 in this regard.

12.18 Registration to non-resident taxable person—Rule 13

1. Application and time limit to apply for registration: Rule 13(1): A non-resident taxable person is required to apply for registration (at least 5 days before the commencement of business) in FORM GST REG-09 and submit a self-attested copy of his valid passport with the application at the common portal either directly or through a Facilitation Centre notified by the Commissioner.

The registration application must be duly signed or verified through an electronic verification code (EVC) by his authorised signatory, who shall be a person resident in India having a valid Permanent Account Number.

Note: If a business entity is incorporated or established outside India, the registration application can be submitted along with its tax identification number (TIN) or unique number on the basis of which such entity is identified by the Government of that country or its PAN, if available.

2. Generation of Acknowledgement (TRN): Rule 13(2): After submitting the application for registration, the non-resident taxable person is assigned a temporary reference number (TRN), which is used to make an advance deposit of tax as per the provisions of section 27, and once the deposit appears in his electronic cash ledger, an acknowledgement is generated in FORM GST REG-02.

3. Applicability of Rules 9 and 10 in case of registration of non-resident taxable person: Rule 13(3): The rules about verification and issue of certificate of registration (which are rule 9 and rule 10 respectively) also apply to this particular situation, with some changes that are necessary to make the rules fit.

Theory Questions

1. Is registration under GST always mandatory? Explain.
2. The threshold limit registration is the same across India. Do you agree?
3. Under what cases is registration mandatory?
4. Is registration within a single State or Union Territory Possible?
5. What are the provisions of registration applicable to non-resident taxable persons and casual taxable persons?
6. Can registration be cancelled by the GST Department?
7. Can a registered person apply for de-registration?
8. What is the procedure for registration?
9. What are the cases in which there is no need to take registration?
10. If someone is liable to get himself registered from a date, then it does not mean he is not liable to pay GST from that date because the registration certificate is received later. Do you agree?
11. What is the significance of the AADHAAR number under the GST registration?
12. What are the provisions of registration for specified organisations?

13

Invoice, Debit Note, Credit Note and Other Documents

13.1 Introduction

Tax invoices, debit notes and credit notes are very important documents. A recipient is not eligible for an input tax credit if he does not possess a tax invoice or debit note. Moreover, these documents are the evidence of the supply and are very useful for accounting, assessment and audit purposes. Sections 31 to 34 are related to these documents.

13.2 Time limit to issue a tax invoice in case of goods—Section 31

Case I: Supply involves movement of goods: Section 31(1)(a): When goods are required to be moved from one place to another so that supply takes place, then this is said that the supply involves the movement of goods. This movement of goods can be undertaken by the supplier or recipient or even a third person. As per section 31(1)(a), a supplier is required to issue a tax invoice **before or at the time of removal of goods** for supply to the recipient.

Case II: Supply DOES NOT involve movement of goods: Section 31(1)(b): When goods are required to be moved from one place to another so that supply takes place, then this is said that the supply involves the movement of goods. This movement of goods can be undertaken by the supplier or recipient or even a third person. As per section 31(1)(b), a supplier is required to issue a tax invoice **before or at the time of delivery of goods or making them available to the recipient** for supply to the recipient.

Example 13.1: On 1 May 2022, a builder sells a furnished home. What should be the time of issue of a tax invoice for selling furniture?

Solution

There is no need to move the furniture to deliver it to the buyer because the house is already equipped. Therefore, the supply of the furniture does not involve movement; hence, up to 1.5.2022, the builder must issue a tax invoice.

13.3 Time limit to issue tax invoice in case of continuous supply of goods—Section 31(4)

Section 2(32) defines continuous supply of goods as a supply of goods which is provided, or agreed to be provided, continuously or on a recurrent basis, under a contract, whether or not by means of a wire, cable, pipeline or other conduits, and for which the supplier invoices the recipient on a regular or periodic basis and includes the supply of such goods as the Government may, subject to such conditions, as it may, by notification, specify.

In case of continuous supply of goods, where successive statements of accounts or successive payments are involved, the invoice shall be issued before or at the time each such statement is issued or, as the case may be, each such payment is received.

Example 13.2: A is a supplier of beverage products. He enters into an agreement with B Ltd. to supply 30 water bottles and 50 lassi bottles per week. As per the agreement, the supplier shall issue a statement of quantities and other details at the end of each month.

Solution

This is the case of a continuous supply of goods. Therefore, as per section 31(4), A must issue an invoice before or at the time of issuing the statement of quantities and other details, i.e., at the end of each month.

13.4 Time limit to issue tax invoice in case of services—Section 31(2) read with Rule 47

Although the invoice may be issued before or after service, as per Rule 47, it must be issued within 30 days (45 days in the case of insurers, banking companies, financial institutions and NBFCs) from of the date of service.

Rule 47 also provides that an insurer, banking company, financial institution, NBFC, telecom operator, or other notified persons making taxable supplies between distinct persons may issue a tax invoice.

(a) before or at the time of recording the supply in books of account or
(b) before the expiry of the quarter during which the supply is made.

13.5 Revised invoice—Section 31(3)(a)

Suppose that the aggregate turnover of Mr. A exceeds ₹20 lakhs on 1.4.2022. He applied for GST registration on 5.4.2022 and received the registration certificate on 10.4.2022. It is obvious that he is liable to pay tax from 1.4.2022 but received GSTIN on 10.4.2022. Now a question arises, i.e., if he is liable to pay GST from 1.4.2022, then how will he issue a tax invoice during the period 1.4.2022 to 9.4.2022 because it is necessary to show the GSTIN number in the invoice and GSTIN is received on 10.4.2022? To answer this question, section 31(3)(a) has been inserted.

The section states that a registered person can issue a revised invoice (in a prescribed manner) against the invoice already issued during the period beginning with the effective date of registration till the date of issue of the registration certificate.

Note: Consolidated Revised Tax invoice may be issued in respect of taxable supplies made to an unregistered person during the relevant period. However, in the case of inter-state supplies, a consolidated revised tax invoice cannot be issued if the value of supply exceeds ₹2.5 lakhs during the relevant period.

13.6 Not necessary to issue tax invoice if the value of supply is less than ₹200—Section 31(3)(b)

A registered person may not issue a tax invoice if the value of the supply is not greater than ₹200. However, if a registered recipient wants a tax invoice, then the registered person shall issue the tax invoice. Moreover, a consolidated tax invoice shall be issued for such supplies at the close of each day.

Example 13.3: Suppose that a registered supplier named ABC Ltd. sells a pack of pens to a registered buyer named XYZ Corp. for a price of ₹150. Since the value of the supply is less than ₹200, ABC Ltd. is not required to issue a tax invoice for this transaction.

However, let us say that XYZ Corp. requires a tax invoice for this purchase in order to claim an input tax credit (ITC) for the GST paid on the pens. In this case, even though the value of the supply is less than ₹200, ABC Ltd. must issue a tax invoice to XYZ Corp. upon request.

13.7 Issue of bill of supply in lieu of tax invoice—Section 31(3)(c)

(a) If a person opts for a composition scheme under section 10, then he is required to issue a bill of supply in lieu of a tax invoice.

(b) The registered person may not issue a bill of supply if the value of the goods or services or both supplied is less than ₹200 subject to such conditions and in such manner as may be prescribed.

(c) Moreover, a registered supplier making exempt supply also issues a bill of supply.

13.8 Receipt and Refund voucher in case of advance payment—Section 31(3)(d)/(e)

1. According to section 31(3)(d), when a supplier receives an advance payment, then he is required to issue a **receipt voucher** or any other document with such details as prescribed by Rule 50.
2. According to section 31(3)(e), if after receiving an advance payment, the supply is not made and no tax invoice is issued, then the supplier is required to issue a **refund voucher**.

Note: Where at the time of receipt of the advance, the rate of tax or nature supply cannot be determined, then the tax rate shall be 18%, and supply shall be inter-state supply.

13.9 Tax invoice and payment voucher in case of Reverse Charge Mechanism—Section 31(3)(f)/(g)

We know that under the reverse charge mechanism, a recipient is liable to pay tax to the Government. According to section 31(3)(f), if the supplier is unregistered, then the recipient is required to issue a tax invoice. Moreover, section 31(3)(g) provides that the recipient shall issue a payment voucher at the time of payment to the supplier.

13.10 Issue of Invoice in case of continuous supply of goods—Section 31(4)

In case of continuous supply of goods, where successive statements of accounts or successive payments are involved, the invoice shall be issued before or at the time each such statement is issued or, as the case may be, each such payment is received.

13.11 Issue of Invoice in case of continuous supply of services—Section 31(5)

(a) Where the due date of payment is ascertainable from the contract, the invoice shall be issued on or before the due date of payment.

Example 13.4: Suppose that Company X and Mr. Y enter into a contract for continuous services where Y will provide graphic design services to Company X for 12 months. The contract specifies that the due date for payment will be the 5th day of the next month. In this example, the due date of payment is ascertainable from the contract of continuous service; therefore, Y is required to issue a tax invoice on or before the 5th day of the next month.

(b) Where the due date of payment is not ascertainable from the contract, the invoice shall be issued before or at the time when the supplier of service receives the payment.

Example 13.5: Let us say that you own a lawn care business, and you have a client who has contracted with you for continuous lawn maintenance services for 36 months. The contract does not specify a due date for payment. In this case, the due date of payment is not ascertainable from the contract of continuous service. As a result, you would need to issue an invoice before or at the time when you receive payment from the client.

(c) Where the payment is linked to the completion of an event, the invoice shall be issued on or before the date of completion of that event.

Example 13.6: Let us say you are a registered freelance web developer, and you have been hired to create a new website for a client. Your contract with the client specifies that payment for your services will be linked to the completion of the website. In this case, the event that triggers the payment is the completion of the website. Once you have finished building the website and the client has approved it, you can issue an invoice to the client. The invoice should be issued on or before the date of completion of the website, as specified in the contract.

13.12 Issue of invoice in case of Cease of Service—Section 31(6)

In a case where the supply of services ceases under a contract before the completion of the supply, the invoice shall be issued at the time when the supply ceases, and such invoice shall be issued to the extent of the supply made before such cessation.

Example 13.7: Suppose that a company has entered into a contract with a service provider to provide IT services for a period of 15 months. The service provider begins providing the IT services in February and continues to provide them until May, at which point they cease providing the services due to unforeseen circumstances. Therefore, the service provider will issue an invoice at the end of May.

13.13 Issue of invoice in case of goods sent or taken on approval basis—Section 31(6)

Notwithstanding anything contained under section 31(1), where the goods being sent or taken on approval for sale or return are removed before the supply takes place, the invoice shall be issued

(a) before or at the time of supply or
(b) Six months from the date of removal,
whichever is earlier.

13.14 Prohibition of Unauthorized Tax Collection—Section 32

An unregistered person cannot collect any tax, and a registered person can collect tax only as per the provisions of the CGST Act or rules made thereunder.

13.15 Amount of tax to be indicated in tax invoice and other documents—Section 33

Notwithstanding anything contained in this Act or any other law for the time being in force, where any supply is made for a consideration, every person who is liable to pay tax for such supply shall prominently indicate in all documents relating to assessment, tax invoice and other like documents, the amount of tax which shall form part of the price at which such supply is made. It simply means that if someone supplies something and charges a tax for it, they have to clearly show the amount of tax on any documents related to the supply. This includes things like invoices and receipts. The tax amount is part of the total price of the item being supplied.

13.16 Credit and Debit Notes—Section 34

Credit Note: Section 34(1)/(2): In the following cases, a supplier may issue a credit note to the recipient in a financial year containing such particulars as prescribed under Rule 53.

(a) excess taxable value has been shown in the tax invoice or
(b) excess tax has been charged in the tax invoice or
(c) the recipient has returned the goods supplied or
(d) where goods or services or both supplied are found to be deficient

The details of such credit note shall be furnished in the return for the month during which such credit note has been issued up to **earlier** of the following dates:

(a) 30 November following the end of the financial year in which such supply was made or
(b) the date of furnishing of the relevant annual return.

Note: The tax liability shall be adjusted in such manner as may be prescribed, and the tax incidence and interest has not been passed to any other person.

Debit Note: Section 34(3)/(4): In the following cases, a supplier may issue a debit note to the recipient in a financial year containing such particulars as prescribed under Rule 53.

(a) less taxable value has been shown in the tax invoice or
(b) less tax has been charged in the tax invoice or

The details of such debit note shall be furnished in the return for the month during which such debit note has been issued, and the tax liability shall be adjusted in such manner as may be prescribed.

13.17 Invoice-cum-bill of supply—Rule 46A

Irrespective of anything contained in Rules 46, 49, 54, where a registered person makes taxable as well as exempt supply to an unregistered person, a single "invoice-cum-bill of supply" may be issued for all such supplies. Moreover, as per *Notification No. 26/2022 Central Tax, dated 26.12.2022*, such invoice-cum-bill of supply shall contain the particulars as prescribed in Rule 46, or Rule 49, or Rule 54 as the case may be.

13.18 Manner of Issuing invoice—Rule 48

(a) In the case of goods, an invoice shall be issued in triplicate (the original is for the recipient, the duplicate is for the transporter, and the triplicate is for the supplier). However, in the case of services, two copies shall be issued (the original one for the recipient and the duplicate copy for the supplier).

(b) The serial numbers of the invoices issued during a tax period shall be furnished in GSTR 1.

Theory Questions

1. What is the time limit to issue a tax in case of goods?
2. What is the time limit to issue a tax invoice for services?
3. What are the circumstances when a debit note can be issued?
4. Under what circumstances can a credit note be issued?

Case-based Questions (Unsolved)

1. Rakesh, a registered supplier, has a grocery store in Delhi. He makes taxable as well as exempt supplies. You are required to advise him on the following matters:
   (a) Whether is he required to issue a tax invoice in all cases, even if he is supplying the goods to the end consumers?
   (b) Since he makes taxable as well as exempt supplies, therefore, is he required to issue two separate invoices or documents?
   (c) Is it necessary to show the tax amount separately in the invoice issued?

   Answer: (a) No, he is not required to issue a tax invoice in all cases—Section 31(1)/(3); (b) No, he is not required to issue to separate invoices or documents—Rule 46A; (c) Yes.

2. Mr. Bittoo makes continuous supply to his client, where the due date of payment is not determinable. No advance has been received on this behalf. Advise him to issue a time limit to issue tax invoices.

   Answer: The invoice can be issued before or at the time when the payment is received by the supplier—Section 31(5).

14

Payment of Tax, Interest, Penalty and Other Amounts

14.1 Introduction

This chapter discusses the aspects of payment of GST, interest, penalty, and other amounts. Sections 49, 50, 51, 52 and 53 are relevant sections.

14.2 Three Electronic Ledgers—Section 49

Before we move further, it is necessary to know the meanings of three ledgers available on GST Common Portal in digital format. These ledgers are as follows:

(a) **Electronic Cash Ledger:** If a registered individual needs to make payments such as tax, interest, penalty, etc., using cash, they do not directly pay from their bank account. Instead, the necessary amount is transferred from their bank account to a digital ledger (known as electronic cash ledger), which is similar to an e-wallet on the GST Common portal, comparable to the one found on Paytm. The registered person maintains their cash balance in this ledger, which can be utilized whenever required. Other relevant points are as follows:

1. Electronic cash ledger is maintained in FORM GST PMT-05.
2. Deposit to an electronic cash ledger can be made by generating a challan in FORM GST PMT-06 (valid for 15 days) and then transfer of money through any of the following modes:

- Internet banking
- Credit card or debit card
- NEFT or RTGS
- Over the counter payment through authorized banks for deposit up to ₹10,000 per challan per tax period, by cash, cheque, or demand draft (DD). However, this restriction is not applicable in the case of some persons mentioned in Rule 87(3).

3. Electronic cash ledger contains two heads classified as major heads and minor heads.

Major Heads	Minor Heads
Integrated tax	Tax
Central tax	Interest
State tax	Penalty
Cess	Fee
	Others

Here is an extract of the electronic cash ledger, which shows how major and minor heads appear in it.

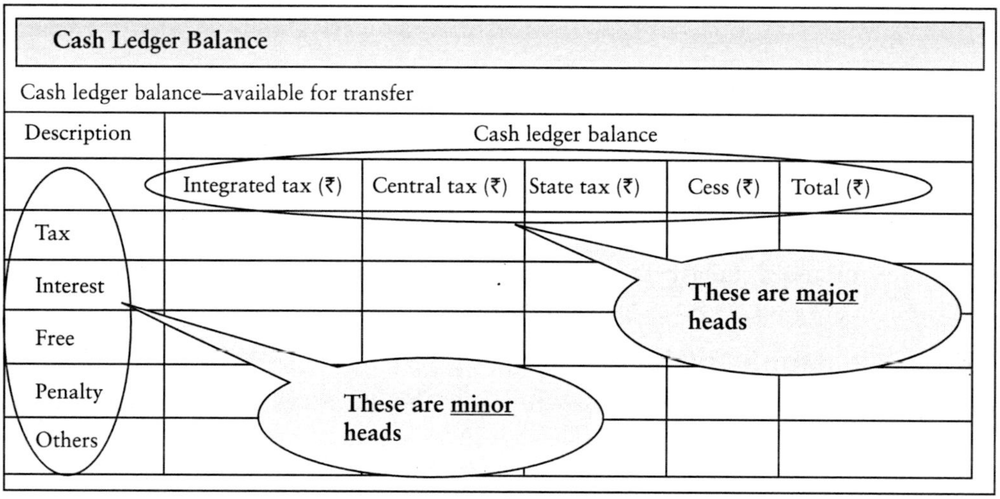

4. It is also possible that due to some human error, a registered person has deposited an amount in a particular minor head of a given major head while it was an item of some other minor head, then the law allows the registered person to transfer from one minor head to another minor head of a given major head. For this purpose, FORM GST PMT-09 is filled.
5. An unregistered person can also deposit to an electronic cash ledger on the basis of a Temporary Identification Number (TIN) generated through a common portal.

(b) Electronic Credit Ledger: The balance of eligible input tax credit available to a registered person is shown by a digital ledger known as an electronic credit ledger. The balance in the electronic credit ledger can be used only to pay tax, not interest. While using the balance in an electronic credit ledger, the conditions and restrictions mentioned under the CGST Act must be kept in mind. Other relevant points are as follows:

On the GST portal, Electronic Credit Ledger looks like this:

Sr. No.	Date	Ref. no.	Tax period, if any	Description (source of credit & purpose of utilization)	Transaction Type (Debit/ Credit)	Credit/Debit					
						Central tax	State tax	UT tax	Integrated tax	Cess	Total
1	2	3	4	5	6	7	8	9	10	11	12

Balance available					
Central tax	State tax	UT tax	Integrated tax	Cess	Total
13	14	15	16	17	18

(c) **Electronic Liability Ledger:** The Electronic Liability Ledger contains details of the amount of tax payable by the taxpayer for each head of tax, such as CGST, SGST, IGST and any interest or penalty that may be applicable.

14.3 How to Pay GST Liability

Tax liability can be paid through two ways or ledgers in digital format, i.e.,

1. Utilising input tax credit balance available in electronic credit ledger. This topic has been explained in Chapter 10 of Input Tax Credit. Sections 49, 49A, 49B, read with Rules 86A, 86B and 88A, are relevant to this topic.
2. Utilising cash balance available in electronic cash ledger.

14.4 Due Date to Pay Tax

This topic is related to GST Returns and, therefore, will be discussed in the next chapter.

14.5 How to Pay Interest, Penalty

Interest and penalty cannot be paid through electronic credit ledger, but they can be paid through electronic cash ledger only.

14.6 Interest on Delayed Payment of Tax—Section 50

1. Who is liable to pay interest: Section 50(1): If a person fails to pay the tax (whether completely or partially) to the Government within the specified time, then he is liable to pay (on his own) interest at the rate notified, which cannot exceed 18% p.a. Presently, the notified rate is 18%. Such interest is calculated for the period for which the tax or any part thereof remains unpaid.

Note: The interest on tax payable in respect of supplies made during a tax period and declared in return for the said period furnished after the due date in accordance with the provisions of section 39, except where such return is furnished after commencement of any proceedings under section 73 or section 74 in respect of the said period, shall be levied on that portion of the tax that is paid by debiting the electronic cash ledger. It simply means that if GSTR-3B is furnished after its due date, then the interest on tax payable on the supplies shown in the return is calculated on that part of the tax, which is paid in cash through the electronic cash ledger. Thus, no interest is levied on the tax paid through the electronic credit ledger. However, this rule is not applicable when a return is filed due to section 73 or 74; thus, in such a situation, interest is levied on the total tax paid through the electronic credit ledger as well as electronic cash ledger.

2. From which date interest is calculated: Section 50(2): The interest under section 50(1) is calculated from the next day to the due date of payment of tax.

3. Interest in case of wrong availment or utilisation of the input tax credit: Section 50(3): Where the input tax credit has been wrongly availed and utilised, the registered person is liable to pay interest on such input tax credit wrongly availed and utilised at a notified rate not greater than 24% and the interest is calculated in a specified manner.

Example 14.1: Suppose that the tax payable for the month of August 2022 was ₹70,000 (CGST+SGST). The date of the invoice raised for the supply of goods was 13 August 2022. If the tax is paid (through electronic cash ledger) on 25 September 2022, then what is the amount of interest under section 50(1)?

Solution

Particulars	Date/Amount
Time of Supply as per Section 12(2) = Date of invoice	13.08.2022
Due date of filing GSTR-3B	20.08.2022
Due date of payment of tax as per section 39(7) of the CGST Act = Due date of filing GSTR-3B	20.08.2022
Actual date of payment	25.09.2022
Period of delay: As per section 50(2) of the CGST Act, the interest is calculated from the next day to the due date to pay tax and as per sections 50(1), interest is charged for the period of delay of the tax, therefore, the period of delay = From 21.08.2022 to 25.09.2022 = 11 days for August + 25 days for September = 36 days	36 days
Interest = Tax x (Period of delay/365)	₹70,000 × (36/365) = ₹6,904

Example 14.2: Suppose that the tax payable for the month of August 2022 was ₹70,000 (CGST+SGST). The date of the invoice raised for the supply of goods was 13 August 2022. If the tax is paid (through electronic credit ledger) on 25 September 2022, then what is the amount of interest?

Solution

Particulars	Date/Amount
Time of Supply as per Section 12(2) = Date of invoice	13.08.2022
Due date of filing GSTR-3B	20.08.2022
Due date of payment of tax as per section 39(7) of the CGST Act = Due date of filing GSTR-3B	20.08.2022
Actual date of payment	25.09.2022
Interest: As per section 50(1), if tax is paid (even after the due date of filing GSTR-3B) through the electronic credit ledger, then no interest is levied.	Not applicable

Example 14.3: Suppose that the tax payable for the month of August 2022 was ₹70,000 (CGST+SGST). The date of the invoice raised for the supply of goods was 13 August 2022. If the tax is paid (80% through electronic credit ledger and 20% through electronic cash ledger) on 25 September 2022, then what is the amount of interest?

Solution

Particulars	Date/Amount
Time of Supply as per section 12(2) = Date of invoice	13.08.2022
Due date of filing GSTR-3B	20.08.2022
Due date of payment of tax as per section 39(7) of the CGST Act = Due date of filing GSTR-3B	20.08.2022
Actual date of payment	25.09.2022
Period of delay: As per section 50(2) of the CGST Act, the interest is calculated from the next day to the due date to pay tax and as per sections 50(1), interest is charged for the period of delay of the tax, therefore, the period of delay = From 21.08.2022 to 25.09.2022 = 11 days for August + 25 days for September = 36 days	36 days
Interest: As per section 50(1), if tax is paid (even after the due date of filing GSTR-3B) through the electronic credit ledger, then no interest is levied, but the portion that is paid through the electronic cash ledger then interest is levied. Therefore, in the present case, only 20% of the tax paid in cash is subject to interest calculation.	₹(20% × 70,000) × (36/365) =₹14,000 × (36/365) =₹1380.82

14.7 Tax Deducted at Source (TDS)

1. Persons Liable to Deduct Tax at Source: Section 51(1): The following persons are liable to deduct tax at source if the **total value of taxable supply (under a contract**) exceeds ₹2,50,000.

1. A department or establishment of the Central Government or State Government.
2. Local authority.
3. Governmental agencies.
4. Notified persons, i.e., (a) An authority or a board or any other body which has been set up by Parliament or a State Legislature or by a government, with 51% equity (control) owned by the government. (b) A society established by the Central or any State Government or a Local Authority and the society is registered under the Societies Registration Act, 1860. (c) Public Sector Undertakings (PSUs).

Notes

- It is compulsory to obtain GST registration for the person who is liable to deduct TDS as per the provisions of section 51 of CGST Act, 2017. Threshold exemption limit is not applicable to such persons. Unique feature of GST registration for the person liable to deduct TDS is that PAN is not mandatory while obtaining GST registration; however, GST registration can be obtained on the basis of existing Tax Deduction and Collection Account Number (TAN).

- When the location of the supplier and the place of supply is in a State or Union Territory which is different from the State or Union Territory of the recipient, then no tax shall be deducted at the source.
- Rate of TDS is 2% (1% for CGST + 1% for SGST/UTGST). TDS is calculated on the value of the taxable supplies.

2. Persons not liable to deduct tax at source: Notification No. 61/2018–Central Tax dated 05.11.2018 and Notification No. 73/2018–Central Tax dated 31.12.2018

(a) One PSU supplying goods or services to any other PSU.

(b) When supply takes place between one person to another person mentioned under section 51(1).

3. Time Limit to Deposit TDS to the zGovernment: Section 51(2)/(3): The deductor shall pay the deducted amount of tax to the account of the Government within 10 days after the end of the month in which such deduction is made in such manner as specified. The deductor shall issue a TDS certificate in FORM GSTR 7A.

4. Section 51(4) (Omitted by the Finance Act, 2020): If the deductor fails to furnish the certificate to the deductee within five days of crediting the amount to the Government, then there is a provision of late fee as follows:

(a) ₹100 per day

(b) Maximum ₹5,000.

5. Claim for Credit of TDS: Section 51(5): The amount of TDS shall be credited to the electronic credit ledger of the deductee and reflected in the return of the deductor furnished under section 39(3) in such manner as may be prescribed.

6. Interest Payable in Case of Failure of Deposit of TDS To the Government: Section 51(6): If the deductor does not deposit the amount of TDS to the Government, then he is liable to pay interest at 18% p.a.

7. Determination of the Amount of Default: Section 51(7): The amount in default under section 51 shall be calculated in the manner specified in section 73 and section 74.

8. Refund: Section 51(7): The case of excess or erroneous deduction of TDS is dealt with under section 54. However, if the amount of TDS has been credited to the electronic cash ledger, then no refund claim is entertained.

Illustration 14.1 showing the summary of TDS provisions

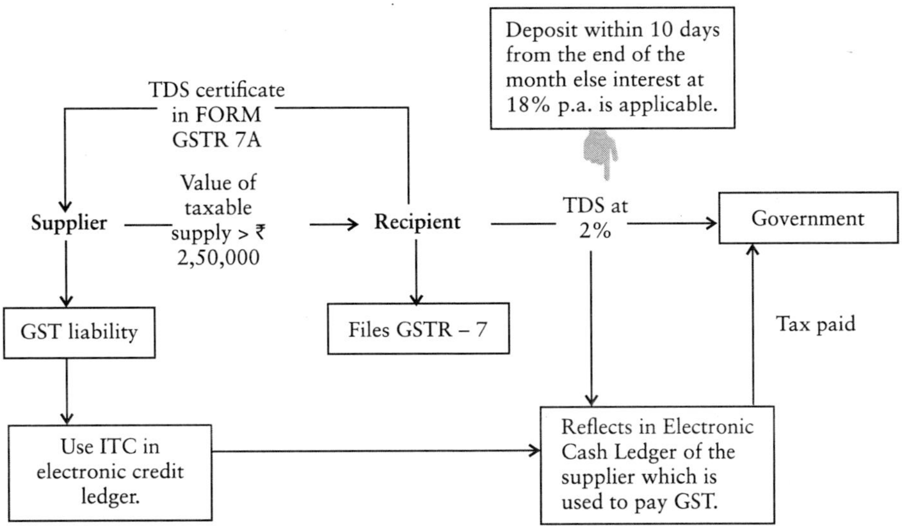

14.8 Tax Collection at Source (TCS)—Section 52

1. Applicability of Tax Collection at Source: Section 15(1): The provisions of tax collection at source are applicable in the case of e-commerce operators only. According to this section, every e-commerce operator like Amazon, Flipkart, Urban Company, Big Basket, etc., is required to collect tax at source at a rate not greater than 1% from a supplier if the following conditions are satisfied:

(a) the supplier is a registered person,
(b) supplies are made through the e-commerce operator, not working as an agent,
(c) the above supplies must not be notified under section 9(5), and
(d) the consideration is collected by the e-commerce operator.

Notes:

1. Net taxable value means the aggregate value of taxable supplies of goods or services or both (excluding services notified under section 9(5)) made during any month by all registered persons through the e-commerce operator minus the aggregate value of taxable supplies returned to the suppliers during the said month. Thus,

Particulars	Amount
Value of taxable supplies (other than notified under section 9(5)	–
Less: Value taxable supplies returned	–
Net value of taxable supplies	–

2. One may question that every person supplying goods or services through e-commerce operators is mandatorily required to take registration, then what is the benefit of giving condition (a)? The answer is Notification No. 65/2017 dated 15.11.2017, which states that a supplier supplying goods or services or both through an e-commerce operator is exempted from registration if his aggregate turnover does not exceed ₹20 lakhs or ₹10 lakhs in special category states.

3. Presently, the rate of TCS is as follows:

Tax	Rate
CGST	0.5%
SGST/UTGST	0.5%
Total GST	**1%**
IGST	1%

Example 14.4: The aggregate value of taxable supplies of goods by a supplier through Amazon is ₹53,10,000, including GST at 18%. Calculate the TCS liability of Amazon. Assume it intra-state supply.

Solution

Particulars	Amount (in ₹)
Value of taxable supplies (other than notified under section 9(5) excluding GST	45,00,000
Less: Value taxable supplies returned	Nil
Net value of taxable supplies	**45,00,000**
TCS (0.5% CGST + 0.5% SGST)	1% × 45,00,000 = 45,000

So, when Amazon pays the consideration to the supplier, then it will deduct its commission and TCS from it.

Example 14.5: The aggregate value of taxable supplies of goods by a supplier through an e-commerce operator is ₹53,10,000, including GST at 18%. The taxable supplies worth ₹1,00,000 were returned. Calculate the TCS liability of Amazon. Assume it intra-state supply.

Solution

Particulars	Amount (in ₹)
Value of taxable supplies (other than notified under section 9(5) before GST	45,00,000
Less: Value of taxable supplies returned	1,00,000
Net value of taxable supplies	**44,00,000**
TCS (0.5% CGST + 0.5% SGST)	1% × 44,00,000 = 44,000

2. Time to Deposit of TCS to the Government: Section 52(3): The e-commerce operator is required to deposit the amount of TCS to the Government within 10 days from the end of the month to which such TCS belongs.

3. Monthly Statement in Form GSTR-8: Section 52(4) read with Rule 67

(a) The e-commerce operator who collects tax at source is required to furnish a statement in FORM GSTR-8 within 10 days after the end of the month in which tax is collected. This statement contains the details of

- outward supplies of goods or services or both made through it,
- the goods or services or both returned through it,
- monthly tax collected,

(b) The above form may be furnished electronically on the common portal or through the facilitation centre.

(c) The commissioner has the power to extend the above time of 10 days by notification, for a notified class of registered persons. However, the reasons for the extension are required to be recorded in writing.

4. Annual Statement in Form GSTR-10: Section 52(5)

(a) The e-commerce operator who collects tax at source is required to furnish a statement in FORM GSTR-10. This statement contains the details of

- outward supplies of goods or services or both made through it during a financial year,
- the goods or services or both returned through it during the financial year,
- annual tax collected during the financial year,

(b) The above form may be furnished electronically on the common portal or through the facilitation centre.

(c) The due date to furnish FORM GSTR-10 is 31 December of the financial year following the financial year to which the above details belong. On the recommendation of the GST council, the commissioner may extend the said time limit by issuing a notification for a notified class of registered persons. However, the reasons for the extension are required to be recorded in writing.

5. Correction in Form GSTR-8: Section 52(6): If some correction is required to be made in FORM GSTR-8 filed, then it is possible to the earlier of the following dates:

(a) 30 November of the financial year following the end of the financial year to which such form is related
(b) Date of filing of annual statement.

Note: If some omission or incorrect particulars are found under scrutiny, audit, inspection or enforcement activity by tax authorities, then correction cannot be made.

6. Credit of TCS: Section 52(7): The amount of tax collected and reflected in FORM GSTR-8 is transferred to the ***electronic cash ledger*** of the supplier of the goods or services or both. Therefore, the supplier can claim the credit for the tax collected.

7. Matching of details of supplies: Section 52(8)/(9)/(10)/(11)

- The details filled in FORM GSTR-8 must match with details of outward supplies furnished by the supplier (under section 37 or 39) within a specified manner and time.
- In case of a mis-match, the e-commerce operator and the supplier shall be communicated about the discrepancy within a specified manner and time.
- If the discrepancy is not corrected by the supplier in his valid return or by the operator in his statement for the month in which the discrepancy is communicated, then there may be two cases:

Case I: Value of supply as per the supplier is more than shown by the e-commerce operator

In such case, the discrepancy is added to the output tax liability of the supplier in his return for the month succeeding the month in which the discrepancy has been communicated. Such a supplier is also liable to pay interest at 18% p.a. on the amount added from the due date of such tax till its payment.

Case II: Value of supply as per the supplier is less than shown by the e-commerce operator

In such case, the discrepancy is added to the output tax liability of the e-commerce operator in his return for the month succeeding the month in which the discrepancy has been communicated.

8. Notice to the Operator: Section 52(12)/(13)/(14): An authority not below the rank of Deputy Commissioner can issue notice to an e-commerce operator asking him to furnish details relating to the volume of goods or services supplied, stock of goods lying in warehouses, godowns, etc., managed by such operator. The e-commerce operator is required to furnish such details within 15 working days of service of the notice. In case an Operator fails to furnish the information, besides being liable for penal action under section 122, is also liable to pay a penalty of up to ₹25,000.

Section 52(15)–A new section: *The operator is not allowed to furnish a statement under section 52(4) after three years from the due date of furnishing of the said statement. However, the Government may, on the recommendations of the Council, by notification, subject to such conditions and restrictions as may be specified therein, allow an operator or a class of operators to furnish a statement under section 52(4), even after the said period of 3 years.* ***[Inserted by section 145 of the Finance Act, 2023]***

Illustration 14.2 showing the summary of TCS provisions

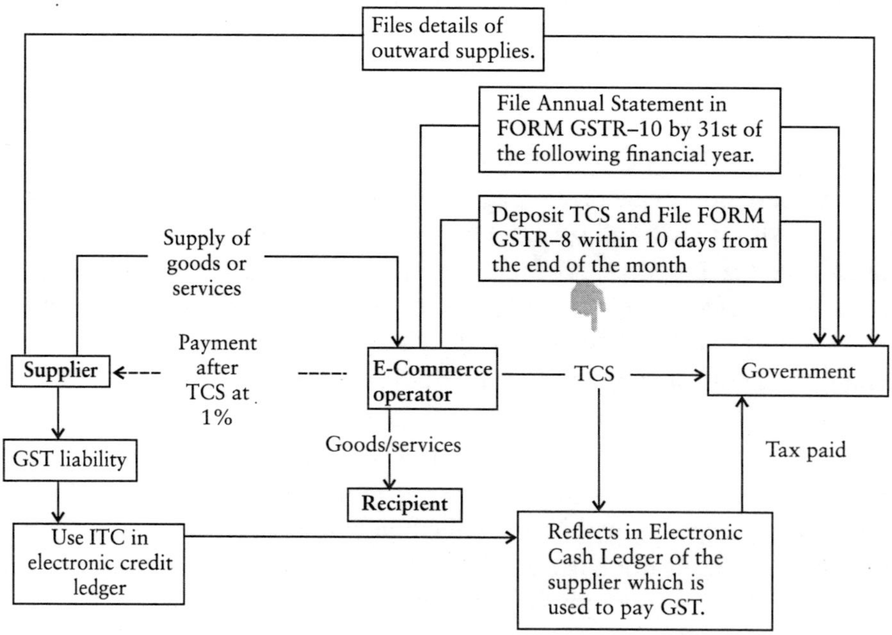

Theory Questions

1. What are electronic ledgers under the GST common portal?
2. What is Tax Collected at Source (TCS)? What are its provisions under the CGST Act?
3. What is Tax Deducted at Source (TDS)? Explain its provisions under the CGST Act.
4. Write a short note on interest on delayed payment of tax.

15
GST Returns

15.1 Furnishing GST Returns—Section 39

1. Who is liable to furnish GST Returns: Section 39(1) read with Rule 61(1: Every registered person (other than those given in the note) shall furnish a return of

(a) inward and outward supplies of goods or services or both,
(b) input tax credit availed,
(c) tax payable,
(d) tax paid and
(e) such other particulars,

in FORM GSTR-3B. Such return shall be filed electronically for every calendar month or part of it by the twentieth day of the next month.

However, the Government has the power to notify certain classes of registered persons where FORM GSTR-3B can be furnished for every quarter or part of it. As per Rule 61(1), the due dates to furnish a return by such class of registered persons are as follows:

Class of registered persons	Due dates
Registered persons whose Principal Place of Business (PPOB) is in the States of Chhattisgarh, Madhya Pradesh, Gujarat, Maharashtra, Karnataka, Goa, Kerala, Tamil Nadu, Telangana, Andhra Pradesh, the Union territories of Daman and Diu and Dadra and Nagar Haveli, Puducherry, Andaman and Nicobar Islands or Lakshadweep.	Twenty-second of the month of the following quarter
Registered persons whose principal place of business (PPOB) is in the States of Himachal Pradesh, Punjab, Uttarakhand, Haryana, Rajasthan, Uttar Pradesh, Bihar, Sikkim, Arunachal Pradesh, Nagaland, Manipur, Mizoram, Tripura, Meghalaya, Assam, West Bengal, Jharkhand or Odisha, the Union territories of Jammu and Kashmir, Ladakh, Chandigarh or Delhi.	Twenty-fourth of the month of the following quarter

Note: Persons not covered under section 39(1) and Rule 61(1)

(a) Input Service Distributor (ISD) or
(b) a non-resident taxable person or
(c) a person paying tax under the provisions of section 10, i.e., composition levy or
(d) those persons liable to deduct tax at source (TDS) under section 51 or
(e) those persons liable to collect at source (TCS) under section 52

2. Furnishing of return by a person who pays tax under composition levy: Section 39(2) read with Rule 62: If a person pays tax under composition levy under section 10, then he shall furnish a return of

- turnover in the State or Union territory,
- inward supplies of goods or services or both,
- tax payable,
- tax paid and
- such other particulars

in FORM GST CMP-08. Such returns shall be filed electronically for every quarter or part of it. The due date is the eighteenth day of the month, just next to the relevant quarter. Apart, an annual return for a given financial year or part of it shall also be filed in FORM GSTR-4. The due date to file such an annual return is 30 April, following the end of the relevant financial year.

3. Furnishing of return by a person liable to deduct tax at source (TDS) under section 51: Section 39(3) read with Rule 66: Those persons who are liable to deduct tax at source under section 51 shall furnish a return in FORM GSTR-7 for the month in which such deductions have been made within 10 days after the end of such month.

4. Furnishing return by Input Service Distributor (ISD): Section 39(4) read with Rule 65: Every taxable person registered as ISD shall, for every calendar month or part of it, furnish a return in FORM GSTR-6 within 13 days after the end of such month. As per rule 65, an ISD shall, on the basis of details contained in FORM GSTR-6A, and where required, after adding, correcting or deleting the details, furnish electronically the return in FORM GSTR-6, containing the details of tax invoices on which credit has been received and those issued under section 20.

5. Furnishing return by a Non-Resident Taxable Person (NRTP): Section 39(5): Every registered NRTP shall, for every calendar month or part of it, furnish, in such form and manner as may be prescribed, a return electronically,

- within 13 days after the end of a calendar month or
- within seven days after the last day of the period of registration specified under section 27(1), whichever is earlier.

6. Power to extend time limit to furnish GST Returns: Section 39(6): The Commissioner has power to extend the time limit to furnish GST returns for specified registered persons. Such extension shall be given by issuing a notification.

Note: Any extension of the time limit notified by the Commissioner of State tax or Union territory tax shall be deemed to be notified by the Commissioner.

7. Due date to pay tax: Section 39(7): Every registered person who is required to furnish a return under

- section 39(1) except the notified persons or
- section 39(3) or
- section 39(5),

shall pay to the Government the tax due as per such return not later than the last date on which he is required to furnish such return. *Thus, the due date of payment of tax is the due date to furnish the GST return.*

However, a notified person [under section 39(1)] shall pay to the Government

(a) an amount equal to the tax due, taking into account
   - inward and outward supplies of goods or services or both,
   - input tax credit availed,
   - tax payable and
   - such other particulars during a month;

or

(b) in lieu of the amount referred to in clause (a), an amount determined in such manner and subject to such conditions and restrictions as may be prescribed.

However, *a person paying tax under composition levy* shall pay to the Government the tax due, taking into account

- turnover in the State or Union territory,
- inward supplies of goods or services or both,
- tax payable, and
- such other particulars during a quarter,

in such form and manner, and within such time as may be prescribed.

8. Furnishing return is compulsory even if the supply is zero: Section 39(8): Every registered person who is required to furnish a return under

- section 39(1) or
- section 39(2)

shall furnish a return for every tax period whether or not any supplies of goods or services or both have been made during such tax period.

9. Correction in the return furnished: Section 39(9): Where any registered person, after furnishing a return under

- section 39(1) or
- section 39(2) or
- section 39(3) or
- section 39(4) or
- section 39(5)

discovers any omission or incorrect particulars in the return (other than as a result of scrutiny, audit, inspection or enforcement activity by the tax authorities), he shall rectify such omission or incorrect particulars in the return to be furnished for the month or quarter during which such omission or incorrect particulars in such form and manner as may be prescribed, but such rectification is subject to payment of interest under the CGST Act.

However, rectification of the omission or incorrect particulars is allowed up to earlier of the following dates:

(a) 30 November following the end of the financial year to which such details pertain or
(b) the actual date of furnishing of relevant annual return

10. Furnishing a return for a tax period is not possible before furnishing the return for the tax period just preceding to it: Section 39(10): A registered person shall not be allowed to furnish a return for a tax period if the return for any of the previous tax periods or the details of outward supplies under section 37(1) for the said tax period have not been furnished by him. However, the Government may notify some registered persons or a class of registered persons who can be allowed.

A registered person is not allowed furnishing a return for a specific tax period after three years have passed from the due date for furnishing that return. However, the government, based on recommendations from the Council, may, through notification and subject to specified conditions and restrictions, grant permission for a registered person or a class of registered persons to submit the return for a tax period even after the aforementioned three-year period has lapsed from the due date [**Inserted by Section 144 of the Finance Act, 2023**].

15.2 Furnishing Annual Return—Section 44 read with Rule 80

Every registered person (other than an input service distributor, a person paying tax under section 51 or section 52, a casual taxable person and a non-resident taxable person, shall furnish an annual return which may include a self-certified reconciliation statement reconciling the value of supplies declared in the return furnished for the financial year, with the audited annual financial statement for every financial year electronically. Such return shall be filed in FORM GSTR-9 (or FORM GSTR-9A in case of composition levy or FORM GSTR-9B in case of e-commerce operator collecting tax at source) on or before the 31st day of December following the end of such financial year.

Notes:

1. As per the first proviso of section 44, the Commissioner may, on the recommendations of the Council, by notification, exempt any class of registered persons from filing annual returns under this section.
2. As per the second proviso of section 44, nothing contained in this section shall apply to any department of the Central Government or, a State Government or a local authority whose books of account are subject to audit by the Comptroller and Auditor-General of India or an auditor appointed for auditing the accounts of local authorities under any law for the time being in force.
3. Every registered person, other than those referred to in the second proviso to section 44, an Input Service Distributor, a person paying tax under section 51 or section 52,

a casual taxable person and a non-resident taxable person, whose aggregate turnover during a financial year exceeds ₹5 crore , shall also furnish a self-certified reconciliation statement as specified under section 44 in FORM GSTR-9C along with the annual return referred to in rule 80(1), on or before the 31st day of December following the end of such financial year.

15.3 Final Return—Section 45 read with Rule 81

Every registered person who is required to furnish a return under section 39(1) and whose registration has been cancelled shall furnish a final return within

(a) three months of the date of cancellation or

(b) date of order of cancellation

whichever is later. Such return shall be filed in FORM GSTR-10.

15.4 Current GST Returns forms and their due dates

Return Form	Description	Frequency	Due date
GSTR-1	This return is filed to give details of outward supply.	Monthly Quarterly under QRMP scheme	11th of the next month 13th of the month following the quarter
GSTR-2	Omitted (w.e.f. 1.10.2022)		
GSTR-3	Omitted (w.e.f. 1.10.2022)		
GSTR-3B	This is a summary return of outward supplies, ITC claimed, payment of tax.	Monthly Quarterly under QRMP scheme	20th of the next month. 22nd or 24th of the month following the quarter
CMP-08	To declare summary of outward supplies and import of services liable to reverse charge mechanism.	Quarterly	18th of the next month.
GSTR-4	It is an annual return for a person opting composition levy.	Annually	30th of the month following a financial year.
GSTR-5	This return is filed by a non-resident taxable person if he does not want to claim Input Tax Credit (ITC).	Monthly	20th of the next month.
GSTR-5A	This return is filed by Online Information and Database Access or Retrieval (OIDAR) service providers outside India for their services to unregistered persons in India.	Monthly	20th of the next month.

Return Form	Description	Frequency	Due date
GSTR-6	This return is filed by Input Service Distributors (ISD) for distribution of ITC to their branches, etc.	Monthly	13th of the next month.
GSTR-7	This return is filed by the entities liable to deduct tax at source. So, it's a TDS return.	Monthly	10th of the next month.
GSTR-8	This return is filed by e-commerce operators.	Monthly	10th of the next month.
GSTR-9	It is an annual return which is filed by all the normal taxpayers.	Annually	31st December of the next financial year.
GSTR-10	This return is filed by the taxpayers, whose GST registration has been cancelled or surrendered.	1 time only when registration is cancelled or surrendered.	3 months from the date of cancellation or the date or date of order of cancellation, whichever is earlier.
GSTR-11	This return is filed by Unique Identity Number (UIN) holders stating the supplied/ received goods and services and to claim a GST refund.	Monthly	28th of the month following the month for which the statement is filed.

15.5 QRMP scheme for small taxpayers

QRPM stands for Quarterly Return Filing and Monthly Payment of Taxes. The term itself defines its feature, i.e., it is an **optional scheme** in which a return is filed quarterly, and payment of taxes is made monthly. This scheme has been introduced for small taxpayers having aggregate turnover not exceeding ₹5 crore in the previous financial year. This scheme allows taxpayers to report their supplies and tax liabilities in a hassle-free manner and to make compliance easier. Tax under the QRPM scheme is paid monthly by furnishing challan in Form GST PMT-06. The due date to pay tax is 25th of the following month.

15.6 Modes of Filing GST Returns

GST Returns are filed online only, i.e., no paper format is used. These are the modes of filing GST returns:

1. Direct using a common portal, i.e., www.gst.govt.in
2. Downloading offline utilities from the common portal.
3. GST Suvidha Providers.

Theory Questions

1. What are the different forms of GST Returns? Explain.
2. What are the due dates to furnish or file GST Returns?
3. What is the due date to pay GST?
4. Write a short note on QRMP.
5. What final return? Is it different from the annual return?

16
E-Way Bill

16.1 Introduction

To make the movement of goods hassle-free and reduce tax evasion, the concept of an e-way bill has been brought into GST law. There are certain cases in which an e-way bill is required to be generated subject to specified conditions. According to Section 68, the Government may require the person in-charge of a conveyance (in which goods are being carried having a value greater than a specified amount) to carry with him spec]ified documents and devices. E-way bill is that specified document under Rule 138. This chapter discusses the concept of the e-way bill and its related aspects.

16.2 Meaning of E-way bill

E-way bill is a document generated electronically on the common portal www.ewaybillgst.gov.in before the movement of the goods. It helps in monitoring the movement of goods. It is generated in FORM GST EWB-01, which consists of two parts:) Part A and Part B, as shown below:

FORM GST EWB-01 (See Rule 138) E-Way Bill		
E-way Bill No.:	E-Way Bill Date:	
Generator:	Valid from:	Valid until:
Part-A		
A. 1	GSTIN of Supplier	
A. 2	Place of Dispatch	
A. 3	GSTIN of Recipient	
A. 4	Place of Delivery	
A. 5	Document Number	
A. 6	Document Date	
A. 7	Value of Goods	
A. 8	HSN Code	
A. 9	Reason for Transportation	
Part-B		
B. 1	Vehicle Number for Road	
B. 2	Transport Document, Number/ Defence, Vehicle No./Temporary Vehicle, Registration, No./Nepal or Bhutan, Vehicle Registration No.	

Tax invoice number, bill of supply number, delivery challan number, etc.

Supply, job work, export, exhibition, etc.

16.3 Who is required to furnish Part A of E-way bill?—Rule 138(1)

Part A is to be furnished by a registered person **who causes the movement of goods (see note 3)** if the consignment value is greater than ₹50,000 and the movement is

(a) in relation to supply or

(b) in relation to other than supply or

(c) due to inward supply from an unregistered person

But, if the registered person authorises, then Part A may be furnished by

(a) the transporter

(b) the e-commerce operator or courier agency if the goods are supplied through such an e-commerce operator or courier agency.

Once Part A is furnished, then a **unique number** is generated, which can be used for furnishing Part B. This unique number remains valid for 15 days.

However, in the following two cases, E-way bill is mandatory irrespective of the value of the consignment.

1. **Inter-state transfer of goods for job work** by principal to job worker. In such case, the E-way bill shall be generated by either the principal or job worker (if registered).
2. **Inter-state transfer of handicraft goods** by a person who is required mandatory registration under section 24 but exempted from registration.

Notes:

1. Consignment value is calculated as follows:

Particulars	Amount
Value of taxable supply (as per section 15 and declared in invoice/bill of supply/ delivery challan)	–
Add: GST (CGST, SGST/UTGST, IGST, Cess)	–
Consignment value	–

Consignment value excludes the value of exempt supply of goods when the invoice is issued for both exempt and taxable supply of goods. Thus, only taxable supply is considered to calculate consignment value if an invoice contains both taxable as well as exempt supply.

2. Handicraft goods mean the goods as mentioned in Notification No. 56/2018-Central Tax–dated 23.10.2018.

3. Meaning of 'who causes movement of goods'

Who causes the movement of goods depends upon the point who undertakes to transport goods and his registration.

- If a registered supplier undertakes to transport the goods, then he causes the movement.
- If a recipient undertakes to transport the goods, then he causes the movement.
- If the goods are supplied by an unregistered supplier to a registered recipient, the movement shall be caused by such recipient if the recipient is known at the time of the commencement of the movement—Rule 138(3).

16.4 Who is required to furnish Part B of E-way bill?—Rule 138(2)/(2A)/(3)

OR

Who is required to generate E-way bill?

Part B contains the transportation details and these details are to be furnished by the person **who transports the goods.** Transportation of goods may be by road, railways, air, or vessel.

Image courtesy–Freepik

Transportation by Road: If a registered supplier (consignor) or recipient (consignee) takes responsibility to transport the goods (whether in his own conveyance or hired or public conveyance) by *road*, then it is said that he causes the movement of the goods, therefore, he is required to furnish required information in Part B and thereafter generate E-way bill—Rule 138(2).

If the E-way bill is not generated by the registered supplier or recipient and the goods are handed over to a transporter (or Goods Transport Agency—GTA) for transport by road, then the registered person shall furnish the information relating to the transporter in Part B on the common portal, and the transporter shall generate the E-way bill—Rule 138(3).

Additional points from rule 138(3):

1. E-way bill can be generated voluntarily even the value of consignment is not greater than ₹50,000.
2. If an unregistered person causes the movement of goods either in his own conveyance or a hired conveyance or through a transporter, then he or the transporter may generate the e-way bill. Thus, to generate e-way bill, it is not required to be registered under the GST.

Transportation by Railways/Air/Vessel: Rule 138(2A): If the goods are transported by railways or by air or vessel, then the registered person (supplier or recipient), either before or after the commencement of movement, is required to furnish the information in Part B and generate an E-way bill. Also, the railways cannot deliver the goods unless the e-way bill is produced to it at the time of delivery.

From the above discussion, it is clear that an E-way bill cannot be generated without furnishing the details in Part B. However, Rule 138(3) says that Part B is not required in case of **intra-state movement** of goods up to 50 kilometres

(a) from place of business of consignor to place of business of transporter for further transportation

or

(b) from place of business of transporter to place of business of the consignee.

16.5 Unique E-way bill number (EBN)—Rule 138(4)

Once an e-way bill is generated, a unique bill number is generated, which is communicated to the supplier, the recipient and the transporter on the common portal.

16.6 Change of conveyance—Rule 138(5)

If conveyance is changed, then the details of the conveyance furnished in part B is required to be updated by the generator or the transporter before the change and further transportation of the goods.

Exception: Where the goods are transported for a distance of upto 50 kilometres within the State or Union territory from the place of business of the transporter finally to the place of business of the recipient, the details of the conveyance may not be updated in the e-way bill.

16.7 Assigning the E-way bill number to another registered person—Rule 138(5A)

The consignor or the recipient, who has furnished the information in Part A, or the transporter, may assign the e-way bill number to another registered or enrolled transporter for updating the information in Part B for further movement of the consignment.

However, after the details of the conveyance have been updated by the transporter in Part B, the consignor or recipient, as the case may be, who has furnished the information in Part A shall not be allowed to assign the e-way bill number to another transporter.

16.8 Consolidated E-way bill—Rule 138(6)

After e-way bill has been generated in accordance with the provisions of rule 138(1), where multiple consignments are intended to be transported in one conveyance, the transporter may indicate the serial number of e-way bills generated in respect of each such consignment electronically on the common portal and a consolidated e-way bill in FORM GST EWB-02 maybe generated by him on the said common portal before the movement of goods.

16.9 Special case—Rule 138(7)

Where the consignor or the consignee has not generated the e-way bill in FORM GST EWB-01, and the **aggregate** of the **consignment value of goods** carried in the conveyance is more than ₹50,000, the transporter (except in case of transportation of goods by railways, air and vessel) shall, in respect of inter-State supply, generate the e-way bill in FORM GST EWB-01 on the basis of invoice or bill of supply or delivery challan, as the case may be, and may also generate a consolidated e-way bill in FORM GST EWB-02 on the common portal prior to the movement of goods:

Provided that where the goods to be transported are supplied through an e-commerce operator or a courier agency, the information in Part A of FORM GST EWB-01 may be furnished by such e-commerce operator or courier agency.

16.10 Information submitted for e-way bill can be used for filing GST Return—Rule 138(8)

A supplier can use the information furnished in Part A of FORM GST EWB-01 to furnish his FORM GSTR-1. However, when the information has been furnished by an unregistered supplier or an unregistered recipient in FORM GST EWB-01, he shall be informed electronically, if the mobile number or the e-mail is available.

16.11 Cancellation of E-way bill is possible—Rule 138(9)

E-way bill can be cancelled within **24 hours** from the time of its generation if goods are not transported or not as per the details furnished. However, it cannot be cancelled if it has been verified under rule 138B.

16.12 Validity period of E-way bill/consolidated E-way bill—Rule 138(10)

Case I	Dimensional Cargo or multimodal shipment in which at least one leg involves by ship
	1 day up to 20 km and thereafter 1 additional day per 20 km or part of it. Mathematically, number of days of validity of the e-way bill can be calculated as follows: = Total distance/20 If the answer comes in fraction, then ignore it and increase the whole number by 1. **Example 16.1:** Suppose that distance is 60 km, then the validity period is 1 day for the first 20 kms, for the next 20 km another 1 day, for the next 20 kms another 1 day. So, total validity period is 3 days. Alternatively, validity = 60/20 = 3 days **Example 16.2:** Suppose that the distance is 62 km, then the validity period is 1 day for the first 20 kms, for the next 20 km another 1 day, for the next 20 km another 1 day and for the next 2 km (a part of 20 km) another 1 day. So, total validity period is 4 days. Alternatively, validity = 62/20 = 3.1 days Since, the result is in fraction, therefore, ignore it and increase the whole number by 1. Thus, validity is 4 days.

Case II	Other case
	1 day up to 200 km and thereafter 1 additional day per 200 km or part of it. Mathematically, number of days of validity of the e-way bill can be calculated as follows: = Total distance/200 If the answer comes in fraction, then ignore it and increase the whole number by 1. **Example 16.3:** Suppose that distance is 450 km, then the validity period is 1 day for the first 200 kms, for the next 200 km another 1 day, for the next 50 kms another 1 day. So, total validity period is 3 days. Alternatively, validity = 450/200 = 2.25 days Since, the result is in fraction, therefore, ignore it and increase the whole number by 1. Thus, validity is 3 days.

Notes:

1. Validity of the first day remains till the midnight of the next day. For example, if an e-way bill (valid for 3 days) is generated at 7.30 pm on 19.03.2022, then its validity starts from 7.30 pm, and its first-day validity remains till midnight of 20.03.2022. Thus, the dates of validity are as follows:

First day	From 7.30 pm, 19.03.2022 till midnight of 20.03.2022
Second day	From 0.00 hrs till midnight of 21.03.2022
Third day	From 0.00 hrs till midnight of 22.03.2022

2. Commissioner may, on the recommendations of the Council, by Notification, extend the validity period of an e-way bill for certain categories of goods as may be specified in the notification.
3. In exceptional cases (including trans-shipment) where the goods cannot be transported within the validity period of the e-way bill, the transporter may extend the validity period after updating the details in Part B of FORM GST EWB-01, if required.
4. The validity of the e-way bill may be extended within eight hours from the time of its expiry.
5. For the purposes of this rule, the expression "Over Dimensional Cargo" shall mean a cargo carried as a single indivisible unit and which exceeds the dimensional limits prescribed in rule 93 of the Central Motor Vehicle Rules, 1989, made under the Motor Vehicles Act,1988.

Image courtesy–Freepik

16.13 Communication of details—Rule 138(11)/(12)

- Part A information is communicated (on the common portal) to the registered supplier if it has been furnished by the recipient or the transporter.
- Part A information is communicated (on the common portal) to the registered recipient if it has been furnished by the supplier or the transporter on the common portal.

The supplier or the recipient is required to communicate his acceptance or rejection of the information furnished. Further, as per rule 138(12), if he does not do so by earlier of the following

(a) 72 hours of the communication on the common portal
(b) the time of delivery of goods, then it is assumed that he had shown his acceptance.

16.14 E-way bill is valid in every State or Union Territory—Rule 138(13)

The e-way bill generated is valid in every state or Union Territory.

16.15 No E-way bill is required in the following cases—Rule 138(14)

Whatsoever rule 138 says, no e-way bill is required in the following cases:

(a) If the following goods are transported:

1.	Liquefied petroleum gas (LPG) for supply to household and non-domestic exempted category (NDEC) customers
2.	Kerosene oil sold under Public Distribution System (PDS)
3.	Postal baggage transported by Department of Posts
4.	Natural or cultured pearls and precious or semi-precious stones; precious metals and metals clad with precious metal (Chapter 71)
5.	Jewellery, goldsmiths' and silversmiths' wares and other articles (Chapter 71) excepting Imitation Jewellery *[As amended by Notification No. 26/2022 Central Tax, dated 26.12.2022]*
6.	Currency
7.	Used personal and household effects
8.	Coral, unworked and worked coral

(b) where the goods are being transported by a non-motorised conveyance (e.g., thela, rickshaw).
(c) where the goods are being transported from the customs port, airport, air cargo complex and land customs station to an inland container depot or a container freight station for clearance by Customs.
(d) in respect of movement of goods within such areas as are Notified under clause (d) of sub-rule (14) of Rule 138 of the State or Union territory Goods and Services Tax Rules in that particular State or Union territory.
(e) where the goods, other than de-oiled cake, being transported, are specified in the Schedule appended to Notification No. 2/2017-Central tax (Rate) dated the 28 June 2017 published in the Gazette of India, Extraordinary, Part II, Section 3, Sub-section (i), vide number G.S.R. 674 (E) dated the 28 June 2017 as amended from time to time.
(f) where the goods being transported are alcoholic liquor for human consumption, petroleum crude, high speed diesel, motor spirit (commonly known as petrol), natural gas or aviation turbine fuel.
(g) where the supply of goods being transported is treated as no supply under Schedule III of the CGST Act.
(h) where the goods are being transported: (1) under customs bond from an inland container depot or a container freight station to a custom sport, airport, air cargo complex and land customs station, or from one customs station or customs port to another customs station or customs port, or (2) under customs supervision or under customs seal

(i)	where the goods being transported are transit cargo from or to Nepal or Bhutan.
(j)	where the goods being transported are exempt from tax under Notification No. 7/2017-Central Tax (Rate), dated 28 June 2017 published in the Gazette of India, Extraordinary, Part II, Section 3, Sub-section (i), vide number G.S.R. 679(E) dated 28 June 2017 as amended from time to time and Notification No. 26/2017 Central Tax(Rate), dated the 21 September 2017 published in the Gazette of India, Extraordinary, Part II, Section 3, Sub-section (i), vide number G.S.R. 1181(E) dated 21 September 2017 as amended from time to time.
(k)	any movement of goods caused by defence formation under Ministry of defence as a consignor or consignee.
(l)	where the consignor of goods is the Central Government, Government of any State or a local authority for transport of goods by rail.
(m)	where empty cargo containers are being transported.
(n)	where the goods are being transported up to a distance of 20 kilometres from the place of the business of the consignor to a weighbridge for weighment or from the weighbridge back to the place of the business of the said consignor subject to the condition that the movement of goods is accompanied by a delivery challan issued in accordance with Rule 55.
(o)	where empty cylinders for packing of liquefied petroleum gas are being moved for reasons other than supply.

16.16 Documents and devices to be carried by a person in charge of a conveyance—Rule 138A

1. The person in charge of a conveyance must carry the following documents:
   (a) the invoice or bill of supply or delivery challan, and
   (b) a copy of the e-way bill in physical form or the e-way bill number in electronic form or mapped to a Radio Frequency Identification Device (RFID) embedded on to the conveyance in such manner as may be Notified by the Commissioner. However, in case of movement of goods by rail or by air or vessel, there is no such requirement.

   Note: In case of imported goods, the person in charge of a conveyance shall also carry a copy of the bill of entry filed by the importer of such goods and shall indicate the number and date of the bill of entry in Part A of FORM GST EWB-01.
2. In case, invoice is issued in the manner prescribed under rule 48(4), the Quick Response (QR) code having an embedded Invoice Reference Number (IRN) in it, may be produced electronically, for verification by the proper officer in lieu of the physical copy of such tax invoice.
3. Where the registered person uploads the invoice under sub-rule (2), the information in Part A of FORM GST EWB-01 shall be auto-populated by the common portal on the basis of the information furnished in FORM GST INV-1.
4. The Commissioner may, by Notification, require a class of transporters to obtain a unique Radio Frequency Identification Device, get the said device embedded on to

the conveyance and map the e-way bill to the Radio Frequency Identification Device before the movement of goods.

5. Irrespective of Rule 138A(1)(b), where circumstances so warrant, the Commissioner may, by Notification, require the person in charge of the conveyance to carry the following documents instead of the e-way bill
   (a) tax invoice or bill of supply or bill of entry or
   (b) a delivery challan, where the goods are transported for reasons other than by way of supply.

16.17 Verification of documents and conveyances—Rule 138B

1. The Commissioner or an officer empowered by him in this behalf may authorize the proper officer to intercept any conveyance to verify the e-way bill in physical or electronic form for all inter-State and intra-State movement of goods.
2. The Commissioner shall get Radio Frequency Identification Device readers installed at places where the verification of movement of goods is required to be carried out and verification of movement of vehicles shall be done through such device readers where the e-way bill has been mapped with the said device.
3. The physical verification of conveyances shall be carried out by the proper officer as authorised by the Commissioner or an officer empowered by him in this behalf:

   Provided that on receipt of specific information on evasion of tax, physical verification of a specific conveyance can also be carried out by any other officer after obtaining necessary approval of the Commissioner or an officer authorised by him in this behalf.

16.18 Inspection and Verification of Goods—Rule 138C

1. A summary report of every inspection of goods in transit shall be recorded online by the proper officer in Part A of FORM GST EWB-03 within 24 hours of inspection and the final report in Part B of FORM GST EWB-03 shall be recorded within three days of such inspection:

   Provided that where the circumstances so warrant, the Commissioner, or any other officer authorised by him, may, on sufficient cause being shown, extend the time for recording of the final report in Part B of FORM EWB-03, for a further period Not exceeding three days.

   Note: The period of twenty-four hours or, as the case may be, three days shall be counted from the midnight of the date on which the vehicle was intercepted.
2. Where the physical verification of goods being transported on any conveyance has been done during transit at one place within the State or Union territory or in any other State or Union territory, no further physical verification of the said conveyance shall be carried out again in the State or Union territory, unless specific information relating to evasion of tax is made available subsequently.

16.19 Facility for uploading information regarding detention of vehicle—Rule 138D

Where a vehicle has been intercepted and detained for a period exceeding thirty minutes, the transporter may upload the said information in FORM GST EWB-04 on the common portal.

Note: The expressions 'transported by railways', 'transportation of goods by railway', 'transport of goods by rail' and 'movement of goods by rail' does Not include cases where leasing of parcel space by Railways takes place.

Theory Questions

1. What do you mean by an E-way bill? Explain its parts.
2. Where is the E-way bill necessary? Are there cases where an E-way bill is not required?
3. Who is liable to generate an E-way bill?
4. Is cancellation of the E-way bill possible?
5. What is the validity period of an E-way bill?
6. What are the powers of the commissioner with regard to the verification of the documents and the conveyance?
7. What are the conditions for generating an E-way bill?
8. What are the documents and devices to be carried by a person in charge of a conveyance?
9. What are the provisions of the consolidated E-way bill?
10. What is EBN?

17

Inspection, Search, Seizure and Arrest

17.1 Introduction

The biggest problem in any tax system is tax leakage or evasion. Although the GST law has been formulated in such a way that tax evasion can be minimised, there are many cases in which people indulge in illegal practices of tax evasion. Therefore, it becomes necessary for the Government to penalize or punish such evaders financially and non-financially. This chapter deals various provisions regarding inspection, search, seizure and arrest.

17.2 Power of inspection—Section 67(1)

The proper officer (with the rank joint commissioner or above) has the power to give authority (in writing) to an officer of central tax to inspect any places of business of a taxable person or the persons engaged in the business of transporting goods or the owner/operator of a warehouse/godown/any other place if the proper officer has reasons to believe that

(a) the taxable person has suppressed (or hidden) any transaction relating to the supply of goods or services of both or the stock of goods in hand or

(b) the taxable person has claimed excess input tax credit or

(c) the taxable person, with the intension of tax evasion, has contravened (or violated) any of the provisions of the CGST Act or the rules made thereunder or

(d) any person who carries the business of transporting goods or an owner or operator of a warehouse or a godown or any other place keeps goods which have escaped tax or has kept his accounts or goods in such manner so that there is a probability of tax evasion.

17.3 Search and seizure—Section 67(2)

Power of search and seizure: If, as a result of an inspection conducted in accordance with section 67(1) or otherwise, the proper officer (whose rank must be at least joint commissioner)

has grounds to believe that there are goods that should be confiscated or documents, books, or other things that may be helpful or relevant to any proceedings under the CGST Act are secreted or hidden in any location, he may authorise in writing a central tax officer to search for and seize those goods, documents, books, or other things. He might search them himself and seize them.

Notes:

(i) **What if the seizure of goods is not feasible due to some reasons like a heavy weight, very large dimensions, etc.?:** If it is not feasible to take any such goods, the proper officer or the authorised officer may serve the owner or custodian of those goods with an order prohibiting removal, disposal, or any other type of handling of the goods without permission.

(ii) **By what time to retain the goods seized?:** The goods seized can be kept/retained by the proper officer/authorized officer for a necessary period of time for their examination and for any inquiry or proceedings under the CGST Act.

17.4 Returning of the documents, books, or things which have not been relied upon—Section 67(3)

There is a possibility that some of the documents, books, or things (seized under section 67(2) or produced by the taxable person or any other person) cannot be relied upon to issue notice under the CGST Act or the CGST rules. In such case, such documents, books, or things are to be returned within 30 days of the date of issue of the notice.

17.5 Power to seal, break open the door, etc.—Section 67(4)

It may happen that the authorized officer is denied to access any premises, almirah, electronic devices, boxes, or receptacles which are suspected to contain (or hide/conceal) any goods, accounts, registers or documents of the person, then the officer can seal or break open the doors of such premises or to break open the almirah, electronic devices, boxes, or receptacles.

17.6 Right to make a copy or take extracts from the documents seized—Section 67(5)

If a person from whose custody the documents are seized under section 67(2) wants to make copies of the documents seized or to take extracts from them, then the person has this right, but this right shall be exercised in the presence of an authorized officer at such place and time as decided by the officer. However, if the officer thinks that making copies or taking extracts from the documents may be harmful to the investigation, then this right can be refused.

17.7 Provisional release of the goods seized—Section 67(6)

- The goods seized can be released on a provisional basis if the concerned person executes a bond and furnishes a security as per Rule 140 or on payment of applicable tax, interest and penalty payable.
- As per Rule 140, the bond is furnished in FORM GST INS-04 and the security is in the form of bank guarantee equal to the amount of applicable tax, interest and penalty payable. In case, the person to whom the goods are released provisionally fails to produce the goods at the appointed date and place indicated by the proper officer,

then the security can be encashed and adjusted against the tax, interest, penalty and fine, if any.

17.8 Notice of the goods seized—Section 67(7)

The department is required to give a notice of the goods seized within six months of the date of seizure. This period of six months can be extended by the proper officer if sufficient reasons are given, but the extension cannot exceed six months. If required notice is not served within the said time, then the goods shall be returned to the person from whose custody they were seized.

17.9 Disposal of the goods seized—Section 67(8)

After considering the following points, the Government may notify the goods which proper officer can dispose of the goods seized in a manner specified in Rule 141.

(a) Perishable/Hazardous nature of goods,
(b) Depreciation in value due to time factor,
(c) Constraints of storage,
(d) Other relevant points.

Note: The Government has notified the following goods:

1. Salt and hygroscopic substances
2. Raw (wet and salted) hides and skins
3. Newspapers and periodicals
4. Menthol, camphor, saffron
5. Refills for ballpoint pens
6. Lighter fuel, including lighters with gas, not having arrangements for refilling
7. Cells, batteries and rechargeable batteries
8. Petroleum products
9. Dangerous drugs and psychotropic substances
10. Bulk drugs and chemicals falling under the Customs Tariff Act, 1975
11. Pharmaceutical products falling under the Customs Tariff Act, 1975
12. Fireworks
13. Red sander
14. Sandalwood
15. All taxable goods falling under the Customs Tariff Act, 1975
16. All unclaimed/abandoned goods which are liable to rapid depreciation in value on account of fast changes in technology or new models, etc.
17. Any goods seized by the proper officer under section 67 which are to be provisionally released, but the provisional release has not been taken within one month from the date of execution of the bond.

17.10 Preparation of inventory—Section 67(9)

The proper officer is required to prepare an inventory of goods specified under section 67(8) or the goods seized under section 67(2)

17.11 Extent of applicability of the Code of Criminal Procedure—Section 67(10)

The provisions of the Code of Criminal Procedure, 1973, relating to search and seizure shall, so far as may be, apply to search and seizure under this section.

17.12 Section 67(11)

If the proper officer has reasons to believe, he may record the reasons in writing, seize the accounts, etc., of any person who has either evaded or is trying to evade payment of tax. The accounts, etc., gathered shall be retained for as long as necessary for prosecution.

17.13 Section 67(12)

The commissioner or authorized officer may cause procurement of supplies from any person in order to check the issue of tax invoice, etc., and on return of such goods, the tax invoice shall be cancelled, and the tax paid shall be refunded.

17.14 Arrest of a Person—Section 69

Power to arrest: Section 69(1)

If the commissioner has grounds to believe that a person has committed any of the offences listed in

- section 132(1)(a)
- section 132(1)(b)
- section 132(1)(c)
- Section132(1)(d),

which is punishable under clauses (i) and (ii) of section 132(1) or section 132(2), then the commissioner has the power to order a central tax officer to arrest that person. Thus, to understand section 69(1), the reading of section 132 is necessary. The relevant portion of section 132 is explained here briefly:

Section	Offence	Amount of tax evasion/ITC/ tax refund above ₹ 5 crore	Amount of tax evasion/ITC/ tax refund up to ₹ 5 crore
132(1)(a)	Supplying goods without issuing an invoice with an intention to evade tax.	• Cognizable and non-bailable under section 132(5), i.e., the person can be arrested without an arrest warrant.	• Non-cognizable and bailable offence under section 132(4), i.e., the person cannot be arrested without an arrest warrant.
132(1)(b)	Supplying goods without issuing an invoice with an intention to evade tax.		
132(1)(c)	• Availing input tax credit on the basis of the above invoice or bill • Fraudulently, availing input tax credit without any invoice or bill.	• Clause (i) of section 132(1)–Imprisonment up to five years plus fine.	• Clause (ii) of section 132(1)—Imprisonment upto three years plus fine if the amount of the case exceeds ₹2 crore, but upto ₹5 crore.
132(1)(d)	Failure in depositing the tax collected even after five months from the due date.		
132(2)	For the second and every subsequent offence.	Imprisonment up to five years plus fine.	

Producing before the Magistrate: Section 69(2)

Where a person is arrested for a **cognizable and non-bailable offence**, then the person arrested will be informed about the grounds of his arrest and he shall be produced before a Magistrate within 24 hours.

Release on bail and the power to grant bail: Section 69(3)

Subject to the provisions of the Code of Criminal Procedure, 1973,

(a) Where a person is arrested under section 69(1) for any offence specified under section 132(4), i.e., non-cognizable and bailable offence, he will be admitted to bail or, in default of bail, forwarded to the custody of the Magistrate.

(b) The bail can be given by the deputy commissioner or assistant commissioner, and the deputy commissioner or assistant commissioner is subject to the same provisions as an officer in-charge of a police station under section 436 of the Code of Criminal Procedure, 1973.

17.15 Power to summon persons—Section 70

Section 70(1): In the same way that is allowed in the case of a civil court under the Code of Civil Procedure, 1908, the proper officer has the power to summon any person whose attendance he believes necessary to present evidence to provide a document, or to produce anything else in any enquiry.

Section 70(2): Whatever inquiry is conducted under section 70(1) is deemed to be a judicial proceeding under the Indian Penal Code.

17.16 Access to Business Premises—Section 71

Access to Business Premises: Section 71(1)

An officer who is authorized by the proper officer (with a rank of joint commissioner or above) has the power to access any place of business of a registered person. The purpose is to inspect

- books of account,
- documents,
- computers,
- computer programs, computer software, whether installed on a computer or otherwise (e.g., already developed software on a CD), and
- such other things as he may require and which may be available at such place, to any audit, scrutiny, verification and checks as may be necessary to save the interest of revenue.

Production of documents or records on demand: Section 71(2)

A person who is in charge of the above-said place is required to make available (within 15 days or extended time) the following documents demanded by the above said authorised officer/ the auditor appointed by the proper officer or a chartered accountant or a cost accountant nominated under section 66.

(a) The records maintained or prepared by the registered person and declared to the proper officer.

(b) Trial Balance.

(c) Statements of Annual Financial Accounts, i.e., Statement of Profit and Loss and Balance Sheet. They must be audited if required.
(d) Cost Audit Report under section 148 of the Companies Act, 2013.
(e) Income Tax Audit Report u/s 44AB of the Income Tax Act, 1961.
(f) Any other relevant document.

17.17 Officers to assist the proper officer—Section 72(1)

The following officers are required to assist the proper officers in implementing the CGST Act.

1. Police officers
2. Railways officers
3. Customs officers
4. Officers engaged in the collection of land revenue, including village officers
5. Officers of State tax or Union territory tax
6. Other notified officers

Theory Questions

1. What are the provisions of search, inspection and arrest under the GST law?
2. State the cases when the GST officers can break the almirah or other relevant boxes.
3. Who are the officers who are required to assist the proper officer during a search, inspection, or arrest?
4. Under what circumstances a person may be arrested under the GST law?
5. Are there officers from other departments or organisations who are required to assist the proper officer while conducting search, seizure and arrest?

18
Advance Ruling

18.1 Introduction

Sometimes, what happens is that a person wants to do a business activity, but some confusion arises about some matters of GST in relation to that business activity, e.g., the matter of time of supply. In that case, he has two options: move ahead with the confusions and do his best. The problem with this option is that if something goes wrong later on, then legal problems may arise even the matter may go to the court of law. Therefore, the best option is the second option, i.e., go for an advance ruling. Advance ruling is a mechanism in which a person takes a ruling from an authority (established by a government) in advance regarding some specified matters only. Sections 95 to 106 of the CGST Act lay down the provisions of advance ruling.

18.2 Important Definitions—Section 95

1. Advance ruling Section 95(a)	Advance ruling means a decision provided by • the Authority or • the Appellate Authority or • the National Appellate Authority to an applicant on matters or on questions specified in • section 97(2) or • section 100(1) or • section 101C (1), in relation to the supply of goods or services or both being undertaken or proposed to be undertaken by the applicant.
2. Appellate Authority Section 95(b)	The Appellate Authority for Advance Ruling referred to in section 99.
3. Applicant Section 95(c)	Applicant means any person registered or desirous of obtaining registration under the CGST Act.
4. Application Section 95(d)	Application means an application made to the Authority under section 97(1).

5. Authority Section 95(e)	Authority means the Authority for Advance Authority referred to in section 96.
6. National Appellate Authority Section 95(f)	The National Appellate Authority for Advance Ruling referred to in section 101A.

18.3 Authority for Advance Ruling (AAR)

1. Qualification and appointment of members of the Authority for Advance Ruling (AAR): The members (not below the rank of Joint Commissioner) of the AAR shall be appointed by the Government.

2. Constitution of AAR: Section 96: The Authority for Advance Ruling is constituted under the provisions of a State GST Act or a UTGST Act. Such an authority is deemed to be authority for advance ruling under the CGST Act.

3. Application for Advance Ruling: Section 97(1): A person who wants to obtain an advance ruling can make an application in form GST ARA-01 with a fee of ₹5,000.

4. Matters specified in Section 97(2): As per section 97(2), these are the issues or matters or questions for advance ruling can be sought:

(a) classification of any goods or services or both
(b) applicability of a notification issued under the provisions of the CGST Act
(c) determination of time and value of supply of goods or services or both
(d) admissibility of input tax credit of tax paid or deemed to have been paid
(e) determination of the liability to pay tax on any goods or services or both
(f) whether applicant is required to be registered
(g) whether any particular thing done by the applicant with respect to any goods or services or both amounts to or results in a supply of goods or services or both within the meaning of that term.

5. Procedure on receipt of application: Section 98(1): On receipt of the application from the applicant, the authority forwards a copy of the application to the concerned officer and demands relevant records. These documents shall be returned by the authority as soon as possible.

6. Acceptance or Rejection of application: Section 98(2): The authority may accept or reject the application by **an order** after examining the application and the records called for. Moreover, where the question raised in the application is already *pending or decided* in any proceedings in the case of an applicant under any of the provisions of the CGST Act, then the authority cannot accept the application. If an application is to be rejected, a proper opportunity to be heard shall be given to the applicant before the rejection, and the reasons for rejection shall be mentioned in the said order.

7. Sending the copy of the order: Section 98(3): A copy of the above order shall be sent to the applicant and the concerned officer.

8. Pronouncement of the ruling: Section 98(4)/(6): After hearing the applicant or his authorised representative and the concerned officer or his authorised representative, the authority is required to pronounce its ruling within 90 days from the date of the application.

9. Difference of opinion: Section 98(5): There may be a difference of opinion between the members of the authority on a question mentioned in the application, then such points of differences are stated, and the case is referred to a higher authority known as Appellate Authority for Advance Ruling (in short AAAR) to decide on such question.

10. Certified copy of the advance ruling is to be communicated: Section 98(7): A copy of the advance ruling is communicated to the applicant, the concerned officer and the jurisdictional officer. Such copy must be duly signed and certified (as per rule 105) by the members of the authority.

18.4 Appellate Authority for Advance Ruling (AAAR)

1. Constitution of AAAR: The Authority for Advance Ruling (AAAR) is constituted under the provisions of an SGST Act or a UTGST Act. Such authority is deemed to be Appellate Authority for Advance Ruling under the CGST Act.

2. Who can appeal to AAR and time limit to file an appeal: Section 100(1)/(2): If the applicant or concerned officer or the jurisdictional officer feels aggrieved by any advance ruling given by the Authority for Advance Ruling, then the aggrieved has the option to appeal to the Appellate Authority for Advance Ruling within 30 days from the date of communication of the ruling. The period of 30 days can be extended by a period not exceeding 30 days if AAAR is satisfied that there were sufficient reasons for the delay.

3. Fee and form for appeal: Section 100(3) read with Rule 106

(a) If the appeal is to be filed by the applicant, then it should be in FORM GST ARA-02, along with a fee of ₹10,000.

(b) If the appeal is to be filed by the concerned officer or jurisdictional officer, then FORM GST ARA-03 is used, and no fee is required.

4. What can be done by AAAR to the order passed by the AAR: Section 101(1)/(2): AAAR may pass an order as it thinks fit. The order may confirm or modify the order passed by the advance ruling authority. Such an order shall be passed within **90 days** from the date of appeal.

5. No advance ruling can be given: Section 101(3): If there is an opinion difference (among the members of AAAR) on any point or points referred to in the appeal or reference, then it is deemed that an advance ruling cannot be given in respect of the question under the appeal or reference.

6. Certified copy of the advance ruling is to be communicated: Section 101(4): A copy of the advance ruling is communicated to the applicant, the concerned officer, the jurisdictional officer and AAR. Such copy must be duly signed and certified (as per rule 105) by the members of the authority.

18.5 National Appellate Authority for Advance Ruling (NAAAR)—Section 101A

1. Power to constitute of NAAAR: Section 101A (1): On the recommendation of the GST council, the Central Government has the power to constitute an authority known as the National Appellate Authority for Advance Ruling for hearing appeals made under section 101B. Such authority shall be constituted by a notification.

2. Appointment of the President and Members of NAAAR: Section 101A (2): The National Appellate Authority shall consist of the president, a technical member (from the centre) and a technical member (from the state). Their eligibility is as follows:

(a) The President
- who has been a Judge of the Supreme Court or
- is or has been the Chief Justice of a High Court, or
- is or has been a Judge of a High Court for a period of at least five years.

(b) A Technical Member (Centre)

An individual who is or has been a member of the Indian Revenue (Customs and Central Excise) Service, Group A, and has completed at least 15 years of service in Group A.

(c) A Technical Member (State)

An individual who is or has been an officer of the State Government not below the rank of Additional Commissioner of Value Added Tax or the Additional Commissioner of State tax with at least three years of experience in the administration of an existing law or the State Goods and Services Tax Act or in the field of finance and taxation.

3. Who will appoint the above president: Section 101A (3): The President of the National Appellate Authority shall be appointed by the Government after consultation with the Chief Justice of India or his nominee. If the office of the president is vacant due to

- his death,
- resignation or
- other reasons,

then the senior most member of the National Appellate Authority shall hold the office of the President until the date on which a new President appointed enters upon his office. Moreover, if the President cannot discharge his functions because of his absence, illness or any other reason, the senior most member of the National Appellate Authority is required to discharge the functions of the President unless the date on which the President resumes his duties.

4. Who will appoint the above Technical Member (Centre and State): Section 101A (4): The Technical Member (Centre) and Technical Member (State) shall be appointed by the Government on the recommendations of a Selection Committee consisting of such persons and in such manner as may be prescribed.

5. Validity of the appointment of the Members: Section 101A (5): The appointment of the Members of the National Appellate Authority cannot be held invalid just because of any vacancy or defect in the constitution of the Selection Committee.

6. Assurance before appointing the President and the members: Section 101A (6): Before appointing any person as the President or Members of the National Appellate Authority, the Government shall satisfy itself that such person does not have any financial or other interests which are likely to prejudicially affect his functions as such President or Member.

7. Salary, allowances, etc.: Section 101A (7)

- The salary, allowances and other terms and conditions of service of the President and the Members of the National Appellate Authority shall be determined in a prescribed manner.

- Moreover, after the appointment of the President or Member of the NAAAR, the salary, allowances, and other terms and conditions of service of the President or Members of the cannot be changed in a way that puts them at a disadvantage.

8. Term of the President's office: Section 101A (8): The President shall hold office for a period of three years from

(a) the date on which he enters upon his office, or
(b) until he attains the age of 70,

whichever is earlier and shall also be eligible for reappointment.

9. Term of the Technical Member: Section 101A (9): The Technical Member (Centre/State) shall hold office for a term of five years from

(a) the date on which he enters upon his office, or
(b) until he attains the age of 65 years,

whichever is earlier and shall also be eligible for reappointment.

10. Resignation by the President or Member: Section 101A (10): The president or any member may give a written notice of resignation to the Government. However, the President or Member shall continue to hold office until

(a) the expiry of three months from the date of receipt of such notice by the Government, or
(b) a person duly appointed as his successor enters upon his office or
(c) the expiry of his term of office,

whichever is the earliest.

11. Removal of the President or Member: Section 101A (11): The Government has the power, *after consultation with the Chief Justice of India*, to remove the President or Member on the following grounds:

(a) He has been adjudged an insolvent or
(b) He has been convicted of an offence which, in the opinion of the Government, involves moral turpitude or
(c) He has become physically or mentally incapable of acting as such President or Member or
(d) He has acquired such financial or other interest as is likely to affect prejudicially his functions as such President or Member or
(e) He has so abused his position as to render his continuance in office prejudicial to the public interest.

Note: In the case of the last two grounds, the President or the Member cannot be removed unless he has been informed of the charges against him and has been given an opportunity of being heard.

12. Removal of the President and Technical Members: Section 101A (12): The Government can remove the President or Technical Members of NAAAR only by an order passed by the Government for the misbehaviour or incapacity of the President and Technical Members. Such misbehaviour or incapacity must be proved under an inquiry made by a Supreme Court judge who shall be nominated by the Chief Justice of India (CJI) on a reference made to him by the Government. However, such a President or Member shall be given an opportunity of being heard.

Note: Section 101A (11) has overrides section 101A (12).

13. Suspension of the President or Technical Member: Section 101A (13): With the agreement of the Chief Justice of India, the Government may suspend the President or Technical Members of NAAAR who is under inquiry by the Supreme Court Judge under section 101A (12).

14. After leaving his position, the President or Member of NAAAR cannot appear, act or plead before NAAAR where he was the President or Member. This is as per the provisions of article 220 of the Constitution of India.

18.6 Appeal to National Appellate Authority—Section 101B

1. Who can appeal?: Section 101B (1): Where the Appellate Authorities of two or more States or Union territories give conflicting rulings on the questions of section 97(2), then any officer authorised by the commissioner (from the States in which such rulings have been given) or the applicant, being a distinct person under section 25 aggrieved by such ruling, may appeal to the National Appellate Authority.

2. Time for Appeal: Section 101B (2)

- The appeal shall be filed (verified and appealed in a prescribed manner and with a specified fee) within 30 days from the date on which the ruling of the Appellate Authority is communicated to the applicants, concerned officers and jurisdictional officers.
- Further, if the appeal is to be filed by the officer authorised by the Commissioner, then he has the time of 90 days from the date on which the ruling is communicated to the concerned officer or the jurisdictional officer.
- However, the National Appellate Authority may increase the above time of 30 days or 90 days, as the case may be, if it is satisfied that there were sufficient grounds for delay, but such increase cannot exceed 30 days.

Note: It is to be noted that the period of 30 or 90 days shall be counted from the date of communication of the last of the conflicting rulings sought to be appealed against.

18.7 Order of National Appellate Authority—Section 101C

1. Power to pass an order confirming and modifying the rulings appealed against: Section 101C (1): The National Appellate Authority may, after giving an opportunity of being heard to the applicant,

- the officer authorised by the Commissioner,
- all Principal Chief Commissioners,
- Chief Commissioners of Central tax,
- Chief Commissioner and Commissioner of State tax of all States and
- Chief Commissioner and Commissioner of Union territory tax of all Union territories,

pass such order as it thinks fit. The order may confirm or modify the rulings appealed.

2. Difference in opinion: Section 101C (2): If there is a difference in opinion of the members of the National Appellate Authority, then the principle of majority shall be exercised to decide the case.

3. Time limit to pass the above order: Section 101C (3): The above order shall be passed as far as possible within 90 days from the date of the appeal under section 101B.

4. Copy of the order to be sent: Section 101(4): A copy of the Advance Ruling pronounced by the National Appellate Authority shall be duly signed by the Members and certified in such manner as may be prescribed and shall be sent to

- the applicant,
- the officer authorised by the Commissioner,
- the Board (i.e., CBIC),
- the Chief Commissioner and Commissioner of State tax of all States and Chief Commissioner and Commissioner of Union territory tax of all Union territories, and
- to the Authority or Appellate Authority, as the case may be.

18.8 Rectification of the order—Section 102

AAR or AAAR or NAAAR may amend any order passed by it under section 98 or section 101 or section 101C, respectively, so as to rectify any error apparent on the face of the record if such error

- is noticed by AAR or AAAR or NAAAR on its own accord or
- is brought to its notice by the concerned officer, the jurisdictional officer, the applicant, the appellant, the AAR or AAAR within a period of six months from the date of the order.

Note: No rectification that has the effect of enhancing the tax liability or reducing the amount of admissible input tax credit can be made unless the applicant or the appellant has been given an opportunity to be heard.

18.9 Applicability of advance ruling—Section 103

1. Who is bound by the advance ruling given by AAR or AAAR: Section 103(1)

(a) The applicant and

(b) The concerned officer or the jurisdictional officer in respect of the applicant.

2. Who is bound by the advance ruling given by NAAAR: Section 103(1A)

(a) the applicants, being distinct persons, who had demanded the ruling under section 101B (1) and all registered persons having the same PAN.

(b) the concerned officers and the jurisdictional officers in respect of the applicants referred to in clause (a) and the registered persons having the same PAN.

3. Time up to which the Advance Ruling is valid: Section 103(2): The advance ruling remains binding as long as the law, facts or circumstance supporting the original advance ruling remain unchanged.

18.10 Cases when Advance Ruling is declared void—Section 104(1)/(2)

1. Where AAR or AAAR or NAAAR finds that the advance ruling given by it has been obtained by the applicant or the appellant by

- fraud or suppression of material facts or
- misrepresentation of facts,

then it has the power to declare such ruling *void ab initio* (invalid from the starting point) by an order, and thereupon, all the provisions of the CGST Act or the rules shall apply to the applicant or the appellant as if such advance ruling was never given but before passing such order an opportunity of being heard is required to be given to the applicant or the appellant.

Note: The period beginning with the date of such advance ruling and ending with the date of order under section 104(1) is excluded while determining the period specified in section 73(2)/(10) or section 74(2)/(10).

2. A copy of the above order is required to be sent to the applicant, the concerned officer and the jurisdictional officer.

18.11 Powers of AAR or AAAR or NAAAR—Section 105(1)/(2)

1. AAR or AAAR or NAAAR have power of

- discovery and inspection,
- enforcing the attendance of any person and examining him on oath,
- issuing commissions and compelling production of books of account and other records,

have all the powers of a civil court under the Code of Civil Procedure, 1908.

2. AAR or AAAR or NAAAR is deemed to be a civil court for the purposes of section 195 but not for the purposes of Chapter XXVI of the Code of Criminal Procedure, 1973, and every proceeding before AAR or AAAR shall be deemed to be judicial proceedings within the meaning of sections 193 and 228, and for the purpose of section 196 of the Indian Penal Code.

18.12 Procedure of Authority and Appellate Authority—Section 106

AAR or AAAR or NAAAR shall have the power to regulate its own procedure.

Theory Questions

1. What do you mean by Advance Ruling? How is it useful for a businessman?
2. What are the powers of Authority for Advance Ruling?
3. What are the cases when the advance ruling given by AAR or AAAR or NAAAR is taken to be void?
4. Can any advance ruling authority rectify its order?
5. Write a short note on the National Appellate Authority for Advance Ruling.
6. What are the questions the answers of which can be decided by the Advance Ruling Authority?
7. What do you understand by Advance Ruling? State the procedure for obtaining an Advance Ruling.

Appendix III

Some of the Advance Rulings given in 2023

The purpose of giving this table is that the students can learn what kind of questions can be raised to take advance ruling.

State/UT	Applicant	Referring section	Question raised
Karnataka	M/s. Marubeni India Private Limited	97(2)(e)	Whether the supply of goods from the Applicant to the overseas customer is taxable under GST as a zero-rated supply or not?
Uttar Pradesh	M/s Gobind Sugar Mills Limited	97(2)(a)/(b)/(e)	Classification of Sugarcane Juice 1. Rate of GST applicable on sale of Sugarcane Juice 2. Applicability of a notification which affects the rate of tax (if any)
Rajasthan	M/s Vishwas Green Energy	97(2)(c)	Is GST applicable to government subsidies? How to Generate GST, including Subsidized Invoices?
Haryana	M/s ARPK Health Care Pvt Ltd	97(2)(b)/(e)/(f)/(g)	1. Whether Fees/charges received by M/s ARPK from M/s Asian are exempt under GST? 2. Whether Fees/charges for Health Care Services received by M/s Asian are exempt under GST.
Orissa	M/s Indian Metal and Ferro Alloys Limited	97(2)(a)/(e)	Whether Service Received by a registered person by way of renting of residential premises used as a guesthouse of the registered person is subject to GST under Forward Charge Mechanism (FCM) or Reverse Charge Mechanism?

Source: https://gstcouncil.gov.in/authority-for-advance-rulings?page=1

19 Offences and Penalties

19.1 Penalties for certain offences

As per **section 122(1)**, where a taxable person who:

(i) Supplies any goods or services or both without the issue of any invoice or issues an incorrect or false invoice.

(ii) Issues any invoice or bill without supply of goods or services or both in violation of the provisions of the CGST Act or the rules framed thereunder.

(iii) Collects any amount as tax but does not pay to the Government beyond three months from the date of due.

(iv) Collects any amounts as tax in contravention of the CGST Act but does not pay to the Government beyond three months from the date of due.

(v) Fails to deduct tax at source or deducts less amount or if deducts right amount but does not pay to the government.

(vi) Fails to collect tax at source or collects less amount or if collects right amount but does not pay to the government.

(vii) Takes or utilizes ITC without actual receipt of goods or services or both, either fully or partially.

(viii) Fraudulently obtains tax refund.

(ix) Takes or distributes ITC in violation of section 20 (Input Service Distributor) or the rules made thereunder.

(x) Falsifies or substitutes financial records or produces fake accounts or documents or furnishes any false information or returns with the intention to evade GST.

(xi) Fails to obtain registration when he is liable for registration.

(xii) Furnishes any false information to obtain registration.

(xiii) Obstructs or prevents any officer in discharging of his duties under the CGST Act.

(xiv) Transports any taxable goods without the cover of documents specified.

(xv) Suppresses his turnover to evade tax.

(xvi) Fails to keep, maintain or retain books of account and other documents in accordance with provisions of the CGST Act or rules made thereunder.

(xvii) Fails to furnish information or documents called for during any proceedings under the CGST Act.

(xviii) Supplies, transports, stores any goods which he has reasons to believe are liable to confiscation under the CGST Act.

(xix) Issues any invoice or document by using the registration number of another registered person.

(xx) Tampers with or destroys any material evidence or document.

(xxi) Disposes of or tampers with any goods that have been detained, seized or attached.

shall be liable to a penalty equal to higher of the following:

(a) ₹10,000

or

(b) Tax evaded or the tax not deducted under section 51, i.e., TDS or short deducted or deducted but not paid to the Government or tax not collected under section 52, i.e., TCS or short collected or collected but not paid to the Government or ITC availed or passed on or distributed irregularly, or the refund claimed fraudulently as the case may be.

Section 122(1A): If a person causes to commit and retains the benefits of any of the offences given below, then he shall be liable for a penalty equal to the tax evaded or input tax credit availed or passed on.

(i) Supplies any goods or services or both without the issue of any invoice or issues an incorrect or false invoice.

(ii) Issues any invoice or bill without supply of goods or services or both in violation of the provisions of the CGST Act or the rules framed thereunder.

(iii) Takes or utilizes ITC without actual receipt of goods or services or both, either fully or partially.

(iv) Takes or distributes ITC in violation of section 20 (Input Service Distributor) or the rules made thereunder.

Section 122(1B): [A new section inserted by section 155 of the Finance Act, 2023.

Where any electronic commerce operator

(i) allows a supply of goods or services or both through it by an unregistered person other than a person exempted from registration by a notification issued under the CGST Act to make such supply,

(ii) allows an inter-state supply of goods or services or both through it by a person who is not eligible to make such inter-state supply or

(iii) fails to furnish the correct details in the statement to be furnished under section 52(4) of any outward supply of goods effected through it by a person exempted from obtaining registration under the CGST Act, then the operator is liable to pay a penalty of higher of the following amounts:

(a) ₹10,000 or

(b) an amount equivalent to the amount of tax involved if such supply were made by a registered person (not being a registered person who has opted composition levy under section 10).

Section 122(2): Any registered person who supplies goods or services or both on which tax has not been paid or short paid or erroneously refunded or where the ITC has been wrongly availed or utilized:

Case I: For any reasons other than fraud or any willful misstatement or suppression of facts to evade tax

Amount of Penalty

(a) ₹10,000 or

(b) 10% of the tax due from such a person.

whichever is higher.

Case II: For any reasons of fraud or any willful misstatement or suppression of facts to evade tax

Amount of Penalty

(a) ₹10,000 or

(b) Tax due from such a person

, whichever is higher.

As per **Section 122(3)**, any person who:

(a) Aids or abets any of the offences mentioned in section 122(1) above.

(b) Acquires possession of, or in any way concerns himself in transporting, removing, depositing, keeping, concealing, supplying, or purchasing or in any other manner deals with any goods which he knows or has reasons to believe are liable to confiscation under the CGST Act or the rules thereunder.

(c) Receives or is in any way concerned with the supply of, or in any other manner deals with any supply of services which he knows or has reasons to believe are in contravention of any provisions of the CGST Act or the rules thereunder.

(d) Fails to appear before the officer of central tax, when issued with a summon for appearance to give evidence or produce a document in an enquiry.

(e) Fails to issue invoice in accordance with the provisions of the CGST Act or rules made thereunder or fails to account for an invoice in his books of account.

shall be liable to penalty of up to ₹25,000.

19.2 Penalty for failure to furnish information return—Section 123

As per section 150 (1), specified persons (e.g., a taxable person, local authority, bank, etc.) are required to furnish an information return of the specified information (e.g., bank details, consumption of electricity, etc.) in respect of such periods, within such time, in such form and manner and to such authority or agency as may be prescribed. If the specified fails to do so, then the commissioner or an officer authorized by him may serve upon the defaulting person a notice under section 150(1) to furnish the information return within a period not exceeding 90 days from the date of service notice.

If the above-said person still does not furnish the information return, the proper officer may direct that such person shall be liable to pay a penalty **lower** of the following:

(a) ₹100 per day till such failure or

(b) ₹5,000.

19.3 Fine for failure to furnish Statistics or return under—Section 124

As per section 151, the Commissioner or an officer authorised by him may, by an order, direct any person to furnish information relating to any matter dealt with in connection with the CGST Act within such time, in such form, and in such manner, as may be specified therein.

If a person requires furnishing statistics or return under section 151

(a) without reasonable cause fails to furnish such information or return as may be required under that section,

or

(b) wilfully furnishes or causes to furnish any information or return that he knows to be false

, then he shall be punishable with a fine which may extend to ₹10,000 and, in case of a continuing offence, to a further fine which may extend to ₹1,000 for each day after the first day during which the offence continues subject to a maximum limit of ₹25,000.

19.4 General Penalty—Section 125

As per section 125, any person who contravenes any of the provisions of the CGST Act or any rules thereunder for which no separate penalty is provided in the Act, shall be liable to a penalty up to ₹25,000.

19.5 General Disciplines Related to Penalty—Section 126

1. No officer under the CGST Act shall impose any penalty for
   - minor breaches of tax regulations or
   - procedural requirements or
   - any omission or mistake in documentation that is easily rectifiable and made without fraudulent intent or gross negligence.

   Note: Minor breach means if the amount of tax is less than ₹5,000.
2. The penalty imposed under this Act shall depend on the facts and circumstances of each case and shall be commensurate with the degree and severity of the breach.
3. Penalty cannot be imposed without giving an opportunity being heard.
4. The penalty order shall specify the nature of the breach and the applicable law, regulation or procedure under which the amount of penalty for the breach has been specified.
5. When a person voluntarily discloses to an officer under this Act the circumstances of a breach of the tax law, regulation or procedural requirement prior to the discovery

of the breach by the officer under the CGST Act, the proper officer may consider this fact as a mitigating factor when quantifying a penalty for that person.

6. The provisions of this section shall not apply in such cases where the penalty specified under the CGST Act is either a fixed sum or expressed as a fixed percentage.

19.6 Power to impose penalty in certain cases—Section 127

Where the proper officer is of the view that a person is liable to a penalty and the same is not covered under any proceedings under

- section 62 or
- section 63 or
- section 64 or
- section 73 or
- section 74 or
- section 129 or
- section 130

then he may issue an order levying such a penalty after giving a reasonable opportunity to be heard to such a person.

19.7 Power to waive penalty or fee or both—Section 128

On the recommendation of the GST council, the Government may notify such class of taxpayers and the circumstances where any penalty under section 122 or section 123 or section 125 or any late fee under section 47 can be waived off completely or partially.

19.8 Detention, Seizure and Release of Goods and Conveyances in Transit—Section 129

1. Conditions to detain, seize and release the goods and conveyance: Section 129(1): Ignoring whatsoever is written in other sections of the CGST Act, if a person transports or stores goods while they are being transported from one place to another in violation of the CGST Act or the rules made under it, the proper officer has the power to detain or seize the goods, the conveyance used to transport the goods, and any documents related to them. However, after the detention or seizure, the goods and conveyance can be released in the following manner:

(a) **Where the owner of the goods comes forward for payment of such penalty:** On payment of a penalty equal to 200% of the tax payable on such goods, but in the case of exempted goods, the penalty payable is lower of the following amounts:

(i) ₹25,000

(ii) 2% of the value of the goods.

(b) **Where the owner of the goods does not come forward for payment of such penalty:** On payment of a penalty equal to higher of the following amounts:

(i) 50% of the value of the goods

(ii) 200% of the tax payable on such goods

However, in the case of exempted goods, the penalty payable is lower of the following amounts:

(i) ₹25,000

(ii) 5% of the value of the goods.

(c) On furnishing a security equivalent to the amount calculated above, as the case may be, in such form and manner as may be prescribed.

Note: The goods or conveyance discussed above cannot be detained or seized without giving an order of detention or seizure to the person transporting the goods.

2. Section 129(2) [Omitted, the Finance Act, 2021]

3. Issue of notice of detention or seizure: Section 129(3): The proper officer detaining or seizing goods or conveyance is required to issue a notice (specifying the penalty payable) within seven days of the detention or seizure. Thereafter, he shall pass an order (within seven days of the date of service of the notice) for payment of penalty under section 129(1)(a)/(b).

4. Opportunity of being heard to be given before penalty: Section 129(4): The concerned person shall be given an opportunity to be heard before determining the penalty under section 129(3).

5. The requirement of serving notice is concluded on payment of penalty: Section 129(5): If the penalty determined under section 129(1) is paid, then it is deemed that the requirement of servicing notice under section 129(3) has been completed.

6. Discard of the goods in case of failure in payment of penalty: Section 129(6): Where the transporter or owner of the goods fails to pay the penalty under section 129(1) within 15 days from the date of receipt of the copy of the order passed under section 129(3), then the goods or conveyance detained or seized may be sold or disposed of otherwise, in a specified manner and time, to recover the penalty. However, the conveyance shall be released if the transporter makes the payment equal to the lower of the following:

(i) the penalty or

(ii) ₹1,00,000

Note: Where the detained or seized goods are perishable or hazardous or are likely to depreciate, then the above period of 15 days may be reduced by the proper officer.

19.9 Confiscation of Goods or Conveyances and Levy of Penalty—Section 130

1. Confiscation for committing a specified act and penalty: Section 130(1)

If any person

(i) makes supply or receives any goods in violation of the provisions of the CGST Act or the rules made under it, and the intension is tax evasion or

(ii) fails to account for any goods on which he is liable to pay tax under the CGST Act or

(iii) makes the supply of taxable goods, but without having applied registration or

(iv) violates the provisions of the CGST Act or the rules made under it with intention of tax evasion or

(v) uses any conveyance to transport goods in contravention of the provisions of the CGST Act or the rules made thereunder unless the owner of the conveyance proves that it was so used without the knowledge or connivance of the owner himself or his agent and the person in charge of the conveyance,

then, all such goods or conveyances are liable to confiscation and the person is liable to penalty under section 122.

2. Option to pay a fine instead of confiscation: Section 130(2)

- Whenever confiscation of any goods or conveyance is authorised by the CGST Act, the officer adjudging it shall give the owner of the goods an option to pay such fine as the said officer thinks fit instead of confiscation. However, such a fine cannot exceed the market value of the goods confiscated, less the tax chargeable thereon.
- Moreover, the sum total of the fine and penalty leviable must be equal to or greater than the penalty of 200% of the tax payable on such goods.
- Furthermore, the owner of any such conveyance who uses it to transport goods or passengers for hire will have the option of paying a fine equal to the tax due on the goods being transported thereon instead of having the conveyance confiscated.

3. Section 130(3) [Omitted, the Finance Act, 2021]

4. Opportunity of being heard to be given before penalty: Section 130(4): The order for confiscation of goods or conveyance or for imposition of penalty cannot be issued without giving the concerned person an opportunity to be heard.

5. What will happen to the title of the goods after confiscation?: Section 130(5): Where the goods or conveyance are confiscated, then such goods or conveyance become the property of the Government.

6. Custody of the things confiscated: Section 130(6): The officer responsible for deciding on confiscation will take and keep possession of the confiscated things. Every police officer, when requested by the said officer, must help in taking and keeping possession of those items.

7. Discarding the goods or conveyance confiscated: Section 130(7): The proper officer in charge can sell confiscated goods or conveyance if they are not needed for any other proceeding under the CGST Act. He must give the person involved a reasonable amount of time, up to three months, to pay a fine instead of having their goods or conveyance confiscated. The money collected from the sale of the goods or conveyance shall be given to the Government.

19.10 Confiscation or penalty not to interfere with other punishments—Section 131

Without prejudice to the provisions of the Code of Criminal Procedure, 1973, no confiscation made or penalty imposed under the CGST Act or the rules made thereunder shall prevent the infliction of any other punishment to which the person affected thereby is liable under the provisions of this Act or under any other law for the time being in force.

19.11 Punishment for Certain Offences—Section 132

1. List of offences under Section 132(1): Whoever commits, or causes to commit and retain the benefits arising out of, any of the following offences:

(a) supplies any goods or services or both without issue of any invoice in violation of the CGST Act or its rules, with the intention of tax evasion,

(b) issues any invoice or bill without supplying goods or services or both in violation of the CGST Act, or its rules and such invoice which can be used for wrongful availment or utilisation of input tax credit or refund of tax,

(c) avails input tax credit using the above invoice or bill or fraudulently avails input tax credit without any invoice or bill,

(d) collects any amount as tax but fails to deposit to the Government beyond three months from the due date of deposit,

(e) evades tax or fraudulently receives a refund, and this offence is other than the above four offences,

(f) falsifies or substitutes financial records or produces fake accounts or documents or furnishes any false information with an intention to evade tax due under the CGST Act,

(g) **[Omitted by Section 156(a) of the Finance Act, 2023]**

(h) acquires possession of, or in any way concerns himself in transporting, removing, depositing, keeping, concealing, supplying, or purchasing or in any other manner deals with, any goods which he knows or has reasons to believe are liable to confiscation under the CGST Act or the rules made thereunder,

(i) receives or is in any way concerned with the supply of, or in any other manner deals with any supply of services which he knows or has reasons to believe are in contravention of any provisions of the CGST Act or the rules made thereunder,

(j) **[Omitted by Section 156(a) of the Finance Act, 2023]**

(k) **[Omitted by Section 156(a) of the Finance Act, 2023]**

(l) attempts to commit, or abets (to help) the commission of any of the offences mentioned in clauses (a) to (f) and clauses (h) and (i) of this section. **[Amended by Section 156(b) of the Finance Act, 2023]**

2. Punishment for the above offences: Section 132(1)

(i) imprisonment up to five years plus a fine if the tax exceeds ₹5 crore.

(ii) imprisonment up to three years plus a fine if the tax exceeds ₹2 crore but is up to ₹3 crore.

(iii) in the case of any an offence mentioned under clause (b) imprisonment up to one year plus a fine if the tax exceeds ₹1 crore but is up to ₹2 crore. **[Amended by Section 156(c) of the Finance Act, 2023]**

(iv) in cases where he commits or assists in the commission of a specific offence mentioned in clause (f) he can be punished with imprisonment for up to six months or with a fine or both. **[Amended by Section 156(d) of the Finance Act, 2023]**

Note: For the purposes of this section, the term "tax" shall include the amount of tax evaded or the amount of input tax credit wrongly availed or utilised or refund wrongly taken under the provisions of the CGST Act, the SGST Act, the IGST Act or the UTGST Tax Act and cess levied under the Goods and Services Tax (Compensation to States) Act.

Thus, the summary of section 132(1) is tabulated below:

S. No.	Amount of tax	Punishment
1.	tax > ₹5 crore	Up to five years jail + fine [cognizable and non-bailable offence—Section 132(5)]
2.	₹2 crore < tax ≤ ₹5 crore	Up to three years jail + fine
3.	₹1 crore < tax ≤ ₹2 crore	Up to one year jail + fine
	For the following offences	
4.	• falsifies or substitutes financial records or produces fake accounts or documents or furnishes any false information with an intention to evade payment of tax due under the CGST Act; • obstructs or prevents any officer in the discharge of his duties under the CGST Act; • tampers with or destroys any material evidence or documents	Up to six months jail or fine or both

3. A person convicted for an offence more than once: Section 132(2): If a person is convicted of an offence, under section 132 more than once, they will be punished with imprisonment for up to five years and a fine for each subsequent offence.

4. Minimum imprisonment: Section 132(3): Unless there are specific and adequate reasons stated in the judgement of the court, then imprisonment mentioned in clauses (i), (ii), and (iii) of section 132(1) or 132(2) must be for a minimum duration of six months.

5. All the offences [other than section 132(5)] under the CGST Act are non-cognizable and bailable: Section 132(4): Irrespective of what is written in the Code of Criminal Procedure, 1973, all the offences under the CGST Act, except the case of section 132(5), are non-cognizable and bailable.

General Knowledge (Optional)

- A non-cognizable offence refers to an offence in which a police officer cannot arrest a person without a warrant, investigate or file a First Information Report (FIR) without the permission or direction of a Magistrate. Non-cognizable offences are generally less serious offences, such as causing minor injuries, minor theft, etc., and are usually punishable with a fine, imprisonment for a short term, or both.
- Examples of non-cognizable offences include simple assault, criminal intimidation, cheating, forgery, defamation, and making a false complaint to the police. The aggrieved person can file a complaint about a non-cognizable offence to the Magistrate, who will then direct the police to investigate the matter.

6. Cognizable and non-bailable offence: Section 132(5): The offences mentioned in clause (a) or (b) or (c) or (d) of section 132(1) and punishable under clause (i) of section 132(1) are cognizable and non-bailable. In simple words, if the amount involved in the offences, mentioned in clauses (a) to (d) of section 132(1), exceeds ₹5 crore, then the offence is cognizable and non-bailable.

Notes:

- A cognizable offence refers to a type of crime that is considered serious enough to warrant the police to make an arrest without a warrant and start an investigation without any prior permission from the court. This means that the police have the power to take immediate action upon receiving a complaint or knowledge of a cognizable offence.
- Under the Criminal Procedure Code (CrPC) of India, cognizable offences are classified as such based on the gravity of the offence and the punishment prescribed for it. Examples of cognizable offences in India include murder, rape, kidnapping, theft, and other serious crimes.
- Once a cognizable offence has been reported to the police, they are required by law to register an FIR (First Information Report) and begin the investigation. The police may arrest the accused and produce them before a magistrate within 24 hours of arrest, and seek remand for further investigation.
- It is important to note that while the police have certain powers to investigate and arrest suspects in cognizable offences, it is also essential to protect the rights of the accused, and they should not be subjected to any kind of mistreatment or unlawful detention.

7. Sanction of the commissioner is a must for prosecution: Section 132(6): A person cannot be prosecuted for any offence under section 132 without the previous sanction of the Commissioner.

Theory Questions

1. What are the various activities that would be considered to be offences under section 122(1) attracting penalties under the CGST Act?
2. State the offences under the CGST Act which are cognizable and non-bailable.
3. Specify non-cognizable and bailable offences under the CGST Act.
4. What is the punishment for an offence under section 132 of the CGST Act?
5. Write down the provisions of confiscation of Goods or Conveyances and Levy of Penalty.
6. What are the different types of offences under GST? Explain the provisions pertaining to penalties regarding these offences.
7. Do you agree with the statement that all the offences under the CGST Act are non-cognizable and bailable?

20

Refund

20.1 Cases of Refund claims

Following are the cases of refund claims.

S. No.	Cases
1.	Export or supply to special economic zone or unit on payment of IGST.
2.	Refund of unutilized input tax credit.
3.	Refund of tax paid on the supply of goods regarded as deemed exports.
4.	Refund of any balance in the electronic cash ledger after payment of tax, interest, penalty, fee or any other amount payable.
5.	Refund on account of tax paid on the supply which did not take place (whether completely or partially) and for which no invoice has been issued. It simply means tax paid on advance payment can be claimed as refund of the transaction did not take place.
6.	Refund of tax paid wrongly collected and paid on the transaction which has been considered to be intra-state supply, but it was an inter-state supply.
7.	Refund of the IGST paid by tourist leaving India on any supply of goods taken out of India by him.
8.	Tax to be refunded as a result of a judgement, decree, order or direction of the Appellate Authority, Appellate Tribunal or any Court.
9.	With reference to provisional assessment, if the final assessment results in less tax to be payable.
10.	Refund of taxes on purchases made by specialized bodies, e.g., United Nations bodies, embassies, etc.
11.	Refund of advance tax paid by casual taxable person or non-resident taxable person.

12.	Refund of taxes to the retail outlets established in departure ear of an international airport beyond immigration counters making tax free supply to an outgoing international tourist.
13.	Refund of excess payment of tax.

20.2 Application for refund claims—Rule 89

S. No.	Cases	Forms
1.	Refund of IGST paid on goods exported out of India	No specific form is required. The shipping bill is treated as a refund claim.
2.	Refund of balance in the electronic cash ledger	No specific form is required. Such refund is claimed in the return filed.
3.	Claim of refund of any tax, interest, penalty, fees, or any other amount	Form GST RED-01 is to be furnished through the common portal or facilitation centre.

20.3 Time period to apply for refund—Section 54(1)

Refund must be claimed within two years from the relevant date by applying in a specified form.

Notes: Relevant date means

(a) in the case of goods exported out of India where a refund of tax paid is available in respect of goods themselves or, as the case may be, the inputs or input services used in such goods,
- if the goods are exported ***by sea or air***, the date on which the ship or the aircraft in which such goods are loaded leaves India; or
- if the goods are exported ***by land***, the date on which such goods pass the frontier; or
- if the goods are exported ***by post***, the date of dispatch of goods by the Post Office concerned to a place outside India;

(b) in the case of supply of goods regarded as deemed exports where a refund of tax paid is available in respect of the goods, the date on which the return relating to such deemed exports is furnished;

(ba) in case of zero-rated supply of goods or services or both to a Special Economic Zone developer or a Special Economic Zone unit where a refund of tax paid is available in respect of such supplies themselves, or as the case may be, the inputs or input services used in such supplies, the due date for furnishing of return under section 39 in respect of such supplies;

(c) in the case of services exported out of India where a refund of tax paid is available in respect of services themselves or, as the case may be, the inputs or input services used in such services, the date of:
- receipt of payment in convertible foreign exchange or in Indian rupees wherever permitted by the Reserve Bank of India, where the supply of services had been completed prior to the receipt of such payment; or
- issue of invoice, where payment for the services had been received in advance prior to the date of issue of the invoice;

(d) in the case where the tax becomes refundable due to a judgment, decree, order or direction of the Appellate Authority, Appellate Tribunal or any court, the date of communication of such judgment, decree, order or direction;

(e) in the case of refund of unutilized input tax credit on account of zero-rated supplies without payment of tax, the due date for furnishing of return under section 39 for the period in which such claim for refund arises;

(f) in the case of provisional refund, the date of adjustment of tax after the final assessment thereof;

(g) in the case of a person other than the supplier, the date of receipt of goods or services or both by such person; and

(h) in any other case, the date of payment of tax.

20.4 Time period to apply for a refund for specialized agency—Section 54(2)

A specialized agency of

- the United Nations Organisation or
- any Multilateral Financial Institution and Organisation notified under the United Nations (Privileges and Immunities) Act, 1947 or
- Consulate or Embassy of foreign countries or
- any other person or class of persons, as notified under section 55,

can claim a refund of tax paid by it on inward supplies by an application for such refund, in such form and manner as may be prescribed, before the expiry of two years from the last day of the quarter in which such supply was received.

20.5 Refund of unutilized ITC—Section 54(3)

Subject to the provisions of section 54(10), a registered person may claim a refund of any unutilized input tax credit at the end of any tax period in the following cases:

(a) zero-rated supplies made without payment of tax,

(b) where the credit has accumulated on account of the rate of tax on inputs being higher than the rate of tax on output supplies (other than nil rated or fully exempt supplies), except supplies of goods or services or both as may be notified by the Government on the recommendations of the Council.

Notes:

1. No refund of unutilized input tax credit shall be allowed in cases where the goods exported out of India are subjected to export duty.
2. No refund of input tax credit shall be allowed, if the supplier of goods or services or both avails of drawback in respect of CGST or claims refund of IGST paid on such supplies.

20.6 Documents—Section 54(4)

The application of refund shall be submitted with the following documents:

(a) such documentary evidence as may be prescribed to establish that a refund is due to the applicant and

(b) such documentary or other evidence (including the documents referred to in section 33 as the applicant may furnish to establish that the amount of tax and interest, if any, paid on such tax or any other amount paid in relation to which such refund is claimed was collected from, or paid by, him and the incidence of such tax and interest had not been passed on to any other person:

Note: If the amount of refund claims is less than ₹2,00,000, it is not necessary to furnish any documentary and other evidences, but he may file a declaration certifying that the incidence of such tax and interest had not been passed on to any other person.

20.7 Refund Order—Section 54(5)/(7)/(8)/(8A)

If the proper office is satisfied that the entire or part of the refund claim is justified, then he may make an order (within 60 days from the date of application) accordingly, and the amount so determined shall be credited to the **Consumer Welfare Fund** as referred to in section 57. However, in the following cases, the refund amount shall be paid to the application instead of transferring the Fund referred to in section 57:

(a) refund of tax paid on exports of goods or services or both or on inputs or input services used in making such exports,

(b) refund of unutilised input tax credit under section 54(3),

(c) refund of tax paid on a supply which is not provided, either wholly or partially, and for which an invoice has not been issued or where a refund voucher has been issued,

(d) refund of tax under section 77,

(e) the tax and interest, if any, or any other amount paid by the applicant if he had not passed on the incidence of such tax and interest to any other person,

(f) the tax or interest borne by such other class of applicants as the Government may, on the recommendations of the Council, by notification, specify.

Note: The Government may disburse the refund of the State tax in such manner as may be prescribed.

20.8 Refund on provisional basis—Section 54(6)

Notwithstanding anything contained in section 54(5), the proper officer has power to release refund on provisional basis in the case of any claim for refund on account of zero-rated supply of goods or services or both made by the registered persons other than the notified persons. Such provisional refund is equal to 90% of the total claim for refund (excluding the amount of input tax credit provisionally accepted). Thereafter, he is required to make an order [under section 54(5)] for final settlement of the refund after due verification of documents given by the applicant.

20.9 Refund as per section 54(8) only—Section 54(9)

Notwithstanding anything to the contrary contained in any judgement, decree, order or direction of the Appellate Tribunal or any court or in any other provisions of the CGST Act or the rules made thereunder or in any other law for the time being in force, no refund shall be made except in accordance with the provisions of section 54(8).

20.10 Refund in case of a defaulter—Section 54(10)

Where any refund is due to a registered person who has defaulted in furnishing any return or who is required to pay any tax, interest or penalty, which has not been stayed by any court, Tribunal or Appellate Authority by the specified date (i.e., the last date of filing an appeal under the CGST Act), the proper officer may:

(a) withhold payment of refund due until the said person has furnished the return or paid the tax, interest or penalty, as the case may be,

(b) deduct from the refund due, any tax, interest, penalty, fee or any other amount which the taxable person is liable to pay but which remains unpaid under the CGST Act or under the existing law.

20.11 Withholding refund if there is a chance of adverse effect in a proceeding—Section 54(11)/(12)

Where an order giving rise to a refund is the subject matter of an appeal or further proceedings or where any other proceedings under the CGST Act is pending, and the Commissioner is of the opinion that the grant of such refund is likely to adversely affect the revenue in the said appeal or other proceedings on account of malfeasance or fraud committed, he may, after giving the taxable person an opportunity of being heard, withhold the refund till such time as he may determine. As per section 54(12), in such case, the taxable person has the right to receive interest at such rate notified by the Government, but not exceeding 6%, if the decision of the appeal or proceeding goes in his favour.

20.12 Refund to Casual Taxable Person or Non-Resident Taxable Person—Section 54(13)

Notwithstanding anything to the contrary contained in this section, if a casual taxable person or a non-resident taxable person has not filed all the required tax returns (under section 39) for the entire period for which the registration certificate was in force, they will not receive a refund for any advance tax they have deposited under section 27(2).

20.13 No Refund if the amount is less than ₹1,000—Section 54(14)

Notwithstanding anything contained in this section, no refund under section 54(5)/(6) is entertained if the amount is less than ₹1,000.

Note: Refund includes refund of tax paid on zero-rated supplies of goods or services or both or on inputs or input services used in making such zero-rated supplies, or refund of tax on the supply of goods regarded as deemed exports, or refund of unutilized input tax credit as provided under section 54(3).

20.14 Interest on delayed refunds—Section 56

Case I: Refund is due to order passed under section 54(5): If the refund is not within 60 days from the date of receipt of an application, interest at such rate notified by the Government, but not exceeding 6%, is payable on such refund for the period of delay after 60 days from the date of receipt of the application to the date of refund. Presently, the interest rate notified is 6%. **[Amended by Section 147 of the Finance Act, 2023].**

Case II: Refund is due to order passed by an adjudicating authority, court, etc.: If any refund arises from an order passed by an adjudicating authority or Appellate Authority or Appellate Tribunal or court is not refunded within 60 days from the date of receipt of application filed consequent to such order, interest at notified rate, but not exceeding 9% is payable on such refund from the 61st day from the date of receipt of application till the date of refund. Presently, interest rate notified is 9%.

Explanation: For the purposes of this section, where any order of refund is made by an Appellate Authority, Appellate Tribunal or any court against an order of the proper officer under section 54(5), the order passed by the Appellate Authority, Appellate Tribunal or by the court shall be deemed to be an order passed under section 54(5).

20.15 Consumer Welfare Fund—Section 57 read with Rule 97

The Government is required to constitute a Fund (known as the Consumer Welfare Fund), and this fund shall be credited with the following:

- the amount referred to in section 54(5),
- any income from investment of the amount credited to the Fund, and
- such other monies received by it,

in such manner as prescribed under Rule 97.

20.16 Utilization of Consumer Welfare Fund—Section 58 read with Rule 97

1. The Fund can be utilised by the Government for the welfare of the consumers in such manner as may be prescribed.
2. The Government or the authority specified by it shall maintain proper and separate account and other relevant records in relation to the Fund and prepare an annual statement of accounts in such form as may be prescribed in consultation with the Comptroller and Auditor-General of India.

20.17 Refund of IGST to a tourist leaving India—Section 15 of the IGST Act, 2017

The IGST paid by a tourist (leaving India) on any supply of goods taken out of India by him is refunded in such manner and subject to such conditions and safeguards as may be prescribed.

Note: For the purposes of this section, the term tourist means a person not normally resident in India, who enters India for a stay of not more than six months for legitimate non-immigrant purposes.

Theory Questions

1. What are the cases where refund can be claimed?
2. Explain the provisions of refund under the CGST Act?
3. Can a foreigner get refund?
4. What are the provisions of refund on zero-rated supply?
5. What is consumer welfare fund?
6. What is the provision of interest on delayed refunds?
7. Can a casual taxable person get refund of the advance tax deposited by him under section 27(2)?

21
Demand and Recovery

21.1 Demand under Section 73

This section deals with the situation where it is to be determined that how much tax has not been (whether whole or part of it) or tax has been refunded erroneously or input tax credit has been wrongly availed, but the intention was not doing fraud or any intentional misstatement or hiding facts.

1. Issue of Show Cause Notice (SCN): Section 73(1): The proper officer shall issue a show cause notice (stating why he should not pay the amount specified in the notice along with interest at 18% p.a. and penalty) to a taxpayer if he feels that

(a) tax has not been paid at all or
(b) if paid, it is short paid or
(c) he has got refund erroneously or
(d) he has availed ITC wrongly,

but the above events happened not because the taxpayer had the intention to evade tax or suppress facts or do fraud. The proper officer may communicate the demand before issuing the SCN to the taxpayer.

2. Time to issue above SCN: Section 73(2) read with Section 73(10)

- The above SCN shall be issued at least three months before the time limit specified under section 73(10) for passing the order determining the amount of tax, interest and any penalty payable.
- As per section 73(10), the said order shall be passed within three years from the due date of filing the Annual Return for the financial to which the tax not paid/short paid/ ITC availed wrongly and in case of erroneous refund, within three years from the date of erroneous refund.

Note: As per section 44(1), the due date to furnish the Annual Return is 31st December of the next financial year.

3. Issue of a Statement: Section 73(3)/(4): After serving the SCN under section 73(1), if it is found that the taxpayer has committed such defaults for a period other than the period mentioned in the SCN, then the proper officer may issue a statement containing the details of tax not paid or short paid or erroneously refunded or input tax credit wrongly availed or utilised. The service of such statement shall be deemed to be service of notice on such person under section 73(1), subject to the condition that the grounds relied upon for such tax periods other than those covered under 73(1) are the same as are mentioned in the earlier notice.

4. Taxpayer comes forward before issue SCN/Statement: Section 73(5)/(6)/(7)

- As per section 73(5), before issuing the SCN/Statement, the taxable person may pay the tax along with interest at 18% p.a. on the basis of his own calculation or the tax as communicated by the proper officer. He will inform the proper officer in writing of such payment.
- As per section 73(6), on receipt of such information, the proper officer shall not issue SCN under section 73(1) or Statement 73(5).
- As per section 73(7), where the proper officer thinks that the amount paid under section 73(5) is short paid, he shall proceed to issue the notice as provided for in section 73 (1) for such amount which falls short of the amount actually payable.

5. No Penalty if the demand is paid within 30 days: Section 73(8): Where any person chargeable with tax under section 73(1) or section 73(3) pays the said tax along with interest within 30 days of the issue of show cause notice, no penalty shall be payable, and all proceedings in respect of the said notice shall be deemed to be concluded.

6. Issue of demand order: Section 73(9): If the taxpayer thinks that he is not liable to pay the tax as shown in the SCN, then he may make representation to the proper officer and the proper officer will, after considering the representation made by the taxpayer, determine the amount of tax, interest and a penalty due from such person and issue an order. The amount of **penalty** is higher of the following amounts:

(a) 10% of tax or

(b) ₹10,000

7. Time period of issuing the above order: Section 73(10): The proper officer is required to issue the order under section 73(9) within three years from the due date of filing the annual return for the financial year to which the tax not paid or short paid or input tax credit wrongly availed or utilised relates to or within three years from the date of erroneous refund.

8. Section 73(11): Whatsoever is written under section 73(6) or section 73(8), penalty under section 73(9) shall be payable if any amount of self-assessed tax or any tax collected but has not been paid within 30 days from the due date of payment of such tax.

21.2 Demand under Section 74

1. Issue of Show Cause Notice (SCN): Section 74(1): The proper officer shall issue a show cause notice (stating why he should not pay the amount specified in the notice along with interest at 18% p.a. and penalty) to a taxpayer if he feels that

(a) tax has not been paid at all or
(b) if paid, it is short paid or
(c) he has got refund erroneously or
(d) he has availed ITC wrongly,

but the above events happened because the taxpayer had the intention to evade tax or suppress facts or do fraud. The proper officer may communicate the demand before issuing the SCN to the taxpayer.

2. Time to issue above SCN: Section 74(2) read with Section 74(10)

- The above SCN shall be issued at least six months before the time limit specified under section 74(10) for passing the order determining the amount of tax, interest and any penalty payable.
- As per section 74(10), the said order shall be passed within five years from the due date for furnishing the Annual Return for the financial to which the tax not paid/short paid/ITC availed wrongly and in case of erroneous refund, within five years from the date of erroneous refund.

Note: As per section 44(1), the due date to furnish the Annual Return is 31 December of the next financial year.

3. Issue of a Statement: Section 74(3)/(4): After serving the SCN under section 74(1), if it is found that the taxpayer has committed such defaults for a period other than the period mentioned in the SCN, then the proper officer may issue a statement specifying the details of tax not paid or short paid or erroneously refunded or input tax credit wrongly availed or utilised. The service of such statement shall be deemed to be service of notice on such person under section 74(1), subject to the condition that the grounds relied upon in the said statement, except the ground of fraud, or any willful-misstatement or suppression of facts to evade tax, for periods other than those covered under section 74 (1) are the same as are mentioned in the earlier notice.

4. Taxpayer comes forward before issue SCN/Statement: Section 74(5)/(6)/(7):

- As per section 74(5), before issue SCN/Statement, the taxable person may pay the tax along with interest at 18% p.a. and a penalty of 15% of such tax on the basis on his own calculation or the tax as communicated by the proper officer. He will inform to the proper officer in writing of such payment.
- As per section 74(6), the proper officer, on receipt of such information, shall not serve any notice under section 74(1), in respect of the tax so paid or any penalty payable under the provisions of the CGST Act or its rules.
- As per section 74(7), where the proper officer is of the opinion that the amount paid under section 74(5) is less than actually payable, he shall proceed to issue the notice as provided for in section 74 (1) for such amount which falls short of the amount actually payable.

5. Demand is paid within 30 days: Section 74(8): Where any person chargeable with tax under section 74(1) pays the said tax along with interest and a penalty of 25% of such tax within 30 days of issue of SCN and all proceedings in respect of the said notice shall be deemed to be concluded.

6. Opportunity of submission of representation by the taxpayer: Section 74(9): If the taxpayer thinks that he is not liable to pay the tax as shown in the SCN, then he may make representation to the proper officer and the proper officer shall, after considering the representation made by the tax payer, determine the amount of tax, interest and a penalty and issue an order regarding this.

7. Time period of issuing the above order: Section 74(10): The proper officer is required to issue the order under section 74(9) within a period of five years from the due date of filing an annual return for the financial year to which the tax not paid or short paid or input tax credit wrongly availed or utilised relates to or within five years from the date of erroneous refund.

8. Section 74(11): Where any person served with an order issued under section 74(9) pays the tax along with interest payable thereon under section 50 and a penalty equivalent to 50% of such tax within 30 days of communication of the order, all proceedings in respect of the said notice (excluding proceedings under section 132) is deemed to be concluded:

Notes: These notes are applicable to section 73 as well as section 74

(a) The expression "*all proceedings in respect of the said notice*" does not include proceedings under section 132.

(b) Where the notice under the same proceedings is issued to the main person liable to pay tax and some other persons, and such proceedings against the main person have been concluded under section 73 or section 74, the proceedings against all the persons liable to pay the penalty under [sections 122 and 125] are deemed to be concluded.

(c) The word "*Suppression*" means non-declaration of facts or information which a taxable person is required to declare in the return, statement, report or any other document furnished under the CGST Act or the rules made thereunder, or failure to furnish any information on being asked for, in writing, by the proper officer.

Summarised Provisions of Sections 73 and 74

S. No.	Situations	Section 73	Section 74
1.	Defaults committed	1. tax has not been paid at all or 2. if paid, it is short paid or 3. he has got refund erroneously or 4. he has availed ITC wrongly.	1. tax has not been paid at all or 2. if paid, it is short paid or 3. he has got refund erroneously or 4. he has availed ITC wrongly.
2.	Intention behind the defaults	Other than tax evasion, fraud, mis-statement, suppression of facts.	Intentional, tax evasion, fraud, misstatement, suppression of facts.
3.	Communication before SCN	The proper officer may communicate about the demand before serving SCN.	The proper officer may communicate about the demand before serving SCN.

4.	Issue of Show Cause Notice (SCN)	At least 3 months before the time limit specified for passing the order determining the amount of tax, interest and any penalty payable. Time limit specified = Order must be issued within three years from the due date for furnishing the Annual Return for the financial to which the tax not paid/short paid/ITC availed wrongly and in case of erroneous refund, within three years from the date of erroneous refund.	At least six months before the time limit specified for passing the order determining the amount of tax, interest and any penalty payable. Time limit specified = Order must be issued within five years from the due date for furnishing the Annual Return for the financial to which the tax not paid/short paid/ITC availed wrongly and in case of erroneous refund, within five years from the date of erroneous refund.
5.	Issue of Statement after the SCN	If similar defaults have been committed in other periods too, then a statement can be issued by the proper officer.	If similar defaults have been committed in other periods too, then a statement can be issued by the proper officer.
6.	If the taxpayer pays the amount of demand before issue of the SCN/ Statement	No penalty is charged and no notice is issued.	Penalty of 15% is charged but no notice is served.
7.	If the taxpayer pays the amount of demand within 30 days after issue of the SCN	No penalty is charged and it is deemed that all proceedings have been completed.	Penalty of 25% of the tax amount is payable and it is deemed that all proceedings have been completed.
8.	If the taxpayer makes representation to the proper officer and after the representation the officer passes an order of demand. The demand is paid within 30 days of the communication of the order	Penalty = 10% of the tax or ₹10,000 whichever is higher.	Penalty = 50% of the tax amount payable
9.	If the taxpayer makes representation to the proper officer and after the representation the officer passes an order of demand. The demand is paid after 30 days of the communication of the order	Penalty = 10% of the tax or ₹10,000 whichever is higher.	Penalty = 100% of the tax amount

21.3 General Provisions relating to determination of tax—Section 75

1. Stay period must not be taken into consideration: Section 75(1): Where the service of notice or issuance of order is stayed by order of a court or Appellate Tribunal, the period of such stay must be excluded while computing the period as specified in section 73(2)/(10) or section 74(2)/(10), as the case may be.

2. Charges in the notice under section 74(1) could not be proved: Section 75(1): If an Appellate Authority or Appellate Tribunal or court finds that the notice issued under section 74(1) cannot be sustained because the charges

- of fraud or
- any wilful-misstatement or
- suppression of facts to evade tax

could not be proved against the person to whom the notice was issued, then the tax amount owed by that person will be determined as if the notice was issued under section 73(1).

3. Time limit to issue order in pursuance of the direction of the Appellate Authority/Appellate Tribunal/Court: Section 75(3): Where the Appellate Authority or Appellate Tribunal directs to issue any order, then such order must be issued within two years from the date of communication of the said direction.

4. Opportunity of hearing: Section 75(4): Where a written request is received from the person chargeable with tax or penalty or where any adverse decision is contemplated against such person, then an opportunity of being heard shall be given to such person.

5. Adjournment of hearing: Section 75(5): The proper officer can grant an adjournment of a hearing if the person liable to pay taxes presents sufficient reasons, and the officer must record the reasons in writing. However, the number of adjournments cannot exceed three during the proceedings.

6. Setting out relevant facts and basis of his decision: Section 75(6): When the proper office passes his demand order, then he is required to set out the relevant facts and the basis of his direction.

7. Limitations on Tax, Interest and Penalty Demands: Section 75(7): The order cannot demand more tax, interest and penalty than what was specified in the notice, and no demand can be confirmed based on grounds other than those mentioned in the notice.

8. Amount of demand modified by the Appellate Authority/Appellate Tribunal/Court: Section 75(8): Where the amount of tax is modified by the Appellate Authority or Appellate Tribunal or court, then the amount of interest and penalty shall stand modified accordingly.

9. Interest on short paid or unpaid Taxes regardless of tax demand order: Section 75(9): The interest on the tax short paid or not paid is payable whether or not specified in the tax demand order.

10. Deemed conclusion of the adjudication proceedings: Section 75(10): If the order is not issued within three years [as stated in section 73(10)] or within five years [as stated in section 74(10)], the adjudication proceedings is deemed concluded or finished.

11. The period to be excluded in case of appeal: Section 75(11): If there is a situation where a decision on an issue has been made by an Appellate Authority, Appellate Tribunal, or High

Court that is unfavourable to the revenue in some other proceedings, and an appeal has been filed against that decision to a higher authority (e.g., the Appellate Authority, the Appellate Tribunal, the High Court or the Supreme Court), the time period between the original decision and the decision of the higher authority shall not be counted when calculating the period referred to in section 73(10) or section 74(10) where proceedings are initiated by way of issue of a show cause notice under the said sections.

12. Self-assessed tax or interest on it remains unpaid: Section 75(12): If the self-assessed tax (as per the return filed under section 39) is unpaid (whether wholly or partly) or any interest on such tax is unpaid, then such amount of tax or interest shall be recovered under section 79 regardless of section 73 or section 74.

Note: The expression *self-assessed tax* also includes the tax payable in respect of details of outward supplies filed under section 37 but not included in the return filed under section 39.

13. Avoidance of duplication of penalty on the same person for the same act: Section 75(13): Once any penalty is imposed under section 73 or section 74, no penalty for the same act or omission shall be imposed on the same person under any other provision of the CGST Act.

21.4 Tax Collected but not paid to the Government—Section 76

1. Liability to pay the tax collected: Section 76(1): Every person who has collected an amount in the name of tax under the CGST Act, but has not paid the same to the Government, then he is required to pay such tax collected to the Government whether or not the concerned supplies were taxable. This sub-section is not affected even anything contrary is contained in any order or direction of any Appellate Authority or Appellate Tribunal or court or in the CGST Act or the rules made thereunder or any other law for the time being in force.

2. Show cause notice (SCN) in case of default to deposit the tax collected but not paid to the Government: Section 76(2): If the tax collected is not paid to the Government, then the proper officer may serve a show cause notice to the person liable to pay such tax. Such notice asks why the said amount, as specified in the notice, should not be paid by him to the Government and why a penalty equal to the amount specified in the notice should not be imposed under the CGST Act.

3. Determination of the amount due after receiving the representation of the SCN: Section 76(3): The proper officer shall consider any arguments or explanations given by the person to whom notice is the above SCN is issued. Based on that, the officer will calculate the amount owed by that person. Once the amount is determined, the person must pay it.

4. Liability to pay interest: Section 76(4): The person who is liable to pay tax under section 76(1) or section 73(3) is also required to pay interest as per section 50. The interest shall be calculated from the date of collection of the tax by him to the date of payment of the same to the Government.

5. Opportunity of being heard to be given: Section 76(5): An opportunity to be heard shall be given where a request is received in writing from the person to whom the show cause notice was given.

6. Time limit to issue demand order: Section 76(6)/(7): The proper officer is required to issue a demand order within one year from the date of issue of the show cause notice. However, where the issuance of the demand order is stayed by a court or Appellate Tribunal, then the period of such stay is excluded in computing the period of one year.

7. The proper officer, in his order, shall set out the relevant facts and the basis of his decision: Section 76(8)

8. The adjustment of the paid to the Government: Section 76(9)/(10)/(11): The amount paid to the Government under 76(1) or section 76(3) shall be adjusted against the tax payable, if any, by the person in relation to the supplies referred to in section 76(1). If after the adjustment, some amount remains left, then the such surplus is either credited to the Consumer Welfare Fund or refunded to the person who has borne the burden of the tax and such person may apply for the refund as per the provisions of section 54.

21.4 Tax wrongfully collected and paid to Central Government or State Government—Section 77

1. Inter-state supply considered to be intra-state supply: If a registered person made a supply and considered it an intra-state supply, therefore, he collected CGST and SGST/UTGST and paid the same to the Government. Later on, it was found that the supply was inter-state supply, then the tax paid shall be refunded in such manner and subject to such conditions as may be prescribed.

2. Intra-state supply considered to be inter-state supply: If a registered person who has paid IGST on a supply considered by him to be an inter-state supply, but, later on, the supply is found to be an intra-state supply, he is not required to pay any interest on the amount of CGST and SGST/UTGST payable.

21.5 Intimation of Recovery Proceedings—Section 78

Any amount payable by a taxable person in pursuance of an order passed under the CGST Act must be paid within three months (which may be reduced by the proper officer due to the reasons to be recorded in writing) from the date of service of the said order and if he fails, then the recovery proceedings shall be started.

21.6 Recovery of Taxes—Section 79

1. Modes of recovery: Section 79(1): Where a person does not pay the Government any amount payable under the CGST Act or its rules, then the proper officer can start the proceeding of recovering the amount payable. The modes of recovery available to him are as follows:

(a) **Deduction from the money under the control of the specified officer: Section 79(1)(a) read with Rule 143:** The proper officer can deduct or instruct another specified officer to deduct the amount payable from the money (owed to the person) which is under the control of the proper officer or the specified officer. For this purpose, FORM GST-DRC-09 is used.

Note: *Specified officer means any officer of the Central Government or a State Government or the Government of a Union territory or a local authority, or of a Board or Corporation or a company owned or controlled, wholly or partly, by the Central Government or a State Government or the Government of a Union territory or a local authority.*

(b) Recovery by auction of goods under the control of the specified officer: Section 79(1)(b) read with Rule 144

- The proper officer may recover or instruct another specified officer to recover the amount payable by detaining and selling any goods (owned by the person) that are under the control of the proper officer or such other specified officer.
- The proper officer is required to prepare a list of the goods to be auctioned and estimate their market value. Only So much of the goods can be auctioned, which is necessary to recover the Government dues, including the administrative expenditure incurred on the recovery process.
- The auction can be started by issuing a notice in FORM GST DRC-10, and the officer can cancel the auction if the government dues are paid by the defaulter.

(c) Recovery from a third person: Section 79(1)(c) read with Rule 145

(i) **Issue of notice to the third person:** The proper officer may serve a written notice to a third person who is to pay (within the time specified in the notice) so much of the money that is sufficient to cover the Government dues or the whole money when it is equal to or less than the amount due. The third person means a person who is

- is debtor or prospective debtor to the defaulter
- holds or may subsequently hold money for or on account of the defaulter.

However, such a third person cannot be bound to pay unless he becomes a debtor or holds money.

(ii) **The recipient of the notice under section 79(1)(c)(i) is bound to comply with it**

- the third person to whom the notice is issued under section 79(1)(c)(i) is bound to comply with the notice.
- where any such notice is issued to a post office, banking company or insurer, it is not necessary to produce any passbook, deposit receipt, policy or any other document for the purpose of any entry, endorsement or the like being made before payment is made, notwithstanding any rule, practice or requirement to the contrary.

(iii) **Deemed defaulter:** If the recipient of the notice does not comply with the notice issued under section 79(1)(c)(i), he is deemed defaulter in respect of the amount specified in the notice and all the consequences of the CGST Act or the rules made thereunder shall be faced by such deemed defaulter.

(iv) **The power to amend/revoke or extend the time of making payment:** The officer issuing a notice under section 79(1)(c)(i) has power that, at any time, to

- amend or revoke such notice or
- extend the time for making any payment in pursuance of the notice.

(v) **Good and sufficient discharge of the liability by the third person to the person in default**

- The third person making the payment in response to the notice issued under sub-clause (i) is deemed to have made the payment on behalf of the person in default, and this payment is deemed a valid payment.

- After such payment is credited to the Government, then it is deemed that the third person has settled his liability payable to the person in default, but to the extent of the amount mentioned in the receipt.

(vi) **The third person is personally liable:** Any person discharging any liability to the person in default after service on him of the notice issued under sub-clause (i) shall be personally liable to the Government to the extent of the liability discharged or to the extent of the liability of the person in default for tax, interest and penalty, whichever is less.

(vii) **Where the third person is relaxed to pay the amount mentioned in the notice:** where a person on whom a notice is served under sub-clause (i) proves to the satisfaction of the officer issuing the notice that the money demanded or any part thereof was not due to the person in default or that he did not hold any money for or on account of the person in default, at the time the notice was served on him, nor is the money demanded or any part thereof, likely to become due to the said person or be held for or on account of such person, nothing contained in this section shall be deemed to require the person on whom the notice has been served to pay the Government any such money or part thereof.

(d) **Power to distrain property belonging to or under the control of the person**

- The proper officer may distrain any movable or immovable property owned by or under the control of such person.
- The proper officer can detain the above property unless the amount due is paid.
- If, after the distress of the property, any portion of the owed amount or the expenses associated with the distress and storage/keeping of the property remain unpaid for a period of 30 days, then the following action can be taken.
- The proper officer may sell the property to recover the amount due. The proceeds from the sale shall be used to cover the amount due as well as any costs incurred during the process, including the expenses related to the sale itself.
- If there is any surplus amount left after satisfying the owed amount and the associated costs, that remaining sum shall be returned to the person.

(e) **Recovery by the Collector of the district**

(i) **The proper officer has the option to prepare a certificate showing the amount payable by such a person and send it**

- to the Collector of the district in which such person
  - owns any property or
  - resides or
  - carries on his business
- to any officer authorized by the Government.

(ii) After receiving the certificate, the Collector or the officer shall collect the amount due from the said person as if it were an arrear of land revenue.

(f) **Submission of application to an appropriate Magistrate for recovery:** Regardless of what is mentioned in the Code of Criminal Procedure, 1973, the proper may submit an application to the appropriate Magistrate, who shall then take action to collect the amount from the person mentioned in the application. This collection will be treated as if it were a fine imposed by the Magistrate.

2. Manner of recovery mentioned in a bond or any other document: Section 79(2): If the terms of a bond or any other document created under the CGST Act or its related rules or regulations state that any money owed can be collected in a manner as laid down in section 79(1), that amount can be collected using the process outlined in that subsection, along with other available methods of recovery.

3. Recovery by the proper officer of State tax or Union Territory tax: Section 79(3)/(4): The proper officer of State tax or Union territory tax has the power to recover tax, interest or penalty (which is payable by a person to the Government under the CGST Act or the rules made thereunder and is unpaid) from the said person. In such a situation, it shall be deemed that it was an arrear of State tax or Union territory tax. The amount so collected shall be credited to the account of the Government. If the amount collected is less than the amount due to the Central Government and State Government, then whatever amount is collected shall be credited to the account of each Government in the ratio of the amounts due to each such Government.

Note: For the purposes of this section, the word person shall include distinct persons as referred to in section 25(4)/(5).

21.7 Payment of tax and other amount in instalments—Section 80

If a taxable person applies to pay the amount due under the CGST Act in instalments, the Commissioner has the authority to grant an extension or allow the payment of any amount due, except for the self-assessed liability as per any return, in monthly instalments not exceeding 24. This decision will be made based on specific reasons that must be documented in writing. However, interest under section 50 must still be paid, and there may be certain conditions and limitations as may be prescribed.

However, if a payment instalment is not made on its due date, the entire remaining balance becomes immediately due and payable. No additional notice is required, and the outstanding amount can be pursued for recovery.

21.8 Transfer of property to be void in certain cases—Section 81

If a person owes any amount and then creates a charge on or parts with (in the form of sale, mortgage, exchange, or any other mode) their property to someone else in order to cheat the government out of the amount they owe, that charge or transfer shall be considered invalid when it comes to any claim related to the unpaid taxes or sums owed by that person. In simple words, you cannot avoid paying your taxes or debts by transferring or selling your property to someone else.

Exception: Such charge or transfer is not void if it is made for adequate consideration, in good faith and without notice of the pendency of such proceedings under the CGST Act or without notice of such tax or other sum payable by the said person or with prior permission from the proper officer.

21.9 Tax to be first charge on property—Section 82

In simple words, regardless of what is written in any law for the time being in force, if any amount is payable by a taxable person or any other person for taxes, interest, or penalties to the Government, the Government shall be given priority in the property of such taxable person or such person, unless stated otherwise in the Insolvency and Bankruptcy Code, 2016.

21.10 Provisional attachment to protect revenue in certain cases—Section 83

1. Provisional attachment of the property: Section 83(1): After the initiation of any proceeding under the following chapters in the CGST Act:

- Assessment,
- Inspection, Search, Seizure and Arrest or
- Demand and Recovery,

the Commissioner thinks that to safeguard the interest of the Government revenue, it is necessary to attach any property (including bank account) of the taxable person or any person specified under section 122(1A), then he may pass an order in writing to attach the property ***provisionally***, in such manner as may be prescribed.

2. End of provisional attachment: Section 83(2): Every such provisional attachment is not effective after the expiry of a period of one year from the date of the order made under section 83(1).

21.11 Continuation and validation of certain recovery proceedings—Section 84

Where any demand notice in respect of Government dues (any tax, penalty, interest or any other amount payable under the CGST Act) is issued to any taxable person or any other person, and any appeal or revision application is filed, or any other proceedings is initiated in respect of such Government dues, then,

(a) **The Government dues are increased in such appeal: Section 84(a)**

- If the amount of Government dues is increased under such appeal, revision, or other proceeding, the Commissioner must send another demand notice to the taxpayer or any other person involved.
- This new demand notice will specify the increased amount of government dues.
- Any ongoing efforts to recover the government dues, which were covered by the original demand notice served before the appeal or revision, can continue without issuing a new demand notice.
- These recovery proceedings will pick up from the point they were at immediately before the appeal or revision was resolved.

(b) **The Government dues are reduced in such appeal: Section 84(b)**

- It is not necessary for the Commissioner to issue the taxable person a fresh notice of demand.
- The Commissioner shall intimate to him and to the appropriate authority with whom recovery proceedings is pending.
- Any recovery proceedings initiated on the basis of the demand served upon him prior to the disposal of such appeal, revision or other proceedings may be continued in

relation to the amount so reduced from the stage at which such proceedings stood immediately before such disposal.

Theory Questions

1. Distinguish between section 73 and section 74.
2. What do you mean by provisional attachment of property? Is it possible under the GST law? If it is possible, then does it remain effective forever?
3. Discuss briefly the time limit for the issue of show cause notice under section 73 and section 74.
4. What are the modes of recovery of tax available to the proper officer?
5. Can the tax or other amount dues be paid in instalments?
6. What are the general provisions relating to tax?

22
Assessment

22.1 Meaning of Assessment

Assessment means the determination of tax liability under GST law. Below are the various types of assessment under GST.

22.2 Self-assessment—Section 59

It means that a registered person assesses/calculates his tax liability and files the GST returns as applicable. This is the first level of assessment.

22.3 Provisional assessment—Section 60

1. Meaning and filing of application for provisional assessment: Section 60(1): Sometimes, an assessee is unable

(a) to calculate the value of goods/services or both or

(b) to find/determine applicable tax rate,

then he may request to the proper officer that he accept the payment of tax on a provisional basis. An application in FORM GST ASMT-01 is filed electronically. The form asks for reasons for payment on a provisional basis. After the acceptance of the application, the proper officer passes an order (within 90 days from the date of application) to the assessee to pay tax on the basis of the value of goods/services or both or such rate as prescribed by the proper officer. Such a type of situation of assessment is called provisional assessment. This situation can be compared with a graduate who receives a provisional certificate from a university to study further, but the final degree will be allotted later on.

2. Execution of a bond: Section 60(2): The assessee is required to execute a bond in FORM GST ASMT-05. Under this bond, the assessee furnishes a security in the form of a bank guarantee for an amount prescribed by the proper officer, and he declares that he will pay the difference in tax after the final assessment and in case he defaults, then the department can take the payment from the guarantor bank.

3. Passing final assessment order: Section 60(3): The proper officer is required to issue a **final assessment order** within 6 months from the date of communication of the provisional assessment order on the basis of the required information. If the joint commissioner or additional commissioner is given proper reasons for delay in passing the final assessment order, then he can extend the said period but not by more than 6 months. However, the commissioner can extend it by a period not exceeding 4 years.

4. Interest payable by the taxpayer: Section 60(4): The taxpayer will have to pay interest on any tax payable under provisional assessment which was not paid within the due date. Interest period will be calculated from the first day when the tax was first due on the goods/services (and not the date of provisional assessment) till the actual payment date, irrespective of payment being before or after the final assessment. Rate of interest will be a maximum of 18%, as given under section 50(1).

5. Interest payable by the department: Section 60(5): If the tax as per the final assessment is less than the provisional assessment, then the taxable person will get a refund. He will also get interest on a refund. Rate of interest will be a maximum of 6%.

22.4 Scrutiny Assessment—Section 61 read with Rule 99

1. Scrutiny of Returns: Section 61(1) and Rule 99(1): Once the return is filed by a registered person, then the proper officer may scrutinize the return to verify the correctness of the return, and if any discrepancy is observed, the proper officer issues a notice to him to obtain the explanations from the registered person. Rule 99 says that the notice shall be served in FORM GST ASMT–10, and if possible, the notice should quantify the amount of tax, interest and any other amount payable in relation to such discrepancy.

2. Reply to the notice: The registered person is required to reply to the notice within 30 days (or extended time) from the date of service of the notice. As per Rule 99(2), he may accept the discrepancy as given in the notice, pay the required amount and inform the proper officer. He may also give an explanation to the proper officer for the discrepancy if he is not ready to accept the discrepancy. Whatever the situation is, the registered person must reply in FORM GST ASMT–11.

3. Action by the Proper officer

(a) **Explanation is found satisfactory:** Section 61(2) and Rule 99(3): If the proper officer is satisfied with the reply submitted by the registered person, the registered person shall be informed accordingly in FORM GST AMT–12, and no further action shall be taken in this regard.

(b) **Explanation is not satisfactory: Section 61(3):** In case no satisfactory explanation is furnished within the specified time or where the registered person, after accepting the discrepancies, fails to take the corrective measure in his return for the month in which the discrepancy is accepted, the proper officer may initiate appropriate action, including those under section 65 or section 66 or section 67, or proceed to determine the tax and other dues under section 73 or section 74.

22.5 Best judgment

The Assessing Officer, under this assessment, has an obligation to make an assessment of the total income or tax of a taxpayer to the best of his judgment in the following cases.

Assessment of non-filers of returns: Section 62

(i) **Section 62(1)**: Notwithstanding anything to the contrary contained in section 73 or section 74, where a registered person fails to furnish the return under section 39 or section 45, even after the service of a notice under section 46, the proper officer may proceed to assess the tax liability of the said person to the **best of his judgement** taking into account all the relevant material which is available or which he has gathered and issue an assessment order within a period of 5 years from the date specified under section 44 for furnishing of the annual return for the financial year to which the tax not paid relates. Also, the readers are advised to refer *Notification No. 06/2023-Central Tax—Dated: 31 March 2023* in this regard. This notification is available on the CBIC website.

(ii) **Section 62(2)**: Where the registered person furnishes a valid return within ***60 days***[1] of the service of the assessment order under section 62(1), the said assessment order shall be deemed to have been withdrawn, but the liability for payment of interest under section 50(1) or for payment of late fee under section 47 shall continue.

> **A new proviso:** Where the registered person does not furnish a valid return within 60 days of the service of the assessment order under section 60(1), then he has option to furnish the same within a further 60 days on payment of an additional late fee of ₹100 for each day of delay beyond 60 days of the service of the said assessment order and in case he furnishes valid return within such extended period, the said assessment order shall be deemed to have been withdrawn, but the liability to pay interest under section 50(1) or to pay late fee under section 47 shall continue. **[Inserted by section 148 of the Finance Act, 2023]**

Assessment of Unregistered Person: Section 63

Notwithstanding anything to the contrary contained in section 73 or section 74, where a taxable person fails to obtain registration even though liable to do so or whose registration has been cancelled under section 29 (2) but who was liable to pay tax, the proper officer may proceed to assess the tax liability of such taxable person to the **best of his judgment** for the relevant tax periods and issue an assessment order within a period of five years from the date specified under section 44 for furnishing of the annual return for the financial year to which the tax not paid relates. However, an opportunity of being heard shall be given before passing such order.

22.6 Summary assessment—Section 64

1. Summary assessment order: Section 64(1): If the proper officer has any evidence showing a tax liability of a person and he has sufficient reasons to believe that any delay may adversely affect the interest of revenue, then he can pass an assessment order, but after taking permission from the Additional Commissioner or Joint Commissioner. Such an order is called a summary assessment. Moreover, if the above-said person is not ascertainable and the liability is related to the supply of goods, then the person who is in charge of such goods shall be deemed to be the taxable person, and therefore, he is liable to be assessed and to pay tax and any other amount due under this section.

1. Section 148 of the Finance Act, 2023 has replaced the earlier time of 30 days with 60 days.

Note: The term "summary" is used because this type of assessment is intended to be a quick and summary determination of the tax liability. It is based on the available information and is conducted without going into the details of the taxpayer's accounts and records.

2. Withdrawal of the summary assessment order: Section 64(2): On an application made by the taxable person within 30 days from the date of receipt of the summary order or on his own motion, if the Additional Commissioner or Joint Commissioner considers that such order is erroneous, he may withdraw such order and follow the procedure laid down in section 73 or section 74.

Theory Questions

1. What are various types of assessment under the CGST Act, 2107?
2. What is the best judgement assessment, and under what circumstances such an assessment is made?
3. Can the summary assessment order be withdrawn?
4. With reference to the scrutiny of returns, what actions can be taken by the proper officer if he finds that the explanations submitted by the taxpayer are not satisfactory?

23
Accounts and Other Records

23.1 Who is liable to maintain books?—Section 35(1)

Every registered person is required to keep and maintain a true and correct account of:

1. production or manufacture of goods;
2. inward and outward supply of goods or services or both;
3. stock of goods;
4. input tax credit availed;
5. output tax payable and paid; and
6. such other particulars as may be prescribed.

Such account shall be kept and maintained at the principal place of business which is mentioned in the certificate of registration. Further, if there is more than one place of business, the accounts related to each such place of business shall be kept at such place of business.

23.2 Owner or operator of a godown or warehouse, etc., and transporter of goods—Section 35(2)

A transporter and an owner or operator of a warehouse or godown or any other place where goods can be stored, then maintaining the records of the consigner, consignee and other relevant details of the goods is mandatory whether such transporter or owner or operator is registered or not.

23.3 Other categories notified—Section 35(3)

The Commissioner may notify a class of taxable persons to maintain additional accounts or documents for such purpose as may be specified therein.

23.4 If certain class of taxable persons is not able to maintain keep and maintain books of account—Section 35(4)

As per this section, if the Commissioner considers that a class of taxpayers is unable to keep and maintain accounts as per section 35(1), he can allow them to maintain accounts in a prescribed manner.

23.5 Failure to maintain books of account—Section 35(6)

Subject to section 17(5)(h), where the registered person fails to account for the goods/services/ both in as per section 35(1), the proper officer shall calculate tax payable on those goods/services/ both that are as if such goods or services or both had been supplied by such person. In such case, section 73 or section 74, as the case may be, shall, *with necessary modifications*, apply to calculate such tax.

23.6 Period of retention of accounts and records—Section 36

Case 1: Normal cases: The accounts and records under section 35(1) shall be kept and maintained by the registered person for 72 months from the due date of filing of the annual return for the year to which such accounts and records are related.

Example 23.1: If the accounts and records belong to the financial year 2022-23, then the due date for filing the annual return is 31 December 2023. Consequently, the accounts and records are required to be kept and maintained up to 31 December 2029.

Case 2: Cases of appeal or investigation: If a registered person is a party to an appeal or revision or any other proceedings before any

- Appellate Authority,
- Revisional Authority,
- Appellate Tribunal,
- Court or

he is under investigation for an offence under Chapter XIX of the CGST Act; then he shall keep the books of account and other records related to the subject matter of the appeal or revision or proceedings or investigation for

(a) One year after final disposal of such appeal or revision or proceedings or investigation

OR

(b) for the period specified in case 1,

whichever is later.

Theory Questions

1. What are the accounts and records to be maintained by a registered person?
2. Is there any time period up to which books of account and other records are to be maintained by the registered person?

24
Audit

24.1 Introduction

The CGST Act, 2017 prescribes two types of audits: (1) an audit by the tax authorities or departmental audit under section 65 and (2) a special audit which is directed by the department but conducted by a Chartered Accountant or Cost Accountant under section 66. Let us see what are various provisions of the audit under the GST law.

24.2 Departmental Audit—Section 65 read with Rule 101

1. Who can undertake the audit?: Section 65(1): The Commissioner or an authorised officer, by passing a general or specific order, may conduct an audit of any registered person. The audit can cover a specific period, occur at a certain frequency, and follow rule 101.

2. Place of audit: Section 65(2): The audit can be conducted

- at the place of business of the taxable person and or
- in their office.

3. Prior notice of audit is required: Section 65(3) read with Rule 101(2): The auditee must be given 15 days prior notice. This notice is given in FORM GST ADT-01.

4. Expectations from the auditor: Rule 101(3)/(4)

1. The authorised officer auditing a registered person's records and books of account is required, along with his team, to verify
   - the documents used to maintain the books of account as well as the returns and statements submitted under the CGST Act and its rules.
   - the accuracy of the turnover, exemptions, and deductions claimed, the tax rate applied to goods or services supplied, the input tax credit utilized, refund claims, and other relevant matters.
2. He is also required to document his findings and observations in his audit notes.
3. He may inform the registered person about the discrepancies found during the audit. The registered person may then reply, and he will finalise the findings after considering the reply.

5. Time to complete audit: Section 65(4): The audit must be completed within three months from the date of commencement of the audit. However, if the commissioner is satisfied that the audit cannot be completed within three months, he has the power to extend the period by a period not exceeding six months, but the reasons for the extension must be recorded in writing.

Note: Date of commencement of the audit means later of the following dates:

(a) the date on which the records and other documents (demanded by the tax authorities) are made available by the registered person or

(b) the actual institution of audit at the place of business.

6. Duty of the auditee during the audit: Section 65(5): On being asked by the authorised officer, the auditee is required

(a) to provide the authorised officer necessary facilities so that the officer can verify the books of account or other documents.

(b) to furnish the information demanded by the officer and assist him so that the audit can be completed in time.

7. On conclusion of the audit: Section 65(6) read with Rule 101(5): At the conclusion of the audit, the proper officer is required to inform the auditee about the findings, his rights and obligations and the reasons for the findings. Such information shall be given within 30 days in FORM GST ADT-02.

8. Initiation of action: Section 65(7): Where the special audit reveals that

- tax has not been paid or
- short paid or
- erroneously refunded or
- input tax credit wrongly availed/utilized,

then the proper officer may take action under section 73 or section 74.

24.3 Special Audit by Chartered Accountant or Cost Accountant—Section 66

1. Who directs for the audit, and who is the auditor?: Section 66(1) read with Rule 102(1): If, during scrutiny, enquiry, investigation or any other proceedings, an officer (Assistant commissioner or above rank) believes that

- the value declared by a registered person is not correct or
- he has availed input tax credit, which is not within normal limits,

then, after taking approval from the commissioner, he can direct such person, in FORM GST ADT-03, to get his books of account audited by a Chartered Accountant or Cost Accountant nominated by the commissioner.

2. Time to submit audit report: Section 66(2): The auditor has time to submit his audit report to the assistant commissioner within 90 days. However, upon request from the auditor or auditee, the assistant commissioner can extend the period not exceeding 90 days, provided reasonable causes are given for the extension.

3. No effect of the audits under any other law: Section 66(3): The special audit is conducted even the accounts have been audited under any other laws.

4. Opportunity of being heard: Section 66(4): The auditee shall be given an opportunity to be heard in respect of any material gathered in the special audit which is proposed to be used in any proceedings against him under the CGST Act or the rules made thereunder.

Illustration 24.1: Showing the provision of audit by tax authorities: Section 65

Image courtesy – Freepik

5. Informing the auditee about the findings: Rule 102(2): At the conclusion of the special audit, the auditee is informed about the findings of the special audit in FORM GST ADT-04.

6. Determination of the cost of the audit and its payment: Section 66(5): The expenses of the special audit (including the auditor's remuneration) are determined and paid by the commissioner. Such determination is final.

7. Initiation of action: Section 66(6): Where the special audit reveals that

- tax has not been paid or
- short paid or
- erroneously refunded or
- input tax credit wrongly availed/utilized,

then the proper officer may take action under section 73 or section 74.

Illustration 24.2: Showing the provision of special audit: Section 66

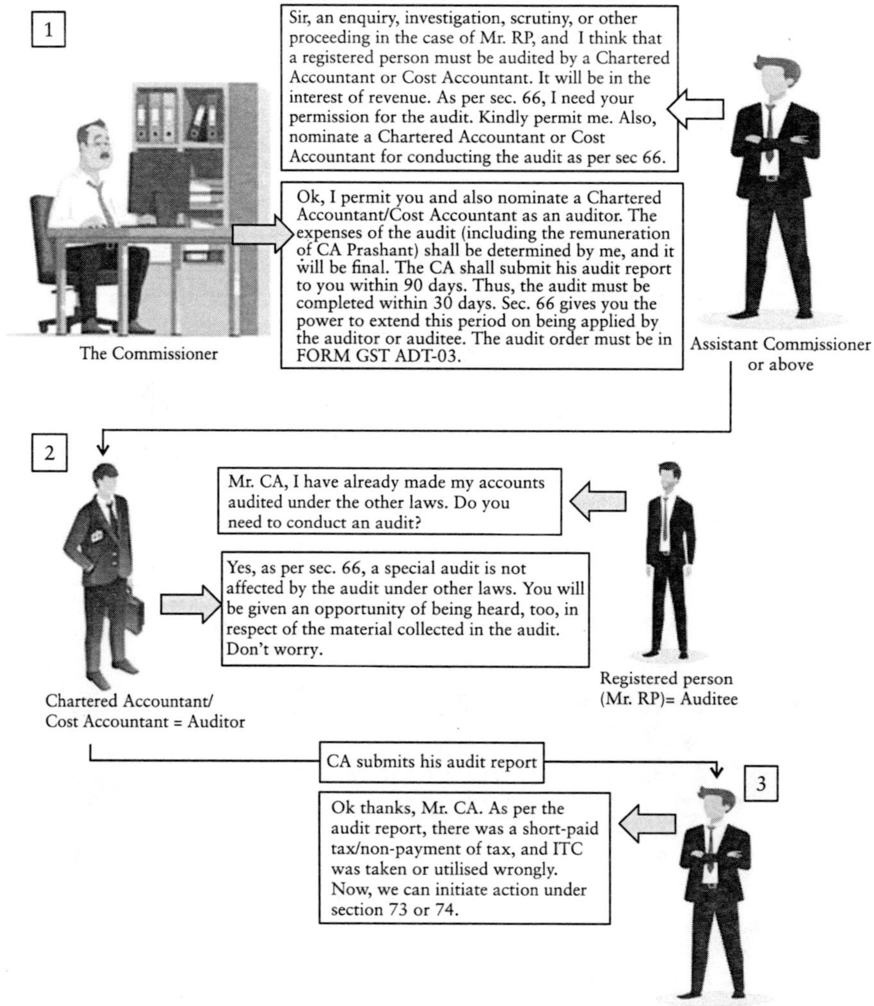

Image courtesy–Freepik

Theory Questions

1. Distinguish between tax audits by tax authorities and special audits.
2. What are the provisions of audit under the CGST Act?
3. Who can conduct a departmental audit and special audit?
4. When can a special audit be conducted?

Appendix IV

Audit Forms

Form GST ADT-01

[*See rule 101(2)*]

Reference No.: Date:

To,

GSTIN ....

Name ....

Address ....

Period - F.Y.(s) - ....

Notice for conducting audit

Whereas it has been decided to undertake audit of your books of account and records for the financial year(s).......... to .... in accordance with the provisions of section 65. I propose to conduct the said audit at my office/at your place of business on ----.

And whereas you are required to:

(i) afford the undersigned the necessary facility to verify the books of account and records or other documents as may be required in this context, and

(ii) furnish such information as may be required and render assistance for timely completion of the audit.

You are hereby directed to attend in person or through an authorised representative on .... (date) at...............................(place) before the undersigned and to produce your books of account and records for the aforesaid financial year(s) as required for audit.

In case of failure to comply with this notice, it would be presumed that you are not in possession of such books of account and proceedings as deemed fit may be initiated as per the provisions of the Act and the rules made thereunder against you without making any further correspondence in this regard.

Signature ....

Name ....

Designation ....

Form GST ADT-02

[*See rule 101(5)*]

Reference No.: Date:

To,

GSTIN ....

Name ....

Address ....

Audit Report No. ....dated ....

Audit Report under section 65(6)

Your books of account and records for the F.Y............... has been examined and this Audit Report is prepared on the basis of information available/documents furnished by you and the findings are as under:

Short payment of	Integrated tax	Central tax	State/UT tax	Cess
Tax				
Interest				
Any other amount				

[*Upload pdf file containing audit observation*]

You are directed to discharge your statutory liabilities in this regard as per the provisions of the Act and the rules made thereunder, failing which proceedings as deemed fit may be initiated against you under the provisions of the Act.

Signature ....

Name ....

Designation ....

Form GST ADT-03

[See rule 102(1)]

Reference No.: Date:

To,

———

GSTIN ....

Name ....

Address ....

Tax period – F.Y(s). ....

Communication to the registered person for conduct of special audit under section 66

Whereas the proceedings of scrutiny of return/enquiry/investigation/........ are going on; And whereas it is felt necessary to get your books of account and records examined and audited by .... (name), chartered accountant/cost accountant nominated by the Commissioner;

You are hereby directed to get your books of account and records audited by the said chartered accountant/cost accountant.

Signature ....

Name ....

Designation ....

Form GST ADT-04

[*See rule 102(2)*]

Reference No.: Date:

To,

———

GSTIN ....

Name ....

Address ....

Information of Findings upon Special Audit

Your books of account and records for the F.Y............... has been examined by ——(Chartered Accountant/Cost Accountant) and his audit report is prepared on the basis of information available/documents furnished by you and the findings/discrepancies are as under:

Short payment of	Integrated tax	Central tax	State/UT tax	Cess
Tax				
Interest				
Any other amount				

[*Upload pdf file containing audit observation*]

You are directed to discharge your statutory liabilities in this regard as per the provisions of the Act and the rules made thereunder, failing which proceedings as deemed fit may be initiated against you under the provisions of the Act.

Signature ....

Name ....

Designation ....

25

Appeals and Revisions

25.1 Introduction

The decisions or orders passed by any authority is ultimately the decisions or orders passed by a human being who may be right or wrong with reference to those decisions or orders. Therefore, the GST law has set up a mechanism for appeals so that an aggrieved person has a proper channel to present his case and arguments so that proper justice can be delivered to him.

25.2 Appeals to Appellate Authority—Section 107

1. Appeal by the aggrieved person: Section 107(1): If a person feels that he is aggrieved by any decision or order passed under the CGST Act/SGST Act/UTGST Act by an adjudicating authority, then he has the option to appeal to Appellate Authority within three months from the date of communication of such decision or order.

2. Appeal by the commissioner: Section 107(2) and 107(3)

(a) If the State or Union tax commissioner requests the commissioner to examine the legality or propriety of the order passed by the adjudicating authority, then the commissioner has the following powers:

- to call for and examine the record of any proceedings in which the Adjudicating Authority has passed the order.
- to direct (by an order) his subordinate officer to apply to the Appellate Authority for the determination of such points as mentioned in his order.

(b) Such application is treated as the appeal by the commissioner, and the authorised officer is treated as the appellant, and the provisions of appeals are applicable to such application.

(c) The above appeal must be made within six months from the date of communication of the order passed by the Adjudicating authority.

Note: It is not necessary that the commissioner can exercise the above powers on being requested by the State or Union tax commissioner, but he can do so on his own motion.

3. Extension of time period of three months/six months: Section 107(4): The Appellate Authority has the power to extend the period of appeal (three or six months) by a maximum one month. However, the authority must be satisfied that there were sufficient reasons for not appealing within the period of three or six months.

4. Verification of the appeal: Section 107(5): Every appeal under section 107 must be in the prescribed form and verified in the manner specified.

5. Compulsory deposit before filing an appeal: Section 107(6): The appellant, under section 107(1), is required to pay the following amount before appeal:

100% of the amount of tax, interest, fine, fee and penalty as admitted by the appellant	–
Add: 10% of the remaining amount of disputed tax, but not exceeding ₹25 crore (₹50 crore in case of IGST)	–

However, if the order passed by the adjudicating authority is under section 129, then the appeal cannot be filed unless 25% of the penalty is paid.

Example 25.1: BAS Entertainment Limited received a notice demanding tax of ₹10,00,000, penalty of ₹10,00,000 and interest of ₹2,00,000. The adjudicating authority passed an order that confirmed the demand. The company admitted the tax liability of ₹4,00,000 and interest of ₹80,000. Therefore, the disputed amount of tax is ₹6,00,000, penalty ₹10,00,000 and interest ₹1,20,000. The company opts to appeal to the appellate authority against the demand order. Calculate the mandatory deposit to be made by the appellant under section 107(6).

Solution

Calculation of the deposit under section 107(6).

Particulars	Amount (in ₹)
100% of the amount of tax, interest, fine, fee and penalty as admitted by the appellant	₹4,00,000 (tax) + ₹80,000 (interest)
Add: 10% of the remaining amount of tax in dispute (but up to ₹25 crore)	₹60,000
Total deposit	₹5,40,000

Note: It has been assumed that the above tax is CGST only. An equal deposit is also to be made for SGST.

6. Stay on the recovery of the balance amount: Section 107(7): Once the amount under section 107(6) is deposited, then the recovery of the balance amount is stayed.

Example 25.2: Calculate the amount, in example 25.1, for which the stay on recovery can be taken under section 107(7).

Solution

Required amount = Total demand – Total deposit = ₹22,00,000 – ₹5,40,000 = ₹16,60,000

7. Opportunity of being heard: Section 107(8): The appellant shall be given an opportunity to be heard.

8. Adjournment of the hearing: Section 107(9): If the appellant authority is satisfied, then it can adjourn the hearing but up to a maximum three times. Also, the reasons for adjournment shall be given in writing.

9. Chance to add any further ground of appeal if omitted: Section 107(10): The appellant authority may allow the appellant to add any ground of appeal not specified in the grounds of the appeal, if it is satisfied that the omission of that ground was not willful or unreasonable

10. Passing the order: Section 107(11): The authority can pass its order confirming, modifying, or annulling the decision or order appealed against, but it cannot send the case back to the adjudicating authority.

Notes:

(i) If the proposed order is to increase any fee or penalty or fine in place of confiscation or confiscating goods of greater value or reduce the amount of refund or input tax credit, then the appellant is given an opportunity to be heard before passing such order.

(ii) Where the Appellate Authority thinks that

- any tax has not been paid or short-paid or
- erroneously refunded, or
- where input tax credit has been wrongly availed or utilised,

then the order requiring the appellant to pay such tax or input tax credit cannot be passed unless the appellant is given show cause notice against the proposed order, and the order shall be passed within the time limit as per sections 73 or 74.

11. The above order must be in writing: Section 107(12): The above order must be in writing and shall mention the points for determination, the decision thereon and the reasons for such decision.

12. Advisory time period to hear and decide the appeal: Section 107(13): The authority is expected to hear and decide the appeal within one year from the date of appeal. However, if a stay is given by any court or tribunal, then such period of stay is excluded while calculating one year.

13. Communication of the above order: Section 107(14)/(15): The order passed by the appellate authority shall be communicated to the appellant, respondent and adjudicating authority. A copy of the order shall be communicated to the Jurisdictional Commissioner or the authority designated by him on this behalf and the jurisdictional Commissioner of State tax or Commissioner of Union Territory Tax or an authority designated by him on this behalf.

14. Communication of the above order: Section 107(16): Every order passed the Appellate Authority (subject to the provisions of section 108 or section 113 or section 117 or section 118) is final and binding on the parties.

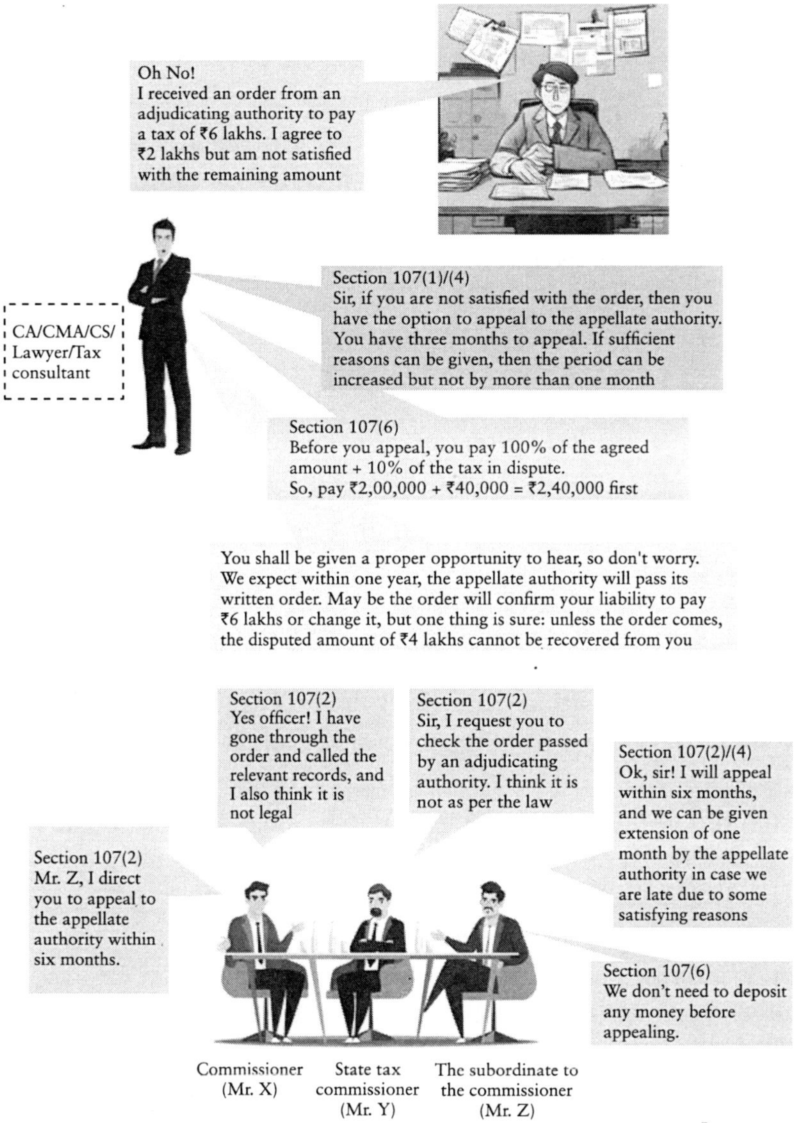

Image courtesy–Freepik

25.3 Powers of Revisional Authority—Section 108

1. Section 108(1)

   (a) The revisional authority can call for and examine the record of any proceedings either on his own motion or upon information received by him or a request from the State tax or Union territory tax commissioner.

   (b) If the revisional authority thinks that any decision or order passed by any officer subordinate to him

   - is erroneous because it is not in favour of the interest of revenue and is illegal or improper,

- material facts have not been considered (irrespective of their availability at the time of issue of the order),
- in consequence of an observation by the Comptroller and Auditor General of India,

then he may stay the operation of such decision or order for such period as he thinks fit. The revisional authority can enhance or modify or annual the said decision or order.

2. When the above powers cannot be exercised: Section 108(2): The revisional authority cannot use his power in the following cases:

(a) An appeal against the order has been made under section 107/112/117/118, i.e., an appeal has been made to the appellate authority/appellate tribunal/a High court/the Supreme Court.

(b) If the period of six months given under section 107(2) has not expired or more than three years have expired from the date of the passing of the decision or order.

(c) The order has already been taken for revision under this section at an earlier stage.

(d) The order has been passed under section 108(1).

Note: The revisional authority may pass an order under section 108(1) on any point that has not been raised and decided in an appeal to the appellate authority/appellate tribunal/a High Court/the Supreme Court before

- the expiry of one year from the date of the order in such appeal or
- the expiry of three years from the date of the initial order.

whichever is later.

3. Section 108(3): Every order passed by the Revisional Authority under 108(1) is subject to the provisions of section 113 or 117 or 118 and is final and binding on the parties.

4. When the above powers cannot be exercised: Section 108(4): The revisional authority cannot use his power in the following cases:

(a) An appeal against the order has been made under section 107/112/117/118, i.e., an appeal has been made to the appellate authority/appellate tribunal/a High Court/the Supreme Court.

(b) If the period of six months given under section 107 has not expired or three years have expired from the date of the passing of the decision or order.

5. Exclusion of the period of stay to calculate the limitation period: Section 108(5): If a court or the Appellate Tribunal gives a stay on the order passed under section 108(1), then the period of stay is not taken into account while calculating the period of limitation of three years.

25.4 Appeal to Appellate Tribunal—Section 112

1. Who can file an appeal?: Section 112(1): Any person aggrieved by an order passed by the appellate authority or revisional authority may appeal to the Appellate Tribunal against such order within three months from the date of communication of the order to be appealed.

2. Possibility of refusal: Section 112(2): The Appellate Tribunal has the discretionary power to refuse the appeal if it finds that

(a) the tax or
(b) input tax credit involved or
(c) the difference in tax or input tax credit involved or
(d) the amount of fine, fee or penalty determined by such order

is up to ₹50,000.

3. Appeal by the Commissioner: Section 112(3)/(4)/(5)/(6)/(7)

(a) If the State or Union tax commissioner requests the commissioner to examine the legality or propriety of the order passed by the adjudicating authority, then the commissioner has the following powers:
- to call for and examine the record of any proceedings in which the **Appellate Authority** or **Revisional Authority** has passed the order.
- to direct (by an order) his subordinate officer to apply to the **Appellate Tribunal** for the determination of such points as mentioned in his order.

(b) Such application is treated as the appeal by the commissioner, and the authorised officer is treated as the appellant, and the provisions of appeals are applicable to such application.

(c) The above appeal must be made within six months from the date of passing of the order against the appeal is to be made.

(d) The appeal must be filed in the prescribed form by paying the prescribed fee.

(e) Once an appeal is filed, the party (against whom the appeal has been made) receives a notice of the appeal. Such party may file a memorandum of cross-objections (against any part of the order appealed) in FORM GST APL-06 within 45 days of the receipt of the notice. The Appellate Authority may accept the memorandum even after 45 days if it is satisfied that there was sufficient reason for the delay.

Note: It is not necessary that the commissioner exercise the above powers on being requested by the State or Union tax commissioner, but he can do so on his own motion.

4. Compulsory deposit before filing an appeal: Section 112(8): The appellant is required to pay the following amount before appeal:

100% of the amount of tax, interest, fine, fee and penalty as admitted by the appellant	–
Add: 20% of the remaining amount of tax in dispute in addition to the amount paid under section 107(6), but not exceeding ₹50 crore (₹100 crore in case of IGST)	–

Example 25.3: PQR Limited received an adjudication order in which the company is required to pay CGST of ₹300 crore and SGST of ₹300 crore. An appeal against the order was filed to the Appellate Authority. The Appellate Authority confirmed the order. Therefore, the entire amount of tax was to be paid. After this, the company appealed to the Appellate Tribunal. Calculate the mandatory deposit to be made with the Appellate Authority under section 107(6) and Appellate Tribunal under section 112(8).

Solution

Deposit under section 107(6)

Particulars	CGST (In ₹ crore)	SGST (In ₹ crore)
100% of the amount of tax, interest, fine, fee and penalty as admitted by the appellant	Nil	Nil
Add: 10% of the remaining amount of tax in dispute (but up to ₹25 crore)	25	25
Total deposit	25	25

Deposit under section 112(8)

Particulars	**CGST (In ₹ crore)**	**SGST (In ₹ crore)**
100% of the amount of tax, interest, fine, fee and penalty as admitted by the appellant	Nil	Nil
Add: 20% of the remaining amount of tax in dispute in addition to the amount paid under section 107(6), but not exceeding ₹50 crore (₹100 crore in case of IGST)	50	50
Total deposit	50	50

5. Stay on the recovery of the balance amount: Section 112(9): Once the amount under section 112(8) is deposited, the recovery of the balance amount is stayed till the appeal is decided.

25.5 Appeal to the High Court—Section 117

1. Who can file an appeal: Section 117(1): Any person who feels aggrieved by a decision made by the *State Benches*[1] of the Appellate Tribunal may appeal to the High Court. If the High Court finds that the case involves a significant question of law, it may accept the appeal.

2. Time period to appeal: Section 117(2): An appeal to the High Court must be filed within 180 days from the date on which the order appealed against is received by the aggrieved person, and it must be in Form GST APL-08, verified in such manner as may be prescribed. If the period of 180 days has expired, nevertheless, the High Court may accept the appeal if it is satisfied with the reasons for being late.

3. Formulation of the substantial question of law: Section 117(3): When the High Court thinks that a substantial question of law is involved in a case, the court formulates the question, and the appeal is heard only on that question, and the respondents, at the hearing of the appeal, are allowed to argue that the case does not involve such question; however, this does not mean that the High Court cannot hear the appeal on any other substantial question of law not formulated by it. If it is satisfied that the case involves such a question, then it can hear it; however, reasons for hearing are to be recorded.

1. Section 152(a)/(b) of the Finance Act, 2023 has amended Section 117(1) and Section 117(5) by replacing the earlier words "*State Bench or Area Benches*" with the words "*State Benches*".

4. Section 117(4): The High Court shall decide the above substantial question of law and give such judgment thereon containing the grounds on which such decision is based and may award such cost as it thinks fit.

5. Section 117(5): The High Court may determine any issue which

(i) is not decided by the State Benches or
(ii) is wrongly decided by the State Benches because of a decision on such question of law as referred to in section 117(3).

6. Section 117(6)/(7): The appeal shall be heard by a bench of at least two judges, and the same shall be decided by majority rule. If there is no majority, then the point of difference is stated by the court and one or more judges are added to the bench so that the point of difference can be decided. The decision will follow the majority rule.

Example 25.4: Suppose that two judges of a High Court, say, Justice A and Justice B, hear three questions, X, Y and Z, in an appeal. Both the judges have different opinions on question Z. Therefore, as per section 117(7), another judge, Mr. C, is added to the bench. Now, Y and Z have the same opinion. Since two judges out of three have the same opinion on question Z, therefore, by majority rule, the judgement of Y and Z will become part of the judgement on question Z.

7. Section 117(8): When the High Court makes a decision in an appeal case filed under this section, both parties can use a certified copy of the judgment to enforce that decision.

25.6 Appeal to the Supreme Court—Section 118

1. When can an appeal to the Supreme Court be made?: Section 118(1): As per section 118(1)

(a) A direct appeal to the Supreme Court can be filed against any order given by the *Principal Benches*[2] of the Appellate Tribunal.
(b) An appeal to the Supreme Court can be filed against any judgment or order given by the High Court in an appeal provided that the High Court certifies to be a fit for appeal to the Supreme Court. The appeal can be made (immediately after the judgment or order) by the High Court on its own motion or on an application made on behalf of or by the aggrieved.

2. Applicability of the Code of Civil Procedure, 1908: Section 118(2): The provisions of the Code of Civil Procedure, 1908, relating to appeals to the Supreme Court, as far as possible, are also applicable here.

3. Enforcement of the decision of the Supreme Court: Section 118(3): Where the judgment of the High Court is changed or overturned by the Supreme Court, the order issued by the Supreme Court will be enforced in the manner provided in section 117 in the case of a judgment of the High Court.

25.7 Sums due to be paid—Section 119

Although an aggrieved may decide to appeal to the High Court or the Supreme Court, he is required to pay the sums due to the Government arising from the order passed by

---

2. Section 153 of the Finance Act, 2023 has replaced the earlier words "*National or Regional Benches*" by the words "*Principal Bench*".

- the *Principal Benches*[3] of the Appellate Tribunal or
- the *State Benches*[4] of the Appellate Tribunal or
- the High Court.

25.8 Appeals in certain cases cannot be filed—Section 120

1. Specifying monetary limits by the Board: Section 120(1): On the recommendation of the GST council, the Board issues orders or instructions or directions specifying such monetary limits so that the filling of appeals by the central tax officers can be regulated.

2. Section 120(1) does not stop filing appeal or application in another case: Section 120(2): If an officer of the central tax does not appeal against a decision or order made under the CGST Act because of section 120(1), then it would not stop him from filing an appeal or application in another case that deals with similar issues or question of law.

3. Contention of lack of opposition by the central tax officer is invalid: Section 120(3): Where a central tax officer has not filed appeal or application because of section 120(1), no party in appeal or application can contend that the central tax officer has agreed without protest to the disputed issue because he has not filed an appeal or application.

4. The Appellate Tribunal or Court should consider the circumstances of not filing an appeal by a central tax officer due to section 120(1) during an appeal: Section 120(4): The Appellate Tribunal or court considering the appeal or application should take into account the reasons why the officer of the central tax did not file it based on the orders, instructions, or directions given under section 120(1).

25.9 Non-appealable decisions and orders—Section 121

No appeal can be filed against the following orders:

(a) an order of the Commissioner or other authority empowered to direct transfer of proceedings from one officer to another officer or

(b) an order of the seizure or retention of books of account, register and other documents, or

(c) an order sanctioning prosecution under the CGST Act; or

(d) an order passed under section 80.

---

3. Section 154(a) of the Finance Act, 2023 has replaced the earlier words "*National or Regional Benches*" with the words "*Principal Bench*".
4. Section 154(b) of the Finance Act, 2023 has replaced the earlier words "*State Bench or Area Benches*" with the words "*State Benches*".

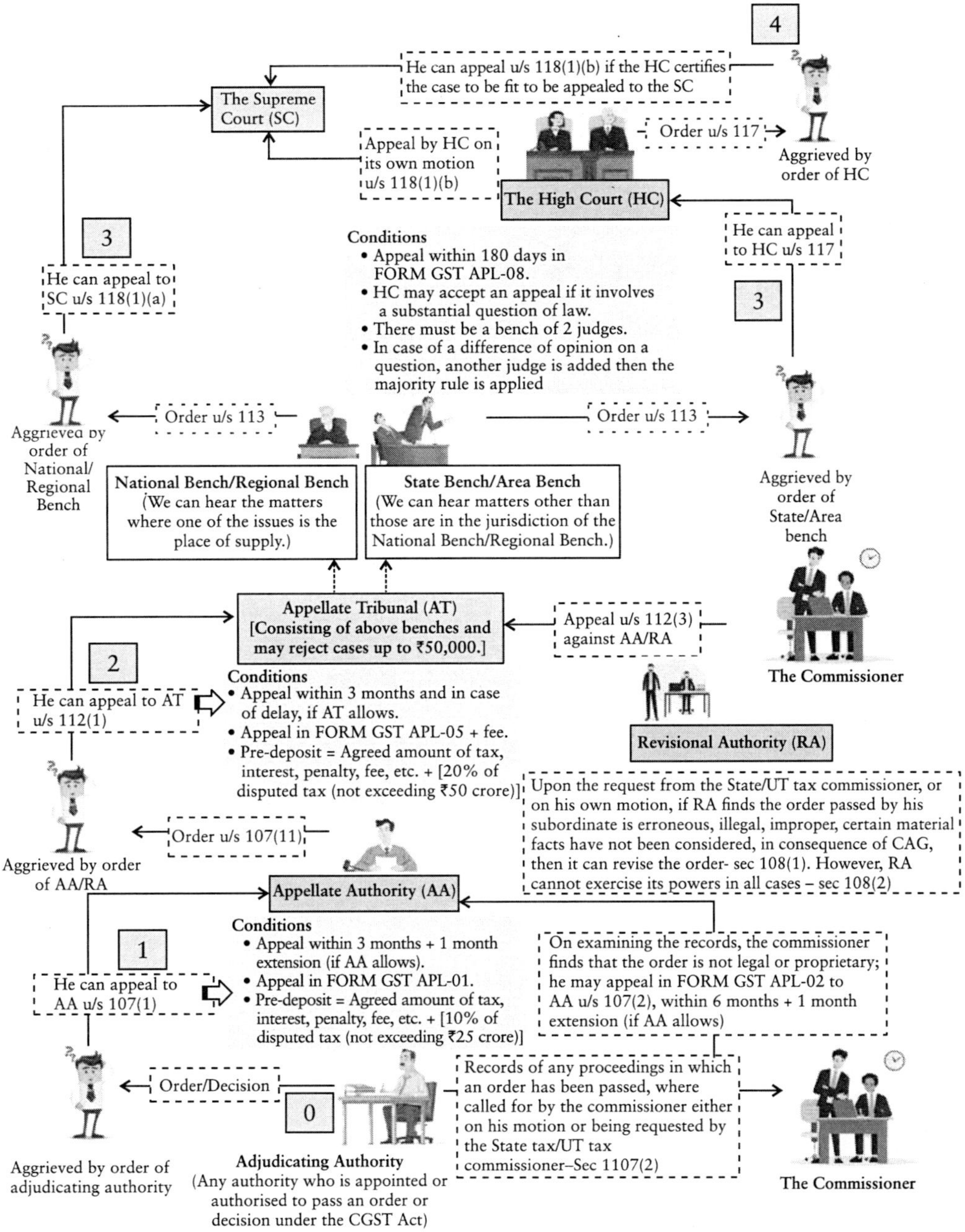

Image courtesy–Freepik

Theory Questions

1. What are the provisions of appeals and revisions under the GST law?
2. When can an aggrieved appeal to the High Court and Supreme Court?
3. What are the powers of revisional authority under section 108 of the CGST Act?
4. Can a revisional authority exercise its powers in all cases?
5. Write a note on Appeal to Appellate Tribunal under section 112.
6. What is a revisional authority?
7. Can an appeal to the Appellate Authority and Appellate Authority be made without any pre-deposit?
8. Can the Appellate Tribunal reject any appeal?
9. What are the powers of Revisional Authority? Describe the cases where these powers cannot be exercised.
10. There are some non-appealable cases. Can you tell what those cases are?
11. Appeals, in some cases, cannot be filed. Do you agree with this statement?
12. When can an appeal be filed to the Supreme Court of India?

26
GST Practioner

26.1 Who is GST Practioner?

A GST practitioner (or GSTP) is a person approved by the Central and State Governments to perform specified functions (as given under section 48, read with Rule 83) on behalf of a taxable person. He is required to fulfil some conditions and possess the qualification as specified under Rule 83, enroll on the common portal in FORM PCT-01, and pass an exam (with at least 50% marks) conducted by the National Academy of Customs, Indirect Taxes & Narcotics (NACIN), Faridabad.

26.2 Provisions regarding GST Practioner—Rule 83

1. Conditions and eligibility to become GSTP: Rule 83(1)

If a person satisfies all of the following conditions

(a) he must be a citizen of India
(b) he must possess a sound mind
(c) he is not declared insolvent
(d) he must not have been convicted at any time by a competent court

and possesses the following qualifications, then the said person can enrol himself as a GST Practitioner on a common portal (www.gst.gov.in) or through the facilitation centre by furnishing **FORM GST PCT-01**.

1. A retired officer of the Commercial Tax Department of any State Government or of the Central Board of Indirect Taxes and Customs, Department of Revenue, Government of India, having worked in a post not lower in rank than that of a Group-B gazetted officer, for a period not less than two years.
2. A registered tax return preparer or a sales tax practitioner for at least 5 years.
3. A graduate or postgraduate or equivalence degree in commerce, law, banking, higher auditing, business administration, business management from any recognized Indian University. Thus, the academic degrees B.Com, BBA, MBA, M.Com, LLB, LLM, etc., are all eligible degrees.

4. A degree received from a foreign university which is deemed to be equivalent to any of the above degrees by any Indian University.
5. The degree of Chartered Accountancy (CA)/Company Secretary (CS)/Cost and Management Accounting (CMA) having a Certificate of Practice.

Note: If we go through the above qualifications, then we find that a graduate or postgraduate in science or humanities or fine arts or social sciences is not eligible for becoming a GST practitioner.

2. Certificate of enrolment and GSTP Exam conducted by NACIN: Rule 83(2) and 83(3): Once a person files FORM GST PCT-01, then the authorized officer goes through the form. If he is satisfied, then he issues a certificate of enrolment as GSTP in FORM GST PCT-01, as shown below. This certificate remains valid unless cancelled. Further, such an enrolled person is required to appear in such examination conducted by a notified authority. At present, the **National Academy of Customs, Indirect Taxes & Narcotics (NACIN), Faridabad,** is the notified agency. Passing percentage of the exam is 50%.

FORM GST PCT-02

[See rule 83(2)]

Enrolment Certificate of Goods and Services Tax Practitioner

	Enrolment number	
	PAN	
	Name of Goods and Service Tax Practioner	
	Address and Contact Information	
	Date of enrolment as GSTP	
Date Authority		Signature of Enrolment
Name and Designation		

3. GSTP found guilty of misconduct: Rule 83(4): If a GSTP is found guilty of misconduct under the CGST Act, then a show cause notice in FORM GST PCT-03 shall be issued to him by the authorised officer, and an opportunity to be heard shall also be given. Thereafter, the authorised officer may pass an order in FORM GST PCT-04 directing that he is disqualified from working as GSTP with immediate effect.

4. Appeal against the above order: Rule 83(5): The person (against whom an order of disqualification has been passed) has the option to file an appeal to the commissioner against the order of disqualification. The time limit to appeal is 30 days from the date of the issue of the order.

5. Authorisation and withdrawal of the authorisation: Rule 83(6): A registered person may give authority to a GSTP to undertake such tasks mentioned in the authorisation. If the registered person wants to withdraw the authority, then it can be withdrawn at any time. Whether the registered person wants to give authority or withdraw it, then FORM GST PCT-05 is filed on the common portal.

6. Confirmation required from the registered person: Rule 83(7): When a GSTP files a statement on behalf of a registered person who has authorised him, then a confirmation email and

SMS are sent to the registered person. The registered person is required to give his confirmation, and if he does not confirm the same till the last date of furnishing of the statement, then it is assumed that he has confirmed. Thereafter, the statement is made available to the registered person on the common portal.

7. Functions which can be performed by a GSTP: Rule 83(8): A GSTP can perform any or all of the following functions on behalf of a taxable person:

(a) furnish the details of outward supplies;
(b) furnish monthly, quarterly, annual or final returns;
(c) make a deposit for credit into the electronic cash ledger;
(d) file a claim for a refund;
(e) file an application for amendment or cancellation of registration;
(f) furnish information for the generation of the e-way bill;
(g) furnish details of challan in FORM GST ITC-04;
(h) file an application for amendment or cancellation of enrolment under rule 58; and
(i) file an intimation to pay tax under the composition scheme or withdraw from the said scheme:

Notes:

(a) As per section 48(3), a GSTP cannot be held liable for the correctness of any particulars furnished in the return or other details filed. The responsibility falls on the person on whose behalf the return and other details are filed.
(b) In the following functions, a confirmation from the registered is also required:
- Application for a refund claim
- Application for amendment or cancellation of registration
- Intimating opting composition scheme of section 10
- Intimating withdrawal of composition scheme.

If the registered person does not confirm, then the application cannot be further proceeded.

8. Functions which can be performed by a GSTP: Rule 83(9): A GSTP can perform any or all of the following functions on behalf of a taxable person:

(a) furnish the details of outward supplies;
(b) furnish monthly, quarterly, annual or final returns.

9. Duties of the registered person: Rule 83(9): If a registered person gets his returns filed by a GSTP, then he is required

(a) to give his consent in FORM GST PCT-05 and
(b) to ensure that the facts given in the return are true and correct.

10. Duties of a GSTP: Rule 83(10): A GSTP is required

(a) to prepare the statements with due diligence and
(b) to affix his digital signature on the statements or verify them using electronic means.

26.3 Conditions for the purpose of appearance—Rule 84

(a) A GSTP cannot appear before any authority (on behalf of a registered or unregistered person) under the CGST Act unless he is enrolled under rule 83.

(b) If a GSTP appears before any authority under the CGST Act, then he is required to produce (before the authority) a copy of the authorization given by the registered person or unregistered person in FORM GST PCT-05.

Theory Questions

1. Who is GST Practioner (GSTP)?
2. What are the qualifications to become a GSTP?
3. What are the functions of a GST Practioner? Or what is the role of GST Practioner?
4. A person has completed his Bachelor in Fine Arts. Is he eligible for GSTP?
5. Can a Goods and Services Tax Practioner appear before any authority to represent a registered person?

Multiple Choice Questions (MCQ)

1. GST is applicable
   (a) on provision of service
   (b) on manufacturing of goods
   (c) on supply of goods
   (d) on supply of goods or services or both
2. The head of the GST Council is
   (a) The state finance minister
   (b) The finance minister of India
   (c) The prime minister of India
   (d) The chief minister of Delhi
3. The constitutional amendment made to impose GST is
   (a) 100th (b) 99th (c) 75th (d) 101th
4. Dhanvi Pvt Ltd (a registered person) purchased some goods costing ₹1,00,000 from a supplier at 18% GST on 18.01.2021. However, the goods will be received in the month of May 2021. What is her eligible amount of input tax credit for the month of January 2021?
   (a) ₹21,600 (b) ₹21,000 (c) ₹18,000 (d) Nil
5. A machine costing ₹47,200, including GST of 18%, was purchased on 1.1.2022. The depreciation on the GST component was not claimed under section 32 of the Income Tax Act, 1961. What is the eligible amount of input tax credit?
   (a) ₹47,200 (b) ₹7,200 (c) ₹40,000 (d) ₹42,200
6. Which of the following is not covered under the scope of GST?
   (a) Natural gas
   (b) Liquor for human consumption
   (c) Petrol
   (d) All of the these
7. A company (registered in GST in UP) purchased a motor vehicle having approved seating capacity, including a driver, is not more than 13, and the firm paid ₹1,00,000 as IGST on its purchase, then choose the correct statement.

(a) The company is eligible to avail the input tax credit of ₹1,00,000 under section 17(5) of the CGST Act, 2017
(b) The credit of ₹1,00,000 is blocked under section 17(5) of the CGST Act, 2017
(c) The credit of ₹1,00,000 is blocked under section 17(1) of the CGST Act, 2017
(d) The credit of ₹1,00,000 is blocked under section 16 of the CGST Act, 2017

8. The primary aim of GST is to remove or lower down
   (a) Cascading effect (b) Corruption
   (c) Administrative costs (d) None of these

9. If the common credit is ₹1,00,000 and 20% of the inputs were exclusively used to effect taxable supply, including zero-rated supply, then what is D2 if the total supply is ₹10 lakhs and exempt supply is 30% of the total supply? Assume that common inputs were used for business as well as non-business purposes.
   (a) ₹30,000 (b) ₹20,000 (c) ₹5,000 (d) ₹10,000

10. You visited a mobile phone showroom in Delhi and purchased a phone on 7.05.2022. At what time should the owner of the showroom issue the tax invoice?
    (a) At the time of delivery of the phone
    (b) 30 days later of the date of delivery of the phone
    (c) 45 days later of the date of delivery of the phone
    (d) Before or at the time of delivery of the phone

11. R purchased some inputs from Y on 1.1.2022 on credit. The cost was ₹1,00,000, and the GST rate was 18%. He availed the tax credit. Y paid 60% of the amount due 10 days later, but the remaining amount was paid on 3.10.2022. Choose the correct option.
    (a) R must repay the remaining balance
    (b) R is required to reverse the input tax credit of ₹10,800 and get re-credit once the payment is made
    (c) R is required to reverse the input tax credit of ₹7,200 along with the interest rate of 18% and get re-credit once the remaining payment is made to Y
    (d) R is required to reverse the input tax credit of ₹18,000 along with the interest rate of 18% and get re-credit once the payment is made

12. Vivek Pvt Limited got itself voluntarily registered under GST on 25.09.2020, while he applied for the same on 21.09.2020. Choose the correction option.
    (a) A is eligible to get credit on the input services availed before 25.09.2020
    (b) A is eligible to get credit on the inputs contained in semi-finished goods available on 24.8.2020
    (c) A is eligible to get credit on the inputs contained in finished goods available on 24.8.2020
    (d) Both (b) and (c)

13. A got himself mandatorily registered under GST on 5.08.2020 while he applied for the same on 1.08.2020 when he became liable to get registered. Choose the correction option.

(a) A is eligible to get credit on the inputs contained in semi-finished and finished goods available on 31.7.2020
(b) A is eligible to get credit on the inputs contained in semi-finished goods available on 4.8.2020
(c) A is eligible to get credit on the inputs contained in finished goods available on 4.8.2020
(d) Both (b) and (c)

14. Wizag Gadgets, a retailer in Delhi, offers the iPhone 13 phone for ₹90,000 (with an exchange offer for any old iPhone). It also offers the same phone without exchange for ₹95,000. Prisha purchases a phone under the exchange offer by exchanging an old iPhone. The value of the old phone is not known. In this case, the value of the supply of iPhone 13 will be

(a) ₹90,000 (b) ₹5,000 (c) ₹95,000 (d) None of these

15. Zee Ltd. manufactures laptops and Y Ltd. manufactures printers. Zee Ltd. sells a laptop to Y Ltd. For this supply, Y Ltd. pays ₹1,00,000 and a printer manufactured by it. The value of the printer is ₹30,000. However, the value of the laptop is not available; value of the supply of the laptop by Zee Ltd. to Y Ltd. will be

(a) ₹12,000 (b) ₹88,000 (c) ₹1,30,000 (d) ₹1,00,000

16. Gyani sells $40,000 at the rate of ₹60 per US $ to a dealer. RBI reference rate on that date for US $ is ₹61.75. The value of taxable supply for GST purposes is

(a) ₹18,00,000 (b) ₹70,000 (c) ₹18,43,500 (d) None of these

17. X purchases a voucher of ₹5,000 from X Ltd. For ₹4,500 (i.e., after a discount of ₹500). This voucher is redeemable against the purchase of any article up to ₹5,000 from any X Ltd. outlet on or before 31 December 2019. The value of taxable supply, in this case, is

(a) ₹5,000 (b) ₹500 (c) ₹4,500 (d) Zero

18. X deals in buying and selling of second-hand goods. On 5 August 2017, he purchases from B a second-hand fridge for ₹14,000. X makes some minor changes. He sells the same fridge for ₹17,000 on 10 August 2017. He does not take any input tax credit on the purchase of a fridge from B (B has not issued any tax invoice to X). The taxable value of supply is

(a) ₹14,000 (b) ₹3,000 (c) ₹17,000 (d) Zero

19. On 2 January 2012, X purchases 6,000 USD from an authorised dealer in exchange for 5400 Euros. RBI reference rate is as follows: 1 USD = ₹68 and 1 Euro = ₹76. The value of taxable supply is

(a) ₹48,000 (b) ₹4,09,000 (c) ₹4,08,000 (d) ₹4,080

20. As per section 15(2) of the CGST Act, 2017, which of the following is not an item of inclusion?

(a) Taxes excluding GST
(b) Incidental expenses
(c) Subsidies provided by the central government and state government
(d) Interest or late fee or penalty for delayed payment on any consideration for any supply

21. X Ltd. supplies a laptop to B Ltd. The Laptop is supplied along with Windows 11, MS Office (licensed versions of both are installed in the laptop), and a laptop bag. Apart, the laptop carries an on site warranty for three years. The laptop is supplied for Rs. 80,000. What kind of supply is this?

    (a) Exempt supply (b) Zero-rated supply
    (c) Mixed supply (d) Composite supply

22. A supply of a package consisting of canned foods, sweets, chocolates, cakes, dry fruits, aerated drinks and fruit juices when supplied for a single price is known as __________.

    (a) Composite supply (b) Exempt supply
    (c) Mixed supply (d) Zero-rated supply

23. I am employed by a grocery store Arman. My salary is ₹50,000 per month. Which of the following statements is correct?

    (a) I will issue a tax invoice to the store because I am rendering a service
    (b) Service given by an employee is covered by the Reverse charge mechanism
    (c) Service given by an employee to the employer is not supply under the GST law
    (d) Service given by an employee to the employer is supply under the GST law

24. The following data is noted from the records of X Ltd. (supplier of services) and Y Ltd. (recipient of services covered by reverse charge mechanism):

    Date of completion of service by X Ltd. to Y Ltd.: 20 November 2017; Date of issue of invoice by X Ltd.: 15 October 2017;

    Date of payment by Y Ltd.: 21 December 2017 (as per books of account by Y Ltd.), and the amount debited by the bank in the current account of Y Ltd. on 20 December 2017.

    What is the time of supply?

    (a) 20 December 2017 (b) 15 December 2017
    (c) 20 November 2017 (d) 15 October 2017

25. Where a tax invoice has been issued for the supply of any goods or services and the taxable value (or tax charged) in the invoice is observed to be exceeding the taxable value (or tax payable) in respect of such supply, then the supplier should issue a

    (a) New tax invoice (b) Retail invoice
    (c) Debit note (d) Credit note

26. With reference to Input Service Distributor (ISD), which of the following is a correct statement?

    (a) ISD is required to get him registered separately apart from its regular registration
    (b) ISD is not required to get him registered separately apart from its regular registration
    (c) ISD can distribute only IGST
    (d) ISD can distribute only CGST and SGST but not IGST

27. The balance in the electronic credit ledger is ₹5000 (IGST), ₹15,000 (CGST), ₹12,000 (SGST). The output liabilities of IGST, CGST and SGST are ₹11,000, ₹8,000 and ₹5000 respectively. The respective balance of IGST, CGST and SGST in the electronic credit ledger is

(a) 0, ₹1000 and ₹7,000
(b) 0, ₹1000 and 0
(c) ₹5000, 0 and 0
(d) 0, 0 and ₹7,000

28. Place of supply means the place of supply as referred to in the
    (a) IGST Act, 2017
    (b) SGST Act, 2017
    (c) CGST Act, 2017
    (d) GST (Compensation to States) Act, 2017

29. Time of supply means the time of supply as referred to in the
    (a) IGST Act, 2017
    (b) SGST Act, 2017
    (c) CGST Act, 2017
    (d) GST (Compensation to States) Act, 2017

30. Which of the following is a taxable event under the GST law?
    (a) Signing the agreement of the transaction
    (b) Payment for the supply
    (c) Supply of goods or services
    (d) All of the above

31. Which of the following schedules is not related to the supply under the CGST Act, 2017?
    (a) Schedule I
    (b) Schedule II
    (c) Schedule III
    (d) Schedule VI

32. Works contract shall be treated as
    (a) Supply of goods
    (b) Supply of services
    (c) Composite supply
    (d) Both (b) and (c)

33. Supply, by way of or as part of any service or in any other manner whatsoever, of goods, being food or any other article for human consumption or any drink (other than alcoholic liquor for human consumption), shall be treated as
    (a) Supply of services
    (b) Supply of goods
    (c) Supply of goods and services, both
    (d) Zero-rated supply

34. Which of the following is supply under the GST law?
    (a) Crematorium services
    (b) Sale of land
    (c) Allowing someone to use the copyright
    (d) Services of an employee to his or her employer

35. A shopkeeper selling storage water bottles along with the refrigerators. Choose the correct option.
    (a) Composite supply
    (b) Mixed supply
    (c) Exempt supply
    (d) Zero-rated supply

36. Prisha manufacturers entered into a contract with X for the supply of readymade shirts packed in designer boxes at X's outlet. Further, Prisha manufacturers would also get them insured during transit. Select the correct option.
    (a) Composite supply
    (b) Mixed supply
    (c) Exempt supply
    (d) Zero-rated supply

37. Dhanvi manufacturers entered into a contract with XYZ for the supply of readymade shirts packed in designer boxes at XYZ's outlet. Further, Prisha manufacturers would also get them insured during transit. Choose the correct option.

(a) Supply of insurance is principal supply
(b) Supply of packing is principal supply
(c) Supply of shirts is principal supply
(d) All the supplies are principal supplies

38. In the case of mixed supply, which of the following is correct?
   (a) GST rate is the highest rate applicable on the supplies
   (b) GST rate is the lowest rate applicable on the supplies
   (c) GST rate is the lowest rate applicable on the principal supply
   (d) None of the above

39. TCS (Tax collected at source) is applicable in the case of
   (a) All suppliers
   (b) E-commerce operators
   (c) All the recipients
   (d) All the recipients under the reverse charge mechanism

40. With reference to e-commerce operators like Amazon, Flipkart, etc., which of the following statements is correct?
   (a) E-commerce operator is required to get compulsorily registered irrespective of aggregate turnover
   (b) Optional registration
   (c) Registration depends upon the aggregate turnover of the previous financial year
   (d) E-commerce operator is not required for registration

41. Jigyasa has earned B.Com. (Hons). With reference to GST Practioner, which of the following statements is correct?
   (a) She is eligible to become a GST practitioner, and no further degree is required
   (b) She may be eligible to become a GST practitioner if she passes M.Com/MBA/CA also
   (c) B.Com. (Hons) and CA are not eligible to become GST practitioners
   (d) Only a Chartered Accountant or Cost Accountant can become a GST practitioner

42. I am a Cost Accountant, and my firm is registered under the GST law in Delhi. I will visit Chandigarh for an audit assignment and stay in a 5-star hotel. The hotel should charge ____________ in the tax invoice.
   (a) No GST because it is an exempt supply
   (b) IGST
   (c) CGST + SGST
   (d) CGST + Chandigarh GST (or UTGST)

43. Sarita has taken a DTH service from Tata Play (regional office at Noida), and the dish antenna was installed at his house in Ghaziabad. Then, the place of supply is
   (a) Mumbai (b) Ghaziabad (c) Delhi (d) Not Defined

44. TCS is collected at
   (a) 0.5% on total value
   (b) 1% on net value
   (c) 1% on total value
   (d) 2% on net value

45. Within how many days is the Authority for Advance Ruling (AAR) required to pronounce its advance ruling?
    (a) 60 days (b) 30 days (c) 50 days (d) 90 days
46. If there is a difference of opinion among the members of the Authority for Advance Ruling (AAR), then what happens?
    (a) The application is dismissed
    (b) The AAR is silent
    (c) The AAR refers the case to the Appellate Authority for Advance Ruling
    (d) The AAR declares its ruling despite the difference in opinions
47. Who is the proper officer to authorise in writing any other officer of central tax to inspect any places of business of the taxable person?
    (a) An officer not below the rank of Additional Commissioner
    (b) An officer not below the rank of Joint Commissioner
    (c) An officer not below the rank of Principal Chief Commissioner
    (d) An officer not below the rank of Chief Commissioner
48. A casual taxable person is required to apply for registration at least ______ prior to commencement of business
    (a) 10 days (b) 4 days (c) 30 days (d) 5 days
49. The appellate authority may, if it is satisfied that the appellant was prevented by sufficient cause from presenting the appeal within three months or six months, then ____________ extension can be given.
    (a) One month (b) Two months (c) Three months (d) 15 days
50. ________________ shall not be treated as supply, but lottery, betting and gambling shall be treated as supply.
    (a) Mixed supply (b) Barter claim (c) Composite supply (d) Actionable claim
51. Composition scheme is
    (a) Alternative method to pay tax (b) Optional scheme
    (c) Both (a) and (b) (d) None of these
52. Capital goods are those
    (a) Inputs
    (b) Which are capitalized in the books of accounts.
    (c) Both (a) and (b)
    (d) None of these
53. The input tax paid on the inputs destroyed by fire is
    (a) Blocked (b) Allowed (c) 70% allowed (d) 50% allowed
54. GSTR-1 is
    (a) Annual GST return for outward supply
    (b) Annual GST return for inward supply

(c) Monthly or quarterly return for outward supply
(d) Monthly or quarterly return for inward supply

55. Who cannot adopt a composition scheme?
(a) Manufacturer of ice cream, pan masala, or tobacco
(b) A person making inter-state supplies
(c) A casual taxable person or a non-resident taxable person
(d) All of the above

56. Time of supply of voucher when we know that the supply can be identified at the time of issue of the voucher, is
(a) The time when the voucher is issued
(b) The time when the voucher is redeemed against the supply identified
(c) The time when the payment for the next purchase is made
(d) The time when the supplier gets the payment

57. I want my GST registration in Jammu and Kashmir, and I deal in goods (other than notified goods) then what is the specified limit for me?
(a) ₹40 lakhs (b) ₹20 lakhs (c) ₹15 lakhs (d) ₹10 lakhs

58. For goods, the specified limit for registration for Mizoram, Tripura, Manipur and Nagaland is
(a) ₹20 lakhs (b) ₹10 lakhs (c) ₹40 lakhs (d) ₹5 lakhs

59. With reference to the apportionment of an input tax credit on goods and services (other than goods), T2 means
(a) ITC attributable to inputs and input services intended to be used exclusively for effecting exempt supply
(b) ITC attributable to inputs and input services intended to be used exclusively for effecting taxable supply
(c) Blocked credit
(d) ITC attributable to inputs and input services intended to be used exclusively for purposes other than business

60. With reference to the audit by tax authorities, the registered person shall be informed by way of notice not less than ____________ working days prior to the conduct of the audit in such manner as may be prescribed.
(a) 30 (b) 15 (c) 10 (d) 45

61. Every decision of the council is taken at its meeting by a majority of at least _______ of the weighted votes of the members present.
(a) 1/3rd (b) 2/3rd (c) 3/4th (d) 1/5th

62. GSTN stands for
(a) Goods and Services Tax Network (b) Goods and Services Tax Nodal
(c) Goods and Services Tax Niyam (d) Goods and Services Tax New

63. Which of the following is a supply under the GST law?
    (a) Sale of land
    (b) Services by a district court
    (c) Services by the member of a legislative assembly
    (d) Restaurant services
64. Which of the following is not a restriction to avail of the composition scheme?
    (a) The supplier is not engaged in manufacturing the notified goods during the preceding financial year
    (b) The words "composition taxable person, not eligible to collect tax on supplies" must be written at the top of the bill of supply issued by him
    (c) The words "composition taxable person, not eligible to collect tax on supplies" must be written
    (d) The supplier cannot make intra-state supply
65. As per Rule 7, what is the total GST rate in case of supplier of services under section 10(2A)?
    (a) 3% of turnover of supplies of goods and services in the State or UT
    (b) 6% of turnover of supplies of goods and services in the State or UT
    (c) 5% of the taxable supplies of goods and services in the State or UT
    (d) 2.5% of turnover of supplies of goods and services in the State or UT
66. Two types of exemptions are
    (a) Absolute and conditional
    (b) Relative and conditional
    (c) Absolute and relative
    (d) None of these
67. Which of the following is not an exempt supply?
    (a) Allowing access to a road or a bridge on payment of toll charges.
    (b) Services by way of loading, unloading, packing, storage or warehousing of rice.
    (c) Coaching to MBA aspirants by a coaching institution.
    (d) Services in the form of storage or warehousing of the following items are exempted services:
    - Cereals
    - Pulses
    - Fruits and
    - Vegetables
68. What is the amount of pre-deposit to appeal under section 112?
    (a) 100% of the disputed tax
    (b) 50% of the dispute tax + the amount of tax agreed
    (c) 100% of the agreed demand + 10% of the disputed tax (but not exceeding 20 crores)
    (d) 100% of the agreed demand + 20% of the disputed tax (but not exceeding 50 crores)
69. What is the amount of pre-deposit to appeal under section 107?
    (a) 100% of the disputed tax
    (b) 50% of the dispute tax + the amount of tax agreed
    (c) 100% of the agreed demand + 10% of the disputed tax (but not exceeding 25 crores)
    (d) 100% of the agreed demand + 20% of the disputed tax (but not exceeding 50 crores)

70. If you find that
    (i) Tax has not been paid at all or
    (ii) If paid, it is short-paid or
    (iii) He has got a refund erroneously or
    (iv) He has availed of ITC wrongly

then choose the correct option
    (a) Demand may be raised under section 73
    (b) Demand may be raised under section 74
    (c) Demand may be raised either under section 73 or section 74, depending upon the intension of the default committe(d)
    (d) Demand cannot be raised at all

71. If I want to know the validity period of an E-way bill, then which rule should I refer to?
    (a) Rule 137 (b) Rule 138 (c) Rule 23 (d) Rule 24

72. With reference to the e-way bill, choose the correct statement.
    (a) E-way bills cannot be generated voluntarily even if the value of the consignment is not greater than ₹50,000
    (b) E-way bills can be generated voluntarily even if the value of the consignment is not greater than ₹50,000
    (c) E-way bill is required only when the value of the consignment exceeds ₹1,00,000
    (d) To generate the e-way bill, it is always required to be registered under the GST

73. QRMP stands for
    (a) Quarterly Return Filing and Monthly Payment of Taxes
    (b) Quarterly Return Furnishing and Monthly Payment of Taxes
    (c) Quad Return Filing and Monthly Paid Term
    (d) Quad Return Filing and Monthly Payment of Taxes

74. Every registered person who is required to furnish a return under section 39(1) and whose registration has been cancelled shall furnish a final return within
    (a) Four months from the date of cancellation
    (b) Three months from the date of the order of cancellation
    (c) Three months from the date of cancellation or date of order of cancellation, whichever is earlier
    (d) Six months from the date of cancellation or date of order of cancellation, whichever is earlier

75. Which of the following is not required to take registration under the GST law?
    (a) An auto driver (not liable for registration under section 22(1)) supplying services through an e-commerce operator
    (b) Supplier of liquor
    (c) A farmer supplying the output out of the cultivation.
    (d) All of the above

Answers

1 (d)	2 (b)	3 (d)	4 (d)	5 (b)	6 (d)	7 (b)	8 (a)	9 (c)	10 (d)
11 (c)	12 (d)	13 (a)	14 (c)	15 (c)	16 (b)	17 (a)	18 (b)	19 (d)	20 (c)
21 (d)	22 (c)	23 (c)	24 (b)	25 (d)	26 (a)	27 (a)	28 (a)	29 (c)	30 (c)
31 (d)	32 (d)	33 (a)	34 (c)	35 (b)	36 (a)	37 (c)	38 (a)	39 (a)	40 (a)
41 (a)	42 (d)	43 (b)	44 (b)	45 (d)	46 (c)	47 (b)	48 (d)	49 (a)	50 (d)
51 (c)	52 (a)	53 (a)	54 (c)	55 (d)	56 (a)	57 (a)	58 (b)	59 (a)	60 (b)
61 (c)	62 (a)	63 (d)	64 (d)	65 (b)	66 (a)	67 (c)	68 (d)	69 (c)	70 (c)
71 (b)	72 (b)	73 (a)	74 (c)	75 (d)					

Index